Communications
in Computer and Information Science   **750**

Commenced Publication in 2007
Founding and Former Series Editors:
Alfredo Cuzzocrea, Xiaoyong Du, Orhun Kara, Ting Liu, Dominik Ślęzak,
and Xiaokang Yang

More information about this series at http://www.springer.com/series/7899

Saroj Kaushik · Daya Gupta
Latika Kharb · Deepak Chahal (Eds.)

Information, Communication and Computing Technology

Second International Conference, ICICCT 2017
New Delhi, India, May 13, 2017
Revised Selected Papers

 Springer

Editors
Saroj Kaushik
Indian Institute of Technology Delhi
New Delhi
India

Latika Kharb
Jagan Institute of Management Studies
Delhi
India

Daya Gupta
Delhi Technological University
Delhi
India

Deepak Chahal
Jagan Institute of Management Studies
Delhi
India

ISSN 1865-0929   ISSN 1865-0937 (electronic)
Communications in Computer and Information Science
ISBN 978-981-10-6543-9   ISBN 978-981-10-6544-6 (eBook)
https://doi.org/10.1007/978-981-10-6544-6

Library of Congress Control Number: 2017954910

Printed on acid-free paper

This Springer imprint is published by Springer Nature
The registered company is Springer Nature Singapore Pte Ltd.
The registered company address is: 152 Beach Road, #21-01/04 Gateway East, Singapore 189721, Singapore

Preface

The International Conference on Information, Communication and Computing Technology (ICICCT 2017) was held on May 13, 2017, in New Delhi, India. ICICCT 2017 was organized by the Department of Information Technology, Jagan Institute of Management Studies (JIMS) Rohini, New Delhi, India. The conference received 219 submissions and after rigorous reviews, 34 papers were selected for this volume. The acceptance rate was around 15.5%. The contributions came from diverse areas of information technology categorized into three tracks, namely: (1) Network Systems and Communication Security; (2) Software Engineering; (3) Algorithms and High-Performance Computing.

The aim of ICICCT 2017 was to provide a global platform for researchers, scientists, and practitioners from both academia as well as industry to present their research and development activities in all the aspects of network systems and communication security, software engineering, and algorithms and high-performance computing.

We thank all the members of the Organizing Committee and the Program Committee for their hard work. We are very grateful to Dr. Vasudha Bhatnagar from the Department of Computer Science, University of Delhi, as keynote speaker, Dr. Maya Ingle from SCSIT, Devi Ahilya Vishwavidyalaya, Indore as Guest of Honor, and Dr. Saroj Kaushik from the Department of CSE, Indian Institute of Technology (IIT) Delhi, Dr. Sonajharia Minz from the Department of SCSS, Jawaharlal Nehru University (JNU), and Dr. Kapil Sharma from the Department of CSE, Delhi Technological University (DTU) as session chairs. We thank all the Technical Program Committee members and referees for their constructive and enlightening reviews on the manuscripts. We thank Springer for publishing the proceedings in the *Communications in Computer and Information Science* series. We would like to congratulate JIMS for organizing such an event and would like to highlight the efforts of Conference Patron Dr. V.B. Aggarwal (Dean-IT) and Conference Conveners Dr. Latika Kharb and Dr. Deepak Chahal who really made it happen. Last but not least, we thank all the authors and participants for their great contributions that made this conference possible.

June 2017

Daya Gupta
Shampa Chakraverty

Organization

General Chair

Daya Gupta — Computer Science and Engineering Department, Delhi Technological University (DTU), Delhi, India

Program Chair

Shampa Chakraverty — Computer Science and Engineering Department, Netaji Subhas Institute of Technology (NSIT), Dwarka, New Delhi, India

Patron

Vijay B. Aggarwal — Jagan Institute of Management Studies (JIMS), Rohini, Sector-05, New Delhi, India

Convener

Latika Kharb — Department of IT, Jagan Institute of Management Studies (JIMS), Rohini, Sector-05, New Delhi, India

Deepak Chahal — Department of IT, Jagan Institute of Management Studies (JIMS), Rohini, Sector-05, New Delhi, India

Technical Program Committee

Wenbing Zhao	Cleveland State University, USA
Abdel-Badeeh M. Salem	Ain Shams University, Abbasia, Cairo, Egypt
Mohd Nazri	Ismail University of Kuala Lumpur (UniKL), Malaysia
Janusz Kacprzyk	Systems Research Institute, Warsaw, Poland
Alexander Gelbukh	Mexican Academy of Sciences, Mexico
Rainier Ngie Ong	De La Salle University, Philippines
Prabhat K. Mahanti	University of New Brunswick, Canada
Markus Santoso	Fraunhofer Institute for Digital Media Technology, Germany
Sanjiv K Bhatia	University of Missouri – St. Louis, Columbia, USA
Mazliza Othman	University of Malaya, Kuala Lumpur, Malaysia
Brett J. O'Brien	University of Texas, Sant Antonio, USA
Rajendra V. Boppana	University of Texas, Sant Antonio, USA
Ramesh Rayudu	Victoria University of Wellington, New Zealand
Chin-chen Chang	Feng Chia University, Taichung, Taiwan
Nikos Komninos	University of London, UK

Chiranut Sa-ngiamsak	University of Manchester Institute of Science and Technology (UMIST), UK
Amirrudin	Kamsin University of Malaya, Kuala Lumpur, Malaysia
Mohamad Nizam Bin Ayub	University of Malaya, Kuala Lumpur, Malaysia
Rosli Salleh	University of Malaya, Kuala Lumpur, Malaysia
Ainuddin Wahid Abdul Wahab	University of Malaya, Kuala Lumpur, Malaysia
Shahaboddin Shamshirband	University of Malaya, Kuala Lumpur, Malaysia
Busyairah Binti Syd Ali	University of Malaya, Kuala Lumpur, Malaysia
Ali Mohammed Mansoor Alsahag	University of Malaya, Kuala Lumpur, Malaysia
Siew Hock Ow	University of Malaya, Kuala Lumpur, Malaysia
Cos Ierotheou	University of Greenwich, London, UK
Mohd Yamani Idna Bin Idris	University of Malaya, Kuala Lumpur, Malaysia
Kouichi Sakurai	Kyushu University, Fukuoka, Japan
Isaac Nti	Auckland University of Technology, Auckland, New Zealand
Ian H. Witten	University of Waikato, Hamilton, New Zealand
Ramesh Lal	Auckland University of Technology, Auckland, New Zealand
Edmund Lai	Auckland University of Technology, Auckland, New Zealand
Sharanjit Kaur	Acharya Narendra Dev College, University of Delhi, India
Manisha Bansal	IndraPrastha College for Women, University of Delhi, India
Muhammad Abulaish	South Asian University, University of Delhi, India
Pradeep Tomar	GBU, Greater Noida, Uttar Pradesh, India
Arpita Aggarwal	P.G.D.A.V College, University of Delhi, India
Khalid Raza	Jamia Milia Islamia, New Delhi, India
Sushanta Karmakar	IIT Guwahati, India
Bijendra Kumar	Netaji Subhas Institute of Technology, New Delhi, India
Ashwani Kush	Kurukshetra University, Kurukshetra, India
Anil Kumar Verma	Thapar University, Patiala, India
V.V. Subrahmanyam	Indira Gandhi National Open University, New Delhi, India
Anita Goel	Dyal Singh College, University of Delhi, India
Rakesh Kumar	National Institute of Technical Teachers Training and Research (NITTTR), Chandigarh, India
Deepak Gupta	NIT Arunchal Pradesh, India
M. Afshar Alam	Jamia Hamdard, New Delhi, India
Dhirendra Pratap Singh	MANIT Bhopal, India
Devesh C. Jinwala	SVNIT Surat, India

Suraiya Jabin	Jamia Milia Islamia, New Delhi, India
Upendra Kumar	BITS Patna, India
Anurag Singh	NIT Delhi, India
Jaya Thomas	NIT Delhi, India
V. Uma	NIT Pondichery, India
Nitin Kumar	NIT Utrakhand, India
Niketa Gandhi	University of Mumbai, India
Yogesh Kumar Meena	MNIT Jaipur, India
Subalalitha C.N	SRM University, Kanchipuram, India
Anurag Jain	GGSIPU, New Delhi, India
Dalton Meitei Thounaojam	NIT Silchar, India
Pranav Dass	Galgotias University, Noida, India
C. Malathy	SRM University Kanchipuram, Chennai, India
Neetu Sardana	Jaypee Institute of Information Technology, Noida, India
Vinod Keshaorao Pachghare	College of Engineering Pune, Pune, India
Ajay Mittal	Punjab Engineering College, Chandigarh, India
Jagannath Vithalrao Aghav	College of Engineering Pune, Pune, India
R. Vishwanathan	Galgotias University, Noida, India
P. Chitra	Thiagarajar College of Engineering, Madurai, India
Sunil B. Mane	College of Engineering Pune (COEP), Pune, India
C. SenthilKumar	Thiagarajar College of Engineering, Madurai, India
Sushama Nagpal	NSIT, New Delhi, India
Izharuddin	Aligarh Muslim University, Aligarh, India
S. Prabakaran	SRM University Kanchipuram, Chennai, India
Parameshachari B D	T G S S S Institute of Engineering & Technology for Women, Mysuru, Karnataka, India
Manas Ranjan Kabat	VSS University of Technology, Burla, India
Vibha Divyesh Patel	Nirma University, Gujrat, India
J. Akilandeswari	Sona College of Technology, Salem, India
Jereesh A S	Cochin University of Science and Technology, Cohin, India
Zayaraz Godandapani	Pondicherry Engineering College, Puducherry, India
E. Grace Mary Kanaga	Karunya University, Coimbatore, India
Aisha Banu	Crescent University, Chennai, India
Diptendu Sinha Roy	NIT Meghalaya, Meghalaya, India
Anala Pandit	Veermata Jijabai Technological Institute, Gujrat, India
Soubhagya Sankar Barpanda	C.V Raman College of Engineering, Orissa, India
Purushothama B R	NIT Goa, Goa, India
Angelina Geetha	Bsa Crescent University, Chennai, India
Ajay S. Patil	North Maharashtra University, Jalgaon, India
Zunnun Narmawala	Nirma University, Ahmedabad, India
S. Revathi	Crescent University, Chennai, India
Arka Prokash Mazumdar	MNIT Jaipur, Jaipur, India

B.B. Meshram	Veermata Jijabai Technological Institute, Mumbai, India
Pinaki Chakraborty	NSIT, New Delhi, India
Anita Singhrova	DCRUST, Murthal, India
Swati Aggarwal	NSIT, New Delhi, India
Ritu Sibal	NSIT, New Delhi, India
A. Amuthan	Pondicherry Engineering College, Puducherry, India
Suman Mann	MSIT, Delhi, India
G. Raghavendra Rao	The National Institute of Engineering, Mysore, India
R. Gomathi	Bannari Amman Institute of Technology, Tamil Nadu, India
Sandra Johnson	R.M.K. Engineering College, Tamil Nadu, India
Abhishek Swaroop	Galgotias University, Greater Noida, India
Bibhash Sen	NIT Durgapur, West Bengal, India
Pradeep Singh	NIT Raipur, Chhattisgarh, India
Pratyay Kuila	NIT Sikkim, Sikkim, India
Rinkle Rani	Thapar University Patiala, Punjab, India
R Sanjeev Kunte	J N N College of Engineering, Karnataka, India
T Sobha Rani	University of Hyderabad, Telangana, India
Arun Solanki	GBU, Greater Noida, Uttar Pradesh, India
Gurjit Kaur	GBU, Greater Noida, Uttar Pradesh, India
Preeti Gulia	MDU Rohtak, Haryana, India
Arun Sharma	IGTDW, Delhi, India
Om Prakash Sangwan	GJU Hissar, Haryana, India
Vijay kumar	Kautilya Institute of Technology and Engineering, Jaipur, India
B. Surendiran	NIT Puducherry, Puducherry, India
Namita Tiwari	MNIT Bhopal, Madhya Pradesh, India
Arambam Neelima	NIT Nagaland, Nagaland, India
Jagdeep Kaur	The NorthCap University Gurugram, Gurugram, India
Jagadeesh Kakarla	Rajasthan Technical University, Kota, Rajasthan, India
Karan Verma	Rajasthan Technical University, Kota, Rajasthan, India
Nishtha Kesswani	Rajasthan Technical University, Kota, Rajasthan, India
Shashank Srivastava	MNIT Bhopal, Madhya Pradesh, India
Kathemreddy Ramesh Reddy	Vikrama Simhapuri University, Andhra Pradesh, India
Jeegar Trivedi	Sardar Patel University, Gujrat, India
Prashant P. Pittalia	Sardar Patel University, Gujrat, India

Contents

Software Engineering

Algorithm and High Performance Computing

Network Systems
and Communication Security

CbdA: Cloud Computing Based DMIS on ANEKA

Shweta Meena[1(✉)], Rahul Johari[2], John Sushant Sundharam[3], and Kalpana Gupta[4]

[1] Delhi Technological University, Delhi, India
shweta82336@gmail.com
[2] USICT, GGSIPU, Delhi, India
[3] StartupFlux, New Delhi, India
[4] C-DAC, Sector-62, Noida, India

Abstract. A cloud computing application possesses the ability to have its processing tasks divided into small independent work units. These work units (in the form of tasks, threads etc.) are made to execute in parallel with complete independence from each other over the cloud. The proposed disaster management information system (DMIS) can be potentially used by amateurs, bureaucrats, technocrats and professionals working in the field or in the disaster affected area to handle any record based information, archive it, analyze it and use it even for forecasting the occurrence of disaster. Designing and deploying such an application over the cloud have given DMIS benefit of wide reach coupled with high performance, high reliability and better security.

Keywords: Cloud · Disaster · Disaster management · Aneka · PaaS · Information system · Task model · Cloud application

1 Introduction

Aneka [1–3] basically provides us a platform for developing cloud based application. There are three types of cloud computing service levels which are infrastructure-as-a-service (IaaS), platform-as-a-service (PaaS), and software-as-a service (SaaS). From the three services which are provided by cloud; Aneka serves as platform-as-service. It is used to build the customized applications and deploying them on either private cloud or on the public cloud. It is a .NET based Application PaaS. It provides an environment where it enables the user to design a customized application using any one of the several models provided by Aneka. Aneka provides its own set of API and libraries which users, if required can use directly. The Aneka integrates the applications which are designed and developed on other platforms. Aneka enables the simultaneous execution of multiple applications in parallel to each other. Aneka provides a runtime environment to the users though which they can create private and public clouds as well as they can create other application by using the several API provided by Aneka.

The key feature of Aneka PaaS is that it preserves the resources on public cloud like Amazon EC2 and on the another side it also provides public cloud resources which can be used for delivering data on the end user desktop.

© Springer Nature Singapore Pte Ltd. 2017
S. Kaushik et al. (Eds.): ICICCT 2017, CCIS 750, pp. 3–10, 2017.
https://doi.org/10.1007/978-981-10-6544-6_1

At the time of Aneka installation, Management Studio and client libraries are use which helps in developing the application using the resources and API provided by Aneka. The Management Studio act as a key component for the Aneka Cloud and it plays a main role in managing the Aneka Cloud.

2 Problem Statement

The objective of current work is to develop a disaster management system for the government, which is capable of handling and dissemination of the information about the number of people affected by disasters over the years. It can be used by the government so that it can provide all the facilities to the families of affected peoples as well as prepare it's citizens for specific disasters in areas which are more prone to them. The main objective behind developing such a cloud based application is to easily provide all the possible facilities to the people who are affected by disaster. The idea was to develop the application as there are very few web applications which can provide complete information at one point of time. One of the crucial advantage of this application is that it saves a lot of a person's time as well as it provides the useful information in reasonable amount of time.

3 Related Work

In [6, 11] the author describes the implementation of a console application named 'Unique Identifier System (UIS)'. The idea, notion and concept presented in this paper closely resembles to the UIS Application. It is a 15 digit code known as the unique identification number (UID) for a person allotted at the time of his birth. With the help of UID a person is recognized all over the world as the code generated contains the person's personal details like his/her country name, state to which he/she belong, gender, age, date of birth et al.

In [7] to use Cloud resources efficiently and gain maximum profit out of it, the author has used a Cloud analyst simulator based on Cloudsim which enables modelling and simulations in cloud's ambience. The paper explains the various cloud computing models like IaaS, SaaS, PaaS and about CloudSim and its simulation in the subsequent topics.

In [8], the author proposes a model for effective utilization of resources among several universities and research institutes located in different continents along with decrease in their infrastructural cost. It includes the concept of Cloud federation and Volunteer Computing. In this model, institutes can avail much higher computing power through cloud federation concept.

In [9] author(s) deals with Scientific Cloud Computing concept meaning thereby that the user has to focus on the application without being too much concerned about the infrastructure required and the installation process. Scientific Cloud is based on Infrastructure as a Service (IaaS) model which provides high performance computing virtual clusters as well as large number of virtual machines on demand.

In [10], for optimal utilization of resources, the author used CloudSim API to monitor the load patterns of various users through a web application. CloudSim is Cloud Simulation framework that is used for simulating the exact environment, visualizing the usage patterns and to monitor the load.

4   Architecture of ANEKA

The Management Studio of Aneka consists of two containers which are Master and Worker container. The adopted approach involved single master and multiple workers. The Management Studio usually manages and configures the Aneka Cloud. The master would basically control all the workers. After developing proposed application it would be analyzed how much time would be taken by the manager and worker container individually? It would then be evaluated whether the time taken by the Master container is less or more than the time taken by the Worker container. Once installation of the Management Studio is over, it is required to set a user credentials through which user would login and then install the available machines as worker container by setting one of the one of the machine as Master container. ANEKA provides a feature to design multiple Master container and multiple worker container that totally depends on type and purpose for which the application is designed and developed. The Management Studio manages the resource allocation of Aneka cloud that means it would decide who can access the resources? What resources can be allocated to the users? All these things are decided on the basis of the permission given to the users at the time of creating users account for Aneka Cloud.

5   Cloud Programming Model

Types of Cloud programming models which are available for the Aneka PaaS are as follows:-

5.1   Task Programming Model

In Task Programming model there are different tasks, as the name itself includes "Task" word. This model will be used if user wants to create a distributed application which contains different independent task. The main parts of this programming model are Execution unit, Work unit and Scheduler. Execution unit is responsible for executing all the independent tasks. The Work unit is responsible for keeping all records or work. Scheduler helps us in scheduling the independent task on work unit. Aneka provide an Execution unit for executing those tasks. In this model, their are three main blocks at the time of coding for developing the application. One key feature of this model is that there is no particular schedule in which tasks are scheduled for execution on the scheduler.

5.2   Thread Programming Model

The Thread programming model [4] basically uses the concept of process and thread. Process as well known is a collection of one or more thread. There are multiple types of thread one is Kernel based threads and another one is User threads. The general definition of thread is "sequence of one or more instructions which are executed in parallel with other instructions". In thread programming model there are only threads and there is no need to deal with any task. The threads which are created by the developers would be executed remotely. There is a concept of multi-threaded environment in which multiple threads which co-exist execute in parallel with all the available threads. So, User will virtualize the multi-threaded application to execute them on locally threaded application. Locally threaded applications are different from multi-threaded applications. This model is used when the user wants to uses the multi-threaded application on locally threaded Application in Aneka.

5.3   MapReduce Programming Model

The MapReduce Model basically consist of two different functions which are used in existing functional languages such as Lisp (1958). In MapReduce programming model there are two operations one is map and another one is reduce. Different key/value pairs are provided as input and output is also obtained in the form of key/value pair. It has two different phases for execution. In the first phase, different key/value pairs are given as input to the map function after execution another set of values corresponding to the inputs that were provided was obtained.

In the second one, all the intermediate values that were obtained after execution in the first phase were merged and they were grouped by keys corresponding to those values at the initial stage. Then reduce function was called once for each key with the associated values and it produced output values as final results of the MapReduce programming model.

6   Proposed Approach

The proposed DMIS application has been designed and developed in 3 stages:

- **Deploying a private cloud using Aneka**. A private cloud was deployed using Aneka over a single machine. For doing this, virtualization was used. Two Virtual Machines with Windows 7 were deployed and a NAT Network was setup between them. Aneka was deployed on these machines followed by the deployment of a master container and a worker container.
- **Gathering and integrating the dataset**. Disaster management information for the year 2001–2013 was acquired from the Open Government Data Platform of India [5]. The data was curated as per the need of the application. The curated data was then integrated into a local instance of a Microsoft SQL Server 2016 database.
- **Developing and deploying the cloud application**. The cloud application was developed using the task programming model. The functions of the application were developed as Aneka tasks which can be processed over the private cloud

deployed earlier. The application is a Windows Forms application based on .NET Framework 4.0 developed using Visual Studio 2015.

7 Experimental Set up: Application Development and Deployment

The Disaster Management Information System has five modules. These modules have been programmed as Windows Forms in C#. These forms are compatible with .NET Framework 4.0 and higher (Fig. 1).

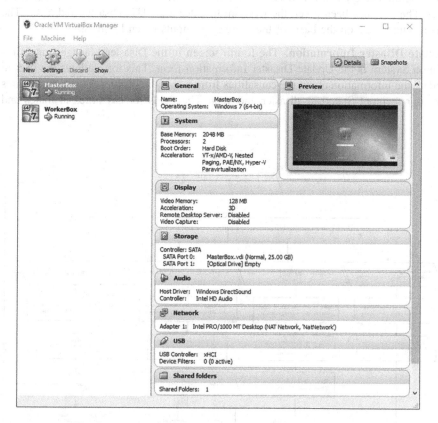

Fig. 1. VirtualBox start screen showing the virtual machines

Main Menu. The first screen in the Disaster Management Information System is the main menu. This menu gives access to all the other screens in the application. The main menu gives a user the functionality to open the add disaster information, view disaster information, update disaster information, delete disaster information and exit the application.

Add Disaster Information. The second screen in the Disaster Management Information System is the Add Disaster Information form. This form allows the user to add information about the causalities in a specific disaster. The user is expected to fill all the information in the form before the form can be submitted. The user needs to enter the name of the State/UT, the disaster and the year in which it occurred. The user also needs to enter the number of casualties in both males and females across different age groups.

View Disaster Information. The third screen in the Disaster Management Information System is the View Disaster Information form. This form allows the user to view information about the casualties in different disasters. The form has different pre-programmed queries which can be individually fired on the basis of the input of the user. The user has been given the freedom to enter State/UT, Disaster and Year. The results shown are on the basis of the number of inputs given by the user.

Update Disaster Information. The fourth screen in the Disaster Management Information System is the Update Disaster Information form. This form allows the user to update the information about the causalities from a specific disaster. The form requires the user to input State/UT, disaster and year. The fields for casualties in males and

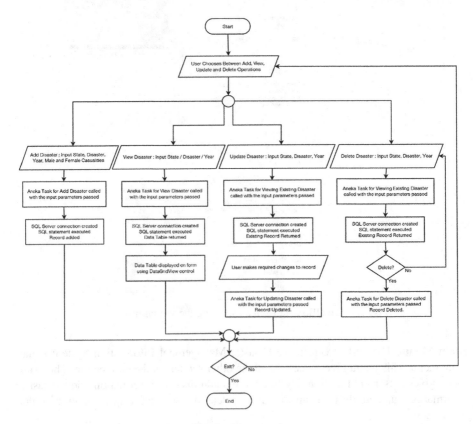

Fig. 2. Flow graph

females get populated on the basis of these inputs. These fields can now be edited to the desired values. The record will be saved after the user has made changes.

Delete Disaster Information. The fifth screen in the Disaster Management Information System is the Delete Disaster Information form. This form allows the user to delete the information about the causalities from a specific disaster. The form requires the user to input State/UT, disaster and year. The fields for casualties in males and females get populated on the basis of these inputs. The user can delete the record after viewing the information in it to ensure that he/she is deleting the correct record.

The flow chart depicting the working of the DMIS application is depicted in Fig. 2 and the Snapshots of the different modules designed and developed as part of Disaster Management Information System has been showcased in Figs. 3, 4, 5 and 6.

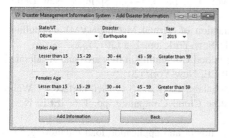

Fig. 3. Add information screen

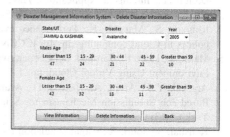

Fig. 4. Delete information screen

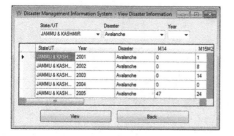

Fig. 5. View information screen

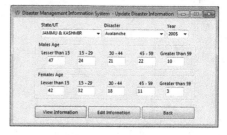

Fig. 6. Update information screen

8   Conclusion and Future Work

The objective of designing, developing and deploying the Disaster Management Information System on the Manjrasoft's Cloud Computing Platform: ANEKA was successfully achieved. In future work, in DMIS user credentials would be integrated so that only particular person that is administrator can only handle all the functionalities of this application. It is also proposed to integrate GIS feature in this application. Through GIS, it would be easy to locate the locations where disaster occurred and then it would fetch the data of that location in reasonable amount of time.

References

1. http://www.manjrasoft.com/download/3/AnekaInstallationGuide.pdf
2. http://www.manjrasoft.com/Aneka-Tutorial-Brief-WSU.pdf
3. Mastering Cloud Computing: Foundations and Applications Programming
4. Thread Model Programming Tutorial
5. Open Government Data (OGD) Platform India. https://data.gov.in/
6. Varshney, K., Johari, R., Ujjwal, R.L.: Unique identifier system using Aneka platform. In: Satapathy, S.C., Mandal, J.K., Udgata, Siba K., Bhateja, V. (eds.) Information Systems Design and Intelligent Applications. AISC, vol. 433, pp. 437–445. Springer, New Delhi (2016). doi:10.1007/978-81-322-2755-7_45
7. Khurana, S., Marwah, K.: Performance evaluation of Virtual Machine (VM) scheduling polices in Cloud computing. In: 4th ICCCNT, New York. pp. 1–5 (2013)
8. Malik, S., Huet, F., Caromel, D.: Cooperative Cloud Computing in Research and Academic Environment Using Virtual Cloud, pp. 1–7. IEEE, New York (2012)
9. Arackal, V.S., Arora, A., Saxena, D., Arunachalam, B., Rao, B.P.: SciInterface: A Web Based Job Submission Mechanism for Scientific Cloud Computing, pp. 1–6. IEEE, New York (2013)
10. Koushal, S., Johri, R.: Cloud simulation environment and application load monitoring. In: IEEE International Conference on Machine Intelligence Research and Advancement, pp. 554–558. IEEE, New York (2013)
11. Gupta, S., Johri, R.: UID C: Cloud based UID application. In: IEEE 7th International Conference on Cloud System and Big Data Engineering, Confluence, New York (2017, to appear)

Design of Task Scheduling Model for Cloud Applications in Multi Cloud Environment

P.K. Suri[1] and Sunita Rani[2(✉)]

[1] Department of Computer Science and Applications, Kurukshetra University, Kurukshetra, India
pksurikuk@gmail.com
[2] Department of CSE & IT, B.P.S.M.V., Khanpurkalan, Sonepat, Haryana, India
sunita.bpsmv@gmail.com

Abstract. Task Scheduling is important part in cloud computing environment for heterogeneous resources. Task scheduling is to allocate tasks to the best suitable resources to increase performance in terms of some dynamic parameters. The proposed scheduling model is constructed for cloud applications in multi cloud environment and implemented in three phases (minimization, grouping & ranking and execution) and considered average waiting time, average turnaround time, completion time and makespan as performance parameters. In this scheduling model, execution time of tasks in cloud applications is generated through normal distribution and exponential distribution. Ranking of tasks is based upon shortest job first strategy (SJF) and results are compared with other ranking method based upon first come first serve (FCFS) and largest processing time first (LPTF). The proposed scheduling model gives better performance as per defined performance parameters.

Keywords: Cloud computing · Scheduling model · Task grouping · Ranking · DAG (Directed Acyclic Graph) · SJF

1 Introduction

Cloud computing is parallel and distributed computing that is collection of inter-connected, dynamic and virtualized resources [1]. Resource Management is a very important issue in cloud computing and some various important factor such as cost, performance, functionality are affected by resource management [2]. Cloud resource management is mainly concerned with two aspects i.e. resource allocation and task scheduling. Resource allocation is to allocating resources to the needed applications as per the availability of resources. Task scheduling is to schedule jobs on the allocated resources achieving maximum profit, efficient resource utilization and to meet user's QoS requirement. Cloud computing resource management model has interconnected shared resources and interdependent, interrelated tasks that fall into workflow application model [3]. Workflow application model can be represented by Directed Acyclic Graph (DAG), where nodes represent task and edges represent interdependency and relationship between these tasks.

© Springer Nature Singapore Pte Ltd. 2017
S. Kaushik et al. (Eds.): ICICCT 2017, CCIS 750, pp. 11–24, 2017.
https://doi.org/10.1007/978-981-10-6544-6_2

In this paper, authors present a cloud task scheduling model in multi cloud environment based on workflow application models is presented. Cloud applications are represented as Directed Acyclic Graph. Execution time of all tasks corresponding to all resources is not known with certainty and the execution time of tasks is probabilistically generated through normal distribution and exponential distribution. This task scheduling model is works in three phases, in the first phase find minimum execution time of tasks, in second phase makes groups and assign ranking as per the SJF strategy and in the third phase execution of these groups are performed. This task scheduling model is compared with other algorithm that follows different ranking strategy i.e. FCFS (First Come First Serve) strategy and LPTF (Largest Processing Time First) strategy. Simulation is performed in MATLAB and a proposed scheduling model outperforms the other two models and minimizes waiting time, completion time and makespan.

This paper is organized as follows: Sect. 2 discusses the related work regarding this scheduling model. Section 3 presents proposed scheduling model and scheduling algorithm and its strategy. Section 4 provides the simulation results on the proposed scheduling algorithm using MATLAB. Section 5 gives the conclusion of this paper.

2 Related Work

Various resource allocation and task scheduling algorithms that are based upon grouping of tasks or jobs are proposed in cloud computing. A dynamic job- grouping scheduling strategy is [4] developed that considered processing requirements of jobs, granularity size and transmission of job groups to the required resources. Granularity size is used for measurement of total jobs executed within a specified time on a particular resource [4, 5]. Granularity is also defined as number of jobs to be grouped at a particular time [5].This scheduling strategy maximized the resource utilization and reduced overhead time of communication and processing of each jobs. An adaptive and parameterized job grouping scheduling algorithm is [5] proposed for grid jobs. Jobs are grouped according to the processing requirements of jobs, resource policies, network conditions and user's QoS requirements. In this scheduling algorithm all jobs are assumed for independent applications and [5] algorithm reduced the total processing time and cost of computational grid applications. An immediate mode scheduling of independent jobs in computational grids [6] that discussed the job allocation and considered makespan, flowtime, resource utilization and matching proximity parameters for performance measurement. This scheduling mode allocated the jobs to available resources for execution as these entered in the system. Fine grained grouping scheduling [7] that grouped lightweight jobs into coarse-grained jobs. Bandwidth-aware job grouping scheduling algorithm [8] proposed that grouped independent jobs with small processing requirements into suitable job groups with large processing requirements and scheduled according to network conditions. This scheduling strategy reduced the total job processing time. An algorithm [9] discussed in which jobs are grouped according to the ability of the resources according to the processing capabilities of resources. Scheduling algorithm [10] proposed that have task grouping, prioritization of bandwidth awareness and SJF algorithm and reduced processing time, waiting time and overhead. In this tasks are generated using Gaussian distribution and resources are created using random distribution. The smoothing concept for organization of tasks in heterogeneous multi-cloud environment [11] represented cloud model as DAG (Directed Acyclic Graph) and scheduling performed in two pass. In the first pass, tasks are divided into batches and in second pass batches are executed. A cost-based job grouping scheduling algorithm for grid computing environment [12] proposed where Job prioritization is done on the base of cost and then job grouping is performed. The fine grained jobs are grouped to coarse grained jobs and minimized the processing time and cost and achieved full utilization of resources. [13] proposed resource allocation algorithm for cloud computing system that have combined two algorithms, one is based on priority and second is based on earliest deadline first scheduling. This scheduling algorithm presented the task migration. In this scheduling, firstly assigned the priority of tasks and allocated the resources according to their priority and migrated the resources whenever they miss their deadline. This approach reduced the execution time and waiting time of preempt-able tasks. A task scheduling algorithm for heterogeneous multi-cloud environment that is based on Min-Min and Max-Min [14] proposed and this scheduling algorithm is executed with two phases and tested synthetic and benchmark data sets. This represented cloud as DAG (Directed Acyclic Graph) and performance is measured in terms of makespan and cloud utilization. A description of resource management and scheduling of cloud computing [15] presented and discussed cloud computing model and resource management model with virtual machine allocation and scheduling issues. Probabilistic availability based task scheduling algorithm (PATSA) [16] proposed where resources are scheduled on the basis of probabilistic availability of resources. This is based on assigning priority for each node by using rank value and application model is represented as DAG. Adaptive deadline based dependent job scheduling (A2DJS) algorithm for cloud computing [17] proposed that consisted job manager and data center. The job manger pointed the dependences among the tasks and eliminated ambiguity and data center comprised of job scheduler. This scheduling algorithm minimized the makespan of job and improved the utilization of the processing speed of the virtual machine. A hierarchical task model is proposed [18] that is associated with task scheduling for real applications in cloud computing. This algorithm considered parallel structure of sub-DAG and improved task execution concurrency and reduced the execution cost. A delay in task scheduling and delay-bound constraint is also discussed.

3 Scheduling Model

Cloud Scheduling Model (CSM) is represented with two parameters p and q, where p is the number of resources that are associated with scheduling model and q is the set of Cloud Applications (CA) that are associated with scheduling model. Cloud application is represented as DAG (Directed Acyclic Graph), i.e. CA = (T, E), where T is the set of nodes represents tasks of cloud application and E as edges represents the communication link between task. Each edge $e_{ij} = (t_i, t_j) \in E$ between task t_i and t_j represents the inter task communication and inter dependency of task.

Let consider CSM has m number of resources $(R_1, R_2, \ldots, R_m)$ and n number of cloud applications $(CA_1, CA_2, \ldots, CA_n)$ and each application with r number of tasks $(T_1, T_2, \ldots, T_r)$. Tasks of each cloud applications are submitted to resources for execution.

Execution Time matrix (ET_{ij}) for each task corresponding to each resource is generated.

Our proposed scheduling model is implemented with three phase. In the first phase, find the minimum execution time of each task corresponding to each resource, i.e. the task has different execution time on different resource (or machine) that has minimum execution time for tasks, for all tasks minimum execution time of resource are selected.

In second phase, makes the groups of tasks according to the minimum execution of tasks. The tasks with minimum execution time corresponding to that resource are placed in the same group. In this phase ranking is performed by mapping of the execution time of each task to a rank value. Ranking is based on the execution time of tasks. Rank value is assigned using Shortest Job First (SJF) strategy. The task with minimum execution time in a group is assigned the first rank, next minimum is assigned second rank and soon assign rank to each task.

Number of groups are formed as per the maximum number of resources, (let assume maximum value of resources is nn, then number of groups will be nn, Group 1, Group 2, ..., Group nn). Group of tasks is represented with two parameters, Group [nn, a], where nn is the resource number and a is the number of tasks encountered in a group.

In third phase, these groups are executed one after another in the ascending numeric order of groups (Group[1, a], Group[2, a'], ..., Group[nn, a''], where a, a', a'' be the number of tasks in Group 1, Group 2, ..., Group nn respectively) using the shortest job first (SJF) strategy, in the group which task has highest rank execute that task first, then second higher rank task and at last with lowest rank of task of that group and then execute second group and same process is repeated until all groups are executed.

3.1 Probabilistic Task Durations of Scheduling Model

In this scheduling model, execution time of tasks corresponding to resources is generated with two different approaches: one is the normally distributed and another one is exponentially distributed.

3.1.1 Normal Distribution
In this approach, execution time of tasks is to have normal distribution, following this distribution execution time is to be: $ET_{ij} = sigma*randn(T,R) + mue;$

Where, ET_{ij} is the execution time of task i on resource j, Sigma is standard deviation, Mue is mean value, T is Number of tasks, R is Number of Resources and randn() is function in MATLAB that generates normally distributed random numbers.

Here, value of sigma and mue is to be assumed for each application.

3.1.2 Exponential Distribution
In this approach, execution time of tasks is to have exponential distribution, following this distribution execution time is to be: $ET_{ij}=exprnd(Mue,T,R);$

Where, ET_{ij} is the execution time of task i on resource j, Mue is mean value, T is Number of tasks, R is Number of Resources and exprnd() is function in MATLAB that generates exponentially distributed random numbers. Here, value of Mue is to be assumed for each cloud application.

3.2   Notations Used in Algorithm

CSM(R,Q) – Cloud scheduling model with R resources and Q cloud applications
CA(T,E)- Cloud applications with T tasks and E communication links between tasks
R- Number of resources,
T- Number of tasks
ET_{ij} – Execution time of task i on resource j.
Rank- Rank Value of each task
CTT_{ij} – Completion Time of task i on resource j
CTG- Completion Time of a group on a resource
CT- Completion Time of all tasks or groups
WT-Waiting Time of task
AWT- Average Waiting Time
TAT- TurnAround Time
TTAT- Total TurnAround Time
ATAT- Average TurnAround Time
SJF-Shortest Job First
FCFS- First Come First Serve
LPTF- Largest Processing Time First

3.3   Scheduling Algorithm

Step1: Input T and R
Step 2: Generate Execution Time matrix $ET_{ij}[T,R]$
CASE 1: With task duration Normal Distribution
ET_{ij}=sigma*randn(T,R)+mue;
Sigma and mue are assumed for each cloud application.
CASE 2: With task duration Exponential Distribution
 ET_{ij}=exprnd(Mue,T,R);
Mue are assumed for each cloud application.
Step 3: Find Minimum execution time of task for resources
Step 4: Make groups of tasks that execute on the same resource due to minimum execution time
Step 5: Assign Rank to each task in each group
Step 6: Execute all groups in ascending order of groups
Step 7: Calculate Total Waiting Time
TWT=WT+TWT;
Step 8: Compute Average Waiting Time
AWT=TWT/T;
Step 9: Calculate Total TurnAround Time
TTAT=WT+ET
Step 10: Compute Average TurnAround Time
ATAT=TTAT/T;
Step 11: Compute Completion Time of each Group
$CTG=CTT_1 +CTT_2+...+CTT_n$; [n number of tasks in a group]
Step 12: Compute Completion time of all tasks
$CT=CTG_1+CTG_2+....+CTG_m$
Step 13: Compute Makespan [19]
Makespan=max $(CTG_1, CTG_2,....,CTG_m)$

4 Results and Discussion

In this paper, task scheduling model for cloud applications in multi cloud environment with Probabilistic Task Duration has proposed and its performance is evaluated. Simulation is performed using MATLAB. A comparison is made among three algorithms, in first one ranking is based on SJF strategy, in second one ranking is based on FCFS strategy, and third one is based on LPTF strategy. Here, we have showed two cases, in CASE 1 Execution Time is generated using Normal Distribution and in CASE 2 Execution Time is generated using Exponential Distribution. Performance is measured with average waiting time, average turnaround time, completion time of all groups and makespan = max $(CTG_1, CTG_2, ..., CTG_m)$ [19].

4.1 CASE 1: Execution Time of Tasks is Generated with Normal Distribution

In this execution time of tasks corresponding to resources is follows normal distribution and ten runs are made with different values of number of tasks and number of resources and different values of mue and sigma, average waiting time, average turnaround time, completion time and makespan is noted down as shown in Tables 1 and 2.

In Fig. 1, average waiting time is compared with different values of T, R, MUE and SIGMA as shown in Table 1, figure shows average waiting time of tasks with SJF ranking strategy is always less as compared to the other two ranking strategy.

In Fig. 2, average turnaround time is compared with different values of T, R, MUE and SIGMA as shown in Table 1, figure shows average turnaround time of tasks with SJF ranking strategy is always less as compared to the other two ranking strategy.

In Fig. 3, completion time of all tasks is compared with different values of T, R, MUE and SIGMA as shown in Table 2, figure shows completion time of all tasks with SJF ranking strategy is always less as compared to the other two ranking strategy.

In Fig. 4, makespan is compared with different values of T, R, MUE and SIGMA as shown in Table 2, figure shows makespan with SJF ranking strategy is always less as compared to the other two ranking strategy.

4.2 CASE 2: Execution Time of Tasks is Generated with Exponential Distribution

In this execution time of tasks corresponding to resources is follows exponential distribution and ten runs are made with different values of number of tasks and number of resources and different values of mue, average waiting time, average turnaround time, completion time and makespan is noted down as shown in Tables 3 and 4.

In Fig. 5, average waiting time is compared with different values of T, R and Mue as shown in Table 3, figure shows average waiting time of tasks with SJF ranking strategy is always less as compared to the other two ranking strategy.

Table 1. Table with normally distributed execution time of tasks in different cloud applications with different values of T, R, Mue and Sigma for average execution time and average turnaround time

Sr. no.	MUE	SIGMA	T	R	Average waiting time			Average turnaround time		
					SJF	FCFS	LPTF	SJF	FCFS	LPTF
Application 1	40.0342	29.9833	50	25	1.3801	3.1824	4.825	4.6622	6.4644	8.107
Application 2	29.7401	19.0356	350	100	0.75764	1.4661	2.1115	1.6193	2.3278	2.9731
Application 3	34.2915	24.9953	500	100	1.0577	2.1491	3.26	1.8808	2.9722	4.0831
Application 4	37.3542	29.3779	500	100	1.1419	2.2081	3.2859	1.9824	3.0486	4.1264
Application 5	42.2735	19.9938	600	150	1.5553	2.9551	4.3691	3.1268	4.5266	5.9406
Application 6	18.6186	6.5901	700	300	0.76688	1.4729	2.1857	2.0062	2.7122	3.425
Application 7	105.3209	48.4132	3000	500	1.85	3.6697	5.7004	3.1087	4.9284	6.9591
Application 8	93.2298	44.3965	3000	500	1.5153	3.0225	4.4857	2.5183	4.0255	5.4887
Application 9	86.4021	38.1572	5000	1000	0.77282	1.5234	2.3214	1.3876	2.1382	2.9362
Application 10	73.6956	34.2227	5000	1000	0.54622	1.0769	1.6587	0.98716	1.5178	2.0997

Table 2. Table with normally distributed execution time of tasks in different cloud applications with different values of T, R, Mue and Sigma for Completion time and Makespan

Sr. no.	MUE	SIGMA	T	R	Completion time			Makespan		
					SJF	FCFS	LPTF	SJF	FCFS	LPTF
Application 1	40.0342	29.9833	50	25	233.108	323.22	405.35	35.2635	45.1	62.306
Application 2	29.7401	19.0356	350	100	566.74	814.72	1040.6	26.6933	41.931	51.511
Application 3	34.2915	24.9953	500	100	940.412	1486.1	2041.5	62.0506	95.269	143.15
Application 4	37.3542	29.3779	500	100	991.188	1524.3	2063.2	73.064	116.75	131.02
Application 5	42.2735	19.9938	600	150	1876.08	2716	3564.3	63.0974	121.51	134.03
Application 6	18.6186	6.5901	700	300	1404.31	1898.5	2397.5	34.8354	54.512	62.551
Application 7	105.3209	48.4132	3000	500	9326.25	14785	20877	88.1595	166.93	210.9
Application 8	93.2298	44.3965	3000	500	7554.97	12077	16466	80.3987	150.99	216.96
Application 9	86.4021	38.1572	5000	1000	6937.98	10691	14681	35.7892	63.018	92.38
Application 10	73.6956	34.2227	5000	1000	4935.79	7589.1	10498	26.3422	48.746	65.765

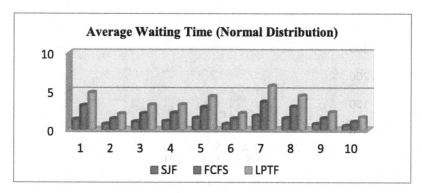

Fig. 1. Average waiting time for normally distributed execution time of cloud applications

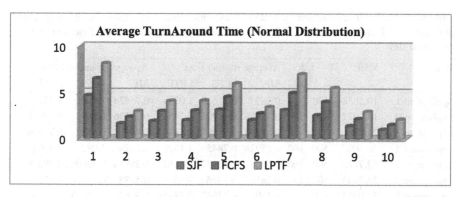

Fig. 2. Average turnaround time for normally distributed execution time of cloud applications

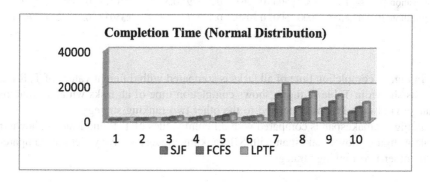

Fig. 3. Completion time for normally distributed execution time of cloud applications

In Fig. 6, average turnaround time is compared with different values of T, R and Mue as shown in Table 3, figure shows average turnaround time of tasks with SJF ranking strategy is always less as compared to the other two ranking strategy.

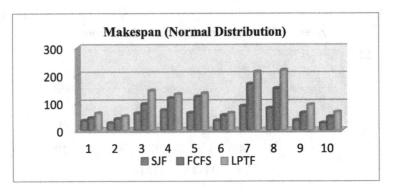

Fig. 4. Makespan for normally distributed execution time of cloud applications

Table 3. Table with exponential distributed execution time of tasks in different cloud applications with different values of T, R and Mue for average execution time and average turnaround time

Sr. no.	MUE	T	R	Average waiting time			Average turnaround time		
				SJF	FCFS	LPTF	SJF	FCFS	LPTF
Application 1	10.5638	100	30	0.382	0.71629	1.0394	0.76624	1.1005	1.4237
Application 2	14.1972	350	100	0.11869	0.24906	0.34515	0.25196	0.38232	0.47841
Application 3	21.89	350	100	0.18712	0.34369	0.58401	0.40219	0.55877	0.79909
Application 4	30.8007	500	100	0.35928	0.78456	1.1576	0.65786	1.0831	1.4562
Application 5	12.7863	500	100	0.16062	0.30157	0.46627	0.28914	0.43009	0.59479
Application 6	38.7043	600	150	0.28152	0.53863	0.83794	0.54884	0.80595	1.1053
Application 7	53.9315	800	250	0.16025	0.34642	0.51156	0.3862	0.57237	0.73751
Application 8	65.9462	1000	300	0.178	0.36543	0.54618	0.39964	0.58707	0.76783
Application 9	44.152	3000	500	0.12632	0.25779	0.38681	0.21218	0.34365	0.47268
Application 10	67.8355	3000	500	0.20992	0.42997	0.63597	0.35037	0.57042	0.77643

In Fig. 7, completion time of all tasks is compared with different values of T, R and Mue as shown in Table 4, figure shows completion time of all tasks with SJF ranking strategy is always less as compared to the other two ranking strategy.

In Fig. 8, makespan is compared with different values of T, R and Mue as shown in Table 4, figure shows makespan with SJF ranking strategy is always less as compared to the other two ranking strategy.

Table 4. Table with exponential distributed execution time of tasks in different cloud applications with different values of T, R and Mue for completion time and makespan

Sr. no.	MUE	T	R	Completion time			Makespan		
				SJF	FCFS	LPTF	SJF	FCFS	LPTF
Application 1	10.5638	100	30	76.6243	110.054	142.366	13.4921	21.6426	22.8266
Application 2	14.1972	350	100	88.1857	133.812	167.445	4.4786	8.3735	8.5562
Application 3	21.89	350	100	140.768	195.568	279.68	6.0347	7.3009	14.8408
Application 4	30.8007	500	100	328.93	541.572	728.092	19.1547	38.7021	45.6242
Application 5	12.7863	500	100	144.568	215.044	297.395	7.1397	11.8357	17.1671
Application 6	38.7043	600	150	329.302	483.569	663.152	11.832	15.2958	22.5624
Application 7	53.9315	800	250	308.963	457.897	590.01	8.8954	14.9909	19.0281
Application 8	65.9462	1000	300	399.642	587.071	767.829	9.5586	14.5679	23.3159
Application 9	44.152	3000	500	636.548	1030.96	1418.03	6.611	12.1458	17.682
Application 10	67.8355	3000	500	1051.12	1711.27	2329.29	11.9007	24.0619	27.4316

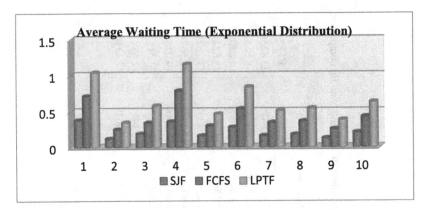

Fig. 5. Average waiting time for exponentially distributed execution time of cloud applications

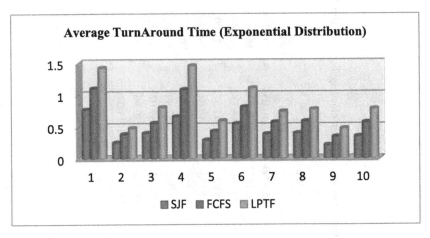

Fig. 6. Average turnaround time for exponentially distributed execution time of cloud applications

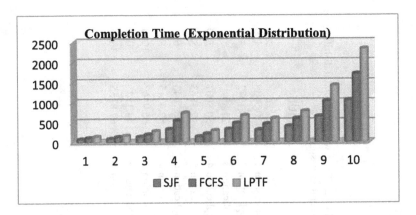

Fig. 7. Completion time for exponentially distributed execution time of cloud applications

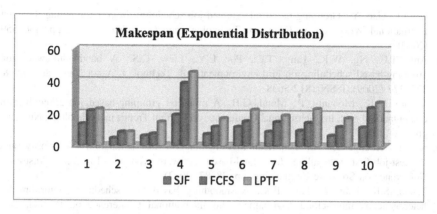

Fig. 8. Makespan for exponentially distributed execution time of cloud applications

5 Conclusion

The presented task scheduling model for different cloud applications in multi cloud environment is simulated in MATLAB and results show the presented algorithm give better performance i.e. minimized average waiting time and turnaround time and minimized completion time and makespan. The simulation results gives two cases, one case is where execution time of task in generated through normal distribution and another is where execution time of tasks is generated through exponential distribution. The simulation results show that presented scheduling model is compared with other two ranking strategy, i.e., first come first serve (FCFS) and largest processing time first (LPTF).

References

1. Buyya, R., Yeo, C.S., Venugopal, S., Broberg, J., Brandic, I.: Cloud computing and emerging IT platforms: vision, type, and reality for delivering computing as the 5th utility. Futur. Gener. Comput. Syst. **25**, 599–616 (2009)
2. Suri, P.K., Rani, S.: Simulator for priority based scheduling of resources in cloud computing. Int. J. Comput. Appl. **146**(14), 10–15 (2016)
3. Lee, Y.C., Subrata, R., Zomaya, A.Y.: On the performance of a dual-objective optimization model for workflow applications on grid platforms. IEEE Trans. Parallel Distrib. Syst. **20**(9), 1273–1283 (2009)
4. Muthuvelu, N., Liu, J., Soe, N.L., Venugopal, S., Sulistio, A., Buyya, R.: A dynamic job grouping-based scheduling for deploying applications with fine-grained tasks on global grids. In: Coddington, P., Wendelborn, A. (eds.) Australasian Workshop on Grid Computing and e-Research (AusGrid2005), Newcastle, Australia. Conferences in Research and Practice in Information Technology, vol. 44. Australian Computer Society, Adelaide (2005)
5. Muthuvelu, N., Chai, I., Eswaran, C.: An adaptive and parameterized job grouping algorithm for scheduling grid jobs. In: ICACT, pp. 975–980 (2008). ISBN 978-89-5519-136-3
6. Xhafa, F., Barolli, L., Durresi, A.: Immediate mode scheduling of independent jobs in computational grids. In: 21st International Conference on Advanced Networking and Applications (AINA 2007) (2007)

7. Liu, Q., Liao, Y.: Grouping-based fine-grained job scheduling in grid computing. In: First International Workshop on Education Technology and Computer Science, pp. 556–559 (2009)
8. Ang, T.F., Ng, W.K., Ling, T.C., Por, L.Y., Liew, C.S.: A bandwidth-aware job grouping-based scheduling on grid environment. Inf. Technol. J. Asian Netw. Sci. Inf. **8**, 372–377 (2009). ISSN 1812-5638
9. Mishra, M.K., Mohanty, P., Mund, G.B.: A modified grouping-based job scheduling in computational grid. In: International Conference on Current Trends in Technology, Nuicone, pp. 1–6 (2011)
10. Ru, J., Keung, J.: An empirical investigation on the simulation of priority and shortest-job-first scheduling for cloud-based software systems. In: 22nd Australian Conference on Software Engineering, pp. 78–87 (2013)
11. Panda, S.K., Nag, S., Jana, P.K.: A smoothing based task scheduling algorithm for heterogeneous multi-cloud environment. In: International Conference on Parallel, Distributed and Grid Computing, pp. 62–67. IEEE (2014)
12. Yadav, S., Agarwal, A., Rastogi, R.: Cost-based job grouping and scheduling algorithm for grid computing environments. Int. J. Comput. Appl. **91**(15), 21–27 (2014). ISSN 0975-8887
13. Gupta, G., Kumawat, V.K., Laxmi, P.R., Singh, D., Jain, V., Singh, R.: A simulation of priority based earliest deadline first scheduling for Cloud computing system. In: First International Conference on Networks & Soft Computing, pp. 35–39 (2014)
14. Panda, S.K., Jana, P.K.: An efficient task scheduling algorithm for heterogeneous multi-cloud environment. In: International Conference on Advances in Computing, Communications and Informatics (ICACCI), pp. 1204–1209 (2014)
15. Bittencourt, L.F., Madeira, E.R., da Nelson, L.S., Fonseca, N.L.S.: Resource management and scheduling. In: Fonseca, N., Boutaba, R. (eds.) Cloud Services, Networking, and Management, 1st edn, pp. 243–267. Wiley, New York (2014)
16. Chitra, S., Prashanth, C.S.R.: Probabilistic availability based task scheduling algorithm. IEEE (2015)
17. Komarasamy, D., Muthuswamy, V.: Adaptive deadline based dependent job scheduling algorithm in cloud computing. In: Seventh International Conference on Advanced Computing (ICoAC), pp. 1–5 (2015)
18. Mao, Y., Zhong, H., Li, X.: Hierarchical model-based associate tasks scheduling with the deadline constraints in the cloud. In: Proceeding of the 2015 IEEE International Conference on Information and Automation, Lijiang, China, pp. 268–273, August 2015
19. Oyetunji, E.O., Oluleye, A.E.: Minimizing makespan and total completion time criteria on a single machine with release dates. J. Emerg. Trends Eng. Appl. Sci. **1**(1), 100–108 (2010)

Analysis of Epidemic Outbreak in Delhi Using Social Media Data

Sweta Swain$^{(\boxtimes)}$ ⓘ and K.R. Seeja

Department of Computer Science and Engineering, Indira Gandhi Delhi
Technical University for Women, Delhi, India
swetaswain86@gmail.com, seeja@igdtuw.ac.in

Abstract. A Social media generates a vast amount of data related to epidemic outbreak every year. Data produced by social media platform such as Twitter for health surveillance applications is exponentially increasing. Chikungunya and Dengue are taking the toll on Delhi in the year 2016 and mining twitter data reflects the status of Chikungunya and Dengue outbreak in Delhi. In this paper, the tweets extracted from twitter over a time period using epidemic - related keyword are classified using a supervised classification technique called Naïve Bayes classifier with manual tagging feature into relevant epidemic - related tweets with 90% accuracy. The relevant tweets classified are enumerated for analyzing the spread and estimating the most affected month during the outbreak and compare it with the health statistics.

Keywords: Social media data · Twitter · Chikungunya · Dengue · Tweets

1 Introduction

With the advent of social media, amount of data on social network increased tremendously. Social media [1] explores vast amount of data for extracting useful information like events, patterns, trends or outbreaks. Social media analytics helps to uncover meaningful information from the available online data and to gain knowledge from the data for understandability of the event. Social media channels, such as Twitter, generate epidemic-related information over a time period which is used to analyze the effect of outbreak and reflects the status of chikungunya outbreak in Delhi. Dengue, a "Flavivirus" and Chikungunya, an "Alphavirus", spread by "Aedes mosquitoes", are transmitted among people at a rapid pace in India every year. "Aedes aegypti" mosquitoes are vectors generally found in "Dengue" and "Chikungunya" virus. In regions where both viruses found, they often spread infection together [2]. Chikungunya, which has never really been a big worry in the north, however the abrupt rise in chikungunya cases in Delhi and a few different parts of north India, has come almost after 10 years in the country [3] .

Twitter [4] is a social media platform provides real-time information. Unlike other information sources, Twitter is up-to-date and provides information about the ongoing news and events around the world. Data generated in twitter being mined to have a glimpse of public views in general, but also within the health sector for monitoring diseases and delivering healthcare services at minimal cost. In this paper, the tweets are

© Springer Nature Singapore Pte Ltd. 2017
S. Kaushik et al. (Eds.): ICICCT 2017, CCIS 750, pp. 25–34, 2017.
https://doi.org/10.1007/978-981-10-6544-6_3

extracted from twitter using hash-tags or keywords as indicators of topics to produce reliable results and classified the tweets into relevant and irrelevant using a supervised machine learning technique. The tweets classified as relevant are used to analyze the epidemic outbreak over a time period and enumerated for estimating the most affected month during the outbreak period in Delhi. The proposed methodology shows a correlation between number of tweets and number of chikungunya – dengue cases which helps to monitor or analyze the spread of epidemic in the Delhi.

2 Literature Review

During the last decades, social media generates large amount of data in terms of users experiences, thinking and feeling and the contents are analyzed using machine learning approach [5]. Social media data is being analyzed to predict or estimate the spread of epidemic outbreak over a region. Various frameworks have been developed for extracting and studying the opinions and views of users on a trending topic. Harunalsah et al. [6] developed such framework for users, manufacturing companies, and enforcement agencies to analyze the views and reaction of users related to brand or product in order to take immediate action with the rise in negative sentiment; the proposed framework focused on analyzing the facebook comment posted by users and data from twitter related to product or brand.

There are certain protocols to be followed to extract and collect tweets from twitter and to analyze the affect of epidemic. The extractions of tweets and to have epidemic outbreak insights from huge amount of data generated through social media which helps healthcare, government officials, and policymakers in decision making process and provides insights and awareness about epidemic outbreaks in present time are described by Yusheng Xie et al. [7]. Lampos et al. [8] proposed a framework for analysis or to monitor tweets from Twitter to track flu rates in the states of U.K and obtain a "flu-score" for each document by analyzing each word and their associated score based on predictive power on held-out data. The result is highly correlated with the statistical report provided by the U.K.'s Health Protection Agency with 92% by using a set of 41 manually selected "markers". Unlike our work, A. Culotta [9], monitor Tweets from Twitter over eight month period and they infer that analyzing a few flu-related keywords permit us to predict influenza rates in future with high accuracy, acquire a 95% correlation with national health report by filtering out misleading tweets.

In our work we will classify the tweets as irrelevant and relevant tweets as Nivedha et al. [10] classifies the twitter data into health and non-health data where as Ishtiaq Ahmed et al. [11] proposes a hybrid system for document classification to detect spam or ham using classifier Naïve Bayes and Apriori Algorithm. They achieve a significant improvement on accuracy 98.7% which outperform the state of the art algorithm. Missier et al. [12] discuss methods to extract relevant content from twitter data using appropriate hash tags or keywords in order to focus on a specific trend using supervised classification and clustering by topic modeling. However, supervised classification segregated good proportion of actionable messages with 80% prediction accuracy. The relevant tweets being classified are analyzed to model the affect of outbreak over the time by spatial analysis as discussed on [13]. Unlike ours work Gomide et al. [14] proposed a dengue surveillance system provide weekly analysis of the content to analyze what is happening in each city in comparison with the last week.

3 Proposed Methodology

In this section, we describe how to extract, process and analyze tweets for estimating the most effected month during epidemic outbreak in Delhi. The steps involved in the proposed methodology are shown in Fig. 1.

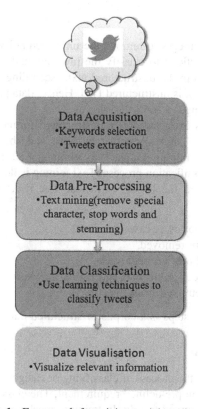

Fig. 1. Framework for mining social media data.

3.1 Data Acquisition

In data acquisition, the tweets are extracted from the twitter using predefined parameters. Twitter, a social media platform that allows users to post 140 character messages (and photos) called as tweets to the world [15]. Trending topics are often denoted using the hash tag, #. The nature of Twitter is to keep the messages length brief and focus on one trending topic at a time. Twitter provides a public API to access their database of tweets, with an average query time of less than 100 ms. This API allow access not just to the text of the tweets, but also to all available metadata including user handle, location, date, language, time created, profile description and others. Data acquisition includes two steps called selecting keywords and extracting tweets.

Selecting keywords - Identify suitable keywords or hashtags for extracting tweets related to the topic to create a corpus for analysis.

Extracting tweets – Twitter provides access to twitter database through application programming interface (API) [16] for extracting tweets using hash tags. For accessibility, create an account on twitter site to create an application for establishing connection with twitter API. Application created provides credentials required for establishing connection for extraction tweets.

3.2   Data Pre-processing

Data Pre-processing is a process to remove the unwanted/noisy information from the tweets extracted as it is difficult to classify the raw data and which helps to uncover meaningful information from the unstructured text. According to Merrill Lynch more than 80% of the information is unstructured [17]. Hence, data pre-processing of tweets is also called as text mining.

Text mining – Tweets extracted are in unstructured format, due to informal conversations, short messages, signs, grammatical error and abbreviations used by the twitter users. Thus, text mining is used to eliminate all special characters and unstructured forms for classification process. Text mining is done to remove noisy and unwanted information from the tweets extracted. The tweet undergoes a series of pre-processing [18] steps:

- Conversion of tweets to lower case character.
- Username and URL are removed.
- Punctuation, links and tabs are removed.
- Removal of white spaces at the start and ending of tweets.
- Stop words are also removed from tweets.

The resultant of above steps is a corpus of structured data.

3.3   Data Classification

Data Classification [10] is the process of classifying or categorizing the data into types, class and category based on pre-defined requirement. The classification of data consist of two phase called training and testing. In training, machine learns the data and their associate class. In testing, machine test the data based on the training to predict the output. Tweets are classified into relevant tweets and irrelevant tweets as shown in Table 1. Relevant tweets include personal tweets, opinions and news and irrelevant tweets includes jokes and sarcastic tweets.

The Text classification using supervised learning techniques has two parts:
1. Training

(1) In training, each input value is transformed to a feature set by feature extractor.

Table 1. Tweets with associated category, description and example.

Category	Description	Examples	Tweet
Personal tweets	Tweet describes the thoughts of a user in a particular situation	"I was suffering from #chikungunya"	Relevant
News	News that reports the no: of cases in a specific areas, report on preventive measures and campaigns	Fogging banish #mosquitoes #Chikungunya #dengue #delhi Peparation for 2017? The truth is out there, somewhere. Delhi civic bodies update official dengue toll to six. https://t.co/JFt3cXSiZZ#dengue#publichealth	Relevant
Jokes	Jokes are irrelevant tweets	You're lucky if you're in Delhi and you don't get #dengueor #chikungunya. It's almost an annual trend & amp; everyone seems to be okay with it	Irrelevant

(2) The feature sets created gather information about each input value which is used for classification.

(3) Feature sets and labels pairs are sustained into the machine learning algorithm to create a model.

2. Prediction

In prediction, for conversion of unobserved to features sets the same feature extractor is used. These feature sets are inputted into the model, which produces predicted labels.

3.3.1 Naïve Bayes Classifier

Naïve Bayes classifier is used for classification of data into relevant and irrelevant. Naïve Bayes is simple classification technique which depends on Bayes theorem with an assumption called strong naïve independence. This assumption deals with each word as a single, independent and mutually exclusive. This model can be described as "Independent Feature Model" [11]. The steps involved in classifying tweets using Naïve Bayes is:

1. Create a document term matrix - It depicts the recurrence of each term in each document in the corpus and performs the transposition of it. The most commonly used document representation is called vector space model (VSDM).
2. Create a training set and test set - The document term matrix is partitioned into train set and test set. trainSize and testSize describes the size of documents in the training set and test set, respectively.
3. Training and Evaluating models - The train_model() is used train the model on the data.

3.4 Data Visualization

Data Visualization helps in inferring the impact of the event or the topic on the pubic easily through graphical means. Visualization [19] presents data and analysis results in context, and thus, it can provide rich evidence that supports or contradicts the analysis results, and consequently, help with data interpretation and result validation. Twitter helps to plot a graph describing the most affected month during outbreak in Delhi.

4   Implementation

For analysis of epidemic outbreak, we extract the tweets from twitter using Twitter API [16]. Twitter provides a public API to access their database of tweets by establishing a connection. For extracting epidemic-related tweets, #Chikungunya, #Dengue and #Delhi was selected as relevant keywords for target topic. 4037 tweets were extracted matching the keywords "Chikungunya" "Delhi" and 3103 tweets were extracted matching the keywords "Dengue" "Delhi" using twitteR [20] package and saved as .CSV file. Subsequently, Data preprocessing removes all the unwanted information from the extracted tweets and create a corpus for applying classification technique using tm [21] package. The other keywords related with the target topic are shown in the wordcloud Fig. 2.

Fig. 2. Keywords associated with the Chikungunya-Dengue outbreak.

Naïve Bayes classifier is used, for classifying the tweet into two specified categories. The cleaned corpus is manually tagged into relevant and irrelevant tweets where 70% of data is considered as train set and rest is considered as test set. The classifier classifies 4037 tweets related to chikungunya as 2631 relevant tweets and 1406 irrelevant tweets with 90% accuracy and dengue related 3103 tweets classified as 2000 relevant and 1103 irrelevant tweets with the accuracy of 92% using package e1071 [22]. The relevant tweets are enumerated so as to analyze the spread and estimate the most effected month during the epidemic outbreak. The number of relevant tweets generated every month from Twitter in the outbreak season is represented using ggplot2 [23] as shown in Figs. 4 and 6.

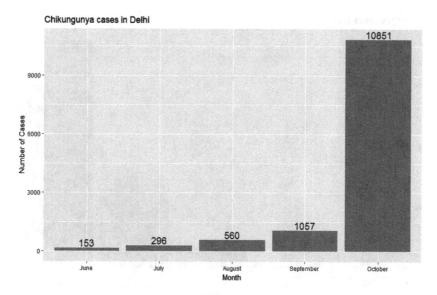

Fig. 3. Reported Chikungunya cases in Delhi [24].

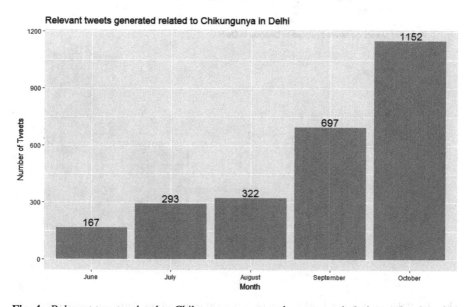

Fig. 4. Relevant tweets related to Chikungunya generated every month during outbreak period.

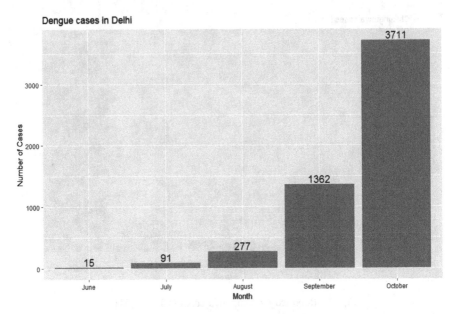

Fig. 5. Reported Dengue cases in Delhi [24].

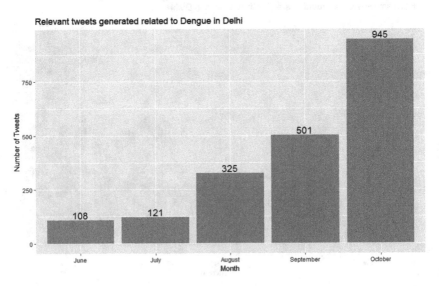

Fig. 6. Relevant tweets related to dengue generated every month during outbreak period.

5 Result

Social media data analysis shows that the high number of tweets related to chikungunya case were generated between the month of September and October in the outbreak period as shown in Fig. 4 where as the number of cases more in the month of

October according to government statistics [24, 25] as shown in Fig. 3. For Dengue, the number of cases of Dengue is more in the month of October by government statistics [24, 26] as shown in Fig. 5 where as the analysis of social media data shows that the high numbers of tweets were generated between the month of September and October in the outbreak period as shown in Fig. 6. The outbreak analysis shows a strong correlation between the number of tweets and the number of chikungunya-dengue cases in Delhi i.e., with the increase in number of tweets, the number of chikungunya-dengue cases also increasing which results in the spreading of epidemic in the capital city.

6 Conclusion

Social media generates great amount of information in a short period of time through liking, chatting, and tweeting in the form of unstructured data due to increase in popularity among people. Social media channel such as Twitter, generate epidemic-related information in the form of tweets and analyzing the tweets evinces the affect of epidemic outbreak in Delhi. In this paper, the unstructured data gathered from twitter is processed using text mining techniques and classified to extract relevant tweets using Naïve bayes classifier; in order to analyze the spread and find the most affected month during chikungunya-Dengue outbreak in Delhi. Thus, social media analytics extracts meaningful information from the large dataset, in order to analyze the effect of the event on the public.

References

1. Batrinca, B., Treleaven, P.C.: Social media analytics: a survey of techniques, tools and platforms. AI Soc. **30**(1), 89–116 (2015)
2. Chahar, H.S., Bharaj, P., Dar, L., Guleria, R., Kabra, S.K., Broor, S.: Co-infections with Chikungunya virus and Dengue virus in Delhi, India. Emerg. Infect. Dis. **15**(7), 1077–1080 (2009)
3. Chikungunya, Dengue sting India, with over 12,000 cases across country and 10 deaths in Delhi. http://www.firstpost.com/living/chikungunya-dengue-sting-india-with-over-12000-cases-across-country-and-6-deaths-in-delhi-3003632
4. Sakaki, T., Okazaki, M., Matsuo, Y.: Earthquake shakes Twitter users: real-time event detection by social sensors. In: Proceedings of the 19th International Conference on World Wide Web, pp. 851–860. ACM (2010)
5. Isah, H., Trundle, P., Neagu, D.: Social media analysis for product safety using text mining and sentiment analysis. In: 14th UK Workshop on Computational Intelligence (UKCI), pp. 1–7. IEEE (2014)
6. Xie, Y., Chen, Z., Cheng, Y., Zhang, K., Agrawal, A., Liao, W.K., Choudhary, A.: Detecting and tracking disease outbreaks by mining social media data. In: Proceedings of the 23rd International Joint Conference on Artificial Intelligence, pp. 2958–2960 (2013)
7. Ye, X., Li, S., Yang, X., Qin, C.: Use of social media for the detection and analysis of infectious diseases in China. ISPRS Int. J. Geo-Inf. **5**(9), 1–17 (2016)

8. Lampos, V., Cristianini, N.: Tracking the flu pandemic by monitoring the social web. In: 2nd International Workshop on Cognitive Information Processing, pp. 411–416 (2010)

9. Culotta, A.: Detecting influenza outbreaks by analyzing Twitter messages. arXiv preprint arXiv:1007.4748 (2010)

10. Nivedha, R., Sairam, N.: A machine learning based classification for social media messages. Indian J. Sci. Technol. **8**(16), 1–4 (2015)

11. Ahmed, I., Guan, D., Chung, T.C.: SMS classification based on Naïve Bayes Classifier and Apriori Algorithm frequent itemset. Int. J. Mach. Learn. Comput. **4**(2), 183–187 (2014)

12. Missier, P., Romanovsky, A., Miu, T., Pal, A., Daniilakis, M., Garcia, A., Cedrim, D., da Silva Sousa, L.: Tracking dengue epidemics using twitter content classification and topic modelling. In: ICWE Workshops, pp. 80–92 (2016)

13. Ye, X., Li, S., Yang, X., Qin, C.: Use of social media for the detection and analysis of infectious diseases in China. ISPRS Int. J. Geo-Inf. **5**(9), 156 (2016)

14. Gomide, J., Veloso, A., Meira Jr., W., Almeida, V., Benevenuto, F., Ferraz, F., Teixeira, M.: Dengue surveillance based on a computational model of spatio temporal locality of Twitter. J. Web Sci. (2011). ACM

15. Twitter. https://en.wikipedia.org/wiki/Twitter

16. Twitter Developers. https://apps.twitter.com/

17. Rosaline, R.A.A., Parvathi, R.: Performance analysis of various text classification algorithms. Int. J. Pure Appl. Math. **101**(5), 625–634 (2010)

18. Text Mining in R. https://rstudio-pubs-static.s3.amazonaws.com/31867_8236987cf0a8844e962ccd2aec46d9c3.html

19. Wu, Y., Cao, N., Gotz, D., Tan, Y.P., Keim, D.A.: A survey on visual analytics of social media data. IEEE Trans. Multimed. **18**(11), 2135–2148 (2016)

20. twitteR package. https://cran.r-project.org/web/packages/twitteR/twitteR.pdf

21. tm package. ftp://cran.r-project.org/pub/R/web/packages/tm/vignettes/tm.pdf

22. e1071 package. https://cran.r-project.org/web/packages/e1071/e1071.pdf

23. ggplot2 package. https://cran.r-project.org/web/packages/ggplot2/ggplot2.pdf

24. Delhi: 10,851 Chikungunya cases in the National Capital. http://indianexpress.com/article/india/india-news-india/delhi-10851-chikungunya-cases-in-the-delhi-national-capitral-3730889/

25. Directorate General of Health Services Ministry of Health and Family Welfare. National Vector Borne Disease Control Program. Chikungunya cases in the country since 2010. http://www.nvbdcp.gov.in/chik-cd.html

26. Directorate General of Health Services Ministry of Health and Family Welfare. National Vector Borne Disease Control Program. Chikungunya cases in the country since 2010. http://www.nvbdcp.gov.in/den-cd.html

Erasure-Coded Network Backup System (ECNBS)

Aatish Chiniah$^{(\boxtimes)}$ ⓘ, Jellina Aishwarta Devi Dhora, and Chaahana Juhinee Sandooram

Computer Science and Engineering Department, University of Mauritius, Reduit, Mauritius
a.chiniah@uom.ac.mu,
{jellina.dhora,chaahana.sandooram}@umail.uom.ac.mu

Abstract. Traditionally File Servers are used as storage medium as Network Attached Storage. However the need for backup servers is a necessity. As a rule of thumb, data in a network environment needs to be replicated on 3 different machines. The amount of data replicated and other issues such as consistency and concurrency maintenance becomes a huge overhead. As a solution to those issues, Erasure Coded Storage is tipped to be the next best alternative. In Erasure Coded Storage, an object (file) is broken down into n blocks, and encoded. Furthermore some redundant parity blocks are created using mathematical formulas, so that redundancy could be provided. In case of loss of original blocks of data, any parity block can be used for recovery. There exist several Erasure Code Techniques, namely Reed-Solomon, Hierarchical, Self-Repairing and Regenerating codes. Each code has its specificity, some look into diminishing bandwidth consumption, while other lesser computational loads. Till date, there are only a few implementations based on erasure codes. Our contribution is that we are proposing a novel architecture for Network Backup System using Erasure Codes in ECNBS that includes three layers. The Interface Layer presents the user with a layout of files similar to windows environment, whereby files are stored in folders and subfolders. The Intermediate Layer (Mapping Layer) stores information about the files and the locations of the related blocks. The Storage Layer is where blocks of data are physically stored. The newly implemented system is fully functional, and has also been compared to the traditionally used File Server.

Keywords: Erasure code · Reed-Solomon · Replication · Network backup system · Hadoop · HDFS

1 Introduction

With the advent of the daily use of computers in every sphere of modern life, the storage of data has become more than necessary. Thus an efficient backup system needs be implemented to keep those data safe. Backup [1] is the process of copying data in order to preserve or recover it in case of data loss. Threats to the IT system such as hardware failures, deliberate or accidental damage and viruses have made backup vital [2]. A backup system replicates data [3, 4]. Data replication is a technique that can be used to copy data over a computer network to one or more remote locations [5]. Thus a backup system is a reliable, consistent and fault tolerant solution. However, data replication has some disadvantages. More storage space is needed

© Springer Nature Singapore Pte Ltd. 2017
S. Kaushik et al. (Eds.): ICICCT 2017, CCIS 750, pp. 35–43, 2017.
https://doi.org/10.1007/978-981-10-6544-6_4

and updating the data can be tedious. So the network backup system will make use of erasure codes to minimize the storage space. Erasure code is a technique used to protect data where data is broken down into fragments. The fragments are then expanded and encoded with redundant data pieces and stored across a set of different locations. The original file can be retrieved even if some fragments are lost in one location. Thus erasure code is a less vulnerable and reliable method.

The remaining parts of the paper are arranged using the following structure: In Sect. 2, we first present a brief on network backup theories, and then in Sect. 3, we describe Erasure Codes and its advantages over Replication. In Sect. 4, we detailed the experimental setup used for the implementation of ECBNS and the succeeding emanating results are laid out in the Outcome section that is Sect. 5. Finally, Sect. 6 contains the conclusion and future works.

2 Network Backup System

Data loss due to hardware, software, or user error can be very inconvenient; or in the worst case, it will result in the wastage of innumerable hours as well as monetary value of lost productivity. The obvious solution to data loss is redundancy, that is, backup [1, 6]. However loss of data is still happening, due to the fact that performing regular backup is inconvenient. Traditionally and until recently the most efficient medium for backup is on Tape. To make the backup process successful, data need to be warehoused away from the source system. This process necessitates the involvement of clumsy removable media or costly, centralized storage systems needing trained personels for its management. Many individuals and organisations cannot upkeep the time or cost of such solutions. The common used Network Backup System are Backup4all [7, 8], UrBackup [9], Mozy [10, 11].

A Network Backup System [12] is a system where data is safeguarded and preserved for future use. It can also be acceded by any backup media, navigating the network to ensure file protection. If the primary data is destroyed, the secondary data will still be available given that it is saved in another location [13].

There are different types of backups namely, full, incremental and differential [14].

2.1 Full Backup

A full backup will back up all files. It is the initial step for a backup process after which incremental and differential backups can be done. Every single information is copied every time which results in fast and simple restore operations. However full backups are mostly done at intervals since they are time consuming and require more storage space.

2.2 Incremental Backup

Incremental Backup is a process where only changes are made to the original file or since the last incremental backup is copied. Since an incremental backup can simply make copies of information as from the latest backup of any type, it may be run as often as desired, with only the most recent changes stored. The benefit of an incremental backup is that they copy a smaller amount of data than a full. Thus, these operations will complete faster, and require less media to store the backup.

2.3 Differential Backup

It is a backup technique found between the full and incremental backups. Differential backup also known as cumulative backup copies all changes made to the last full backup. Differential backup will store more data than incremental backup but less than a full backup. They also require more space and time to complete than incremental backups.

3 Erasure Codes

Erasure coding (EC) refers importantly to the data protection process through which fragmentally split data are expanded and classified into codes for retention across different storage locations or media [5, 15]. It is meant to detect data erasure and recover the erased parts using redundant data pieces.

With the expansion and complexity of storage systems the importance of Erasure Coding for storage applications is gathering momentum [16]. Erasure Code may prove useful in dealing with massive data protection in regard to any systems that needs to tolerate failures, namely data grids, distributed storage applications, and the archives. The cloud storage system is currently in use for Erasure coding [5].

Erasure Coding has different characteristics namely; The variable "k" which is the original amount of data or symbols; The variable "m" which stands for the extra or redundant symbols that are Erasure Coded Network Backup System added to provide protection from failures; The variable "n" which is the total number of symbols created after the erasure coding process and the rate of a code R is $R = n/(n + m)$ [5, 17].

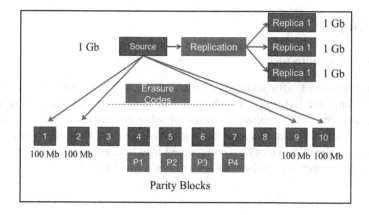

Fig. 1. Principle of erasure codes

Erasure Code splits an object into m fragments and then produces n redundant fragments, where n > m [18]. The key property of erasure codes is that the original object can be reconstructed from any m fragments. For example, in a 10 of 16 configurations, six extra symbols (m) are added to the 10 base symbols (k). The resulting 16 data fragments (n) would be spread across 16 drives, nodes or geographic locations. The original file could therefore be reconstructed from 10 fragments as shown in Fig. 1. [5, 19].

3.1 Erasure Codes vs. Replication

Data replication is the process of storing data in more than one site or node. HDFS [20] (a java based file system providing efficient and scalable data storage) and Google File System use a 3 way replication system [21, 22].

The data is stored on a namenode and it is replicated on 3 datanodes. The secondary replicas are rarely used; thus data replication causes a 200% storage overhead [23, 24] as shown in Fig. 1.

With Reed-Solomon [22, 25, 26], different values for k and m can be chosen in order to adjust data durability and storage cost. The proportion of data blocks to those of the parity blocks defines the storage efficiency [23] by $m/(k + m)$.

Typical Reed Solomon configurations such as RS (6, 3) and RS (10, 4) provide higher files robustness and bigger storage proficiency as opposed to the three blocks replication, since RS can accept up to 3 or 4 failures correspondingly and perform all this, with <50% storage overhead [22] as shown in Table 1.

Table 1. Efficiency of erasure codes [27]

	Data durability	Storage efficiency (%)
Single replica	0	100
3-way replication	2	33
XOR with 6 data cells	1	86
RS (6, 3)	3	67
RS (10, 4)	4	71

4   ECNBS

4.1   Layered Architecture

The Architecture of ECNBS has been constructed in a Layered Model that includes three layers. The Interface Layer presents the user with a web interface having a layout for browsing files similar to windows environment, whereby files are stored in folders and subfolders. The Intermediate Layer (Mapping Layer) stores metadata about the files and the locations of the related blocks. The Storage Layer is where blocks of data are physically stored. An overview of the Architecture is shown in Fig. 2.

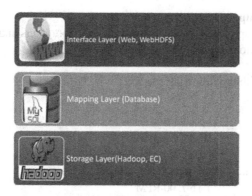

Fig. 2. Layered architecture of ECBNS

4.1.1 Interface Layer

In the Interface Layer, we implemented a web interface using web related languages such as HTML, CSS, Javascript and PHP. The design of the web interface is simple, user-friendly and yet with all necessary functionalities of a Network Backup System. In addition to the primitive types of backup, namely, full, differential and incremental, we provided some additional choices. For examples, if the user wants to backup videos and pictures only, or any specific folder.

4.1.2 Mapping Layer

In the Mapping Layer, we stored metadata related to the user and their specific files. Information such as owner, original location, date created, date modified and so on, are stored. These are stored in a database to ease the searching processing.

4.1.3 Storage Layer

The Storage Layer has been constructed using Hadoop and HDFS. HDFS, being a file system that allows large files and large amount of data to be stored. And also HDFS is cloud-ready, which will allow easy migration to the cloud when the system needs scaling up. Data is stored in blocks that are erasure coded using the Reed-Solomon algorithm, to able to provide Reliability as well as fault-tolerance all that maximizing storage capacity as explained in Sect. 3.1.

4.2 Experimental Set-up

The implementation part of this project consists of setting up a Linux cluster using commodity hardware and the development of a web system for the deployment of the backup system. Below we provide the hardware details of the components that have been used for the setting up of the cluster.

4.2.1 Cluster Setup

The cluster is made up of both specialised hardware (Computers and switch) and software. The Specifications for both are provided below:

Hardware:

4 Computers with the following specs:

Part	Specification
Processor	Dual Core (Intel)
Memory	DDR2 667 MHz Upgraded to 4 GB
Motherboard	Single motherboard with Socket 478
Hard disk	1 Tb 7200-RPM
Network	100 Mbps Network Port

Software:

We installed the following software on the cluster:

- Linux Ubuntu 10.4
- Hadoop Version 0.22
  The version of Hadoop used in this project, is one updated by facebook that includes the libraries of Erasure Codes with the XOR and RS implementation. HDFS-RAID contains the 'Raidnode' feature, which will be used to raid the file. The Namenode and datanode can be used to verify the status of nodes of in a cluster. It provides a web interface whereby the file system can be browsed. Addition of clusters is easy since it is highly scalable [8, 9].
- HDFS (Hadoop File System)
  Underlying Cloud File System that supports distributed storage and raid through Erasure Codes.
- Apache Web Server.

4.3 Web Interface

The Web Interface of the ECNBS has been developed in PHP and using WebHDFS API for easy and user-friendly access to the cluster.

WebHDFS API. WebHDFS delivers a modest, regular means to implement Hadoop filesystem processes by an peripheral nodes that does not essentially works on the Hadoop system. The prerequisite for WebHDFS is that the connecting nodes must have a uninterrupted link to namenode and datanodes via the predetermined ports. Hadoop HDFS over HTTP – that was drawn by HDFS Proxy – overcomes the short comings by having a proxy layer working on preconfigured Tomcat bundle [28].

5   Outcome

5.1   Replication vs. Erasure Codes

Replication really absorbs a lot of storage capacity as we increase the replication factor for more fault tolerance. From Fig. 3, we denote the availability of 2 Tb (50%), 1.25 Tb (31%) and 1 Tb (25%) of storage space out of the 4 Tb for Replication Factor of 1,2 and 3 respectively. However the extra storage capacity needed in ECNBS for providing a fault tolerance of 3, is only about 30%. Recovery time is constant in replication and less than in replication, however in ECNBS, the more there are failures, the more repair time, and hence the recovery time linearly varies with the number of failures.

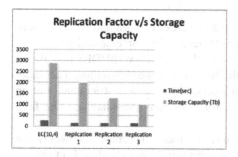

Fig. 3. Replication factor vs storage capacity

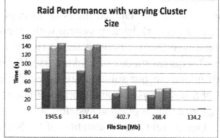

Fig. 4.   Performance: Raid with varying cluster size

5.2   Experimental Results

First, we evaluate raid performances in terms of the number of nodes being used, recovery time while raiding and recovery time after raiding. Figures 3, 4, 5 and 6, shows the encoding time of blocks depending on the number of data node available. Figure 3 shows linear variation between file size and raid time. It is also observed that the more nodes are available, the more the raiding time, since encoded blocks needs to be transferred to the increasing number of clusters.

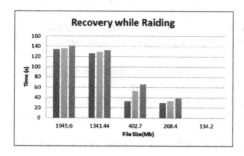

Fig. 5. Performance: Recovery while raiding

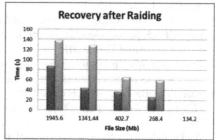

Fig. 6. Performance: Recovery after raiding

Figures 4 and 5, shows the raiding and recovery time, if ever one or more nodes fail while raiding a file. If a node fails during raiding, first of all, it has to be detected, and blocks have to be redirected to other nodes in a balanced manner. The extra amount of time for the additional processes mentioned is almost constant irrespective of the number of failures.

The amount of time required for the recovery of blocks when a node is done, well after the raiding process has been completed, is shown in Fig. 6. Here we find only 2 columns, as if there is 3 node failures, recovery will not be possible as there will be too many blocks lost.

6 Conclusions

In this work, we tackled the issue of application of erasure codes and having a fault tolerant network backup system with storage efficiency. We implemented a full functional web interface connected to Hadoop and HDFS through WebHDFS that allows the 3 required modes of backup, namely full, incremental and differential. The major advantages of our solution are especially pronounced in the user –friendliness of an HDFS based system, and storage efficiency through erasure codes having more fault tolerance than replicated systems.

Our current implementation of ECNBS runs in a local environment, however can easily be migrated to the cloud since it has been primitively been built in Hadoop. As future enhancement, we intend to further elevate the system by taking advantage of the processing power of the clusters in cloud infrastructure, and thus, scale the system.

References

1. Aardvark, A.: Incremental vs. differential backup—what is the difference? Exchange & Office 365 Admin's Blog (2015). http://www.codetwo.com/adminsblog/difference-differential-incremental-backup/. Accessed 16 Sep 2015
2. Msdn.microsoft.com.: Chapter 1—Backup and Restore Design (2002). https://msdn.microsoft.com/en-us/library/bb727086.aspx. Accessed 8 Dec 2015
3. Introduction to HDFS Erasure Coding in Apache Hadoop. [Blog] Cloudera (2015). https://blog.cloudera.com/blog/2015/09/introduction-to-hdfs-erasure-codingin-apache-hadoop/. Accessed 15 Dec 2015
4. Shenoy, A.: In: Storage Developer Conference (2015). http://www.snia.org/sites/default/files/SDC15_presentations/datacenter_infra/Shenoy_The_Pros_and_Cons_of_Erasure_v3-rev.pdf. Accessed 12 Dec 2015
5. Rouse, M.: What is erasure coding?—Definition from WhatIs.com. SearchStorage (2014). http://searchstorage.techtarget.com/definition/erasure-coding. Accessed 13 Sep 2015
6. SearchDataBackup.: What is cloud backup (online backup)?—Definition from WhatIs.com (2013). http://searchdatabackup.techtarget.com/definition/cloudbackup. Accessed 9 Oct 2015
7. Backup4all, (n.d.). Screenshots. [image]. http://www.backup4all.com/backup4all-prof.html. Accessed 1 Oct 2015
8. Backup4all.com (n.d.). Network backup. http://www.backup4all.com/kb/network-110.html. Accessed 9 Oct 2015

9. UrBackup.: Client screenshots. [image] (2016). https://www.urbackup.org/
impressions.html. Accessed 10 Oct 2015

10. Mozy.com (n.d.). Mozy is a cloud based online backup provider backed by EMC. https://
mozy.com/product/overview. Accessed 10 Oct 2015

11. Mozy.com (n.d.). Personal, Small business, and Enterprise online cloud backup. https://
mozy.com/product/mozy. Accessed 10 Oct 2015

12. Daisy.: What is network backup? 2016. http://www.todo-backup.com/backup-resource/
network-backup.html. Accessed 9 Sept 2016

13. Todo-backup.com (n.d.). What is network backup?—EaseUS Backup Resource. http://
www.todo-backup.com/backup-resource/network-backup.htm. Accessed 10 Sep 2015

14. Backup.info.: Difference between: Full, Differential, and Incremental Backup I Backup
(2008).   http://www.backup.info/difference-between-full-differentialand-incremental-
backup. Accessed 15 Sep 2015

15. Manning, L.: Word of the day: Erasure Coding (EC). [Blog] Redpalm Technology Services
(2015). http://blog.redpalm.co.uk/2014/12/02/471/. Accessed 15 Dec 2015

16. Huang, C., Simitci, H., Xu, Y., Ogus, A., Calder, B., Gopalan, P., Li, J., Yekhanin, S. (n.d.).
Erasure Coding in Windows Azure Storage. http://research.microsoft.com/en-us/um/people/
chengh/papers/LRC12.pdf. Accessed 3 Mar 2016

17. Plank, J., Luo, J., Schuman, C., Xu, L., Wilcox-O'Hearn, Z.: A performance evaluation and
examination of open-source erasure coding libraries for storage. In: 7th USENIX Conference
on File and Storage Technologies (2009). http://web.eecs.utk.edu/~plank/plank/papers/
FAST-2009.pdf. Accessed 14 Dec 2015

18. Nychis, G., Andreou, A., Chheda, D., Giamas, A. (n.d.). Analysis of erasure coding in a peer
to peer backup system. http://www.andrew.cmu.edu/user/gnychis/DS/p2peur.pdf. Accessed
16 Dec 2015

19. O'Reilly, J.: RAID Versus Erasure Coding I Network Computing. Networkcomputing.com
(2014).   http://www.networkcomputing.com/storage/raid-vserasure-coding/1792588127.
Accessed 3 Sep 2015

20. Hortonworks (n.d.). HDFS & Hadoop. http://hortonworks.com/hadoop/hdfs/. Accessed 20
Mar 2016

21. Dimakis, A.: Erasure Codes for Large Scale Distributed Storage. [video] (2013). https://
www.youtube.com/watch?v=TPZyW_CnXGQ. Accessed 17 Sep 2015

22. Zhang, Z., Jiang, W.: Native erasure coding support inside HDFS. In: Strata+Hadoop World.
[online]   (2015).   http://cdn.oreillystatic.com/en/assets/1/event/132/Native%20erasure
%20coding%20support%20inside%20HDFS%20Presentation.pdf. Accessed 16 Dec 2015

23. Introduction to HDFS Erasure Coding in Apache Hadoop (2015). [Blog] Cloudera. https://
blog.cloudera.com/blog/2015/09/introduction-to-hdfs-erasure-codingin-apache-hadoop/.
Accessed 15 Dec 2015

24. Khan, O., Burns, R., Plank, J., Pierce, W., Huang, C. (n.d.). Rethinking Erasure Codes for
Cloud File Systems: Minimizing I/O for Recovery and Degraded Reads. http://
www.cs.jhu.edu/~okhan/fast12.pdf. Accessed 2 Feb 2016

25. Wikipedia (n.d.). Reed Solomon error correction. https://en.wikipedia.org/wiki/Reed
%E2%80%93Solomon_error_correction. Accessed 4 Mar 2016

26. Hadoop.apache.org.: HDFS Users Guide (2013). https://hadoop.apache.org/docs/r1.2.1/
hdfs_user.html. Accessed 3 Mar 2016

27. Hadoop.apache.org.: Overview (2013). https://hadoop.apache.org/docs/r1.2.1/. Accessed 5
Mar 2016

28. NellaVijay.: BigHadoop (2013). https://bighadoop.wordpress.com/2013/06/02/hadoop-rest-
api-webhdfs/. Accessed 09 Sept 2016

Morphological Analysis and Synthesis of Manipuri Verbs Using Xerox Finite-State Tools

Ksh. Krishna B. Singha[✉] [iD]

Department of MCA, TIAS, New Delhi 110085, India
drkrishna_bsingha@hotmail.com

Abstract. One of the basic components of any natural language processing applications is the morphological analyzer where the analyzer produces the constituent morphemes of a given word. As all the world languages have its own unique morphological features, approaches to analyze each of these languages may vary. Manipuri, a Tibeto-Burman language, is an agglutinative language. Its verbal morphology is considered to be very rich and complex because of its features on morphosyntax, morphophonemic alterations, long distance dependency, reduplication, etc. Developing a morphological analyzer and generator of words for such a language is a challenging task especially when a standard documentation on the grammar and spelling rules for this language is not available. This paper presents the morphological analysis of Manipuri verbs using the finite-state techniques and tools and shows how the same analyzer can be used to generate/synthesize words with given verb roots and probable lexical tags.

Keywords: Finite-State morphology · Manipuri · Morphological analysis and generation · Morphophonemic alteration · Morphosyntax · xfst

1 Introduction

Morphology is the study of internal structure of words of a language. The constituents of a word, called morphemes, are the smallest meaningful units in a language. Morphemes can transform a word from one grammatical category to another, in addition to changing its meaning. Linguistically, morphological analysis of a language is the exploration of the constituent morphemes in the word structure of the language. In any Natural Language Processing (NLP) application, morphological analysis and generation of valid word forms is probably the basic and most fundamental component in the application. Correct analysis and generation of surface word forms is an important key to the success of natural language based software that facilitates parts of speech (POS) tagger, spell checker, information retrieval, machine translation, etc. Basically the morphological analyzer of an NLP application takes a word as input and gives out the structure components of the word in terms of its morpheme constituents as its output. And a generator does the reverse of it- given the lexicalized form of a word, along with its grammatical constituents as per some pre-specified order; it generates the output as the surface form of the given constituents. In most of the languages,

© Springer Nature Singapore Pte Ltd. 2017
S. Kaushik et al. (Eds.): ICICCT 2017, CCIS 750, pp. 44–56, 2017.
https://doi.org/10.1007/978-981-10-6544-6_5

morphemes are just concatenations of the symbols from the alphabet of the language and words in turn are the concatenations of the morphemes. The words thus produced by the raw concatenation operation on the morphemes may not produce valid word forms every time, due to some restriction constraints (read morphophonemic alternation) for different combinations of the morphemes. Also the ordering of the morphemes in the word structure of a language is according to some pre-specified rule. So while modeling a system with a perception to do morphological analysis and generation of valid word forms of a language, there are two challenges to meet-

(1) Identifying the morpheme ordering, i.e. the morphosyntax or morphotactic rules of the language
(2) The morphophonemic alternation rules for grammatically well-formed surface words.

Depending upon the type of the language, there are various mechanisms available in the literature to do the analysis and generation. Since Kimmo Koskenniemmi's dissertation "Two-Level Morphology: A General Computational Model for Word-Form Recognition and Production", 1983 [1], the two-level morphology formalism has ever become popular and many languages mainly the European languages such as Turkish, Finnish, English, Russian, French has been modeled using this formalism. In agglutinative languages like Finnish, Basque, Manipuri, Turkish, etc. many word-forms are produced with the help of the concatenation operation on morphemes. A single word in such languages may represent a full-fledged average length English sentence. Finite-state networks can represent the concatenating nature of morphemes and the application of finite-state methods to phonological and morphological analysis has brought about spectacular progress in computational morphology over the last several years [2]. A finite-state automaton represents a regular language and a finite-state transducer represents regular relation between two regular languages. Koskenniemmi's two-level model of morphology maps the surface form of a word into its corresponding grammatically lexicalized form and vice verse for analysis and generation respectively.

Manipuri is one of the less researched languages among the languages of India from Computational point of view. Research from this perspective is very less, though some works are available online in the literature. Being an agglutinative language, Manipuri resembles similarity with other agglutinative language like Finnish, Turkish, Tamil, etc. in terms of its concatenative and complex word structure. Manipuri has mainly two word classes- nouns and verbs, others are derived from verbs. It is also possible to derive nouns from verbs with the help of affixes. Affixation and compounding are two main word formation processes to form new word forms or derived words from a base word class. Adjectives, adverbs, and some nouns are derived from verb class. The language has around sixty affixes and a single word form may comprise of up to ten morphemes concatenated together showing the language's agglutinative natures. Of the two word classes, the word structures of verbal words are more complex compared to the other class. For a language without a proper standard documentation and with such a complex word structure, the task of morphological analysis and generation of word forms is a very challenging one.

The morphological analysis and generation of the verb class with the help of Xerox finite-state tool is presented here. As with any finite-state morphological transducer, our Manipuri morphological analyzer and generator is bidirectional; taking a word as input and producing lexicalized components for analysis and producing the surface form of a word after accepting the lexical components of the word. The paper is structured as follows. Section 2 gives an overview of the morphology of Manipuri verbs with examples, showing the complexities involved in morpheme concatenation of this class. Section 3 outlines automata and transducers and shows how they are fit to sketch the morphology of an agglutinative language like Manipuri, etc. Section 4 discusses the morphosyntax to create lexicon and the notation for replace rules for morpheme alternations for spelling changes in xfst notations. Section 5 discusses the details of implementation of the generator and analyzer using Xerox FST tools. The last Sect. 6 discusses the result accomplishment and draws a conclusion with a note on future scope for extending the work on its shortcomings and enhancement.

2 Verbal Morphology of Manipuri

All the Manipuri verbs are bound roots, that is, without proper attachment of suitable affix/es to it, it does not qualify to be a valid word form. Both inflectional and derivational morphology are observed in the verbal word structure of the language. Inflectional morphology is the study of how inflections or attachment/deletion of morphemes to a word's most basic form, changes meaning, without changing the class of the word; The word class does not change due to the attachment/deletion of inflectional affixes to/from the base word. Derivational morphology, on the other hand, semantically changes the meaning of the word which may or may not change the category of the word after attachment/removal of derivational affixes.

2.1 Affixes in the Language

The language has two types of affixes- prefixes and suffixes. Manipuri verbs take both prefix as well as suffixes. A verb root can take a single prefix at the most while it is more than one in case of suffixes. The following Fig. 1 shows the different category and subcategory of affixes in the language.

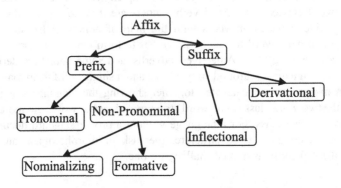

Fig. 1. Category of affixes in Manipuri

2.1.1 Prefix

The prefixes are divided into two categories according to its function in a given context-

(i) Pronominal prefix

Pronominal prefixes are meant for nominal categories to mean my, your and his/her. As we are interested only in verbal morphology here, we'll extend our discussion about pronominal prefix and its usage no further.

i, nə, and mə

(ii) Non Pronominal prefix

Non pronominal prefixes are attached to verb roots to derive it to either an adjective or to a nominal category word form. These prefixes are again divided into two more parts- Nominalizing and Formative or attributive (Table 1).

Table 1. Verbal prefixes

Nominalizing		Formative									
khu	mə	ə	i	mə	tə	thə	puŋ	pən	cə	shuk	khəŋ

The nominalizing prefixes khu and mə are attached to verb roots to form de-verbal noun. The syntax for attaching these prefixes are:

$$PNZR(\text{Nominalizing Prefix}) + VR(\text{Verb Root}) \tag{1}$$

So when khu is attached to the verb root ca (to eat), it becomes

$$khu + ca \rightarrow khuca \qquad / \text{mode of eating.} \tag{2}$$

Likewise mə is another nominalizing prefix that can be attached to a verb root to form a de-verbal noun. These de-verbal nouns take all the suffixes of the nominal category words as per the morphotactics of that category.

Let's see the use of formative prefix with the following example[1]

$$\text{ə+cət} \rightarrow {}^{*}\text{əcət} \tag{3}$$

The above form is invalid and must be followed by nominalizer suffix bə to validate it. So there is a constraint that says whenever a ə is attached to a verb root, bə suffix is essential immediately after the verb root. The resulting word category out of this morpheme concatenation operation is an adjective [4]. i.e.[2]

$$^{\clubsuit}\text{ə+cət+bə} \qquad / \text{the one who goes.} \tag{4}$$

---

[1] *: Incomplete word form.

[2] ♣: Wrong word form due to morphophonemic alteration.

Above word form needs more refinement to produce a valid surface form; however, it is a case of allomorphy and can be sorted out by applying an appropriate rule suitable to the context (see Sect. 5).

$$\text{ə+cət+pə is the result after applying the rule.} \tag{5}$$

Uses of i, mə, tə, thə, puŋ, pəŋ, suk, khəŋ, are for the purpose of reduplicating the verb root. The prefix i is used for partial reduplication.

i + (cət) (cət)+te, here the verb root cət is reduplicated in a negative environment. See [3, 5] for more on this.

2.1.2 Suffix

The verb roots can concatenate with up to ten suffixes at a time clearly showing the agglutinative nature of the language. Most of the suffixes in the language have allomorph, i.e. they change their forms depending on the context they occur.

Following is an example showing the agglutinative nature of words in the language:

$$\text{pusinbihənləmgədəbəni} \tag{6}$$

There are nine morphemes in the above word that are concatenated together; they are

$$\text{pu/sin/bi/hən/ləm/gə/də/bə/ni} \tag{7}$$

The morphemes in their lexical forms are tabulated in the following Table 2:

Table 2. Morphemes with lexical category of the above example (6)

Morphemes	Lexical category
pu →	Verb root
sin →	Directional
bi →	Honorific
hən →	Causative
ləm →	Deictic
gə →	Irrealis
də →	Dubitative
bə →	Nominalizer
ni →	Copula

Both inflectional as well as derivational morphology is exhibited by the verb roots. It is interesting to note that other word categories, such as adjective, adverb, verbal nouns, etc. are derived from verb roots. They inflect and other categories are derived with the help of affixes.

The common practice of forming adjectives in Manipuri is to concatenate the suffix nominalizer bə and a prefix ə to a verb root.

$$\text{əp}^\text{h}\text{əbə} \qquad \text{/ good} \tag{8}$$

More suffixes can come in between the verb root and the suffix bə and this no more requires the formative prefix ə. For instance

$$cətkədəbə \qquad (9)$$

where kə and də suffixes are inserted in between.

On the other hand, adverbs are formed with the help of the adverbial suffix right after the verb root like

$$cətna \qquad /by\ going \qquad (10)$$

$$səkna,\ etc. \qquad /by\ singing \qquad (11)$$

It has been identified that the number of suffixes that can be attached to a verb root are more than that of other categories in the language. The following Table 3 shows the name of suffixes along with its lexical category:

Table 3. Verbal suffixes with lexical category

Suffix type	Lexical tag	Suffix name (allomorphs)
Simple aspect	SASP	i, ŋi, mi, pi, li
Progressive aspect	PRGASP	ri, li
Perfect aspect	PASP	re, le
Irrealis	IRASP	gəni, kəni
Mood	MOOD	niŋ
Negative	NG	te, de, roi, loi, gum, kum, nu, tə, də
Imperative	IMP	o, mo, po, ŋo, u, mu, pu, ŋu, yu, ro, lo, ru, lu
Deictic	DCT	rə, ru, rək, lək, khi
Intentive	INT	ke, ge
Suggestive	SUGG	si
Concessive	CONC	sənu
Adverbial	ADV	nə
Nominalizing	NOM	bə, pə
Copula	COP	ni
Directional	DIR	Sin, cin, ʃin, thok, dok, tok, khət, gət, kət, thə
Goal Centric	GOA	rə, lə, mə, ŋə, pə
Destructive	DEST	khai, gai, kai, thət, dət, tət, thek, dek, tek
Reciprocal	RECI	nə
Together	TOG	min
Excessive	EXC	mən, məl
Causative	CAUS	hən, həl
Reflexive	REFL	cə, ʃə
Honorific	HON	bi, pi
Endearment	END	ko, co
Habitual	HAB	kən, gən
Superiority	SUP	hət

(continued)

Table 3. (*continued*)

Suffix type	Lexical tag	Suffix name (allomorphs)
Doubt	DOUBT	Kum, gum
Evidential	EVI	rəm, ləm
Start	BEGIN	hou
Assumption	ASSUM	dou, tou

3 Two-Level Morphology and Finite-State Transducers for Language Representation and Analysis/Synthesis

A finite-state automaton is a mathematical model of behavior consisting of states and conditional state transitions. They are used to recognize regular languages and can accept or reject an input string. If the input string is in the language it is said to be accepted and recognized otherwise rejected. Such a model in NLP applications is called a recognizer. An example of a finite-state automaton to represent the language car, cat and their plurals is shown below (Fig. 2):

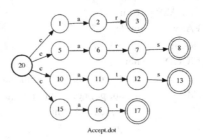

Fig. 2. FSA representing the language car, cat, cars, cats. *Courtesy: Lauri Karttunen*

One such example in Manipuri might be the language cakhi, cagəni, cakhigəni, cabə, cai

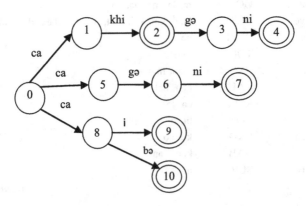

Fig. 3. FSA for the language cabə, cai, cagəni, cakhi and cakhigəni

Finite-state machines can be extended such that they produce strings or weights as output in addition to recognizing text and speech. Such finite-state machines are called finite-state transducers (FST). FSTs can represent relation between two regular languages. So the arcs in an FST are represented by a two-way symbol, upper and lower. The upper symbol represents a symbol from the upper language and the lower symbol from the lower language.

Koskenniemi's (Kimmo Koskenniemi, 1983) two-level morphology was the first practical general model in the history of computational linguistics for the analysis of morphologically complex languages [8]. The formalism requires two way representations of words of a language i.e. a surface form and a corresponding lexical form and a relation between this representations. So the process of morphological analysis and synthesis is reduced to building an FST to map between the lexical and surface forms of Kimmo's 2-level morphology and vice-verse. The FST for the language of Fig. 3 is:

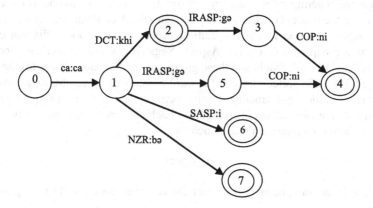

Fig. 4. Compact FST for Fig. 3

In the above Fig. 4, each arc in the network of Fig. 3 is represented by a pair of symbols from input and output alphabets separated by a colon (:). The upper symbol represents the lexical and the lower symbol represents the surface realization of the word. For analysis the mapping is done from lower to upper and the reverse for synthesis of word forms. So if we want morphological analysis of the word cakhigəni, the result is a mapping from lower language to upper language:

$$
\begin{array}{c}
\text{ca} + \text{DCT} + \text{IRASP} + \text{COP} \\
\uparrow \qquad \uparrow \qquad \uparrow \qquad \uparrow \\
\text{ca} + \text{khi} + \text{gə} + \text{ni}
\end{array}
\tag{12}
$$

The conventional way of analysis is that word categories are actually mapped to own and are attached with a tag signifying its category at the upper level but mapped to a zero at the lower level label. i.e.

$$\begin{array}{ll} \text{Lexical form:} & \text{ca+VR+DCT+IRASP+COP} \\ \text{Surface form:} & \text{ca + 0 + khi + gə + ni} \end{array} \qquad (13)$$

FSTs are bidirectional and can be used for analysis as well as synthesis of Manipuri words.

4 Morphosyntax and Morphophonemic Alternations

4.1 Creating Lexicon and Defining Replace Rules

The morpheme ordering rules, called morphosyntactic rules or morphosyntax can be captured using the concept of continuation class in xfst. A continuation class is a group of morpheme/(s) that can follow a specific morpheme. e.g. mood suffix niŋ can be followed by a group of suffixes, viz. Aspect, Negative, Deictic, Adverbial, Nominalizer, Excessive, Habitual, Doubt and these groups are continuation classes for the mood suffix. Verifying valid surface forms of a word requires checking the arrangement of the morphemes in the word structure. For the purpose we can define a lexicon which is a repository of roots and affixes of a language. Each entry in the lexicon has two parts- a morpheme and a continuation class, such as

niŋ Aspect;

Here niŋ is the morpheme and Aspect the continuation class. The template of a lexicon is-

```
Lexicon Root
        entry1        Continuation_class1;
        entry2        Continuation_class2;
        .

Lexicon Continuation_class1                    (14)
        entry3        Continuation_class3;

        .

Lexicon Continuation_class2
End
```

It always starts with the root lexicon. A definition of the continuation class is required once it is specified. Consider the following example lexicon-

```
Lexicon Root
        tou     Verb
Lexicon Verb
        ^VR:0           Mood;
Lexicon Mood
        ^MOOD:niŋ       Aspect;                    (15)
Lexicon Aspect
        ^SASP:i         #;
        ^PASP:re        #;
    END
```

Here the morpheme part of the entry is a two-way symbol representing lexical and the surface forms of a word to accommodate the idea of an FST. The # is a special continuation class to mark the end of a word equivalent to a final state in the finite-state network.

4.2 Morphophonemic Alternations

The spelling changes occur at the morpheme boundary for various reasons. In Manipuri morphophonemic alternations are due to

(i) Voicing Assimilation (VA): one instance of replace rule (in xfst notation) is-

$$bə -> pə \ || \ \{kəlbəltəlpə\} \ \_ \ ;   (16)$$

bə is replaced by pə in the context following a k, tə or a pə.
(ii) De-aspiration (D Rule):

$$khət -> gət \ || \ \{ng\} \ \_ \ ;   (17)$$

(iii) Trilling Rule

$$rə -> lə \ || \ \{pəlləltəlkə\} \ \_ \ ;   (18)$$

There are thousands of such spelling rules which require morphophonemic alternations in specified contexts.

5 Implementation of the Analyzer and Generator Using Xerox FST Tools

The xfst tool is used for compilation of the lexicon file, which is a text file, into a finite-state network. The file contains lexicons and sub-lexicons to define continuation classes of each morpheme entry in the lexicon. Also each of the spelling change rules is compiled individually to form finite-state networks. Composition operation is applied to all the networks at a time to compose a single finite-state network.

As an example, the lexicon file (VerbLex.txt) that consists of the verb root, the mood suffix niŋ and its continuation classes (Aspect, Negative, Deictic, Adverbial, Nominalizer, Excessive, Habitual, Doubt, etc.) is shown below:

```
Multichar_Symbols
+VR +SASP +NG +MOOD +NG +DCT +ADV +NOM +EXC +HAB +COP niŋ cat de
ba ca
LEXICON VERB
        ca:ca   VERBTag;
        cat:cat         VERBTag;
LEXICON VERBTag
        +VR:0   MOOD;
LEXICON MOOD
        +MOOD:niŋ       MOODContinue;
LEXICON MOODContinue
        ASPECT;
        NEGATIVE;
        DEICTIC;
        ADVERBIAL;
        NOMINALIZER;
        EXCESSIVE;
        HABITUAL;
        DOUBT;
LEXICON ASPECT
        +SASP:i         #;
LEXICON NEGATIVE
        +NG:de #;
LEXICON DEICTIC
        +DCT:rəm                DCTSuffix;
LEXICON ADVERBIAL
        +ADV:nə         #;
LEXICON NOMINALIZER
        +NOM:bə         # ;
        +NOM:bə         COPULA;
LEXICON EXCESSIVE
        +EXC:mən        ASPECT;
LEXICON HABITUAL
        +HAB:gən                HABSuffix;
LEXICON DOUBT
        +DOUBT:gum      #;
LEXICON DCTSuffix
        +SASP:i         #;
LEXICON HABSuffix
        +NOM:bə         #;
        +SASP:i         #;
LEXICON COPULA
        +COP:ni #;
END
```

(19)

The screenshot after compilation of the above lexicon is as shown below:

```
xfst[0]: read lexc <VerbLex.txt
Opening input file 'VerbLex.txt'
December 01, 2016 08:43:33 GMT
Reading UTF-8 text from 'VerbLex.txt'
VERB...2,  VERBTag...1,  MOOD...1,  MOODContinue...8,  ASPECT...1,
NEGATIVE...1,   DEICTIC...1,   ADVERBIAL...1,   NOMINALIZER...2,
EXCESSIVE...1,   HABITUAL...1,   DOUBT...1,   DCTSuffix...1,
HABSuffix...2, COPULA...1
Building lexicon...Minimizing...Done!
3.0 Kb. 22 states, 30 arcs, 20 paths.
Closing 'VerbLex.txt'
xfst[1]:
```

When the word caniŋi is analyzed:

```
xfst[1]: up caniŋi
ca+VR+MOOD+SASP
xfst[1]:
```

To synthesize the same, supply the verb root and the required lexical tags as:

```
xfst[1]: down ca+VR+MOOD+SASP
caniŋi
xfst[1]:
```

6 Conclusion

In this paper I presented a verbal morphological model capable of Morphological Analysis and synthesis of the Manipuri verbs using Finite-State techniques and have been experimented using the xfst tool. The model has been tested on verbal morpheme concatenations of up to seven morphemes on thirty verb roots. Though the result has been encouraging there are works yet to be done in respect of morpheme alteration rules and their order while compilation. Any world language is ever changing and evolving day by day. Also languages are influenced by English and other local and indigenous languages; so the problem of dealing with loan words and foreign words is a big issue here. Long distance dependency and reduplication are two major issues exhibited by verbal morphemes in the language that should also be addressed while designing the morphosyntax of the language. While reduplication has been successfully addressed [5] using Compile-Replace [6] technique, the former issue is still a challenge for researchers in this area. Being an agglutinative language and the verbal morphology the utmost complex, developing a nearly complete lexicon representing the verbal morphology will require a lexicographer's help while designing a full-fledged morphological analyzer for Manipuri verbs and Manipuri language as a whole.

References

1. Koskenniemi, K.: A general computational model for word-form recognition and production. In: Proceedings of the 10th International Conference on Computational Linguistics, pp. 178–181. Association for Computational Linguistics (1984)
2. Karttunen, L.: Finite-state constraints. The Last Phonological Rule, pp. 173–194 (1993)
3. Yashwanta Singh, Ch.: Manipuri Grammar. Rajesh Publications, New Delhi (2000)
4. Singha, K.K.B., Singha, K.R., Purkayastha, B.S.: Morphotactics of Manipuri adjectives: a finite-state approach. Int. J. Inf. Technol. Comput. Sci. (IJITCS) 5(9), 94 (2013)
5. Singha, K.K.B., Singha, K.R., Purkayastha, B.S.: A morphological analyzer for reduplicated Manipuri adjectives and adverbs: applying compile-replace. Int. J. Inf. Technol. Comput. Sci. (IJITCS) 2, 32–40 (2016)
6. Beesley, K.R., Karttunen, L.: Finite-State Morphology. CSLI Publications, Stanford University, Stanford (2003)
7. Pradel, M.: Finite-State Transducers- Seminar on Natural Language Processing, 6 July 2007
8. Karttunen, L., Beesley, K.R.: Twenty-five years of finite-state morphology. In: Inquiries into Words, a Festschrift for Kimmo Koskenniemi on his 60th Birthday, pp. 71–83 (2005)

Bi-objective Cross-Layer Design
Using Different Optimization Methods
in Multi-flow Ad-Hoc Networks

Ridhima Mehta[(⊠)] and D.K. Lobiyal

School of Computer and Systems Sciences, Jawaharlal Nehru University,
New Delhi, India
mehtar1989@gmail.com, lobiyal@gmail.com

Abstract. In this paper, we employ three different optimization methods to solve a bi-objective cross-layer design problem in ad-hoc networks. These methods are active-set, interior-point and sequential quadratic programming (SQP) methods. Specifically, we formulate the proposed problem as a nonlinear optimization problem subject to the underlying network operating conditions. The two objectives considered for optimization include minimizing the aggregate link powers and maximizing the overall network utility. For this, two different ad-hoc topology scenarios with multi-flow network design are used to implement the proposed problem. The simulation results demonstrate the convergence process of various iterative methods to their optimal solutions within finite number of iterations. The maximum convergence rate achieved in our scheme is as high as 76.5%.

Keywords: Active-set · Ad-hoc network · Cross-layer design · Interior-point · Sequential quadratic programming

1 Introduction

An ad-hoc network can be defined as a system comprised of autonomous and identical wireless nodes that communicate with each other without any backbone infrastructure support. Self-configuration and rapid deployment make these networks suitable for many intriguing applications including hybrid wireless networks, military communications, ubiquitous computing, emergency medical situations, data and device networks. The network design and operation is influenced by major factors of power conservation, throughput maximization, channel errors, bandwidth-constrained and variable capacity links. The application performance of these networks can be broadly classified into two types. The first category involves minimization of power-based performance objective. This in turn minimizes the interference among contending links and enhances the lifetime of the network composed of nodes relying on power-delimited batteries. The second type comprises rate-based performance objective, whose goal is to maximize the overall network utility fairness among the competing end-users. In this work, we have focused on and analyzed these two objectives in the framework of bi-objective cross-layer optimization.

© Springer Nature Singapore Pte Ltd. 2017
S. Kaushik et al. (Eds.): ICICCT 2017, CCIS 750, pp. 57–67, 2017.
https://doi.org/10.1007/978-981-10-6544-6_6

Recent research studies have demonstrated the significance of employing cross-layer design to achieve consequential performance objectives in the modern heterogeneous wireless ad-hoc networks. This cross-layering methodology exploits the interchange of relevant layer-specific parameters between various layers of the network stack [7]. The authors in [1] proposed a joint cross-layer design between medium access control (MAC) and network layers to enhance the energy-based performance in wireless ad-hoc networks. A novel multi-variable cost function was adopted in [2] to implement the cross-layer optimization algorithm between application and network layers. Debbarma et al. [3] presented a cross-layer formulation to jointly solve power conservation and congestion control issues by improving the link quality. Attada, and Setty [4] developed a cross-layer design based paradigm to provide Quality of Service (QoS) support and congestion control in a reactive routing protocol of mobile ad-hoc networks. In [5], a multi-criterion optimization mechanism was elaborated for random access wireless ad-hoc networks. The proposed problem aimed at maximizing the network utility and minimizing energy via Lagrange dual decomposition. The work in [6] proposed an algorithm to find an optimal solution set by optimizing two objectives of spectrum allocation and power consumption for cognitive radio networks. Moreover, the authors in [8] employed interior-point optimization technique for maximizing user throughput under packet loss probability constraint for delay sensitive applications. Rashtchi et al. [9] used interior-point solver in order to determine optimal power control, subchannel schedule and communication routes in OFDMA-based wireless ad-hoc networks. Z. Chen et al. [10] investigated a SQP algorithm to solve the formulated joint source-channel coding problem. This problem aimed to find a strict local minimum solution to minimize the total power consumption at all the transmitters. Furthermore, the proposed optimization algorithm in [11] was implemented using the interior-point method based on local information for a tree wireless sensor network.

The feasible-point active-set method iteratively solves a sequence of constrained quadratic programs by predicting the active set of equality constraints to start the algorithm. Also known as the barrier function method, the interior-point method reaches a point in the solution set by traversing the interior of the problem's feasible region. In a more competitive SQP algorithm, a quadratic model of criterion function is minimized subject to linearized system constraints using exact second derivatives. Also referred to as the successive or recursive quadratic programming method, this method can be viewed as a generalized form of Newton's method for solving problems with significant nonlinearities. In our framework, we employ these three standard optimization techniques that iteratively solve the proposed bi-objective cross-layer design problem in ad-hoc networks. These methods globally converge to the optimal solution of the minimization problem in a centralized manner with different convergence rates. This is due to the difference in the number of problem function (and its gradient) evaluations and the Hessian approximation required in each of these methods.

The purpose of this paper is twofold. First, we perform a bi-objective cross-layer design between physical and transport layers of protocol stack using three different widely-used methods for general nonlinear optimization. Second, we provide a comparison of the convergence rate behavior of these methods in attaining the global optimal solution of the proposed optimization problem through numerical results.

The remainder of the paper is organized as follows. In the next section, the system model is discussed. In Sect. 3, we provide formulation of the proposed bi-objective optimization problem in multi-flow ad-hoc networks. Section 4 contains the simulation results for two ad-hoc topology scenarios. Finally the paper is concluded in Sect. 5.

2 System Model

Suppose a multi-flow ad-hoc network is represented by a directed graph $G = \{N, E\}$. The set of nodes in the network denoted by N transmit data through their neighbors using a set of E internode communication links. A link $e \in E$ representing a one-hop transmission of data traffic between the distinct nodes i and j ($i, j \in N$) is alternatively denoted with an ordered pair $e = (i, j)$. The transmitting and the receiving nodes of each link, $e \in E$, are denoted by $tx(e)$ and $rx(e)$, respectively. Suppose M denotes the set of multiple information sources supported in the network, such that each source node $m \in M$ uses a predetermined ordered subset of links $E(m) \subseteq E$ as a route to transmit its data. We use r_m bits per second (bps) as the data transmission rate for source m and also assume that no loops exist in its communication route.

2.1 Wireless Channel Model

The general expression for signal-to-interference plus noise ratio (SINR) measured at the receiver $rx(e)$ due to transmission from the previous-hop node $tx(e)$ is given by:

$$\gamma_e = \frac{F_{ee}G_{ee}P_e}{\sum_{f \neq e} F_{ef}G_{ef}P_f + \sigma_{rx(e)}}, \qquad \forall e, f \in E$$

It determines the quality level of communication over each link e. Here P_e denotes the signal power received at $rx(e)$ and varies with the distance between $tx(e)$ and $rx(e)$. P_f is the power resulting from interference by links $f \neq e$, and $\sigma_{rx(e)}$ is the unintended thermal noise power spectral density at receiver $rx(e)$. Associated with network topology graph G is the link gain matrix, $G \in \mathbb{R}^{|E| \times |E|}$. Note that the set cardinality is indicated by $|.|$. The diagonal terms G_{ee} of this matrix represent the corresponding instantaneous path gain on link e. These gain parameters characterize the wireless channel conditional statistics and are determined by channel estimation techniques such as path loss, fading, shadowing, coding gain, antenna gain patterns, etc. The off-diagonal terms G_{ef} ($f \neq e$) denote the effective channel interference coefficient from $tx(f)$ to $rx(e)$. The terms F_{ee} denote the fading components on the single channel embodied by link e, while F_{ef} indicate the fast fading parameters on distinct paths between the nodes consisting of links e and f. Here, we make the assumption of slowly-varying or time-invariant channel with relatively stable network topology between source and relay nodes. As a consequence, the time diversity coefficients F_{ef} can be considered negligibly small, and can be absorbed into the independent channel gain terms G_{ef} used for modeling the slow fading channel characteristics. Thus the simplified expression for SINR is given by:

$$\gamma_e = \frac{G_{ee}P_e}{\sum_{f \neq e} G_{ef}P_f + \sigma_{rx(e)}}$$

We assume that each link, $e \in E$, follows the additive white gaussian noise (AWGN) channel capacity model. In this discrete-time channel model, the noise and the interference are drawn independent and identically distributed (iid) from a Gaussian distribution with covariance $\sigma_{rx(e)}$. Subsequently, the Shannon channel capacity [12] per unit frequency bandwidth associated with a link e can be obtained as:

$$C_e(P) = W \log_2(1 + \alpha\gamma_e(P))$$

where $P = [P_1, P_2, \ldots, P_{|E|}]^T$ is an $|E| \times 1$ vector of non-negative transmitter powers. The system constant $\alpha = -1.5/(\log(5BER))$ and is incorporated into the diagonal entries of the matrix G for ease of exposition. All the channel gain terms G_{ef} are assumed fixed over the time-scale of interest. In addition, we assume that the baseband bandwidth W of the transmitted signal equals one with tolerable BER of 10^{-3} using MQAM modulation. Hence, for links operating at proximately high values of SINR, i.e. when $\gamma_e \gg 1$, $C_e(P)$ can be approximated as:

$$C_e(P) \approx \log_2(\gamma_e(P)) = \log_2\left(\frac{G_{ee}P_e}{\sum_{f \neq e} G_{ef}P_f + \sigma_{rx(e)}}\right)$$

This shows that the link's achievable data-rate C_e is a non-linear function of the operating SINR value and the link transmission power levels. Also, the valid range of the transmission power of each link $e \in E$ is constrained by peak transmit power P_e^{max}, and is lower-bounded by the minimum required power P_e^{min} for proper signal detection, such that:

$$P_e^{min} \leq P_e \leq P_e^{max}, \qquad \forall e \in E$$

2.2   Multi-flow Network Model

In this work, we implement a multi-commodity flow model for data routing in which multiple traffic connections are characterized by different source-destination sessions in the network. These source nodes transfer different data to the respective destinations in a multi-hop and multi-path routing fashion. Suppose a source node wishes to transmit data to a destination node via a number of intermediate nodes. Let $r = [r_1, r_2, \ldots, r_{|M|}]^T$ be the $|M| \times 1$ vector of non-negative amount of end-to-end bit rates allocated to the set of data transmission sources in the network. For simplicity, we define a link-route incidence matrix $T \in \mathbb{R}^{|E| \times |M|}$ to represent the interactions between network commu-nication sessions and link-by-link data flows in accordance with a specific routing algorithm. This binary matrix describes the network topology of G. A matrix entry t_{em} associated with link e and session m, is of the following form:

$$t_{em} = \begin{cases} 1 & \textit{if the route associated with session m uses link e,} \\ 0 & \textit{otherwise.} \end{cases}$$

Moreover, the limited bandwidth constraint at the network links is expressed as the flow rate at each link e bounded by the average link capacity. This bandwidth conservation constraint can be written as:

$$t_{em}r_m \leq C_e(P), \qquad \forall e \in E, m \in M$$

If r_m^{min} and r_m^{max} denote the minimum and maximum data-rate requirement of each information source $m \in M$, then the following rate validity constraint is enforced for each source m:

$$r_m^{min} \leq r_m \leq r_m^{max}, \qquad \forall m \in M.$$

3 Problem Formulation

Each communication link $e \in E$ acquires a utility function $U_e(P_e)$ when allocated a transmit power of P_e. Likewise, each source node $m \in M$ attains a utility function $V_m(r_m)$ by transmitting information at data-rate r_m. Here the utilities U_e, V_m: $\mathbb{R}_+ \rightarrow \mathbb{R}$ are additively separable in the desired variables of interest. Mathematically, the non-linearly constrained optimization problem for multi-user cross-layer design can be cast as follows:

$$\text{minimize} \quad \sum_{e \in E} U_e(P_e) - \sum_{m \in M} V_m(r_m)$$

$$\text{s.t.} \quad t_{em}r_m \leq C_e(P), \qquad \forall e \in E, m \in M$$

$$r_m^{min} \leq r_m \leq r_m^{max}, \qquad \forall m \in M$$

$$P_e^{min} \leq P_e \leq P_e^{max}, \qquad \forall e \in E$$

In this problem, the first objective function is modeled as a linear utility function. Associated with the physical layer, it represents power optimality characteristics in the network according to the application demands. Due to the negative sign, the second objective maximizes the sum rate of user data communicated along point-to-point links in the network. Realization of this objective is accomplished by the routing flows from multiple sources to different destinations across the multi-flow network. Associated with the transport layer, we consider the second objective function $V_m(r_m) = w_m \log r_m$, where $w_m > 0$ is the weight associated with the utility of source m. This particular logarithmic utility function corresponds to TCP Vegas protocol and guarantees proportional fairness among different network flow commodities. The first constraint enforces the bandwidth conservation at each communication link. The second and third constraints specify the lower and the upper bounds for the system variables r_m and P_e, respectively. Observe that the first criterion decreases with decrease in powers allocated to each link, while the second criterion increases with increasing data-rates assigned to each source. Both the utility functions are assumed to be smooth, twice continuously differentiable and strictly increasing. Therefore this problem can be precisely and efficiently solved using the well-known iterative algorithms [13] designed for handling nonlinear minimization problem via Hessian updates. We employ the built-in fmincon function included in MATLAB's Optimization Toolbox [14] to implement the above problem using active-set, interior-point and SQP algorithms.

4 Numerical Results

In our numerical analysis, we have used two ad-hoc network topologies to perform simulation of the proposed optimization model. As mentioned earlier, this model is implemented using the three nonlinear optimization methods. The numerical results for the cross-layer design model are obtained using the MATLAB software [14] and its optimization toolbox. The parameters used in the simulation experiment are summarized in Table 1.

Table 1. System parameters for the simulation experiment.

Simulation parameter	Value
Simulation software	MATLAB
Channel type	Wireless channel
Transport protocol	TCP Vegas
Network protocol	IP
MAC layer protocol	IEEE 802.11 DCF
Antenna model	Omni directional
Radio propagation model	Two-ray ground
SINR threshold	10 dB
Topology scenarios	Linear, hierarchical
Number of nodes	5, 8
Number of sessions	2, 4
Initial transmit power of each link	500 mW
Minimum transmit power of each link	10 mW
Maximum transmit power of each link	1000 mW
Initial data-rate of each source	8 Kbps
Minimum data-rate of each source	5 Kbps
Maximum data-rate of each source	100 Kbps

4.1   Linear Topology

We first conduct simulations of the proposed optimization model in a linear network topology comprising 5 nodes and 2 sessions as shown in Fig. 1. Figure 2 illustrates the bi-objective minimization process using the active-set method. This method accomplishes the maximum convergence rate of 76.5%. In Fig. 3, we plot the objective function values vs. the number of iteration indices obtained via the interior-point method, with mean convergence rate of 63.95%. Finally, Fig. 4 traces the evolution of optimal solution attained using the SQP method with a convergence rate of around 69.45% on an average. Although the optimized objective value retrieved with each method is −5.598, the number of iterations required to achieve this value is different in these three techniques. From these figures, we conclude that among the three methods, the convergence is fastest in active-set method (i.e. 7 iterations) and slowest with interior-point method (i.e. 12 iterations).

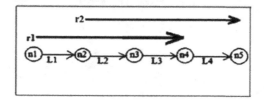

Fig. 1. Linear network topology comprising 5 nodes and 2 sessions.

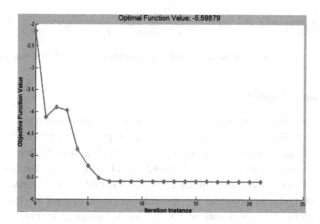

Fig. 2. Convergence of active-set method in linear topology.

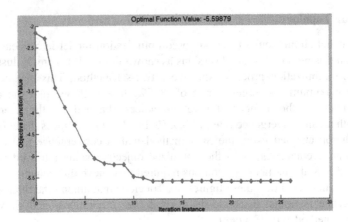

Fig. 3. Convergence of interior-point method in linear topology.

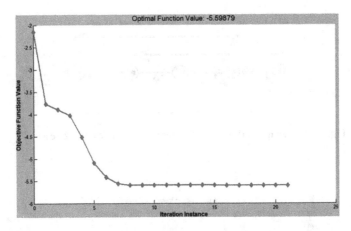

Fig. 4. Convergence of sequential quadratic programming method in linear topology.

4.2   Hierarchical Topology

In this experiment, the simulation scenario consists of 8 nodes arranged hierarchically as shown in Fig. 5. The number of source-destination pairs that communicate data over the network is taken as four. Figure 6 depicts the evolution of bi-objective solution using the active-set method. It can be observed from the figure that the convergence is achieved after 27 iterations, with mean convergence rate of approximately 66.25%. Likewise, the convergence process for the interior-point method is demonstrated in Fig. 7, having the convergence rate of 63.75% on an average. In Fig. 8, we plot the utility objective function values vs. the number of iteration indices obtained via the SQP method, with mean convergence rate of 70%. In this topology scenario, it can be inferred that the best-case performance is acquired using the SQP method (i.e. 23 iterations) and the worst-case performance with the interior-point method (i.e. 30 iterations).

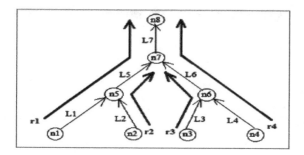

Fig. 5. Hierarchical network topology comprising 8 nodes and 4 sessions.

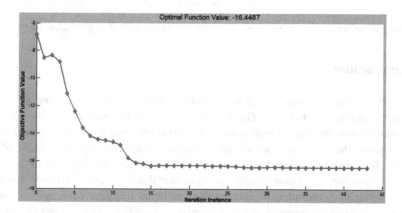

Fig. 6. Convergence of active-set method in hierarchical topology.

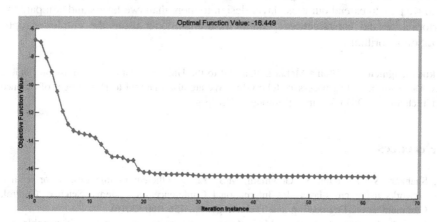

Fig. 7. Convergence of interior-point method in hierarchical topology.

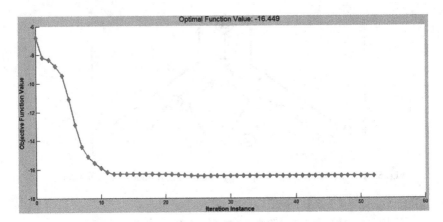

Fig. 8. Convergence of sequential quadratic programming method in hierarchical topology.

5   Conclusions

This paper addresses a cross-layer iterative optimization in multi-flow ad-hoc networks using three standard techniques. The proposed model is formulated as a bi-objective optimization problem which jointly minimizes the power consumption of network links and maximizes the aggregate source utility. We present the convergence process of the optimal utility objective values to their unique solution obtained using each of the three methods. From the simulation results, we conclude that SQP and active-set methods perform better than the interior-point method in terms of faster convergence. More precisely, the highest convergence rate achieved is more than 70% in both the ad-hoc topology scenarios. In future the proposed model can be further explored to consider the effects of unreliable propagation channel conditions such as shadowing and fading. Also we plan to extend our cross-layer design to more than two layers and compare the performance and convergence speed of resulting model using the employed optimization algorithms.

Acknowledgments. Ridhima Mehta is thankful to the University Grants Commission (UGC), New Delhi for providing necessary fellowship. We are also thankful to Department of Science and Technology (DST) for support through PURSE grant.

References

1. Shahana, S., Yuvarani, S., Gowtham, M.S.: Energy-efficient routing design for ad hoc networks using cross-layer. In: International Conference on Systems, Science, Control, Communication, Engineering and Technology, pp. 456–460 (2016)
2. Le, T.A., Nguyen, H., Nguyen, M.C.: Application-network cross layer multi-variable cost function for application layer multicast of multimedia delivery over convergent networks. Wirel. Netw. (Springer) (2015). doi:10.1007/s11276-015-0940-1

3. Debbarma, J., Roy, S., Pal, R.K.: Cross-layer design approach with power consciousness for mobile ad hoc networks. Int. J. Wirel. Mobile Netw. (IJWMN) **4**(3), 51 (2012)
4. Attada, V., Setty, S.P.: Cross layer design approach to enhance the quality of service in mobile ad hoc networks. Wirel. Pers. Commun. **84**(1), 305–319 (2015)
5. Han, X.J., Zhang, X.M., Lv, J.: Optimal rate allocation and power control in wireless ad hoc networks with random access. In: Proceedings of International Conference on Communications and Networking in China (Chinacom) (2008)
6. Jiang, H., Bao, Y., Li, Q., Huang, Y.: Multi-objective optimization of cross-layer configuration for cognitive wireless network. In: Eighth IEEE International Conference on Dependable, Autonomic and Secure Computing (2009)
7. Srivastava, V., Motani, M.: Cross-layer design: a survey and the road ahead. IEEE Comput. Commun. **43**(12), 112–119 (2005)
8. Adebola, E., Olabiyi, O., Annamalai, A.: Cross-layer throughput optimization for delay and QoS constrained applications. In: IEEE Military Communications Conference (2012)
9. Rashtchi, R., Gohary, R.H, Yanikomeroglu, H.: Joint routing, scheduling and power allocation in OFDMA wireless ad-hoc networks. In: IEEE International Conference on Communications (ICC) (2012)
10. Chen, Z., Ho, P.H., She, J.: Energy minimization for multiresolution multirelay multicast networks. IEEE Trans. Wirel. Commun. **15**(2):1063–1075 (2016)
11. Tantawy, A., Koutsoukos, X., Biswas, G.: Model-based design of tree wsns for decentralized detection. Sensors **15**(8), 20608–20647 (2015)
12. Rappaport, T.S.: Wireless Communications: Principles & Practice. Prentice Hall Inc., Upper Saddle River (1996)
13. Bazaraa, M.S., Sherali, H.D., Shetty, C.M.: Nonlinear Programming: Theory and Algorithms, 3rd edn. Wiley, New York (2006)
14. MATLAB. http://www.mathworks.com/products/matlab/description1.html

Power Analysis of a Network Using DECAP Algorithm by Varying Network Sizes and Users

Anup Bhola$^{(\boxtimes)}$ (ID) and C.K. Jha

Banasthali University, Tonk, Rajasthan, India
anupbhola@gmail.com, ckjhal@gmail.com

Abstract. Green Networking is of recent interest. Network devices like access points, switches, computer, server etc. are the major source of energy consumption. To eliminate the problem of energy wastage of Access Points switched on all the time an algorithm is introduced. In this paper, an algorithm is developed to save energy and to avoid wastage of energy due to continuously ON Access Point switches. This algorithm is applied to the centralized controller, which maintains the whole network information and configuration of Access Point, Switches, and Clients etc. A log file is also maintained to keeps track of the Sleep mode timing of the Access Points. Controller is a device that stores the information by linking the client, cluster head, secondary Access Points simultaneously. Communication between all modules (client, cluster head, secondary AP) is done by sending the packets from source to destination. In order to validate the algorithm, experiment has been carried out in Banasthali Vidyapith by varying network size, users, number of Access Points deployed etc. The presented approach works in two phase's first is the association phase and second one is the disassociation phase. From the results, it is inferred that the proposed algorithm saves large amount of energy.

Keywords: WLAN · Clustering · Access point · Controller · Cluster heads

1 Introduction

Wireless technology is used to simplify the network by enabling multiple devices at the same time. In basic term, wireless simply means connecting devices without wires. And WLAN means connecting devices in the single organization, office, municipality etc. Wireless possesses all the features of wired network except the concept of wires. As the data is transmitted over the medium, the medium presents in wireless network is in the form of electromagnetic radiation. Widest use media for local area application is radio waves which can penetrate through walls, overcome obstruction thus provide a broad coverage area.

In large universities, there is a requirement of dense wireless network to be deployed which requires the basic configuration of APs, Switch, and Controller. 100 and 1000 of APs are connected to a large network and they are in idle position most of the time and consume as much energy as in transmitting and receiving the data.

© Springer Nature Singapore Pte Ltd. 2017
S. Kaushik et al. (Eds.): ICICCT 2017, CCIS 750, pp. 68–75, 2017.
https://doi.org/10.1007/978-981-10-6544-6_7

To ensure network coverage, all the APs in the WLANs are powered-on and this causes huge energy wastage.

Wireless Controller: A controller is a centralized controller in which each and every operation performed in the network has to put all the information on to the controller. In a network controller is placed appropriately which configure all the basic information from the Access Point as well as from the client/users.

Access Point: Access Point is a wireless device used in WLAN networks which acts as a bridge between the wired and wireless networks. Access Point has its own coverage areas depending on the type of and features. It provides connectivity to the areas where wired devices cannot operate.

Power Meter: RegExper IT-24 also has power meter feature: it can be used to measure the output power of any device that transmit the frequency range 2300–2600 MHz. When troubleshooting a WiFi system, this feature can be used to measure the output power of WiFi access point.

Algorithm

Step1: Input: Client request for AP_I

Step2: Request goes to controller

Step3: Controller checks the requests for AP_I

Step4: If request is for Association_phase

    {

        If (Status== Active)   \\Check the status of AP_I (Active/sleep)

        {

            Request goes to AP_I

            Status: Connected

        }

      else

        {

            For (Scan all the nearby Active APs of AP_I)

            {

            // Display the list of nearby APs

            If (AP_J _Load$\leq$(T_h* AP_{Atv} ^ AP_{Atv}< AP_{tot}) && ($C_u \subset R$) && ($S_{Sth} > S_{Sth\,Min}$))   // Check the load and signal strength of the AP

            {

```
                    Request goes to APₗ
                    Status: Connected
            }
        else
            {
                    ON AP from power save mode
            }
        }
    }
Else (Disassociation_phase)
    {
            Request goes to APᵢ
            Status: Disconnected

    If (User < Tₕon APᵢ)        //Check the users connected to APᵢ
        {
            // Display the list of nearby APs
            If (APⱼ _Load ≤ (Tₕ* APₐₜᵥ ^ APₐₜᵥ< APₜₒₜ) && (Cᵤ ⊂ R)
            && (Sₛₜₕ > Sₛₜₕ ₘᵢₙ))

                    // Check the load and signal strength of the AP

                    {
                    Request goes to APⱼ
                    Status: User Shifted
                    }
        }
        else
                    {
                    Status: User not Shifted
                    }
```

Flow Chart of Algorithm

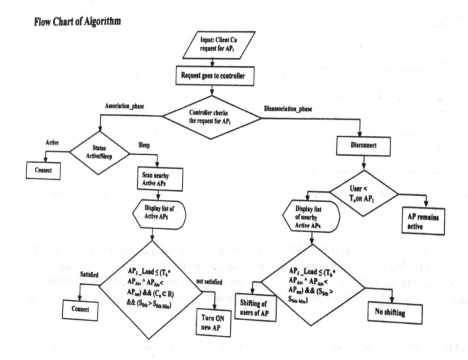

2 Experimental Setup

In this, we performed a number of experiments on different department, and hostels of Banasthali University by varying the network size, coverage, number of Access Point etc. to analyze different conditions with different timings. Experiment is done on the computer science and mathematical and applied science department (AIM & ACT) of Banasthali Vidyapith as shown in Fig. 1 and the basic configuration are described in Table 1 including the number of AP in the network, controller, number of clients, area covered etc.

Second experiment is done on one of the hostels (Shri Shanta Agaar) of Banasthali Vidyapith as shown in Fig. 2 which covers the large area handles large number of users to make the successful implementation of the algorithm. The configuration of the whole network set up is shown in Table 2.

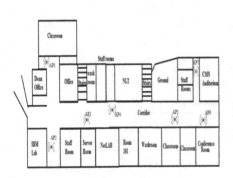

Fig. 1. AIM & ACT department with 7 APs deployed

Fig. 2. Shri Shanta Aagar Hostel

In order to test the result two different buildings are used for experiment to define the results in timing and non- timing constraints. Because of the certain timings defined in the University for Hostels to access the internet that is in morning 6:00 am to 10:00 am and in the evening from 6:00 pm to 1:00 am. These are fixed timings operated on regular basis.

Table 1. AIM & ACT department network configuration

S. N	Item	Configuration
1	AP	7
2.	User	200
4.	Channel	1, 6, 11
5.	Controller	1
6.	Cluster	2
7.	Time	1 day (24 h)
8.	Location	AIM & ACT Dept.
9.	Total area	44 * 8 m, 352 m^2

Table 2. Aagar hostel network configuration

S. N	Item	Configuration
1	AP	31
2.	User	750
4.	Channel	1, 6, 11
5.	Controller	1
6.	Cluster	10
7.	Time	6:00 am to 10:00 am, 6:00 pm to 1:00 am (11 h)
8.	Location	Agaar Hostel
9.	Total area	42 * 43 m, 1806 m^2

3   Results

To calculate the energy consumption in the real scenario, the above network setup results are determined. Log file is used to conclude the amount of power saving by the AP by storing all its sleep mode activity.

The power consumption of the 7 APs in general can be calculated over the year is 613.2 kWh. The average power consumption of the AIM & ACT department without applying any algorithm is 0.09 kWhr for one day whereas implementing our proposed algorithm the network consumes 0.07 kWhr of energy in one day. In the AIM & ACT dept. during college hours all APs remain active all the time but our algorithm saves the energy when APs are in low traffic period and in the lunch timings.

We are deploying 31 APs in the network (Aagar hostel) and the total estimated cost is Rs 32587.2 for one year. And the power consumption for one year estimated is 2715.6 kWhr. One day average power consumption of the network without algorithm is .31 kWhr but using our centralized algorithm this power reduces to 0.24 kWhr.

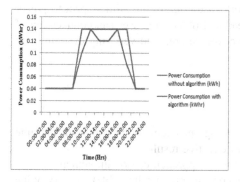 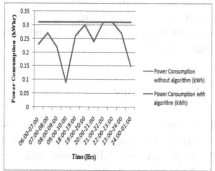

Graph 1. Combined power consumption of AIM & ACT

Graph 2. Combined power consumption of Aagar Hostel

Graph 1 depicts that during high traffic periods there is no or less power saving from 10:00 am to 12:00 noon and 2:00 pm to 6:00 pm. But during low traffic periods a certain amount of energy conserved i.e. from 12 noon to 2:00 pm (during break hours) and from 6:00 pm to 8:00 pm (in evening hours).

Graph 2 illustrates that the power consumption of the APs without using our algorithm is same for every hour i.e. .31 kWhr as none of the APs from 31 APs goes into Sleep mode. But using our algorithm most of the power is saved in morning hours i.e. from 06:00 am to 07:00 am and 9:00 am to 10:00 am in which there are less users present in the network because of the college timings and most of the APs are in sleep mode by using our algorithm. During 08:00 pm to 09:00 pm because of the dinner timings the number of APs gets reduced.

4   Conclusion and Future Work

The proposed work will be implemented and it serves a culminating option for the organizations and the campuses which diminish the cost to a great extent and it also made our environment greener. Provide an effective and efficient way to work with WLAN.

We propose a new method which connects the mobile users meandering in the network. We also propose an algorithm regarding the energy consumption and lead to intensify the performance parameters such as delay, load, hysteresis, transmission power and Throughput. While shifting the users to other APs; two parameters i.e. load and signal strength not be affected. A better signal strength is achieved by the user which leads in enhancing the performance. When working with low users performance enhances in the network while working with more number of users leads to increase the traffic thus reduces the performance. If users come in the sleep period for example: between 2:00 am to 5:00 am, algorithm works accordingly but with respect to power save mode. In a cluster with one cluster head and other APs, user can connect any of the AP in the cluster if it comes under the coverage area and verifying the minimum signal strength.

5 Future Scope

(1) In order to improve performance and storage problem of the controller multiple controllers can be used which provides effective results.
(2) In place of centralized approach, distributed approach can be implemented.
(3) To avoid the Duplication of data on the controller (controller table) memory of the controller can be increased.

References

1. Islam, M.E., Funabiki, N., Nakanishi, T.: Extensions of access-point aggregation algorithm for large-scale wireless local area networks. Int. J. Netw. Comput. 5(1), 200–222 (2015)
2. Lu, Y., et al.: A new green clustering algorithm for energy efficiency in high-density WLANs. KSII Trans. Internet Inf. Syst. (TIIS) 8(2), 326–354 (2014)
3. Debele, F.G., et al.: Experimenting resource-on-demand strategies for green WLANs. ACM SIGMETRICS Perform. Eval. Rev. 42(3), 61–66 (2014)
4. Bianzino, A.P., et al.: A survey of green networking research. Commun. Surv. Tutor. IEEE 14(1), 3–20 (2012)
5. Tang, S., et al.: Wake-up receiver for radio-on-demand wireless LANs.EURASIP. J. Wirel. Commun. Netw. 1, 1–13 (2012)
6. Yoo, J.W., Park, K.H.: A cooperative clustering protocol for energy saving of mobile devices with WLAN and Bluetooth interfaces. Mobile Comput. IEEE Trans. 10(4), 491–504 (2011)
7. Bolla, R., et al.: Energy efficiency in the future internet: a survey of existing approaches and trends in energy-aware fixed network infrastructures. Commun. Surv. Tutor. IEEE 13(2), 223–244 (2011)
8. Litjens, R., Jorguseski, L.: Potential of energy-oriented network optimisation: switching off over-capacity in off-peak hours. In: 2010 IEEE 21st International Symposium on Personal Indoor and Mobile Radio Communications (PIMRC). IEEE (2010)
9. Anastasi, G., et al.: 802.11 power-saving mode for mobile computing in Wi-Fi hotspots: limitations, enhancements and open issues. Wirel. Netw. 14(6), 745–768 (2008)

10. Murty, R., et al.: Designing high performance enterprise Wi-Fi networks. NSDI **8**, 73–88 (2008)
11. Jain, A., et al.: Exploiting physical layer power control mechanisms in IEEE 802.11b network interfaces. Technical report CU-CS-924-01, University of Colorado, Boulder, CO (2002)
12. Benini, L., Glynn, P., De Micheli, G.: Event-driven power management (2001)

Green Communication: An Emerging Telecommunication Technology-Its Research Challenges, Techniques and Applications

Sasi Kiran Sajja and Padmavathy N.[✉]

Department of Electronics and Communication Engineering, Vishnu Institute of Technology,
Bhimavaram, AP, India
ssasikiran.stu@vishnu.edu.in, padmavathy.n@vishnu.edu.in

Abstract. Today human life without telecommunication is beyond belief. The technology development has an exponential growth that proportionally increases with the rate of the telecommunication usage over the recent years and will keep growing to connect all individual entities either through a wired (wireless) media. However, the increasing demand, constant development, rapid expansion for continuous production of new and advance devices has significant effect on the global environment in terms of energy consumption, life-loss due to radiation effects, biological changes and disappearance of living species etc. The most prevalent aforementioned issues have motivated the research community towards green communication. This review paper elaborates on the concepts of the green communication providing a clear insight on its research challenges, techniques adopted to have a green future.

Keywords: Green communication · Energy consumption · Energy efficiency · Spectral efficiency · GreenStar Network · Carbon emission reductions · Greenhouse gases · Radiation effects · Wireless networks

1 Introduction

In the present worldwide scenario, network and technological expansions, low cost, and exponential growth in applications have accelerated the growth of Information and Communication Technology (ICT). Moreover mobile communications technology, in particular, has spread much faster than the anticipated, enabling millions of people to be digitally connected covering nook and corners of the earth. Because of this, there had been an increasing energy demand in several areas viz., telecommunications; manufacturing industries; constructions; power generation and distribution. However, the surroundings of the human lives are considerably affected by all the aforementioned domains. Because of the exponential growing demand of communication technology (e.g., data networks, cellular networks, arbitrary networks) and the digitalization as well, issues like energy efficiency, polluted environment, radiation effects, global warming etc. are very much prevalent. Statistics shows that almost 15% of the overall energy is consumed by data center networks and cellular networks consume about 70%. In few

© Springer Nature Singapore Pte Ltd. 2017
S. Kaushik et al. (Eds.): ICICCT 2017, CCIS 750, pp. 76–84, 2017.
https://doi.org/10.1007/978-981-10-6544-6_8

literatures there has been a mention of energy consumption for cooling, short product life cycle and e-waste etc., which negate the environment directly. Figure 1 gives a clear picture of the levels of energy consumption in different sectors.

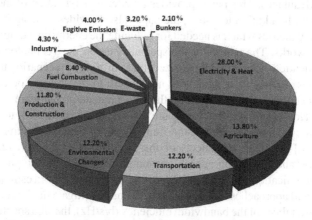

Fig. 1. Energy consumption statistics

From the Fig. 1 it is clear that more than 65% of the energy consumption is due to electricity sectors, production sector, and areas that are prominent of pollution. Green communication is a solution to the above issues which is still at its infancy and however it has received considerable attention over the past decade. Therefore, the primary research focus of this futuristic technology is to achieve low energy consumption; mitigate CO_2 emission; environment protection from hazardous disasters. Accordingly, there are several extensive interesting surveys from slightly different viewpoints that summarize the prior work related to the above concept.

Reference [1] provides a comprehensive treatment of recent green communication techniques focusing on green codes. Green Codes helps short-distance communication at low energy levels across a noisy channel. The proposed model studies the amount of decoder energy using sphere-packing bounds approach. The authors claim that the implementation complexity reduces with low energy consumption when compared to the conventional approach [2]. Have conducted an extensive survey on specialized areas of green communication projects (Mobile Broadband Communication Networks). The main area of focus in this paper was to enhance the energy efficiency without any comprise on the coverage area, QoS of EARTH (Energy Aware Radio and networking tecHnologies) using holistic system view design [3]. Addressed that use of PIC microcontroller based embedded system along with relays help in monitoring and automatically controlling the parameters (Temperature, Humidity, Light Intensity, and Frequency) to maintain and improve the ecological balance especially by reducing the CO_2 emission.

ICT infrastructures viz., telecommunication networks, optical networks, non-renewable and renewable energy sources are major contributors of yearly energy consumption (3%) and CO_2 emissions reduction (2%). [4] highlighted issues related to Green Wireless Communications with a perspective of Cognitive Radios (CRs) in terms of energy efficiency, efficient spectrum usage and simultaneously maintaining a trade-off with the fusion of cognitive dimension and wireless systems. [5] discusses about the issue of energy efficiency techniques prevalent in communications networks with their advantages and disadvantages. This paper provides a better understanding of the techniques and applicability. In addition to above, the paper also provides an insight of choice of energy efficiency metrics which is needed for reducing the energy consumption in future green radio networks. The editors of the special issue on the Technologies for green radio communication networks emphasized that, in today's scenario, technological development has reached its heights with no concern to the serious societal problems such as energy shortages, cost, impact on the environment, global warming and health related issues. However, the technologies are developed using different techniques and further few of the techniques consume more energy due to their algorithmic complexity.

Reference [6] discusses the effects of the surroundings (atmosphere; water, soil minerals, waste, and ozone) on energy consumption, power consumption, life cycle impact on communication networks of ICT technologies that helps in estimating the ICT consumptions and approaches like material recycling to mitigate the footprint issues. A comprehensive analysis of the bandwidth efficiency (b/s/Hz), the area spectral efficiency (b/s/Hz/m^2), the power efficiency (b/TENU), the power efficiency (b/s/Hz/W), and the green efficiency ((b·m)/s/Hz/W) of a wireless link is carried out in [7]. The researchers of this paper defined energy efficiency in terms of time; frequency; space; code and power for efficient transmission through robust encoding and modulation technique. Results were validated by comparing with other efficiency types. [8] proposed Green Heterogeneous Networks using the approaches energy-cognitive cycle, Energy efficient framework for HetNets. These methodologies improve the network energy efficiency, and also avoid the implementation of adaptive mechanisms. [9] explored the recent developments and approaches in the field of green networking. This paper provides a detail study of FP7 framework like EARTH (Energy-Aware Radio and neTworktecHnologies), OPERA-Net, ECONET (Energy COnsumption NETwork), TREND (Towards Real Energy-efficient Network Design), EIT and GREEN., [10] have discussed about the growing concern about the energy efficiency and various approaches like Sleep Scheduling, Orthogonal Frequency Division Multiplexing Access networks, Multi input multi output techniques, relay transmission and resource allocation for signal transmission [11]. Presented an overview of the unique challenges and opportunities viz., interoperability, new infrastructure requirements, scalability, demand response, security and privacy etc., which is being faced by smart grid communications as per European standards. However the smart grid future depends heavily on the communication infrastructure, devices, enabling services and software.

2   Research Issues and Review

Research in green communication technology explores issues pertaining to challenges related to communication networks (4G/5G) like energy efficiency, RF pollution, bandwidth efficiency, spectral efficiency, power efficiency, power consumption, MAC protocols, frequency reuse deployment strategies, spectrum policy, CO_2 emission [2, 4, 12].

The subsequent paragraphs give a brief description on the methodologies adapted to address the above issues.

2.1 Energy Efficiency

The energy efficiency [13] is a major challenge of concern for future generations of the wireless technology because of the computational complexity of advanced techniques and growing size of base station sites for transmission of high data rates. The need of providing demanded high data rates and smarter applications in wireless communication require large amount of energy that grows rapidly. The increasing energy consumption has significant impact on the global environment. Hence, it is essential to develop energy efficient technologies which enable green communication for safe environment. However a clear understanding on energy consumption is essential so as to develop an energy efficient solution.

$$\eta = \frac{E_0}{E_i} \tag{1}$$

Energy efficiency (1) of wireless network link [12] is the consumed energy over the information rate (bits/joule) of energy deployed into the network or as floating-point operations per second (FLOPS) in DSP systems or million instructions per second in computer systems. The evaluation of efficiency is quantitative as a result of novel architecture design, energy efficient metrics and models [14].

Holistic design approaches or green metrics [15] like facility level, equipment-level, network-level have been adapted in projects viz., EARTH, HetNet, OPERA-Net, ECONET, TREND to improve energy efficient communication and networking [9] Facility level metric relates to high-level systems like datacenters, ISP networks that are deployed. Equipment-level metric evaluates the individual equipment performance. The equipment performance considering bandwidth and geographical area are assessed by network-level metrics. Several projects like EU FP7; EARTH; C2POWER; Mobile VCE Green Radio were initiated to increase the energy efficiency by reducing the energy consumption. ECONET allows energy saving when devices are not in use by adopting a dynamic adaptive technology.

2.2 Spectral or Bandwidth Efficiency

The most important and critical design constraint of a design engineer for any communication systems was the network bandwidth in terms of efficiency. Therefore network bandwidth and QoS are essential parameters that make wireless communication is becoming a very important in the present scenario. Therefore above mentioned parameters are to be optimized to improve the system performance. Literature survey exhibits [15] that power consumption increasing with band width and there is always a trade-off between the two parameters according to Shannon Capacity. As power consumption increases it has a significant negative impact on the environment. Hence, it is essential to develop spectral efficient and power efficient technologies which in turn enable green communication for safe environment.

According to the Shannon-Hartley theorem, the bandwidth efficiency of a communication system is defined as the number of bits per unit bandwidth [7] which in the case of single-input single-output (SISO) systems corresponds to bit-per-second-per-Hertz (b/s/Hz), while in multiple-input multiple-output (MIMO) systems is equivalent to bit-per-second-per-Hertz-per antenna (b/s/Hz/antenna).

Different network deployments have been well investigated to improve area spectral efficiency (ASE), e.g., optimization of the number of base stations (BSs) in cellular networks [16] and the placement of relay nodes in relay systems. Also many advanced communication techniques, such as orthogonal frequency division multiple accesses (OFDMA), multiple-input multiple output (MIMO) techniques, and relay transmission, have been fully exploited in wireless networks to provide high spectral efficiency (SE).

Also improving bandwidth efficiency by superimposed training is proposed [17] and adapts a multiple carrier frequency [18] for modulation (OFDM) of signal transmission through fading channels at high data rates. Transmission of data via such channels has good BW efficiency. In some applications, cognitive radio technique has been applied to increase the efficiency. Another approach as seen in [19] can be used to increase the efficiency after combine oversampling technique and MIMO techniques. Finally; [20] this paper focuses on the maximum achievable spectral efficiency, (under various constraints of transmitter/receiver knowledge and input signaling).

2.3   Carbon Emission Reductions

The trade-off between performance, energy saving and quality of services are the parameters dealt with carbon emission reduction. Almost 23–30% of greenhouse gases can be mitigated by adapting the latest industries related with Information and communication technologies.

To test the carbon emissions of telecom products throughout their life cycles, a Life Cycle Assessment (LCA) on its own equipment such as base stations in the mobile network and broadband access products in the fixed network was conducted [21] Further the authors concluded that the release of carbon (80%) is more prevalent during the equipment operation period because of vast electricity usage. Hence in order, to have negligible carbon release, it is essential to develop equipment or technology that consumes less energy. Green communications research challenges and a description of ongoing international efforts to standardize methodologies that accurately quantify the carbon abatement potential of ICTs were discussed and a mitigation of carbon impression of network architecture based research issues and essential solution to the reduction has been described [22]. In support of the above, various initiatives with respect to green ICT test beds; policies promote the concept of power on demand (other words opposite to power "always on"); made the green ICTs more authenticated networks with low energy consumption. Middleware services and light wave communication are the main features of Green networks that enable virtualization.

Drop in Green House Gas production using a concept of virtual machines (VMs) or high-speed optical networks and protocols (NAP) allow virtual remote infrastructure which are powered by renewable energy sources. The fundamental part of the arrangement is to exchange services from vitality wasteful to "greener" gadgets which can be accomplished by assigning convention handling operations to servers situated at green controlled virtual networks. The authors have also mentioned on THE GREENSTAR NETWORK (GSN) PROJECT.

GSN is the a emerging technology raised out of the collaboration of 6 countries (Canada, US, Spain, Ireland, Australia, China) in association with some leading companies, universities and École de Technologie Supérieure (ÉTS) a leading partner of Montreal. The performance (reliability) of GSN is same as that of the conventionally used resources of today. These collaborators aimed at creating a technology and standards for reducing the carbon footprint of ICT by migration of applications and data over the network with a keen interest in optimizing energy utilization by following the green power availability and deploying green data Centre's near renewable power sources interconnected by a high speed network.

All the GREENSTAR Network nodes (HEAnet; NORDUnet, i2CAT, SURFnet, WICO, Smart Village CalIT2, UCSD) are power driven by renewable energy source (solar, hydel and wind power). All these networks were linked by six light paths to GreenStar Network nodes in Canada and the USA through Canarie and ESNet networks (See Fig. 2). In addition, these nets are also connected to Europeans nodes is done via GEANT Network. The source of energy to power these nets were received from renewable energy sources (sun, wind and hydroelectricity) and the use of renewable source reduce the greenhouse gas emission. The purpose of the GreenStar Network is that it helps in a real-time monitoring.

Fig. 2. GreenStar Network worldwide

3   Fundamental Principle of GSN (4Ms)

Mobility helps in understanding the data and services migration between nodes that are distributed in a geographical area.

Measurement accounts and records information on carbon emissions associated with services.

Management optimizes the virtual resources

Money is the significant criteria for creation of innovative commercial opportunities in the sector of ICT services and technologies.

4   Fundamental Components of GSN

Networking and computational infrastructure; Middleware and Carbon Protocol are the three main components of GSN. The first one at geographically distributed facilities uses CANARIE network; while the second one was developed to provide services to applications and users via cloud and the last for the ICT industry to quantify the CO_2 emission reductions based on the ISO14064 standards. Vivid reasons like zero or low carbon sources of electricity; powering this equipment using higher carbon-intensive electricity sources; increasing compute efficiency; use of direct cooling, higher efficiency servers can all help in reducing carbon emission.

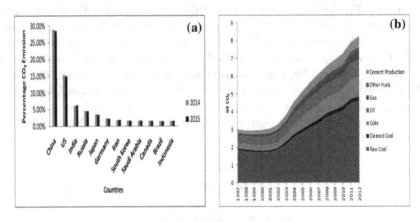

Fig. 3. CO_2 emission by (a) major contributors (b) major sources in China

The total CO_2 emission by the major contributors and sources in China has been depicted in Fig. 3(a) and (b). However, sources [23] have shown that the carbon emission in China over a period of 40 years has drastically reached almost 80% resulting in hazardous pollution in the environment. The reason for this exponential increase in carbon emission is that China is the huge manufacturing hub with major heavy industries (cement (60%), steel (51%), coke (65%)) etc., that constitute to the hike in emission (see Fig. 3(b)). Further, in India, the hike in CO_2 emission had been small (say 1.5%) when compared China over the same duration. Moreover, India are the consumers of the china products, due to which the virtual emission gets added up by its own emission rate resulting in an emission of up to 7% (see Fig. 3(a)). The measures taken by china to reduce the CO_2 emission include the renewable energy; and formulation of cap-and-trade policy. The cap-and-trade policy enforces the manufacturing industry to limit the CO_2 emission up to a permissible level and is termed as Cap. When this permissible level is exceeded, it implies a failure in the today's competitive situation. However when the manufacturers are within the permissible, selling of unused permissible level is allowed and is called Trade. In other words, the cap is a limit on the amount of pollution (billions of tons/year) that can be released into the air and trade helps a manufacturer to pay less for less emission, else vice-versa.

5   Conclusions

This paper briefs on what is Green communication and why it is important. Furthermore an extensive literature study on green communication provides an insight to the summary of enhancements that have occurred. Moreover, this area is still in its nascent stage and hence has high research motivation. A review study on few research challenges (Power efficiency; spectral efficiency and CO_2 emission) have been covered in this paper.

References

1. Grover, P., Sahai, A.: Green codes: energy-efficient short-range communication. In: Proceedings of the 2008 IEEE Symposium on Information Theory Toronto, Canada (2008)
2. Strinati, E.C., De Domenico, A., Herault, L.: Green communications: an emerging challenge for mobile broadband communication networks. J. Green Eng. **267**, 267–301 (2011)
3. Srudhi Lakshmi, V., Roshni, R., Victor, P.B., Rohini, D.: Green radio technology for energy saving in mobile towers. Int. J. Inf. Electron. Eng. **3**(1), 39–43 (2013)
4. Gür, G., Alagoz, F.: Green wireless communications via cognitive dimension: an overview. IEEE Netw. Mag. **25**(2), 50–56 (2011)
5. Alsharif, M.H., Nordin, R., Ismail, M.: Survey of green radio communications networks: techniques and recent advances. J. Comput. Netw. Commun. **2013**,1–13 (2013)
6. Vereecken, W., Van Heddeghem, W., Colle, D., Pickavet, M., Demeester, P.: Overall ICT footprint and green communication technologies. In: The Proceedings of 4th International Symposium on Communications, Control and Signal Processing (ISCCSP), pp. 1–6 (2010)
7. Zhao, L., Cai, J., Zhang, H.: Radio-efficient adaptive modulation and coding: green communication perspective. In: VTC Spring 2011. Budapest, Hungary, pp. 1–5 (2011)
8. Mahapatra, R., De Domenico, A., Gupta, R., Strinati, E.C.: Green framework for future heterogeneous wireless networks. Comput. Netw. **57**(6), 1518–1528 (2013)
9. Penttinen, A.: Green Networking - A Literature Survey. Aalto University, Department of Communications and Networking, Aalto (2012)
10. Kumar, A., Singh, T., Verma, P., Liu, Y.: Various approaches to achieve energy efficiency in mobile wireless communication networks. In: International Conference on Alternative Energy in Developing Countries and Emerging Economies (2013 AEDCEE), Bangkok, Thailand, 30–31 May 2013
11. Fan, Z., Kulkarni, P., Gormus, S., Efthymiou, C., Kalogridis, G., Sooriya Bandara, M., Zhu, Z., Lambotharan, S., Chin, W.: Smart grid communications: overview of research challenges, solutions, and standardization activities. IEEE Commun. Surveys Tutor. **99**, 1–18 (2012)
12. Premalatha, J., Anitha, U., Manonmani, V., Ganesan, P.: Survey on energy saving methods for green communication network. Indian J. Sci. Technol. **8**(19), 1–5 (2015)
13. Fettweis, G., Zimmermann, E.: ICT energy consumption: trends and challenges. In: Proceedings of the 11th International Symposium on Wireless Personal Multimedia Communications, Finland, 8–11 September 2008, pp. 1–4 (2008)
14. Yan, C., Zhang, S., Xu, S., Li, G.Y.: Fundamental trade-offs on green wireless networks. IEEE Commun. Mag. **49**(6), 30–37 (2011)

15. Hasan, Z., Boostanimehr, H., Bhargava, V.: Green cellular networks: a survey, some research issues and challenges. IEEE Commun. Surveys Tutor. **13**(4), 524–540 (2011)
16. Li, G.Y., Xu, Z., Xiong, C., Yang, C., Zhang, S., Chen, Y., Xu, S.: Energy-efficient wireless communications: tutorial, survey, and open issues. IEEE Wirel. Commun. Mag. **18**(6), 28–35 (2011)
17. Chen, N.: Bandwidth efficiency and power efficiency issues for wireless transmissions. Ph.D. thesis, Georgia Institute of Technology, USA (2006)
18. Edfors, O., Sandell, M., Van de Beek, J.-J., Landström, D., Sjöberg, F.: An Introduction to Orthogonal Frequency Division Multiplexing, pp. 1–58. Luleå Tekniska Universitet, Luleå (1996)
19. Lehnert, J., Shea, J., Shroff, N., Stark, W., Wong, T.: Utilizing spectrum efficiently (USE). Technical report, pp. 1–36 (2011)
20. Verdu, S.: Spectral efficiency in the wideband regime. IEEE Trans. Inf. Theory **48**, 1319–1343 (2002)
21. Huawei Whitepaper: Save energy and reduce emissions to achieve sustainable development and improve corporate competitiveness (2012)
22. Despins, C., Labeau, F., Le Ngoc, T., Labelle, R., Cheriet, M., Thibeault, C., Gagnon, F., Leon-Garcia, A., Cherkaoui, O., Arnaud, B.S., Mcneill, J., Lemieux, Y., Lemay, M.: Leveraging green communications for carbon emission reductions: techniques, testbeds, and emerging carbon footprint standards. IEEE Commun. Mag. **49**(8), 101–109 (2011)
23. Liu, Z.: China's Carbon Emissions Report 2015. Harvard Kennedy School, Cambridge (2015)

A 1.25 THz High Gain Hybrid Circuit with CNT Model Performance Optimization for Radar Sensors Application

Sandeep Kumar [ORCID], Van-Ha Nguyen, Won-young Jung, and Hanjung Song[✉]

Department of Nanoscience and Engineering,
Center for Nanomanufacturing, Inje University, Gimhae, Republic of Korea
fedrer.engg@gmail.com, vie.hanguyen89@gmail.com,
wonyoung.jung77@gmail.com, hjsong@inje.ac.kr

Abstract. This work focuses on a novel approach of hybrid circuit topology with carbon nanotube (CNT) model which provides higher gain at 1.25 THz for radar sensors application. A single walled CNT provides RF circuit model and demonstrates its ability to resonant at terahertz frequencies. The hybrid structure provides a circuit topology which achieves wide impedance bandwidth of 0.33 THz within range of 1.07 to 1.42 THz. A transmission line radiator used as a compensator in order to cancel parasitic capacitance and achieves more than 30 dB forward gain. A minimum noise figure of 0.4 dB is also achieves with tuning effects for inductor of RF circuit model at 1.25 THz. The whole circuit topology is implemented in advanced design system with RF simulator using 45 nm predictive technology model. This fascinating work approach first attempts to make circuit topology at THz for parameters of soil measurement application.

Keywords: Carbon nanotube · RF circuit · Berkeley Short Channel (BSIM) · Microstrip transmission line

1 Introduction

Today, a lot of attention requires for sensing applications such as soil measurement where radar sensors has playing very important role. A new approach is grown in the area of proximal soil sensing with use of terahertz (THz) electromagnetic waves. The ground penetrating radar sensors is an established and still developing methods how to measure soil properties [1]. The radar sensors include antenna, low noise amplifier, mixers, detectors, oscillators, switches, transmitters, receivers etc. In recent times radar sensors are operated in domain of THz technology whose wavelength range from 1 mm to 100 μm. To detect the finer, more gradual variations of soils in a quantitative way the use of shorter wavelength could be beneficial. Till now, very few authors showed his research on circuit topology at terahertz frequencies using carbon nanotubes FETs. But still few possibilities are not achieved yet. First moment in this work proposes: (1) RF performance analysis of hybrid structure with single walled CNT at circuit level (2) Observed higher gain over wide impedance bandwidth of 0.33 THz (3) Proposed circuit topology acts as an amplifier that can used in radar sensors for measurement of soil parameters. In [2] given ac performance of nanoelectronics towards a ballistic THz

© Springer Nature Singapore Pte Ltd. 2017
S. Kaushik et al. (Eds.): ICICCT 2017, CCIS 750, pp. 85–94, 2017.
https://doi.org/10.1007/978-981-10-6544-6_9

nanotube transistor but his research is limited to predicted theory level. Medical applications based THz imaging, short range, high speed and narrow band communications are just a few items of numerous THz applications [3–7]. Analysis and design of terahertz and millimeter wave integrated circuits using carbon nanotubes achieved gain of 21.4 dB but its sacrifices noise analysis and S22 parameter which above −10 dB [8]. A new transistor structures such as FINFET, carbon nanotube field effect transistor CNTFET have been established to maintain scaling with the same rate [9]. In this paper, 1.25 THz RF performance analysis of hybrid single walled CNT with BSIM45 nm at circuit level is proposed. The RF circuit model for carbon nanotubes with BSIM model are simulated and achieved impedance bandwidth of 0.33 THz with high gain of 31 dB and also succeed 0.4 dB of noise figure. The paper is organized as follows. A 1.25 THz RF circuit model analysis is presented in Sect. 2. Section 3 describes design consideration with microwave approach at circuit level. Section 4 represents results with discussion and Sect. 5 is shown brief conclusion.

2   Resonant Mechanism for CNT Model

Figure 1 is shown RF circuit model for single walled carbon nanotubes [10]. This model used for dc and capacitive contacted geometries. By modelling the nanotube as transmission line, it is possible to extract inductor and capacitor LC network. The components of extracted network naming as distributed kinetic inductance (Lk), Quantum capacitance (CQ) and Electrostatic capacitance (CES) respectively. It is observed that predicted real impedance from single walled nanotube is almost constant of 20 KΩ after 1 THz. Resulting RF circuit model demonstrates its ability to resonant at 1.25 THz using this impedance as an input. A very sharp peak below −10 dB at 1.25 THz resonant frequency is shown in Fig. 2. The details description of hybrid circuit topology will be discussing in next section.

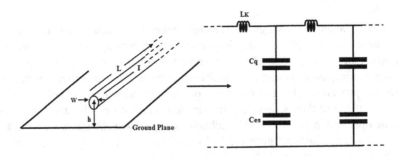

Fig. 1. Conventional RF circuit model for carbon nanotube

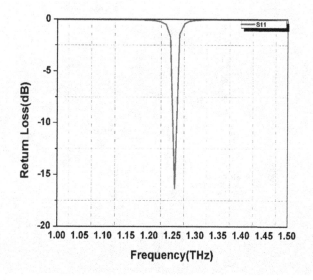

Fig. 2. Proposed variation of return loss vs frequency

3   Design Consideration with Microwave Approach

This section describes a microwave approach within proposed circuit topology which is shown in Fig. 3. The circuit topology consists of single walled CNT, BSIM model, transmission line and LC output matching network respectively. Our purpose is to develop amplifier which can be used in radar sensors at terahertz frequencies. An impedance matching is much essential between single walled CNT and BSIM transistor model which is to relaxed 50 Ω condition throughout the design. An RF signal enables to CNT for resonant at 1.25 THz with 50 Ω matching constraints. A single walled CNT found calculated impedance of Z = 48.5 + j0.45 Ω with smith chart analysis.

This impedance matched to another impedance of Z = 51.5 + j0.52 Ω which is provided by BSIM model transistor at 45 nm and provides a broader bandwidth at the output region. Moreover, microstrip transmission line is used for compensation between gate and drain terminals. This compensation technique cancels out the parasitic capacitances effects and improves the gain. In specification of transmission line (MSL) includes Z = 78 Ω, theta = 90° and F = 1 THz respectively. This MSL plays a vital role to whole topology at terahertz frequencies. It is observed that a current bypass through MSL that added to output current of CNT walled which enables to BSIM transistor for operating resonant frequency of terahertz and which could be provide ballistic performance at circuit level. Subsection 3.1 show detail design procedures of proposed structure which is follow same as in [8].

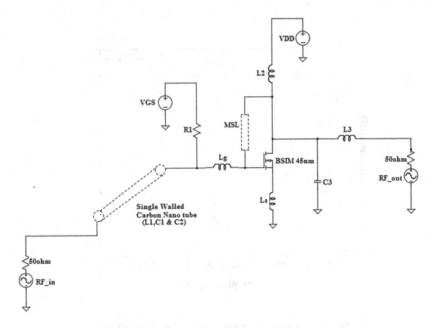

Fig. 3. Proposed schematic diagram of hybrid SWCNT with circuit topology

3.1 Design Procedures of High Frequency Amplifier

Firstly, calculating the real power (p_r) for BSIM model transistor according to equation given below [8].

$$\frac{p_r}{|V_1||V_2|} = \left(\text{Re}[Y_{11}]Q^{-1} + \text{Re}[Y_{22}]Q\right) - |Y_{12} + Y_{21}^*| \text{ X Cos}\left(\text{angle of }[Y_{12} + Y_{21}^*] + \omega\right) \quad (1)$$

where, $Q = \dfrac{|V_2|}{|V_1|}$, ω = angle of $\dfrac{V_2}{V_1}$ and Y is hybrid parameters respectively. It is observed that for maximization of Q and ω, it must be

$$Q = Q_{opt} = \sqrt{\frac{\{\text{Re}Y_{11}\}}{\{\text{Re}Y_{22}\}}} \quad (2)$$

$$\omega = \omega_{opt} = (2K + 1)\pi - \text{angle of }\left(Y_{12} + Y_{21}^*\right) \quad (3)$$

Here k is arbitrary integer. Now decide our operating frequency for circuit topology and it calculated using Eqs. (2) and (3) respectively. In next step, move towards analysis of amplifier with s-parameter which is used to determine whether transistor is potentially or unconditionality stable. It is possible to find out using K-factor and Δ. The amplifier will be unconditionality stable if K > 1 and |Δ| < 1 and its relation are shown below in Eqs. (4) and (5) respectively.

$$K = \frac{1 - |S_{11}|^2 - |S_{22}|^2 + |\Delta|^2}{2|S_{12}S_{21}|} > 1 \tag{4}$$

$$|\Delta| = |S_{11}S_{22} - S_{12}S_{21}| < 1 \tag{5}$$

It is found that higher K values make for safer designs. Another important parameter for which device will be unconditionally device that is μ should be greater than one and relation can be find out in Eq. (6) [8].

$$\mu = \frac{1 - |S_{11}|^2}{\left(|S_{22} - \Delta S_{11}^* + |S_{12}S_{21}||\right)} > 1 \tag{6}$$

The above said relations K, Δ and μ are calculated and can be seen in Figs. 4, 5 and 6. The variation of K-factor is shown in Fig. 4. The dimension values of components used in circuit topology are shown in Table 1.

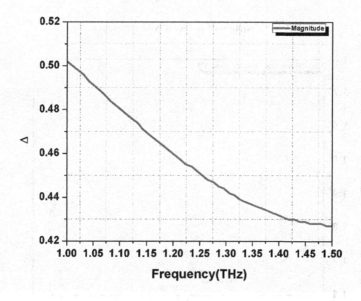

Fig. 4. Variation of Δ (parameter) with frequency

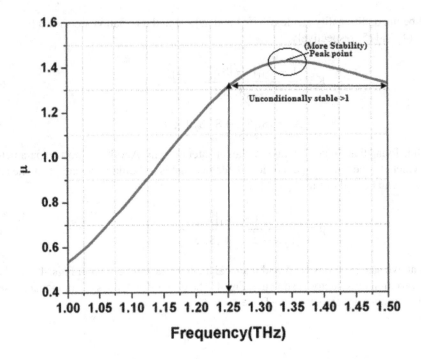

Fig. 5. Variation of K-factor with frequency

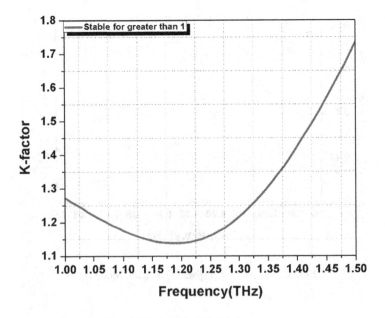

Fig. 6. Variation of μ with frequency

Table 1. Dimensions of proposed circuit topology

Components	Values
R1	67.6 Ω
L1	0.95 nH
L2	64 nH
L3	15.84 pH
W	32 μm
C1	0.013 fF
VGS	0.7 V
VDD	0.9 V

4 Results and Discussion

In this section, results of proposed circuit topology would be discussed and analyzed. Figure 7 is shown s-parameter analysis that includes return loss, forward gain, backward gain and reverse isolation respectively. By improving impedance matching between nano transmission line and BSIM, it is possible to achieve wide bandwidth of 0.33 THz within range of 1.07 to 1.42 THz with resonant frequency of 1.25 THz. The rest parameter (S22 and S12) show satisfactory values at desired frequency band of operation. An

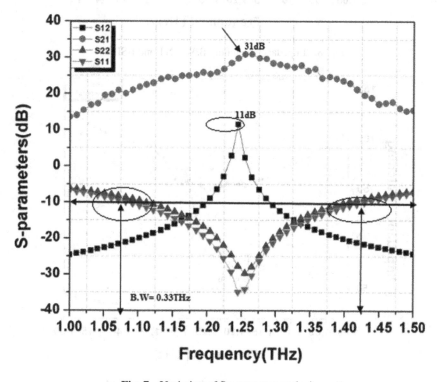

Fig. 7. Variation of S-parameter analysis

achievement of circuit topology to achieves higher forward gain is about to be 31 dB. This is due to insert transmission line between drain and gate regions for compensation. Another important parameter is noise analysis which can be seen in Fig. 8. The minimum noise figure of 0.3 dB at the input is achieved using tuning parameter values of inductors

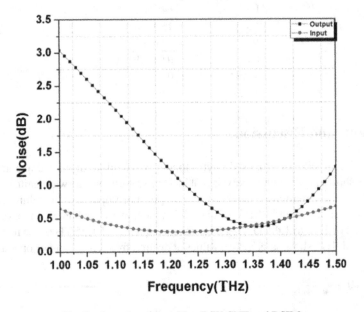

Fig. 8. Impedance matching B/W CNT and BSIM

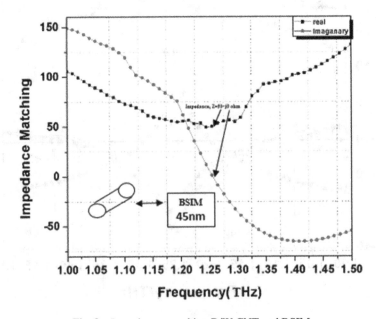

Fig. 9. Impedance matching B/W CNT and BSIM

in RF circuit model of single walled CNT. While in Fig. 9 has shown the impedance matching parameter of $(50 + j0)$ Ω condition at 1.25 THz. The comparison of present work with previous is shown in Table 2.

Table 2. Comparison of current work with previous

Parameters	[11]	[5]	[8]	Current work
Technology	CNTFET	CMOS	CNTFET	CNT with CMOS
Frequency (THz)	0.165	0.103	1.01	1.25
Impedance bandwidth (THz)	NA	NA	1–1.02	1.07–1.42
Gain (dB)	16.61	12.2	21.4	31
NF (dB)	0.25	6.5	NA	0.3

*NA-Not Available

5   Conclusion

In this paper, analysis of hybrid CNT walled with BSIM model transistor at RF for measurement of soil parameters has been presented. This circuit topology achieves wide bandwidth of 0.33 THz within range from 1.07 to 1.42 THz.

Acknowledgements. This research was supported by the Basic Science Research Program through the National Research Foundation of Korea (NRF) funded by the Ministry of Education, Science and Technology (NRF-2015R1D1A1A01057495). This research was also supported by Korea Electric Power Corporation through Korea Electrical Engineering and Science Research Institute (R15XA03-66). This CAD tools was supported by IC Design Education Center (IDEC), Korea.

References

1. Dworak, V., Augustin, S., Gebbers, R.: Application of terahertz radiation to soil measurements: initial results. J. Sens. **11**, 9973–9983 (2011)
2. Burke, P.J.: AC performance of nanoelectronics: towards a ballistic THz nanotube transistor. Solid State Electron. **48**, 1981–1986 (2004)
3. Han, R., et al.: 280 GHz and 860 GHz image sensors using Schottky-barrier diodes in 0.13 μm digital CMOS. In: Proceedings of IEEE International Solid-State Circuits Conference (ISSCC), pp. 254–256 (2012)
4. Crowe, T.W., Bishop, W.L., Porterfield, D.W., Hesler, J.L., Weikle, R.M.: Opening the terahertz window with integrated diode circuit. IEEE J. Solid-State Circuits **40**, 2104–2110 (2005)
5. Heydari, B., Bohsali, M., Adabi, E., Niknejad, A.M.: Millimeter-wave devices and circuit blocks up to 104 GHz in 90 nm CMOS. IEEE J. Solid-State Circuits **42**, 2893–2903 (2007)
6. Sandstrom, D., Varonen, M., Karkkainen, M., Halonen, K.A.I.: W-band CMOS amplifiers achieving +10 dBm saturated output power and 7.5 dB NF. IEEE J. Solid-State Circuits **44**, 3403–3409 (2009)

7. Moghadami, S., JalaiBidgoli, F., Ardalan, S.: A systematic methodology to design high power terahertz and submillimeter-wave amplifiers. In: Proceedings of 27th IEEE International System-Chip Conference (SOCC) (2014)
8. Moghadami, S., JalaiBidgoli, F., Ardalan, S.: Systematic approaches for analysis and design of teraherz and millimeter-wave integrated circuits using carbon nanotube FETs. Can. J. Electr. Comput. Eng. **39**, 92–102 (2016)
9. Cavin, R.K., Lugli, P., Zhirnov, V.V.: Science and engineering beyond Moore's law. In: Proceedings of the IEEE, vol. 100, pp. 1720–1749 (2012)
10. Burke, P.J.: An RF circuit model for carbon nanotubes. IEEE Trans. Nano Technol. **2**, 55–58 (2003)
11. Makni, W., Barrage, I., Samet, H., Masmoudi, M., Najari, M.: Low noise high frequency CNTFET amplifier. In: ICDT of Integrated Systems in Nanoscale Era 2013, pp. 45–49

Image Based Password Composition Using Inverse Document Frequency

K.P. Arun[✉] and Arun Mishra

Department of Computer Science, Defence Institute of Advanced Technology,
Pune 411025, India
arunkp1986@gmail.com

Abstract. Password remains one of the main authentication methods in today's time. The challenge with password as authentication system is due to its dependency on humans. Its strength and weakness is decided by the alphanumeric string set by users. A number of the websites demand users to use strong passwords even though they do not safeguard any critical information assets. This results in an unnecessary cognitive burden on users. It can be reduced by minimizing the number of strong passwords that he/she has to remember. A password composition scheme that considers criticality of information asset is required for this purpose. This article presents one such scheme using inverse document frequency. Users are authenticated based on a valid English sentence. Sentences leave alphanumeric strings behind in recall due to their semantic nature. Users select their authentication sentence by using an image as context. Humans are good at recalling context based information.

Keywords: Password · Authentication · Inverse document frequency · Human computer interaction

1 Introduction

Password remains one of the major authentication methods even decades after its invention. According to its inventor Fernando Corbato, password has become kind of nightmare with the World Wide Web [1]. Number of passwords that a user has to remember is increased exponentially over years. Alternative schemes like fingerprints, smartcards, and retina-scan fail to retain full set of benefits of legacy password [2]. These schemes provide significant security benefits but increase cost to deploy and difficulty to use. Password will remain as one of the major authentication methods in coming years as well due to its acceptance among common users.

The shortcoming of password authentication is due to its dependency on humans to set strong passwords. It is a challenge for humans to remember multiple strong passwords. They resort to weak passwords as a coping mechanism. Humans are better at recalling things which can be encoded in multiple ways [3]. Memorability of password can be improved by associating it with a context like an image.

Password authentication system involves a trade-off; cryptographically strong passwords are difficult to remember where as easy to remember passwords are not strong

© Springer Nature Singapore Pte Ltd. 2017
S. Kaushik et al. (Eds.): ICICCT 2017, CCIS 750, pp. 95–105, 2017.
https://doi.org/10.1007/978-981-10-6544-6_10

enough. Password composition rules followed by websites are historic in nature. Most of these rules do not protect users from current threats. Cryptographically strong passwords protect users only from brute force attacks. Strong passwords do not protect users from keylogging or phishing attacks [4]. Demand for cryptographically strong passwords for all websites that a user come across only increases his cognitive burden. Password composition rules followed by websites are not based on the criticality of their information assets. A good password policy should find a balance between usability and security. This paper proposes a password composition scheme with better usability to reduce user's cognitive burden.

In present work, users choose a valid English sentence for authentication instead of an alphanumeric string. Sentence used for authentication has better recall ratio and strength as compared with ordinary passwords [5]. Users select an image from a set of images provided by the authentication system and use it as context to set their sentence. Humans are good at recalling context-based information. This image is displayed at login time to assist users in recall of their authentication sentence.

Authentication sentences of different users may have overlap since multiple users may select same image as context. Overlap occurs since users use common attributes of cue image in their sentence. If overlap between sentences is allowed, it improves usability since users are allowed to reuse common attributes of the image. Inverse document frequency (idf) [6] is used to quantify any such overlaps. When the user sets an authentication sentence, it is scored by comparing with all sentences in the corpus. The sentence is accepted only if it's score is above a threshold value decided by admin.

It is natural for a user to make mistakes while recalling a sentence. A survey is conducted in our university to study on categories of deviations that users make while recalling a sentence. It showed 9 categories of deviations. Details of these deviations are provided in Table 1. Usability of sentence based authentication scheme is further improved by allowing a predefined set of deviations in recalled sentences. Access is granted if recalled sentence contains only allowed set of deviations. Any other deviations result in denial of access.

Scheme proposed in this paper improves overall usability of password authentication system by scoring overlap in user's authentication sentences and allowing deviations in recalled sentence. It reduces cognitive burden on users of systems with noncritical information assets.

2   Related Works

Roman and Alexander [7] proposed PassShapes to authenticate users by simple geometric shapes. PassShapes are composed of strokes. Users use eight different strokes on a touch screen. Authors argue that it create more complex and secure authentication tokens with less cognitive burden on users. The eight strokes are encoded with **U, 9, R, 3, D, 1, L** and **7**.

Richard et al. [8] evaluated requirement feedback, guidance, and insertion to help users under strict password requirements. Users struggle to create passwords under strict requirements. Authors conducted an online study with 6435 participants to examine the effect of feedback on usability. They found that requirement feedback helped users to reduce errors and create strong passwords which meet complex composition requirements but the strength of the passwords created under this scheme is reduced. Authors conclude by saying that feedback instructions should be designed carefully to bring balance between usability and security.

Cynthia et al. [9] studied the strength of mnemonic phrase-based passwords to conclude that majority of users select phrases which are publicly available like lyrics, movie quotes. This may lead to specialized attacks by creating a dictionary for publicly available phrases. In word association [10], users are authenticated based on response to cue selected at random from cues. Telepathwords [11] predicts next character based on the common behaviour users exhibit while choosing passwords.

Dinei et al. [12] explored how to manage a portfolio of passwords. Users select weak or reuse passwords as coping strategy to minimize the difficulty to manage large password portfolio. Authors found that password reuse by grouping accounts can reduce memorization burden by a factor of five. Authors suggested that optimal grouping is done with accounts having similar PL values. This way higher value accounts will be grouped in smaller groups and lower value accounts in larger groups. Authors concluded by saying that efficient password management should try to minimize sum of loss and effort rather than loss alone.

To understand variations in requirements, Dinei et al. [13] examined password composition rules of 75 different websites including universities, banks, and brokerage and government websites. Features of websites are compared to identify characteristics which are correlated to stronger policies. Authors found that there is no strong correlation between security policies and website characteristics like number of users, value of the assets or frequency of attacks. Websites which publish advertisements or sponsored links use strong password composition policies which are superfluous.

Jianxin et al. [14] conducted an experiment involving 400 participants to compare the effect of giving alternative advice for password selection. Participants were divided into three different groups and given different password composition advice to each group. Authors conducted an attack on snapshot of password files to dismiss the general belief that random passwords are better than those based on mnemonics phrases.

Shirley and Edward [15] conducted a study on 49 undergraduate students to quantify number of passwords and reuse frequency. Over time password reuse has increased as users created new accounts. Authors observed in this study that participants reused their passwords even though they had relatively few accounts. In this study, participants responded "Easier to remember" as the major reason to reuse passwords. It is a natural tendency of users to categorize websites and use same password for websites in same category. Authors conclude by saying that there is gap between how technology could help in password management and what it currently provides.

Sonia et al. [16] reported on a laboratory study comparing recall of multiple text based password with multiple click-based graphical password. Authors looked into memory interference of passwords, how remembering password of one system affects memory of password for another system. Authors conducted an experiment with 65 participants in which participants created six distinct passwords for different accounts by using text-based or click-based graphical passwords. After two weeks participants faced difficulty in recalling text-based as well as graphical based passwords even though graphical based password performed better in short term. Authors also observed that text-based passwords performed better after two weeks if participants used some association to set them. Authors concluded by saying, cueing mechanism can be added to text-based passwords to take best of both systems.

Yishay and Jacob [5] proposed a new approach to use pass-sentence instead of passwords. This method uses a code based on semantics. According to authors, It provides significantly more memorability and less vulnerable than passwords. Pass-sentence uses a sentence with semantic meaning. Authors conducted an experiment to estimate the ease of recalling pass-sentence as compared to regular passwords. Participants were asked to remember two passwords and one pass-sentence. Experiment results showed that users can remember pass-sentence better than passwords for a longer period. Users chose pass-sentence with a number of attributes greater than characters in their password.

3   Proposed Scheme

People fail to recall not because information in storage is destroyed but because it becomes inaccessible. Tulving, Endel, and Zena Pearlstone [17] analysed non-recall of learned items by making a distinction between availability and accessibility of information. Authors conducted an experiment in which participants were asked to learn categorized word lists and recall them in the presence and absence of category names. Experiment results showed higher recall under cued than the non-cued condition. This suggests that specific information is available in the storage even if it is not accessible under non-cued condition.

This paper proposes a scheme in which users use a valid English sentence instead of an alphanumeric string for authentication. The memory advantage of sentence over the alphanumeric string is discussed by Yishay and Jacob [5]. In order to assist users further in their recall, an image is used as a cue to recall authentication sentence. Cued recall outperforms non-cued recalled as discussed by Tulving, Endel, and Zena Pearlstone in [17].

The system maintains a set of images to be used as cue. The user selects an image of his/her choice from this publicly available set while creating authentication sentence. The sentence is constrained to be a valid English sentence with nouns and verb. The same image is displayed as memory cue in each login attempt. It can happen that multiple users choose same image as their context. This may lead to overlaps between authentication sentences of different users since they tend to use common attributes of cue image. A survey is conducted to quantify any such overlap between sentences.

3.1   Survey to Study Overlap Between Sentences

The Survey was aimed at understanding user behaviour in selecting a valid English sentence based on image and possible overlap between sentences. It was hosted using

Google forms. Participants were asked to enter their age and a valid English sentence by using Fig. 1 as context.

Fig. 1. Image used as cue for survey

The survey received 80 responses from students, teaching, and nonteaching staffs. Sentences collected by this survey covered a wide range even though single image is used as a cue for all participants. Some of the sample sentences are as follows

1. Mom is supervising two kids.
2. A happy and blessed family.
3. Happy children with tutor
4. A mother teaches her kids.
5. There are 3 human beings in the picture

Survey results showed an average length of 30 characters per sentence. A sentence with 30 characters provides better protection than eight characters long alphanumeric passwords. According to Richard Shay et al. [11] password policies requiring length leads to more usability and security than passwords created with strict policies. Passwords with minimum 16 characters are found to be more secure than those created under letter, digit and symbol combination policy with 8 characters. Further details on length statistics of survey results are provided in Table 3.

Inverse document frequency (idf) [6] is used to quantify overlap between sentences. Idf measures uniqueness of words in the sentence. Idf of a word in the sentence is calculated by using number of sentences in corpus containing that word as shown in Eq. (1). Corpus of sentences is maintained for each cue image. Idf gives less weight to a word occurring in many sentences as compared to one in fewer sentences. Overall idf of the sentence is calculated by taking sum of word idfs. Overall idf will be high for a sentence with unique words and approaches zero with increase in number of commonly occurring words in the corpus.

Present work proposes a scheme which helps system administrators to measure the overlap between sentences created by using same image cue. System administrator decides allowed percentage of overlap between sentences based on the value of his information asset. Low %overlap indicates sentences with unique collection of words and hence suited for critical information systems. When the user sets an authentication sentences, it is scored and compared with a threshold. Sentence is accepted if its score is above threshold. Allowed %overlap is used to set the threshold value as shown in Eq. (2).

3.2 Survey to Study Deviations in Recalled Sentence

The usability of this scheme is further improved by allowing variations in recalled sentence. A second survey is conducted in our university to categorize deviations that users make while recalling their sentences. It is carried out in two phases. In first phase, users were asked to register and set a sentence by using an image as context. These images were collected from users during registration. The second phase was scheduled after 1 week, in which users were asked to recall their original sentence by displaying the same image as context. Deviations in recalled sentences collected through survey are grouped into 5 categories by doing a qualitative analysis of survey data. These categories are Case_Difference, Order_Difference, Symbol_Difference, Tense_Difference and Noun_Difference

Case_Difference category indicates upper/lower case changes in recalled sentence. Order_Difference is used to record change in word order in recalled sentence. Symbol_Difference indicates addition/omission of symbols like {., ! ; : }. Tense_Difference and Noun_Difference record changes in verb tense and singular/plural variation of nouns in recalled sentence.

Allowed deviations in recalled sentence are recorded in deviation vector (DV). System administrator decides entries in DV based on value of his information asset. DV contains deviation categories with flags initialized to 0. When user recalls his sentence by using image as cue, it is compared with original sentence to identify the variations. Flags in DV are set to 1 for identified deviation categories in recalled sentence. If it contains deviations other than the allowed ones then flag for "Others" category is set to 1 and authentication fails.

As an example, if the user sets "Mom is supervising two kids." for authentication using Fig. 1 as cue and recalls "mom supervises two kids" for access, flags in DV are set as shown in Table 1. System access is allowed in this case since "Others" category in DV is not set.

But if user recalls "Mom is supervising her kids." for access, "Others" flag in DV is set to 1 due to the addition of "her" word and missing of "two" word in recalled sentence. System access is denied in this case.

Table 1. Deviation vector of recalled sentence

Deviation categories	Flag
Case_Difference	1
Order_Difference	0
Symbol_Difference	1
Tense_Difference	1
Noun_Difference	0
Others	0

4   Theory and Calculation

Inverse document frequency (idf) [6] of a term indicates its uniqueness in sentence corpus.

$$idf(t) = log\frac{N}{df(t)} \qquad (1)$$

N indicates total number of sentences in corpus associated with an image, df(t) indicates number of sentences in which term 't' is appearing. Thus the idf of a rare term is high, whereas the idf of a frequent term is likely to below.

The system administrator decides allowed %overlap between sentences based on criticality of his information asset. %overlap is used to define idf_threshold. Users are allowed to set a sentence only if it is scored above idf_threshold.

If corpus contains N sentences, and x indicates allowed %overlap between sentences then ni corresponds to number of sentences in corpus containing words W1 to Wm where m indicates total number of words in sentence.

$$ni = N * \frac{x}{100}$$

$$idf(wi) = log(\frac{N}{ni})$$

$$idf\_threshold = \sum\nolimits_{i=1}^{m} idf(wi) \qquad (2)$$

Scoring of user's authentication sentence is done by using calculate_score function. Pseudo code is given below

```
Function Name: calculate_score
Inputs: A dictionary of words with frequency, Authentication sentence
Output: score
Initialization: score = 0
Step01: remove stopwords from sentence
Step02: for each word in sentence
Step03:         if dictionary contains word
Step04:             ratio = Number of sentences in corpus/ dictionary [word]
Step05:             score= score+ log (ratio)
Step06:         else
Step07:             ratio =Number of sentence in corpus
Step08:             score=score + log (ratio)
Step09: return score
```

Stopwords are removed from a sentence in step01. Stopwords include words such as a, an, the, at, with etc. They are filtered out from sentence to avoid skew in score calculation. Stopwords are avoided in the dictionary as well since they appear more frequently in sentences than other words.

Each word in the sentence is looked up against words in the dictionary in step03. If word is present in the dictionary, frequency is fetched and ratio is calculated by dividing total number of sentences in corpus with frequency of word in step04. Logarithm of ratio is calculated in step05 to get inverse document frequency (idf) of that word.

If word is not present in dictionary then sentence frequency is 1 since it is appearing for the first time in corpus. Ratio in this case is equal to total number of sentences in corpus. Idf is calculated same as before in step08. idf values of each word in sentence is aggregated together to get score of input sentence.

Function 'calculate_score' uses a dictionary containing list of words with sentence frequency. Sentence frequency indicates number of sentences in corpus containing that word. A snippet of dictionary created from sentences collected through survey is given in Table 2. Complete dictionary contains 145 words with corresponding sentence frequencies. Score of any new sentence based on Fig. 1 is calculated using this dictionary.

Table 2. Snippet of dictionary created from survey responses

Words	Sentence frequency
Children	23
Kids	22
Mother	19
Drawing	10
Time	8

As final step, dictionary is updated to include new words and increase word frequencies. update_dictionary function is used for this purpose. Its pseudo code is given below.

Function: update_dictionary
Input: Accepted sentence
Output: updated dictionary

Step01: remove stopwords from sentence

Step02: for each word in sentence
Step03:   if dictionary contains word
Step04:   dictionary [word] = dictionary [word] + 1
Step05:   else
Step07:   add word to dictionary
Step08:   dictionary [word] = 1
Step09: return dictionary

As in calculate_score function, stopwords are removed from sentence in Step01. Each word in sentence is looked up against dictionary and frequency is incremented by 1 in step04 if it exists. New words are added to dictionary with frequency value set to 1 in step 07, 08. Updated dictionary is returned as output.

5   Results and Discussion

80 responses are collected from students, teaching, and nonteaching staffs in the survey which was conducted to study overlap between sentences. Sentences collected by this survey encompassed a wide variety of entries even though single image is used as context for all participants. Age wise sentence length statistics are shown in Table 3. Average length of sentences in different age categories are above 28 characters.

Table 3. Survey sentence length statistics

Age	Max	Min	Median	Mean	Stdev
20–39	111	9	27	28.51	15
40–59	100	18	34	45	30
Overall	111	9	27	30.15	17

Proposed scheme works in two stages. In the first stage, idf_threshold is set for approved %overlap by considering number of words in sentence and in second stage score of the input sentence is calculated based on word frequencies in sentence corpus of the image. User's authentication sentence is accepted only if its score is above idf_threshold.

Example

If system administrator allows 10% overlap between sentences and the corpus contains 80 sentences, then idf_threshold for a sentence with 4 words is calculated as

$$n_1 = \frac{80 \times 10}{100} \qquad idf(w_1) = 1$$

$$n_1 = 8 \qquad idf\_threshold = \sum_{i=1}^{4} 1$$

$$idf(w_1) = \log(80/8) \quad idf\_threshold = 4$$

In this system, if the user sets a sentence *"Mom is supervising two kids"*, score is computed by using calculate_score function. Dictionary entries for words in this sentence are shown in Table 4

Table 4. Words in dictionary

Words	Sentence frequency
Mom	8
Supervising	1
Two	6
Kids	22

Sentence frequency of *"supervising"* is 1 since its appearing for the first time in corpus. *"is"* word is removed from calculation since it is a stopword.

$$\text{score} = \log(\frac{80}{7}) + \log(80) + \log(\frac{80}{5}) + \log(\frac{80}{21})$$

$$\text{score} = 1 + 1.9 + 1.2 + 0.6$$

$$\text{score} = 4.7$$

The user is allowed to set "Mom is supervising two kids" as his authentication sentence since its score is greater than idf_threshold.

6   Conclusion

The challenge with password as an authentication system is due to its dependency on human's recall capacity. Its strength is decided by "how many strong passwords can be remembered for a long time". Human's memory is not good at this task. The demand for strong passwords by some websites like online newspapers are unnecessary since these websites do not safeguard any secret user information. These unnecessary demands for strong passwords with the tremendous increase in online accounts have increased user's cognitive burden. Users are in a critical situation today by using weak passwords or by reusing passwords for accounts where security is the main concern.

Today's password management scheme requires a clear distinction between critical and noncritical information assets. Usability should take front seat of password management for noncritical information assets. Password management scheme proposed in this article is making this distinction by increasing usability of passwords. This scheme takes advantage of human's recall capability of context-based information. It uses a valid English sentence to authenticate users. Authentication sentence is set by using an image selected from a publicly available list of images. Sentence is scored based on its overlap with other sentence in the corpus. User is allowed to set a sentence only if its score is above a threshold value set by system admin. In addition to this, usability is improved by allowing deviations in recalled sentence. These allowed deviations are decided by the system administrator.

The dictionary which is created and updated using sentences from the corpus is the heart of scoring algorithm. The size of this dictionary increases proportionally to number of words in accepted sentences. Future scope of this work is to optimize dictionary lookup time for words. In addition to this scoring of sentences can be modified to incorporate frequency of co-occurring words in the corpus.

References

1. The Man Who Invented The Computer Password Admits That It's Become A Nightmare. http://www.businessinsider.in/The-Man-Who-Invented-The-Computer-Password-Admits-That-Its-Become-A-Nightmare/articleshow/35484027.cms
2. Bonneau, J., et al.: The quest to replace passwords: a framework for comparative evaluation of web authentication schemes. In: 2012 IEEE Symposium on Security and Privacy (SP). IEEE (2012)
3. Paivio, A.: The empirical case for dual coding. In: Imagery, Memory and Cognition, pp. 307–332 (1983)

4. Florêncio, D., Herley, C., Coskun, B.: Do strong web passwords accomplish anything? HotSec **7**(6) (2007)

5. Spector, Y., Ginzberg, J.: Pass-sentence—a new approach to computer code. Comput. Secur. **13**(2), 145–160 (1994)

6. Robertson, S.: Understanding inverse document frequency: on theoretical arguments for IDF. J. Documentation **60**(5), 503–520 (2004)

7. Weiss, R., De Luca, A.: PassShapes: utilizing stroke based authentication to increase password memorability. In: Proceedings of the 5th Nordic Conference on Human-Computer Interaction: Building Bridges. ACM (2008)

8. Shay, R., et al.: A spoonful of sugar? The impact of guidance and feedback on password-creation behavior. In: Proceedings of the 33rd Annual ACM Conference on Human Factors in Computing Systems. ACM (2015)

9. Kuo, C., Romanosky, S., Cranor, L.F.: Human selection of mnemonic phrase-based passwords. In: Proceedings of the Second Symposium on Usable Privacy and Security. ACM (2006)

10. Smith, S.L.: Authenticating users by word association. Comput. Secur. **6**(6), 464–470 (1987)

11. Komanduri, S., et al.: Telepathwords: Preventing Weak Passwords by Reading Users' Minds. USENIX Security (2014)

12. Florêncio, D., Herley, C., Van Oorschot, P.C.: Password Portfolios and the Finite-Effort User: Sustainably Managing Large Numbers of Accounts. Usenix Security (2014)

13. Florêncio, D., Herley, C.: Where do security policies come from? In: Proceedings of the Sixth Symposium on Usable Privacy and Security. ACM (2010)

14. Yan, J., et al.: The memorability and security of passwords–some empirical results. No. UCAM-CL-TR-500. University of Cambridge, Computer Laboratory (2000)

15. Gaw, S., Felten, E.W.: Password management strategies for online accounts. In: Proceedings of the Second Symposium on Usable Privacy and Security. ACM (2006)

16. Chiasson, S., et al.: Multiple password interference in text passwords and click-based graphical passwords. In: Proceedings of the 16th ACM Conference on Computer and Communications Security. ACM (2009)

17. Tulving, E., Pearlstone, Z.: Availability versus accessibility of information in memory for words. J. Verbal Learn. Verbal Behav. **5**(4), 381–391 (1966)

Dynamic Threshold-Based Dynamic Resource Allocation Using Multiple VM Migration for Cloud Computing Systems

Sonam Seth[1(✉)] and Nipur Singh[2]

[1] Kanya Gurukul Campus, Dehradun, Uttarakhand, India
sethsonam@gmail.com
[2] Department of Computer Science, Kanya Gurukul Campus, Dehradun, Uttarakhand, India
nipursingh@hotmail.com

Abstract. As compared to traditional distributed computing systems, cloud computing systems are more reliable, dynamic, and scalable. In recent trend the challenge is managing the resources to maintain the scalability in dynamic environment. The need is to improve the performance of cloud computing systems by provisioning and allocation of on-demand resources to reduce the time. Some of the existing methods are based on static parameters such as CPU utilization threshold, resources, and workload that give less efficient results and there is lack in handling the over-provisioning and under-provisioning situations. In this paper we propose resource allocation model on the basis of dynamic parameters. The proposed method, dynamic threshold-based dynamic resource allocation can optimize the resource utilization and time. The proposed model is implemented on CloudSim and experimental results show the proposed model can improve resource utilization and time.

Keywords: Cloud computing · Dynamic resource allocation · VM migration · CPU utilization · Dynamic threshold

1 Introduction

The Cloud computing model leverages virtualization of computing resources allowing customers to provision resources on-demand on a pay-as-you-go basis [1]. Resource allocation and scheduling using static computing assigns and selects the resources among fixed set of resources to the application to satisfy fixed load balancing. These methods are not suitable for optimal utilization of resources because some resources are under-utilized and some are over-utilized that consume more power. Cloud computing offers the flexibility of handling the dynamic load using dynamic resource allocation methods based on virtualization technology. Virtualization provides modular approach to handle dynamic load. Using virtualization technology cloud data centres multiplex the virtual resources onto physical resources and these virtual resources share single physical resource and allocated to the users. In recent trend, it is the challenge to provide the better solution for resource allocation in dynamic manner. Using hypervisors like Xen mapping of virtual resources onto physical resources takes place.

© Springer Nature Singapore Pte Ltd. 2017
S. Kaushik et al. (Eds.): ICICCT 2017, CCIS 750, pp. 106–116, 2017.
https://doi.org/10.1007/978-981-10-6544-6_11

Resource allocation is the process of assigning available resources to fulfil the demand. Dynamic resource allocation is the process of satisfying the scalable demand. Virtual resources are created on-demand to manage the variable load. Virtual machine migration is the mechanism of migration of virtual resource from one host to another host. Using virtual machine migration techniques utilization of resources increase. Threshold based dynamic resource allocation method provides the efficient use of resources and handles under-utilization and over-utilization of resources.

Load balancing is a technique that helped networks and resources by providing a maximum throughput with minimum response time. Load balancing is dividing the traffic between all servers, so data can be sent and received without any delay with load balancing. Load balancing is used to distributing a larger processing load to smaller processing nodes for enhancing the overall performance of system. In cloud computing environment load balancing is required distribute the dynamic local workload evenly between all the nodes. Under provisioning and over provisioning are also two major issues in load balancing.

Resource provisioning has two steps, (1) Static planning: create VM list and then classify the VMs and map to physical hosts. (2) Dynamic resource Allocation: on-demand VM creation and migration dynamically.

Some issues are considered by an optimal Resource Allocation Strategy.

A. Resource contention: It is the situation where two or more applications try to access the same resource at the same time.

B. Scarcity of resources: This situation arises due to Limited resources. System may get shutdown before complete execution of all tasks.

C. Resource fragmentation: This situation arises when resources are isolated. In such situation, there are enough resources available but still resource allocation strategy can not fulfil the application requirements.

D. Over-provisioning: This arises when application gets more resource than it needed.

E. Under-provisioning: This arises when fewer resources are assigned to application than it needed.

It is the challenge for the cloud service provider to predict the dynamic nature of user demands and the workload. Cloud resources are limited and heterogeneous; also the resource demand is dynamic. Hence we need an efficient dynamic resource allocation strategy [2].

The paper is organized as follows, in Sect. 1, we discuss the recent challenge in cloud computing and the need for dynamic resource allocation policy based on threshold value using virtual machine migration. In Sect. 2, we discuss some existing resource allocation policies. In Sect. 3, we discuss system model, procedure of system model and its simulation flow is explained in this section. In Sect. 4, we discuss proposed method, dynamic threshold based dynamic resource allocation using virtual machine migration for cloud computing. In Sect. 5, we discuss implementation of proposed scheme using CloudSim and simulation of experiment and analyze the experimental results to evaluate the performance of proposed method and in Sect. 6, we conclude the work.

2 Related Work

In cloud computing, few resource allocation policies have been proposed.

In paper [2] Authors proposed an automated resource allocation model based on static threshold for resource utilization using virtual machine migration. Using heuristic method reallocation of resources gives the effective results. Due to migration SLA performance remains unaffected. Over-utilized host leads performance degradation and under-utilized host gets shutdown before completion of task that lead high power consumption.

In paper [4] Authors proposed heuristic method for dynamic provisioning of resources. Optimization of virtual machine allocation is done in two phase. In first phase, VM to be migrated is selected and in second phase the destination server is selected based on Modified Best Fit Decreasing (MBFD) algorithm. Heuristics are based on the upper and lower utilization threshold. VM migration is done based on threshold violation.

In paper [5] Authors proposed dynamic resource allocation strategy based on the priority. Tasks have been assigned the priority. When a task arrives with higher priority, execution of task with lower priority is preempted. New VM is created when no-preemption. Task will be placed in the waiting queue if resources are not available. When the VM will be free then task from waiting queue is selected and executed. Priority assignment is static and preemption is done based on priorities which is not efficient when tasks are of different size.

In paper [6] Authors proposed two tiered resource allocation strategy that includes local as well as global optimization. Local and global schedulers are used to implement the proposed resource allocation mechanism. Local Resource Scheduler controls allocation of resources to VMs within local server. Resource utilization is optimized by adjusting the CPU time slots, memory assigned based on the resource utilization, quality and activity of application. Activity is defined as the threshold of resource allocation. When resource utilization reaches the threshold, few additional resources are allocated to the VM. Resource allocation of the application in the entire system is controlled by Global Resource Scheduler. It adjusts the activity of applications in each local scheduler. The efficiency of this resource allocation strategy depends on how well algorithm can predict the resource utilization and number of requests arrived. This scheme is not suitable for dynamic environment.

In paper [7] Authors proposed threshold-based dynamic resource allocation policy that consists of two procedures Datacenter and Broker. The Datacenter procedure manages the physical resources such as CPU and RAM. On requests from brokers if additional resource is needed request is revoked, in result unable to manage dynamic load effectively. The Broker procedure is based on threshold and manages reallocation. These two procedures communicate with each other to manage the virtual resources in dynamic environment for cloud computing systems. As compares the threshold-based dynamic resource allocation with static resource allocation scheme resource utilization improves, total resource cost reduced. The policy is based on static threshold.

In paper [8] Authors proposed heuristic method for energy and performance enhancement using dynamic consolidation of VM in cloud Datacenters. Single VM migration method is used to optimize cost. In this paper four VM allocation and selection policies are discussed (1) static threshold VM allocation maximum correlation selection, (2) static threshold VM allocation minimum migration time, (3) static threshold minimum utilization, and (4) static threshold random selection. Authors proposed the strategy to detect host overloaded and host under-loaded conditions.

In paper [9] Authors proposed an energy-efficient auto-adjusted threshold based dynamic resource management strategy with heterogeneous physical nodes. The proposed system model contains two tier local manager and global manager. The task of local manager is managing the migration according to workload and global manager manages the overall resource utilization. In this paper power, cost of VM live migration and SLA metrics are optimized. System model has two operation VM selection and VM placement. The proposed VM selection is based on dynamic utilization threshold and VM placement is based on NP-hard bin packing problem that is modified in proposed method Modified Best Fit Decreasing (MBFD).

3 System Model

3.1 Procedure of System Model

- Server consolidation
- Host detection based on dynamic threshold
- Over-utilized host detection
- Under-utilized host detection
- Dynamic resource allocation
- VM migration
- VM selection and allocation

System model is explained in following terms.

A. Server Consolidation

Server consolidation is a technique that converts physical server or physical machine into virtual server or virtual machine (VM) and mapping of VM to physical machine increases the resource utilization and reduces the number of physical machine.

B. Host Detection

Physical server or physical machine is called host. CPU utilization value of host is called threshold that defines the utilization limit for effective use of physical resources. When CPU or RAM utilization reached above the threshold is called over-utilized host and when CPU or RAM utilization reached below the threshold is called under-utilized host. Host is detected for resource utilization based on threshold. In our proposed work host is detected on the basis of dynamic threshold as discussed in Algorithm 1. After detection of host VM is ready for reallocation to meet SLA requirement.

C. VM Migration

Applications have dynamic workload so there are some runtime issues with consolidated server environment. The performance of application degraded due to dynamic workload because of hosts are underutilized and over-utilized. Existing algorithms do not meet SLA requirements; do not support effective use of physical resources, and time constraint as a result VMs may need to be reallocated by using VM migration policy. VM migration approach is carried out in an iterative manner which improves the existing solution. VMs are migrated from over-utilized host to target host based on threshold.

D. VM Selection and Allocation

VM selection for reallocation is based on various policies such as maximum correlation, minimum migration time, minimum utilization, minimum migration cost, and random selection.

Maximum Correlation Policy

Maximum Correlation (MC) [8] policy selects the VM as higher the correlation between resources running on over-utilized host. VM is selected to be migrated with maximum correlation of CPU utilization compared with other VMs.

Minimum Migration Time

Minimum Migration Time (MMT) [8] policy selects the VM with minimum migration completion time compared with other VMs. Migration time is calculated as RAM utilization.

Minimum Utilization

Minimum Utilization policy selects the VM to be migrated on the basis of minimum utilization of resource to optimize the resource utilization.

Random Selection

Random Choice (RC) [8] policy selects the VM to be migrated on the basis of random variable using Random method.

Minimum Migration Cost

Minimum Migration Cost policy selects the VM for migration on the basis of minimum migration cost compared with other VMs. Migration cost can be calculated as product of CPU utilization vector and cost vector.

3.2 System Flow

System flow is explained in paper [3]. This figure shows the backend process of simulation flow.

4 Proposed Method

We propose dynamic threshold based dynamic resource allocation using VM migration to enhance the performance of cloud computing systems. Our method is used to enhance the resource utilization. Method is based on dynamic threshold that try to reduce the energy consumption, number of VM migrations, SLA performance degradation due to migration, and mean time. We have used heuristic approach proposed in paper [2, 3, 8].

The proposed system model consists of five hosts and eight virtual machines. Host has proposed configuration parameters such as network bandwidth, CPU capacity, disk storage, RAM and VM has proposed configuration parameters such as RAM, network bandwidth, CPU capacity. Each host and virtual machine has its own configuration as shown in Tables 1 and 2 respectively in next section. Hosts are independent and virtual resources are correlated using correlation policy and workload is dynamic.

Proposed work is based on following criteria:

- Which VM is to be allocated to cloudlets.
- When VM is migrated from one host to another host.
- When VM is reallocated.
- Which VM is migrated.
- Which host is used as source or target for migration.
- When host is over-utilized or under-utilized.

Static threshold based method is not able to manage dynamic workloads effectively. Dynamic threshold based proposed method can manage dynamic and unpredictable workloads. CPU utilization of host can be taken dynamically within the range varies from 0.1 to 0.9. VM migration can takes place on the basis of under-utilized and over-utilized threshold of hosts. In case of over-utilization of host, VMs with higher correlation are selected for migration using Maximum Correlation Policy (Mc) [8]. First we select VMs from over-utilized host migrated to target host to balance the over-utilized hosts then we select VMs from under-utilized host migrated to target host to manage the under-utilized hosts. The VMs are set for migration to the determined target hosts, and the source host is switched to the sleep mode once all the migrations have been completed. If all the VMs from the source host cannot be placed on other hosts, the host is kept active. This process is iteratively repeated for all hosts that have not been considered as being overloaded.

Over-utilized and under-utilized hosts are detected using given algorithm 1.

Algorithm1. Dynamic Threshold Based Host Detection
Input: HostList
Output: over_utilizedHost List, under-utilizedHost List
1. Define two new lists over_utilizedHost List, under-utilizedHost List
2. get HostList
3. initialize dThreshold = 0.0
4. for each host in HostList
5. get cpuUtilization and ramUtilization
6.   do
7.   if cpuUtilization > dThreshold || ramUtilization > dThreshold
            Then add host to over_utilizedHost List
8.   End if
9.   if cpuUtilization < dThreshold || ramUtilization < dThreshold
            Then add host to under-utilizedHost List
10.   End if
11.   While(dThreshold <= 0.9)
12. End for
13. return over_utilizedHost List
14. return under-utilizedHost List

Following steps explain the overall process of the system:
Phase I

  i. VM mapping on host (physical server) using hypervisor Xen.
 ii. Receive request for resource.
iii. Check request can be fulfil.
 iv. If available resources are sufficient to fulfil the request then allocate resource to request using Dynamic resource allocation method.
  v. If resources are not available to fulfil the request wait for reallocation in next phase.

Phase II
When resources are not allocated to requests in phase I then reallocation of resources to un-serviced requests is carried out in this second phase.

  i. Detect over-utilized host using Dynamic Threshold Based Host Detection method.
 ii. Define set of VM from over-utilized host.
iii. Receive request which is not allocated in phase I.
 iv. Select VM to be migrated using Maximum Correlation policy.
  v. Check whether VM satisfies the request.
 vi. If satisfies then reallocate resource to request.
vii. Repeat the process in phase II until resources are available.
viii. If not satisfy then move to next phase III.

Phase III

i. Detect under-utilized host using Dynamic Threshold Based Host Detection method.
ii. Define set of VM from under-utilized host.
iii. Receive request which is not allocated in phase II.
iv. Maintain the host utilization using migration policy.
v. Check whether VM satisfies the request.
vi. If satisfies allocate the resource to request.
vii. Repeat the process in phase III until all requests are serviced.
viii. Shut down hosts.
ix. End the process.

5 Experimental and Simulation Results

5.1 Experimental Configuration

We have evaluated dynamic threshold based VM migration algorithm to handle under-utilization and over-utilization of resources using CloudSim. CloudSim is a tool used to implement our algorithm and simulate the results.

Experimental Host and VM configuration is given in Tables 1 and 2 respectively.

Table 1. Host configuration

Parameter	Value
RAM (MB)	2048
MIPS (MB)	1000
Storage (GB)	1000000
BW (mbps)	10000
Number of hosts	5

Table 2. VM configuration

Parameter	Value
Image size (MB)	10000
RAM (MB)	512
BW (mbps)	1000
MIPS (MB)	1000
VMM	Xen
Number of VM	8

5.2 Simulation Results

We have simulated our algorithm with given configuration in Table 1 and 2. Simulation results are shown in Table 3. In Table 3, column 1 shows the results those are based on static method at static threshold value that is at 0.8 and column 2 shows the results those are based on dynamic method at dynamic threshold value that varies from lower threshold value 0.1 to upper threshold value 0.9. In existing method it is found that some hosts are over-utilized and some hosts are under-utilized so the VM migrations take place to handle over-utilization and under-utilization situations. The situation when host utilization is up to 100% and low to 0% results in the SLA degraded performance and energy consumption increases. Then we simulated using dynamic threshold method using VM migration. We found many VM migrations from one host to another host due to host over-utilization and host under-utilization. Figure 1 shows that some hosts are under-utilized and some hosts are over-utilized.

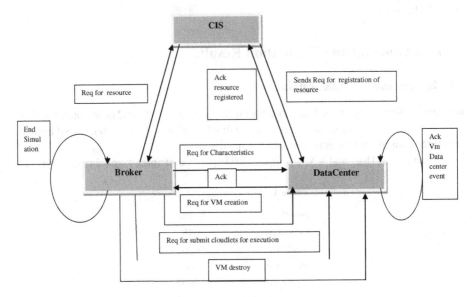

Fig. 1. Backend procedure of system flow

Table 3. Simulation results

S. No.	Parameter	Static threshold based	Dynamic threshold based
1	Energy consumption	6.49 Kwh	6.14 Kwh
2	Number of VM migrations	388	381
3	SLA performance degradation due to migration	0.16%	0.15%
4	Mean time before a VM migration	1652.17 s	1496.19 s
5	Mean time before a host shutdown	19.55 s	19.29 s

6 Conclusion

In this paper we have worked on dynamic threshold based dynamic resource allocation using multiple VM migration to handle host over-utilization and under-utilization. Proposed model is based on multiple correlated VM migration rather than single VM migration. Migrated VM is selected on the basis of correlation factor. Our given method can achieve effective use of resources that helps in minimizing energy consumption, reduces number of VM migrations, reduced mean migration time, reduced mean access time, and upgraded SLA performance. We have done experiment at different static threshold values and results are compared with experiment done at dynamic threshold value then we get results are approximately same on variations. Figure 2 shows host utilization using Static and Dynamic threshold based methods.

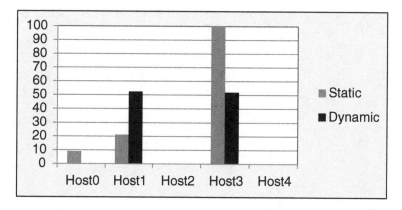

Fig. 2. Host utilization in % using static and dynamic threshold based method for VM migration

References

1. Buyya, R., Yeo, C.S., Venugopal, S., Broberg, J., Brandic, I.: Cloud computing and emerging IT platforms: vision, hype and reality for delivering computing as the 5th utility. Future Gener. Comput. Syst. **25**(6), 599–616 (2009)
2. Ighare, R.U., Thool, R.C.: Threshold based dynamic resource allocation using virtual machine migration. Int. J. Curr. Eng. Technol. **5**(4), 2603–2608 (2015)
3. Calheiros, R.N., Ranjan, R., Beloglazov, A., Rose, C.A.F.D., Buyya, R.: CloudSim: a toolkit for modelling and simulation of cloud computing environments and evaluation of resource provisioning algorithms. Softw. Pract. Exp. **41**, 1–24 (2010)
4. Beloglazov, A. Buyya, R.: Energy efficient allocation of virtual machines in cloud data centers. In: 10th IEEE/ACM International Conference on Cluster, Cloud and Grid Computing (CCGrid), pp. 577–578 (2010)
5. Pawar, C.S., Wagh, R.B.: Priority based dynamic resource allocation in Cloud computing with modified waiting queue. In: International Conference on Intelligent Systems and Signal Processing (ISSP), pp. 311–316 (2013)
6. Song, Y., Sun, Y., Shi, W.: A two-tiered on-demand resource allocation mechanism for VM-based data centers. Serv. Comput. IEEE Trans. **6**(1), 116–129 (2013)

7. Lin, W., Wang, J.Z., Liang, C., Qi, D.: A threshold based dynamic resource allocation scheme for cloud computing. SciVerse Sci. Direct **23**(2011), 695–703 (2011)
8. Beloglazov, A., Buyya, R.: Optimal online deterministic algorithms and adaptive heuristics for energy and performance efficient dynamic consolidation of virtual machine in cloud data centers. Concurr. Comput. **24**(13), 1397–1420 (2011)
9. Beloglazov, A., Buyya, R.: Adaptive threshold-based approach for energy-efficient consolidation of virtual machines in cloud data centers. In: Proceedings of the 8th International Workshop on Middleware for Grids, Clouds and e-Science, pp. 1–6. ACM (2010)

3D Weighted Centroid Localization Algorithm for Wireless Sensor Network Using Teaching Learning Based Optimization

Gaurav Sharma[1](✉) and Ashok Kumar[2]

[1] Department of Electronics and Communication Engineering,
CVR College of Engineering, Hyderabad 501510, Telangana, India
ergaurav209@yahoo.co.in
[2] Department of Electronics and Communication Engineering,
National Institute of Technology, Hamirpur 177005, Himachal Pradesh, India
ashok@nith.ac.in

Abstract. The purpose of this paper is to improve the localization accuracy of range-free algorithm in three-dimensional (3D) space for wireless sensor networks (WSNs). In this paper, weighted centroid localization algorithm using teaching learning based optimization (WCL-TLBO) is proposed to improve the positioning accuracy in 3D space of WSN. In range-free algorithms, only received signal strength (RSS) information between nodes is sufficient to determine the position of target nodes. RSS value gives the clue to find out the distance between sensor nodes but shows non-linearity between RSS and distance. To overcome this non-linearity, fuzzy logic system (FLS) is used. Edge weights of WCL are modelled using FLS. Further to reduce the errors, TLBO is applied to optimize these edge weights. Simulation results establish the superiority of the proposed algorithm in terms of localization accuracy to other existing range-free algorithms in similar scenario.

Keywords: Centroid algorithm · FLS · Range-free localization · TLBO · WSN

1 Introduction

Recent advancement in micro-electro-mechanical systems (MEMS) and communication technology have led to development of inexpensive, multi-functional, extremely small and smart sensor nodes [1]. The capabilities of these sensor nodes include sensing the physical phenomenon i.e. light, pressure, temperature, humidity, etc. These sensor nodes have capabilities to communicate with other nodes in wireless medium. Sensor nodes sense the data; pass this data to a central unit known as base station or sink node through multihop fashion. This complete process forms a network known as wireless sensor network (WSN).

A number of sensor nodes (from hundreds to thousands) are deployed according to application in the region of interest. These nodes sense the desired data and report it to the base station through multihop fashion in wireless medium. Deployment of nodes varies from application to application. Manual deployment of sensor nodes can be done where it is easy to approach the area, whereas random deployment is taken place in inaccessible area i.e. forests, mountains, sea, etc. through aircraft or any other method.

© Springer Nature Singapore Pte Ltd. 2017
S. Kaushik et al. (Eds.): ICICCT 2017, CCIS 750, pp. 117–127, 2017.
https://doi.org/10.1007/978-981-10-6544-6_12

In random deployment, it is hard to find the position of the nodes. Localization is defined as the process of determining the physical location of the sensor nodes in the sensing field. WSNs have a number of perspective applications in the field of structural monitoring, healthcare applications, habitat and environmental monitoring, military applications, surveillance, etc. Most of the applications need precise location of the nodes to make the data meaningful, because sensed data without location information is meaningless. User needs not only to know what happens but also where it has happened. Due to this, localization of nodes in WSN has become one of the critical issues. Since the addition of Global Positioning System (GPS) [2] device to the nodes is not viable in such a large area network due to cost and energy consumption factors. Sometimes, GPS may not work in non-line-of-sight (NLOS) environment. Therefore, alternate of GPS is needed to localize the nodes. Small amount of nodes known as anchor nodes are deployed in the network, which know their coordinates either by GPS or manual placement. Coordinates of location unaware nodes known as target nodes can be determined with the help of anchor nodes.

Many localization algorithms have been described in literature in last decade. Generally, localization algorithms in WSN can be broadly categorized in two types: range-based localization algorithms and range-free localization algorithms. Range-based schemes are comparatively more precise but they need an extra hardware and easily affected by noise and fading. But for large area network, it is not viable to accommodate extra hardware on each sensor node, which makes it bulky and costly. Also using range-based techniques, nodes consume more power which affects the overall lifetime of the network as these nodes run on small battery. In many applications sensor nodes are deployed in environments which are inaccessible. In that case sensor nodes are scattered through aircrafts or any other way. Therefore, after node deployment it is very difficult to replace the batteries or access the nodes. So energy of the nodes should be utilized in efficient way to enhance the lifetime of WSN. On the other hand, range-free schemes show relatively poor localization accuracy, but there is no need of extra ranging hardware as only connectivity information between nodes is sufficient for localization process. Due to drawbacks of range-based schemes, researchers mainly attract towards range-free schemes. Mobility also has a significant impact on localization process as mobile nodes change their position frequently. Due to this, complexity of the algorithm is increased. In this paper, we are not considering the effect of mobility.

Most of the localization research has been done in literature for two-dimensional (2D) WSN. Now the work is being carried out to improve accuracy in three-dimensional (3D), because in real practice, nodes are deployed in 3D. Localization in 3D is more genuine and complicated as compared to 2D localization in WSN. Towards moving in this direction, we have proposed a weighted centroid localization (WCL) algorithm using fuzzy logic system (FLS) with integration of teaching learning based optimization (TLBO) [9] in 3D space. Since the centroid algorithm is very basic and effective range-free location algorithm, which is most widely used. In this paper, only RSS (received signal strength) value is required to estimate the distance between anchor nodes and target nodes. To model and to overcome the non-linearity between RSS and distance, FLS is used. Further to reduce errors, TLBO is used. Simulation results establish superiority of our proposed algorithm viz. WCL-TLBO in terms of localization accuracy to other existing algorithms.

Section 2 presents related works. In Sect. 3, proposed algorithm has been described. Simulation results and conclusion will be discussed in Sects. 4 and 5 respectively.

2 Related Works

Many range-free schemes have been proposed in the literature to improve the localization accuracy. Typical range-free algorithms are centroid localization algorithm (CLA) [4], approximate-point in triangle (APIT) [7], distance vector hop (DV-Hop) [10], convex position estimation (CPE) [3], etc. Currently, research on 3D localization in WSN is being carried out as it is closer to the reality.

CLA is simple and having low computational and communication cost. In this, nodes are placed in grid configuration [4]. Normal nodes get their locations by estimating the centroid of the coordinates of the neighbouring anchors. Since the accuracy of CLA depends on percentage of anchor nodes in the network. When anchor nodes distribution is regular then it shows good localization accuracy. Also the localization accuracy of CLA is proportional to anchor node distribution in network.

In [6], an extension of CLA is presented in terms of adding weights to the coordinates of the anchors to improve the accuracy. These weights are known as edge weights of anchor nodes which can be determined according to the distance between anchors and target nodes i.e. large distance is given a low weight and higher weights are given to nearby anchors. This algorithm is popularly known as weighted centroid localization (WCL) algorithm. Accuracy is improved as compared to centroid algorithm up to some extent. There are also many algorithms in literature related to WCL, but each method is different for weight calculation.

In [8], soft computing approaches and some optimization techniques are applied on different localization algorithms. H-best particle swarm optimization (HPSO) and biogeography based optimization (BBO) performed better in terms of localization accuracy and computational time. BBO shows the slow convergence with high accuracy and HPSO shows fast convergence with low accuracy. These algorithms show the effect of noise variance and radio irregularity property on the localization accuracy.

In [11], an improved DV-Hop (distance vector-hop) algorithm for three-dimensional space in WSN is presented. The concept of degree of coplanarity is also introduced for improving localization accuracy. Up-gradation of target nodes to assistant anchor nodes is also described for better positioning coverage. It is shown by the simulation that localization accuracy and positioning coverage have been improved up to an extent in [11].

Algorithms for 3D localization presented in the literature are more complicated, slow and less accurate. Taking into the consideration of these drawbacks, we have proposed WCL-TLBO in this paper.

3   Proposed Algorithm

This section presents the proposed algorithm viz. weighted centroid localization algorithm using teaching learning based optimization (WCL-TLBO) with the help of fuzzy logic system (FLS). In literature, many optimization techniques have been proposed to improve localization accuracy in WSN i.e. genetic algorithm (GA), PSO, HPSO, BBO, firefly algorithm (FA), etc. Some of these optimization techniques show fast convergence but low accuracy and vice versa. The main limitation of these optimization techniques is that in these techniques computational complexity increases with increase in search space dimension. For this purpose, we propose efficient optimization technique i.e. TLBO which shows fast convergence and high accuracy as there is no algorithm controlling parameters. The following sections present an overview of FLS and TLBO.

3.1   Fuzzy Logic Systems

In 1965, Lofti Zadeh proposed firstly the concept of fuzzy logic [5]. Fuzzy logic reflects how people think. The logic used in FLS, describes fuzziness. Fuzzy logic is the theory of fuzzy sets, which calibrates ambiguity. In the fuzzy logic operations, precise inputs are not required. However, system complexity increases with increase in inputs and outputs.

The fuzzy inference system (FIS) is a FLS in which inputs are processed according to rules. A FIS consists of a fuzzifier unit some fuzzy IF-THEN rules knowledge base unit, an inference decision making unit and a defuzzifier unit. In this paper, we used Mamdani inference system due to its solid defuzzification, which leads to give results in consistent form.

3.2   Teaching Learning Based Optimization

In 2011, Rao et al. firstly proposed TLBO. It is population based optimization technique like other optimization techniques i.e. GA, BBO, PSO, DE, FA, etc. Performance of all these optimization techniques except TLBO depends on the algorithm controlling parameters. Optimal selection of these parameters ensures the optimal solution. But it is also a challenging work to find the optimal values of these parameters. On contrary, TLBO is parameter free algorithm i.e. there is no algorithm controlling parameters. TLBO shows fast convergence and high stability with good accuracy because there is no algorithm controlling parameters.

Working of TLBO is similar to teaching and learning process in the school. Generally, a teacher is considered as highly educated. A group of learners are considered as the population. The teacher makes efforts to teach the learners in best way to have good result. But the quality of teacher affects the result of the class. There is a substantial impact of the teacher on the output of the learners in the class, which depends on the teaching factor of the teacher. Working of TLBO mimics according to two phases: teacher phase and learner phase. In teacher phase, learners gain knowledge from the teacher and in learner phase, learners learn from the interaction between themselves. If any learner is comparatively less healthy than other then it will gain knowledge from healthier learner and this process continues till satisfaction criterion is satisfied. For complete process of TLBO, readers should advise to read [9].

3.3   Node Localization Using FLS and TLBO

In range-free localization, only connectivity information between nodes is sufficient to estimate the distance between anchor nodes and target nodes. In WCL-TLBO, RSS information between the nodes gives clue to find the distance between nodes. Since the RSS value is having uncertainty, it varies with environmental factors, which leads to make non-linearity between RSS and distance value. To overcome this non-linearity, we have used FLS in our proposed algorithm. In our proposed algorithm, edge weights of anchors are defined, which is modelled using FLS. To further improve the localization accuracy, TLBO is used to optimize these edge weights. Nodes are randomly distributed in 3D space. In the process of WCL-TLBO, following assumptions are taken, as follows:

1. Anchor nodes know their coordinates either by the manual deployment or by the system administrator or through GPS. These anchor nodes help in determination of target nodes' coordinates.
2. Radiation pattern of communication range of all nodes is considered perfectly spherical i.e. anisotropic property is not considered in proposed algorithm.

The following steps are performed for the proposed algorithm in 3D space, as:

1. Each anchor broadcasts a beacon message in the network.
2. Target nodes collect the beacon message and find their neighbouring anchor nodes and check the number of neighbouring anchor nodes.
3. Check if number of neighbouring anchor nodes ≥ 4.
4. Each target node maintains a list of RSS value from their neighbouring anchor nodes.
5. Determine the edge weights of anchor nodes according to their RSS value.
6. FLS is used to model the edge weights and TLBO is used to optimize these edge weights.
7. After edge weights calculation, determine the coordinates of the target nodes according to the formula given in [6], as follows:

$$(x_t, y_t, z_t) = \left[\frac{(w_1 x_1) + \ldots (w_n x_n)}{\sum\limits_{i=1}^{n} w_i}, \frac{(w_1 y_1) + \ldots (w_n y_n)}{\sum\limits_{i=1}^{n} w_i}, \frac{(w_1 z_1) + \ldots (w_n z_n)}{\sum\limits_{i=1}^{n} w_i} \right] \quad (1)$$

where (x_t, y_t, z_t) are the coordinates of tth target nodes $(x_1, y_1, z_1), (x_2, y_2, z_2) \ldots (x_n, y_n, z_n)$ are the coordinates of the neighbouring anchor nodes for corresponding t^{th} target node, $w_1, w_2 \ldots w_n$ are the edge weights between each considered target node and corresponding n^{th} neighbouring anchor node.

3.4 Fuzzy Modelling

RSS value is having uncertainty; it varies according to the environmental factors, which leads to make non-linearity between RSS and distance value. To reduce this non-linearity, we use FLS in our proposed algorithm. Since RSS value gives the clue to find distance between anchor nodes and target node.

RSS value of anchors is taken as the input variable in rule base of Mamdani fuzzy model and it is taken in the interval of $[0, RSS_{max}]$, where RSS_{max} is 100 dB (i.e. maximum RSS value). Five membership functions have been used to map input variable RSS i.e. VLOW, LOW, MEDIUM, HIGH, VHIGH as shown in Fig. 1(a). Edge weight is taken as output variable and the values used for edge weight is in the interval of $[0, w_{max}]$, where w_{max} is 1 (i.e. maximum edge weight). Further edge weights are optimized using TLBO as shown in Fig. 1(b). The rules used for determining the distance are shown in Table 1.

Table 1. Fuzzy mapping rules of edge weights

Sr. No.	IF: input (RSS)	THEN: output (edge weights)
1.	VLOW	VLOW
2.	LOW	LOW
3.	MEDIUM	MEDIUM
4.	HIGH	HIGH
5.	VHIGH	VHIGH

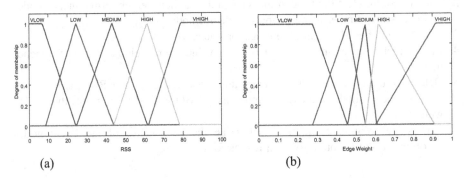

(a)   (b)

Fig. 1. Membership functions of (a) RSS (b) edge weights optimized by TLBO

4 Performance Evaluations

In this section, simulations of our proposed algorithm viz. WCL-TLBO are presented, which is done using MATLAB 8.1 to evaluate the performance in terms of localization accuracy. Performance of proposed algorithm is compared with centroid algorithm [4], weighted centroid algorithm [6] and range-free localization using fuzzy logic based on HPSO (RFHPSO+fuzzy) [8].

4.1 Performance Metrics and Simulation Parameters

To evaluate the performance of our proposed algorithm, following metrics are considered.

- *Localization Error (LE):* It is the difference between actual coordinates and estimated coordinates of nodes. LE of each target node can be calculated as follows:

$$LE = \sqrt{(x_e - x_a)^2 + (y_e - y_a)^2 + (z_e - z_a)^2} \tag{2}$$

where (x_e, y_e, z_e) and (x_a, y_a, z_a) are the estimated and actual coordinates of target nodes respectively.

- *Average Localization Error (ALE):* It is the ratio of total localization error to the number of target nodes *(n)*. In this paper, ALE is taken as the performance metric to measure the localization accuracy of the algorithms Mathematically, it can be expressed as:

$$ALE = \frac{\sum_{i=1}^{n} \sqrt{(x_e - x_a)^2 + (y_e - y_a)^2 + (z_e - z_a)^2}}{n} \tag{3}$$

In simulations, a total of 150 nodes are randomly deployed in three-dimensional space along with 30% of anchor nodes in the fixed area of $150 \times 150 \times 150$ m^3 as shown in Fig. 2. We have evaluated the performance of all algorithms in sparse random topology. Each node is having a communication range of 40 m. Simulation parameters are shown in Table 2. There is no need to set any parameter in TLBO, since it is free from algorithm parameters. We have taken initial population as 50, as very small population

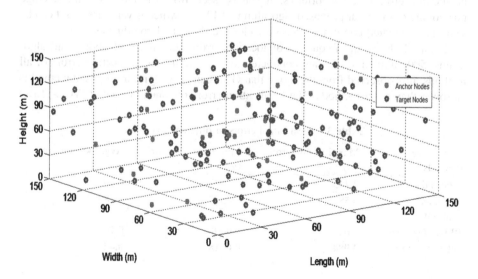

Fig. 2. A typical example of node distribution in 3D

Table 2. Simulation parameters

Parameters	Value
Total number of nodes	50–400
Area	$150 \times 150 \times 150 \text{ m}^3$
Communication range	40 m
Percentage of anchor nodes	2%–50%
DOI	0
Maximum iterations	500
Simulation runs	50
Initial population	50

gives premature results and large population size affects the algorithm complexity and computational time. Fifty simulation runs are conducted to optimize the edge weights of the anchor nodes.

4.2   Simulation Results

To check the effectiveness of our proposed algorithm, we have calculated ALE with respect to variations in anchor nodes and node density. Figure 3 shows the average localization accuracy with respect to variations in number of anchor nodes. Anchor nodes are tuned from 2 to 50% with a total of 150 nodes. It is observed from the results that ALE decreases with increase in the percentage of the anchor nodes. It is due to the reasons that more target nodes are covered by more anchors, resulting higher accuracy. All algorithms are simulated in similar environment. It is also noticed from the results that WCL-TLBO achieves better localization accuracy compared to existing algorithms due to edge weight optimization. Table 3 shows the maximum, minimum and average positioning error of all algorithms. It can be seen from the table that the average positioning error of our proposed algorithm is 0.424 m, which is very less and it can be said that calculated coordinates are very close to the actual coordinates.

Figure 4 shows the frequency of location errors occurrence of above said algorithms. 500 simulation runs are conducted to measure the mean location errors of all methods. It is observed from the figure that Gaussian curve for our proposed method is narrower than other methods. The localization errors obtained in case of WCL-TLBO

Table 3. Localization errors of different algorithms

Range free methods	Max. location error (m)	Min. location error (m)	Avg. location error (m)
Centroid	7.245	0.1097	2.002
Weighted centroid	6.587	0.0572	1.289
RFHPSO+fuzzy	5.025	0.0098	0.709
WCL-TLBO	**3.984**	**0.0018**	**0.424**

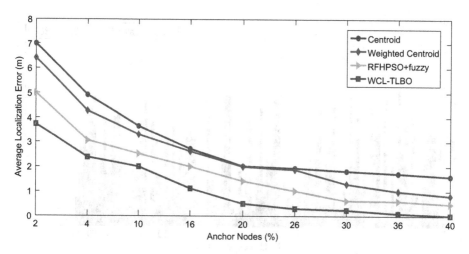

Fig. 3. Average localization errors with respect to different percentage of anchor nodes

algorithm is from 0 to 0.5 m, which indicates the stability and consistency of our proposed algorithm. Figure 5 shows the location error of each target node of WCL-TLBO for a single simulation run at any instance. It is noticed from the figure that maximum location error of WCL-TLBO is 3.984 m and minimum location error is 0.0018 m, which is very less location error compared to other algorithms.

Figure 6 shows the average localization errors with variation in number of sensor nodes. Sensor nodes are tuned from 50 to 350 with 30% of anchor nodes. It is observed from the result that ALE decreases with increase in number of sensor nodes. This is due to the reasons that with increase in node density, network connectivity also increases,

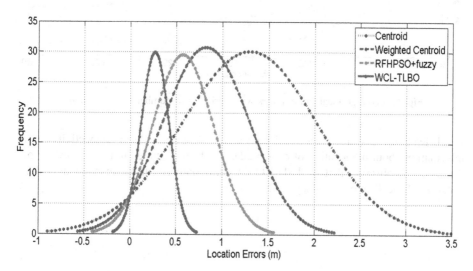

Fig. 4. Frequency of location errors occurrence of different range free algorithms

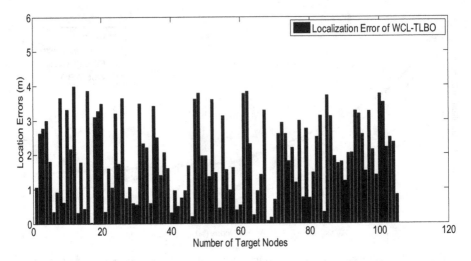

Fig. 5. WCL-TLBO based localization errors of each target node

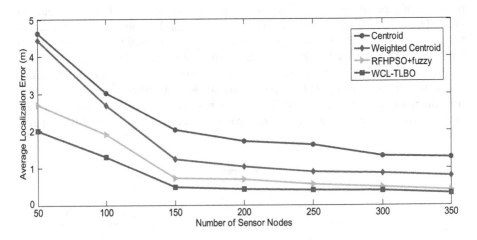

Fig. 6. Average localization errors with variation in number of sensor nodes

which leads to good accuracy of all algorithms. With increase in connectivity, more information about the location of other nodes has been scattered in the network. From the result it is observed that WCL-TLBO algorithm outperforms the existing algorithms in terms of localization accuracy.

5 Conclusions

Due to advantages over range-based localization algorithms, range-free schemes have been proved more efficient and popular as only connectivity information between nodes is sufficient for position calculation of target nodes. Since range-free methods show poor localization accuracy. In order to improve the localization accuracy in range-free methods for three-dimensional WSN, weighted centroid localization algorithm using teaching learning based optimization (WCL-TLBO) for three-dimensional space is proposed in this paper. Only the RSS value is sufficient to determine the position of target nodes as RSS value gives the clue to find approximate distance between nodes. To model the edge weights of anchor nodes, FLS is used. To further reduce the localization errors, TLBO has been applied to optimize the edge weights. Simulation results establish the superiority of the proposed algorithm in terms of localization accuracy to other existing localization algorithms. On average, WCL-TLBO achieves about 46% more accuracy than traditional centroid algorithm in 3D space.

References

1. Akyildiz, I.F., Su, W., Sankarasubramaniam, Y., Cayirci, E.E.: A survey on sensor network. IEEE Commun. Mag. **40**(8), 102–105 (2002)
2. Hofmann-Wellenfof, B., Lichtenegger, H., Collins, J.: Global Positioning System: Theory and Practice. Springer, Wien (1993)
3. Doherty, L., Kristofer, S.J., Laurent, E.: Convex position estimation in wireless sensor networks. In: Proceeding of INFOCOM, Anchorage, AK, vol. 3, pp. 1655–1663 (2001)
4. Bulusu, N., Heidemann, J., Estrin, D.: GPS-less low-cost outdoor localization for very small devices. IEEE Pers. Commun. **7**(5), 28–34 (2000)
5. Zadeh, L.: Fuzzy logic: computing with words. IEEE Trans. Fuzzy Syst. **4**(2), 103–111 (1996)
6. Kim, S.Y., Kwon, O.H.: Location estimation-based on edge weights in wireless sensor networks, inform. Commun. Soc. **30**, 10A (2005)
7. Zhou, Y., Ao, X., Xia, S.: An improved APIT node self-localization algorithm in WSN. In: 7th World Congress on Intelligent Control and Automation (WCICA 2008), Chongqing, China, pp. 7582–7586 (2008)
8. Kumar, A., Khosla, A., Saini, J., Singh, S.: Range-free 3D node localization in anisotropic wireless sensor networks. Appl. Soft Comput. **34**, 438–448 (2015)
9. Rao, R.V., Savsani, V.J., Vakharia, D.P.: Teaching–learning-based optimization: a novel method for constrained mechanical design optimization problems. Comput. Aided Des. **43** (3), 303–315 (2011)
10. Niculescu, D., Nath, B.: Ad Hoc Positioning System (APS). In: Proceedings Global Telecommunications Conference (Globecom 2001), vol. 1, pp. 292–293 (2001)
11. Chen, X., Zhang, B.: Improved DV-Hop node localization algorithm in wireless sensor networks. J. Distrib. Sensor Netw. Int. (2012). doi:10.1155/2012/213980

An Approach to Build a Sentiment Analyzer: A Survey

Singh Dharmendra⬡, Bhatia Akshay[✉]⬡, and Singh Ashvinder⬡

Department of Computer Science, Atma Ram Sanatan Dharma College,
University of Delhi, New Delhi, India
Singh88dk@gmail.com, Akshaybhatia95@gmail.com,
Ashvindersinghdhariwal@gmail.com

Abstract. With the increase in the use of social networking sites like Twitter anyone can share or express his or her views with each other on a common stage. Twitter sentiment analyzer is a tool which is used to find out whether a corpus of data is positive, negative or neutral. Our work focuses on the steps involved in this Opinion Mining problem necessary to fetch opinions out of a corpus. We also aim to look at the strengths and scope for future research in the field of Twitter sentiment analyzer.

Keywords: Opinion mining · Sentiment analysis · Twitter · Social networks

1 Introduction

Sentiment Analysis is a methodology that is involved in taking out the sentiments (positive, negative and neutral in this article). People buy things, read articles, watch movies, generating large amounts of data and thus expressing their opinions. Expressing people's opinion about a particular topic or product has become necessary for product based companies especially e-commerce websites to augment the user experience. Doing this manually is a very tedious task. To make the task easier, sentiment analyzers have been developed to parse opinions on social media. Twitter is a powerful medium where people share their experiences using hashtags which can, in turn, be used to find data about any particular topic and people's opinion is mined.

The paper is defined as follows – Sect. 2 of our report gives a brief explanation of related work in the field of opinion mining. Section 3 deals with general concepts involved in building a sentiment analyzer and specify the rule based approach and machine learning approach. It gives an overview of machine learning algorithms such as Naïve Bayes and Linear Support Vector Machines which are the most popular machine learning algorithms used in sentiment analysis. Section 4 describes the steps involved in making a sentiment analyzer that derives its corpus from Twitter, the famous social networking website. Section 5 deals with the applications/future scope of sentiment analysis. Section 6 concludes the paper.

2 Background Work

There has been much research in the field of opinion mining on Twitter and has shown promising application. In this domain, the biggest challenge is to translate and compute

© Springer Nature Singapore Pte Ltd. 2017
S. Kaushik et al. (Eds.): ICICCT 2017, CCIS 750, pp. 128–136, 2017.
https://doi.org/10.1007/978-981-10-6544-6_13

the abbreviations and slangs used in the social networking world. Use of Twitter as a corpus for opinion mining has been cited by Pak and Paroubek [1]. They have used a three-way classification method which classifies the tweets into positive, negative and neutral. Kumar et al. [2] augmented this approach by using five emotions namely happiness, anger, fear, sadness and disgust. Hasan et al. [3] have used a Naïve Bayes based approach to design a classifier in both English and Bangla. Bhatia et al. [4] have presented a system flow model in opinion mining which points the crucial steps that a text should go through to get a trustworthy opinion from the internet. Balahadia et al. [5] have presented a Teacher Evaluation Architecture which can be used to measure not only the quantitative aspects but also the qualitative aspects of reviews from students to evaluate their Teachers. Fang et al. [9] have used opinion mining techniques on a set of data obtained from Amazon. They have used sentiment analysis to give product reviews.

3 Approaches Used in Building a Sentiment Analyzer

Two different approaches are involved in the construction of a sentiment analyzer:

3.1 Rule-Based Approach

Use of human judgment to find a relationship between sentences, sorting of words as positive or negative and manually doing lexical analysis is known as a rule-based approach. The major steps in rule-based approach consist of:

1. Identifying every word in the document as positive or negative
2. If the number of positive words is more than negative words, then classify the document as positive and vice versa.

VADER: Vader is a tool which uses rule-based methods to do opinion mining work on social media text.

A lexicon and rule-based sentiment analysis tool, i.e., VADER (Valence Aware Dictionary and sentiment Reasoner) is designed to manage the sentiments expressed on the social networks. It is sensitive both to the difference and the intensity of the sentiments voiced in the social networks. It is a cumbersome task to create sentiment lexicon manually and can be erroneous as well, hence opinion mining researchers are using already existing lexicons as their resource.

The below example shows how VADER sentiment is used in one's application.

> 1. "Mohan is smart and intelligent."   Positive sentence example
> 2. "Mohan is smart and intelligent!"   Punctuation emphasis

VADER can analyze the inputs provided into negative, neutral and positive. It also provides a compound value which lies between −1 (Extremely negative) and +1 (Extremely positive).

Mohan is smart and intelligent.
{'neg': 0.0, 'neu': 0.244, 'pos': 0.756, 'compound': 0.8326}
Mohan is smart and intelligent!
{'neg': 0.0, 'neu': 0.247, 'pos': 0.752, 'compound': 0.8439}
Mohan is VERY SMART and INCREDIBLY INTELLIGENT!!!
{'neg': 0.0, 'neu': 0.284, 'pos': 0.716, 'compound': 0.9469}

3.2   Machine Learning Based Approach

Machine Learning based approach is used to classify a document as positive or negative. There are many Machine Learning based algorithms, two of which are the Naïve Bayes Classifier and the Support Vector Machine. We will discuss these shortly but first, let us have a look at the steps to be followed in an ML-based approach –

Input – Input can include any documents or text. Here the ML-based classifier gets trained on the corpus of pre-classified texts. Once the classifier gets trained, it can easily classify the document as positive or negative as is shown in Fig. 1.

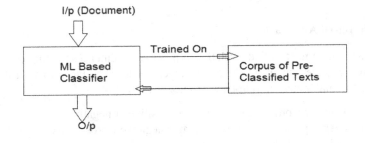

Fig. 1. Flowchart of a basic sentiment analyzer.

Several human annotated corpora are available that are used as training data. These corpora are already marked as positive or negative. They are used to train the ML-based classifier.

Training data include two columns – Text column and a label column which classifies a text as positive or negative (See Table 1)

Table 1. Columns of training data

Text	Label
Pride	Positive
Annoyed	Negative
.	Positive
.	.
.	.
.	.
.	.

Now, convert the trained text into numerical attributes.

e.g. "I Love Delhi" is converted to (3,0,1). Where the first attribute signifies a total number of words, the second one tells the number of negative words and the third one tells the number of positive words. This way features are developed which include all the numerical attributes.

Now, features and labels are added to the algorithm to train it so that it can further be used for analysis of new corpus as is shown in Fig. 2.

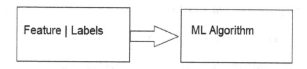

Fig. 2. Features and Labels are fed to a machine learning algorithm.

Finally the new text can now be fed to the algorithm which converts it into a positive or negative entity.

Overview of Naïve Bayes Classification: This is a machine learning based approach used to categorize a document as positive or negative. The simplest way to do so is to look at the individual words in the document.

With this algorithm, we compute the posterior probability. Given some evidence, we compute the probability that the document is positive or negative. Here the evidence is the words present in the document, so we will compute the conditional probability given the words in the document.

$$P \text{ (Document is Positive|Words)} = (P \text{ (document is positive)} * P \text{ (Word 1|document is positive)} * P \text{ (word 2|document is positive)} * \ldots)/(P \text{ (word 1)} * P \text{ (word 2)} * \ldots) \tag{1}$$

$$P \text{ (Document is Negative| Words)} = (P \text{ (document is negative)} * P \text{ (Word 1|document is negative)} * P \text{ (word 2|document is negative)} * \ldots)/(P \text{ (word 1)} * P \text{ (word 2)} * \ldots) \tag{2}$$

Here, P (document is positive) or P (document is negative) are prior probabilities that the document is positive or negative which is number of positive or negative documents in entire corpus divided by total number of documents. We multiply the prior probability with the conditional probability of words given that document is positive or negative and we multiply the probability of each word given that the words are independent of each other.

This is an assumption which is not true for most real life problems, but it has been proved that this algorithm works well with most classification problems. No attention is being given to the denominator which is the probability of a word occurring in a document. This is because we only need to know which of these probabilities is greater for the document. This classifier can also be used to classify the document into multiple classes like positive, negative or neutral.

Overview of Linear Support Vector Machine: Support Vector Machine or SHM is a supervised machine learning classifier which unlike Naïve Bayes is not probabilistic. SHM is binary and thus can only classify text as positive or negative, good or bad. It cannot introduce a third category. For example, the text can be categorized as positive, negative or neutral. In LINEAR SHM, we cannot introduce this third category.

Also, the SHM makes a decision on the basis of a linear function of the point's coordinates. If a point is

$$X = \left(X_1, \ X_2, \ X_3 \dots \dots X_n\right) \tag{3}$$

Then a linear equation would look like

$$F(X) \ = \ aX_1 + bX_2 + cX_3 + \dots + zX_n \tag{4}$$

where a, b, c...z are constants that play a key role in classifying.

Then the support vector machine would run a test:

```
If F(x)>0 then the sentence is positive
Else negative;
```

The linear equation above represents an N−1 dimensional hyperplane in an N-dimensional Hypercube space. SHM does not involve any assumptions about probability distributions of the points involved, unlike Naïve Bayes. SHM involves a training stage when the model "learns" from a set of training data (Fig. 3).

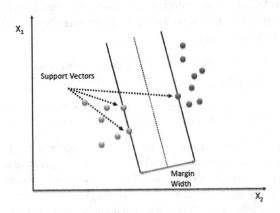

Fig. 3. Support vectors being separated by a hyperplane [7].

One has a bunch of corpus text that is already marked as negative and positive. Take these words and represent them as points in N-dimensional space. The hyperplane neatly separates the two cluster of points marked as positive or negative.

The hyperplane is the linear function that the SHM tries to find. This hyperplane can then be used to classify new data as positive or negative.

How SHM Constructs this Hyper-Plane?

The equation of the set of points on a hyperplane is always Linear. For three-dimensional space, the equation is

$$A.x + B.y + C.z = D \tag{5}$$

All points on the plane will satisfy the equation.
All points on one side would satisfy the condition,

$$A.x + B.y + C.z > D \tag{6}$$

Moreover, the other side would satisfy,

$$A.x + B.y + C.z < D \tag{7}$$

There might be many planes that divide the points into a set of two clusters, but there is only one specific plane that the SHM identifies. It depends on the distance of the point from the hyperplane.

Let a set of points be (x_1, y_1, z_1) then distance from hyperplane is calculated as:

$$\frac{Ax_1 + By_1 + Cz_1 - D}{(A^2 + B^2 + C^2)^{1/2}} \tag{8}$$

The best hyperplane is found by maximizing the sum of the distances of the nearest points on either side while making sure that two clusters are on opposite sides. The plane found is called the maximum margin hyperplane. Support vectors are simply the nearest points on either side of the hyperplane.

4   Twitter Sentiment Analysis Approach

The purpose of a Twitter sentiment analyzer is to accept data from Twitter as input and find the current sentiment on that input. We have used the machine learning based approach.

Accepting a Search Term and Downloading a Certain Number of Tweets for that Term:

Step1: (I) Twitter provides output in a difficult interpreting manner, therefore it is important first to convert it into a readable form using a language like Python.
(II) First, create a new application using the Twitter API that is registered with Twitter. API credentials are provided that are utilized in the program to provide authenticity.
Step2: Create a function whose argument is the search string that the user inputs. The string is used as a keyword to fetch tweets. Python has an inbuilt function API. Getsearch (String search, count = 100) that takes in the string and the number of tweets you want to your data.
Step3: Classify the 100 tweets as positive or negative manually or use an already available corpus to use as TRAINING DATA. Save the tweets into a Comma Separated Variable file. If one is using a pre-defined corpus, then one will need to process it further as Twitter will only provide tweet IDs and not the tweet text. To extract Tweet text, one will need to write a function that will read the Comma Separated Variable

and loop through each tweet ID downloading the corresponding tweet text from Twitter and gain writing it to another CSV file.

Pre-Processing the Tweet Text

Step1: Create a class to preprocess all the tweets, which can be used for both training and test data. We used regular expressions (Python regex) and NLTK (python natural language toolkit) for preprocessing.

Step2: Write a function that removes stopwords, for instance, a, an, the which do not contribute to the polarity of the text. These stop-words are recognized using NLTK in Python. Also, it will tokenize the tweets word by word.

Step3: Define a function that processes the tweets as follows:

Convert all terms to lower case. Example: BEAUTY to beauty.

Substitute the links if any in the tweet with the word URL.

Replace @username with "AT_USER. "Remove both URL and "AT_USER" as they are stop-words using the function defined above.

Remove hashtags with only the text following hashtags. For example, #sunny is replaced with sunny. Figure 4 Shows the possible combination of # removal regex.

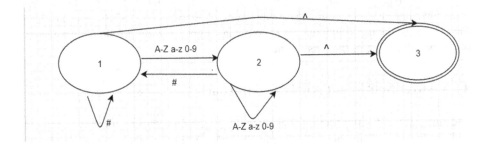

Fig. 4. Possible combination of # removal regex

Using A Machine Learning Classifier:

Step1: Extract features for both the test and training data. Do experimentation using different data.

Step2: Train a classifier on training data.

Step3: Use the classifier to classify the problem instances as positive or negative.

Naïve Bayes Feature Vector:

Step1: Build a vocabulary which is the list of all words in training data.

Step2: Represent each tweet with presence/absence of these words in the tweet.

For example: "Your Pasta is best in the world." is a sentence in vocabulary.

"Pasta is best." is a tweet. The feature vector for Naïve Bayes would be

[0, 1, 1, 1, 0, 0, 0], Here 1 is used to represent data that is there in the vocabulary and 0 is used to denote absence of that word.

Step3: Use NLTK built-inclassifier to train data.

SVM Feature Vector:

The first two steps are the same as Naïve Bayes.

Step3: Weight each word with SentiWordNet [6] subjectivity score which is a lexical resource for opinion mining used for various research and industrial purposes. It provides us with a positive score and negative score for every synonym set (which contains all words which are similar in meaning). Use the first synonym set for the word in SentiWordNet as the first contains the most used words with most common meanings. One could also take an average of the synonym sets. The following logic can be used to represent how positive and negative scores may be set as a weight for synonym set:

```
If pos_score > neg_score, use
pos_score as weight
If pos_score<neg_score, use
(-) neg_score as weight.
```

Feature vector for the above example in SVM would be [0, 0, 0, 1, 0, 0, 0], Pasta is 0 in this case as it is neither positive nor negative and therefore has a subjectivity score 0.

Finally take the majority preference and the percent of tweets with that sentiment and print it as output.

5 Applications and Future Scope

1. Computing customer satisfaction metrics

Sentiment analyzer is exploited in product based companies which rather than manually checking feedbacks can use a sentiment analyzer which could tell whether the product reviews are positive or negative. They can then segregate the positive and negative reviews, focusing on the negative reviews they can try to make their product better.

2. Prediction of elections

The corpus for the reaction of speeches and ideologies of the contesting candidates can be collected and can be categorized as positive or negative collectively or individually, hinting the candidate which the general public is supporting. It could be used by the politicians well to strengthen their campaign by mining the reaction of the masses to his offerings.

3. Stock market

Sentiment about a company could be analyzed from the latest corpus and using that data, trends in the rise and fall of a company's stock can be carried out, mining the news and public reaction to products/services of a company can indicate a rise or fall in the share prices. Sentiment analysis can be exploited well by stock investors.

6 Conclusion

The work presented in this document describes the ways to create a Twitter Sentiment Analyzer. The paper explains the two techniques used for opinion mining. First one is

Rule-based, and the other one is Machine learning based approach. Both the methods have their own advantages and disadvantages. Two of the machine learning based algorithms – Naïve Bayes and SVM - is explained in length. This document annotates the process of opinion mining which has several applications in social media platforms, review related websites or in business intelligence (companies want to know customer's reaction to a product or service).

As a prospective direction for future research and the scope of the analyzer, we intend to use the technique of machine learning for other social media platforms like Facebook. Government officials can also take the benefits of the analyzer for the creation of policies for future.

References

1. Pak, A., Paroubek, P.: Twitter as a corpus for sentiment analysis and opinion mining. In: Proceedings of the 7th International Conference on Language Resources and Evaluation. Valletta, Malta, pp. 1320–1326 (2010)
2. Kumar, A., Dogra, P., Das, V.: Emotion analysis of Twitter using opinion mining. In: 8th International Conference on Contemporary Computing (IC3), Noida, India. IEEE Press (2015)
3. Hasan, K.M.A., Sabuj, M.S., Afrin, Z.: Opinion mining using Naïve Bayes. In: International WIE Conference on Electrical and Computer Engineering (WIECON-ECE), Dhaka, Bangladesh. IEEE Press (2015)
4. Bhatia, S., Bhatia, K.K., Sharma, M.: Strategies for opinion mining - a Survey. In: 2nd International Conference on Computing for Sustainable Global Development (INDIACom), New Delhi, India. IEEE Press (2015)
5. Balahadia, F.F., Fernando, Ma, C.G., Juanatas, I.C.: Teacher's performance evaluation tool using opinion mining with sentiment analysis. In: Region 10 Symposium (TENSYMP), Bali, Indonesia. IEEE Press (2016)
6. SentiWordNet. http://sentiwordnet.isti.cnr.it/
7. University of Toronto, Faculty of Applied Science and Engineering. http://chem-eng.utoronto.ca/~datamining/dmc/support_vector_machine.htm
8. Kumar, A., Sebastian, T.M.: Sentiment analysis of Twitter. Int. J. Comput. Sci. Issues 9(4), 372–378 (2012)
9. Fang, X., Zhan, J.: Sentiment analysis using product review data. J. Big Data 2, 5 (2015). doi: 10.1186/s40537-015-0015-2

Malicious PDF Files Detection Using Structural and Javascript Based Features

Sonal Dabral[1]([⊠]) [iD], Amit Agarwal[2], Manish Mahajan[1], and Sachin Kumar[3]

[1] Computer Science and Engineering, Graphic Era University, Dehradun, India
sonaldabral26@gmail.com, manish.mhajn@gmail.com
[2] Computer Science and Engineering, Indian Institute of Technology, Roorkee, India
amitagrawal1909@gmail.com
[3] Centre for Transportation Systems, Indian Institute of Technology, Roorkee, India
sachinagnihotri16@gmail.com

Abstract. Malicious PDF files recently considered one of the most dangerous threats to the system security. The flexible code-bearing vector of the PDF format enables to attacker to carry out malicious code on the computer system for user exploitation. Many solutions have been developed by security agents for the safety of user's system, but still inadequate. In this paper, we propose a method for malicious PDF file detection via machine learning approach. The proposed method extract features from PDF file structure and embedded Java-Script code that leverage on advanced parsing mechanism. Instead of looking for the specific attack inside the content of PDF i.e. quite complex procedure, we extract features that are often used for attacks. Moreover, we present the experimental evidence for the choice of learning algorithm to provide the remarkably high accuracy as compared to other existing methods.

Keywords: Machine learning · PDF · JavaScript · Malware

1 Introduction

Portable document format (PDF) is an electronic document format and it was released in 1993 by Adobe System Inc, which allows publishing and exchange of documents [1]. Nowadays, PDF is very popular because it is preferred as a mean of exchange different documents between different organizations, peoples i.e. students and professionals. Due to its high popularity, flexible structure and versatile functionality, it has become a popular malware distribution strategy for user exploitation ranging from server side to client side attack. The interest of miscreants has currently switched from server side to client side attacks, because it gives well opportunity to the attacker to exploit client applications (e.g. PDF readers) that are not up-to-date where the goal is to take advantage from lack of security knowledge of users by fooling them into opening a malicious PDF document using applications found on most user's computers [2].

© Springer Nature Singapore Pte Ltd. 2017
S. Kaushik et al. (Eds.): ICICCT 2017, CCIS 750, pp. 137–147, 2017.
https://doi.org/10.1007/978-981-10-6544-6_14

One of the most popular client applications is adobe reader for reading and exchanging of documents. Attackers may exploit specific vulnerabilities of the reader application. In addition to exploitation of the PDF reader's vulnerabilities, the attackers also take the advantages of the many advanced features of PDF such as '/Launch' which can automatically run an embedded script to manage OS specific events, or the '/GoTo' and '/URl' which can automatically open remote resources for creating risk that are in internet [3]. Attackers often use JavaScript code to distract usual execution flow to malicious code, it can be done by Buffer overflow, Heap spraying and Return Oriented Programming (ROP) [4]. In order to bypass detection, attackers mainly use advanced encryptions techniques so that they can easily hide the malicious code or embedded files in PDF [1].

The recent academic works over the malicious PDF file detections are categorized into two methods: dynamic and static. First Detection of malicious JavaScript code within PDF files using both methods dynamic and static [5–7]. Another structural based approaches for malicious PDF detection using static analysis [4, 9]. The advantage of this method over the JavaScript analysis is that they are capable of detection of non-JavaScript attacks and not affected by code obfuscation because it does not a focus on analyzing content itself. However, further research showed that attacker exploits the system through deliberate attacks [10]. Therefore, work has focused again on malicious JavaScript code detection [11].

This paper propose a method based on machine learning technique for malicious PDF files detection where we combine PDF structure feature vector to the JavaScript feature vector which are extracted from the PDF file structure and embedded JavaScript in the PDF file respectively. The set of PDF structure features includes general characteristic of the PDF structure as well as dynamic characteristic of PDF structure in terms of keywords such as '/JavaScript', '/openAction' and '/URL' etc. and the JavaScript features obtained from JavaScript code in the PDF file. As recent research shows that the vast majority of PDF related vulnerabilities do rely JavaScript, hence we also analyze JavaScript code inside the PDF file. But instead of looking for the specific attack inside the JavaScript code, we extract features from JavaScript code which can conduct attack through JavaScript. The extraction process is efficiently carried out using PDF analysis tool, namely, Origami that overcome the parsing related weakness presented in prior work. It provides significant features to the classifier for effective and enhance detection of Malicious PDF file. We employed different ensemble machine learning techniques to choose the classifier for our experiment. The good choice of ensemble classifier gives a significant improvement on malicious PDF file detection.

1.1 The PDF File Structure

PDF file is a hierarchical structure of objects that are logically connected to each other. The structure of PDF file determines how objects are accumulated in a file, how objects accessed and updated [1]. The PDF file structure is made by four parts shown in Fig. 1.

- **Header:** represents the version number of PDF used by the file.
- **Body:** It contains large part in PDF file structure which constitutes all the PDF objects and contains the data or information that is shown to user.

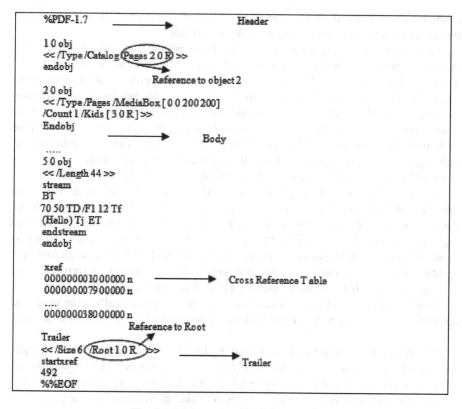

Fig. 1. An example of PDF file structure

- **Cross reference table (CRT):** It indicates the position of every indirect object and these single objects are represented by one entry in the table.
- **Trailer:** It gives the location of CRT and information about root object.

2   Related Work

The increased prevalence of malicious documents has generated interest in techniques to perform malware analysis of such documents over the years. Previous research focused on two methods for malicious PDF detection: static and dynamic. Li et al. and Shafiq et al. [12, 13] present a method for detection of embedded malcode in word document through static analysis using n-gram and introduced novel dynamic run-time test that shows assertion but also remains limited due to the size of malcode. Particularly this work is not designed for PDF file but they specially focused on another file format such as docs, exe etc. There are possibilities to evade detection by modern obfuscation methods like AES encryption [1], and other methods to exploit vulnerability like Heap Spraying, Return Oriented Programming (ROP) [4]. These exploiting methods are performed using embedded JavaScript code in PDF file. Therefore researchers mainly targeted JavaScript code in PDF file.

Laskov and Srndic [6] developed a tool *PJScan* which is closely related to static analysis techniques, used to detect the malicious PDF documents through lexical analysis of JavaScript code. They used a machine learning approach, One-Class Support Vector Machine automatically generate models from the available data for classification of testing data. However this approach showed lower detection rate and not able to analyze obfuscated code that behave maliciously during execution time. To overcome such limitation Snow et al. [14] proposed ShellOS, based on dynamic analysis to detect code injection attacks, during runtime. It uses hardware virtualization that provides faster and precise analysis of code and also enables to detect obfuscated code.

Moreover Tzermias et al. [7] demonstrated that the antivirus systems for the detection of malicious PDF documents are less effective. To make more reliable detection system, they used the combination of both static and dynamic analysis and introduced a standalone malicious PDF file scanner MDScan that specially focus on vulnerabilities. A similar approach adopted by Schmitt et al. [15] presented a tool PDF Scrutinizer is used to detect current malicious PDF file, however it showed a low false-positive rate. It is mainly focuses on JavaScript- based attacks.

Dynamic analysis of JavaScript code may be computationally expensive and complex. To reduce cost factor and increase speed, research again focused on static analysis.

Maiorka et al. [4] introduced a tool, PDF Malware Slayer (PDFMS) based on static method which analyze the structure of PDF files by keywords and their occurrence. They have performed test set on Naive Bayes, SVM, J48 and Random Forests classifiers. The results showed Random forests provided the highest accuracy which is better than others. However, it has some structural weaknesses.

Instead of looking for specific content, the analysis of structure of PDF provided a higher detection rate. However current work Maiorca et al. [10] showed that such detectors may be bypass, due to complexity in parsing mechanism.

Due to some structural weaknesses, work focused again on analysis of malicious JavaScript code. Corona et al. [11] presented LuxOR "Lux 0n discriminant References", a new approach for the malicious JavaScript code detection using characterization of JavaScript code by its API references. And Liu et al. [16] introduced a context-aware approach for the detection of malicious JavaScript in PDF based on static document instrumentation and runtime behavior monitoring.

3 Materials and Methods

In this section, the paper explain a method based on machine learning approach through static analysis where we combine PDF structure feature vector with JavaScript feature vector, which are extracted from the PDF file structure and embedded JavaScript code within PDF file, respectively. Our system architecture is shown in Fig. 2.

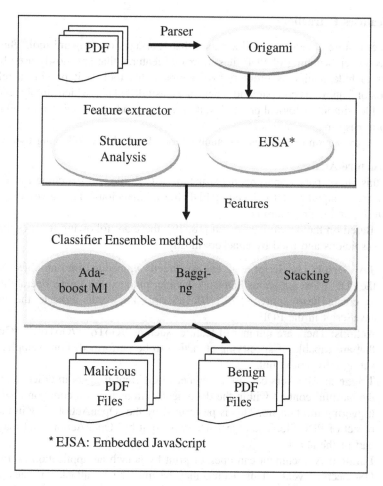

Fig. 2. Architecture of our system

3.1 Dataset Used

We have collected dataset both malicious and benign PDF files from real and up-to date samples. We have collected around 4807 malicious file and 3745 benign files. Malicious PDF file samples are collected from the Contagiodump [9] is a popular depository which contains the information about the trending vulnerabilities and attacks in PDF files. And the benign PDF Samples are collected from the Yahoo search engine API. When collecting data from source websites it gives no assurance that some data may be malicious. The existence of malicious files in the benign dataset will generate undesirable results on the designed experiments. To diminish the risk, whole benign dataset was scanned using antivirus.

3.2   Features Extraction

To extract features, we developed a parser that leverages on Origami tool. This tool performs a deep scanning of PDF files to extract features that are mostly used by the attackers to hide malicious property. We adopted this tool as it provide a reliable extraction of features as compared to others, such as PdfID [17], which simply analyzes the PDF file without its logical properties, it may give good opportunity to the attackers to perform easy manipulations.

For the extraction of features, we analyze each PDF file by following two ways:

(1) **Structure Analysis**

In this phase, parser analyzes the structure of PDF file and searching for features which are significant for labeling PDF file as malicious. This gives the set of features and their occurrence.

Based on the previous research [18, 19], these are following features that can be suspicious and used by attackers mostly.

- **JavaScript:** JavaScript code can be directly embedded into an object within the PDF. Most malicious PDFs use JavaScript to exploit Java vulnerabilities or to create heap sprays. '/JS', '/JavaScript' keywords indicate the use of JavaScript in the PDF.
- **Actions:** There are number of features such as '/GoTo', '/GoToR', '/GoToE' that are capable of specifying an action to be performed. For example: Activating a hypertext link.
- **Triggers:** Attackers can use a number of different triggers in order to execute the harmful content within the documents. An action is a common method to triggering mechanism. This is performed by the 'OpenAction' key in the root object of PDF file. The object which is point by 'OpenAction' that may be a part of the attack.
- **Launch:** A document can open or print by launch an application, to manage OS-specific events. This feature may be misused by attacker to steal confidential data of any organization whenever they access that suspicious PDF file.
- **Form Action:** PDF Reader allow the '/SubmitForm' action from client to server. So in order to take advantage of the weakness of the victim browser, this action perform a request to corrupt sites that will automatically show on the victim browser and can perform a malfunctioning.

(2) **JavaScript Code Analysis**

Our parser extract objects contain JavaScript from the body part of the structure of PDF file. Then it extracts embedded JavaScript code and searching for the features labeled with JavaScript code that are often followed in carrying out an attack. Based on the previous study [6, 19, 20], we describe following set of features used in our system.

- **eval_length:** This function is used by malicious scripts to dynamically interpret code and to calculate the length of the longest string passed to eval() function call.

- **max_string:** It is use to define the length of the longest string. Malware writer use the strings for shell code is very long as compared to string used in legitimate JavaScript.
- **stringcount:** It is used to count the no. of strings that are defined in scripts. To obfuscate the script malware writer break the strings into many paltry strings.
- **replace:** This function calculate the uses of the javascript replace() function. Often it is used to obfuscate JavaScript code in malicious scripts.
- **substring:** This function can be used to measure the uses of the javascript substring() function. It is mostly used to obfuscate the JavaScript code.
- **Eval:** This function call used by the malicious scripts to measure the uses of the javascript eval() function and to dynamically interpret JavaScript code.
- **fromCharCode:** It coverts Unicode values to the characters. It is mostly used to obfuscate the code.
- **setTimeOut():** can be used to replace the eval() to run random javascript code after the particular timeout.
- **document. write and document. createElement:** which indicate the use of dynamic code executions.

3.3 Classification

To classify PDF files, extracted features run by a classifier that can be create by any learning algorithms. But in previous, researchers have used the method of combining the predictions of multiple learners to produce better results than could be produced from any individual learning algorithm [8]. In this sense we tested ensemble methods such as Adaptive Boosting (AdaBoostM1), Bagging, stacking [8]. These algorithms combine weak classification tree models with a particular weight to create a stronger and precise classifier. As a weak model we define a simple decision trees (J48) (supervised learning approach, Quinlan, 1996) because an ensemble of trees gives more robustness compared to a single tree. In addition we decided to give exhaustive experimental evidence in order to know which ensemble method has ability to improve the accuracy on our dataset.

4 Results and Discussion

In this Section, we provide two experiments. The first one demonstrated the features extraction process. And the second experiment presented experimental evidence as to which classification method has ability to improve the accuracy of detection. In order to do this, first the only PDF structure features was run through different classifiers. Than we experimented how the accuracy was improved when JavaScript features were combined with structure features. Furthermore, we compare the performance of proposed method with previously developed tools for malicious PDFs detection.

4.1   Experiment 1: Features Extraction

The goal of the experiment is to extract the feature vector from PDF file. Origami tool performs a deep scanning of PDF files to extract features that are often used by the miscreants. After running the scan over one by one PDF file in malicious and benign dataset, the results were achieved as shown in Fig. 3.

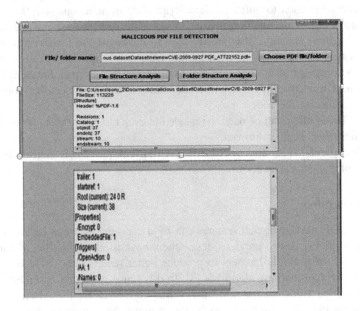

Fig. 3. Structure based features extraction result

After completing the structure feature vector extraction, we realized that a huge number of the malicious PDF files used JavaScript to perform malicious actions. In our own dataset we found around 92.3% malicious samples contained JavaScript. Thus we performed JavaScript features extraction process by origami tool. The Results were shown in Fig. 4.

4.2   Experiment 2: Detection Accuracy

Our test was conducted on Adaboost M1 (used as a boosting ensemble), Bagging (used as a bagging ensemble) and stacking with two learning algorithms (J48 and IBk, and Logistic Regression used as the Meta classifier), using 10-folds Cross Validation repeated 10 times. We show our results with regards to confusion matrices (the number of benign and malicious files with correct and incorrect classifications).

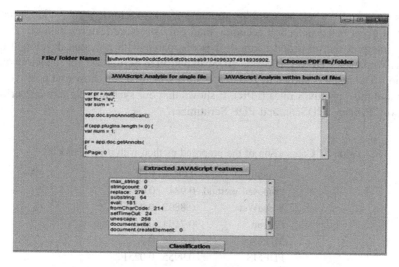

Fig. 4. JavaScript based features extraction result

First the structure feature vector dataset was run through different classifiers. This gives the following results (Table 1).

Table 1. Result of structure features

	AdaBoostM1	Bagging	Stacking
True positives	4498	4471	4493
False positives	309	336	314
True negatives	2990	2936	2976
False negatives	755	809	767
TP rate	0.876	0.866	0.873
FP rate	0.141	0.152	0.144
ROC area	0.945	0.934	0.940
Detection accuracy	87.5584%	86.6113%	87.3363%

Further we tested how well the complete feature vector dataset (structure feature and JavaScript features) performed at the classification task. And the dataset gives the following results as shown in Table 2.

Table 2. Result of complete features (structure features and JavaScript based features)

	AdaBoostM1	Bagging	Stacking
True positives	4753	4742	4744
False positives	54	65	63
True negatives	3666	3603	3670
False negatives	79	142	75
TP rate	0.984	0.976	0.984
FP rate	0.017	0.0287	0.017
ROC area	0.998	0.993	0.995
Detection accuracy	98.4448%	97.5795%	98.3863%

As we can see, when we combine structure feature vector to the JavaScript feature vector, it gives better detection accuracy than only structure features dataset.

To interpret the proposed method, it is compared with previous developed tools such as Wepawet, PDFMS, PJScan, MDScan and PDF Scrutinizer for malicious PDFs detection. The result is shown in Table 3. For each method, we show true positives rate (TPR) and false positives rates (FPR). It shows that our system definitely outperforms Wepawet, PJScan, MDScan and PDF Scrutinizer.

Table 3. Comparison of the proposed method with previous tools.

System	TPR	FPR
Proposed method	0.984	0.017
WepaWet	0.8892	0.032
PJScan	0.7194	0.011
MDScan	0.8934	0
PDFMS	0.9955	0.0251
PDF scrutinizer	0.9	0

PJScan, MDScan and PDF Scrutinizer show the smallest FPR, but detection rate is very low compared to the other tools. PDFMS shows the highest TPR but gives a lower FPR as compared to proposed method. It can be also observed that the proposed method works better than WepaWet in both TPR and FPR terms. Moreover, it is indicating that the proposed method is better than all these tools.

5   Conclusions

In the past few years malicious PDF file has become one of the most crucial threats which originate a very effectual attack vector for malware writers. In this paper, we have proposed a method using machine learning techniques for the malicious PDF file detection. Instead of only relying on structure property of PDF file, we also presented the JavaScript based features to improve the accuracy of detection. In addition, we also showed experimental evidence as to which learning algorithm has ability to improve the accuracy of detection. Finally, we show the comparison of our method with the other academic tools. And the high detection accuracy of our method has to be proved it is more accurate to other tools.

References

1. Adobe: PDF reference, adobe portable document format version 1.7 (2006)
2. Symantec: malware security report: protecting your business, customers, and the bottom line. Symantec (2010)
3. Filiol, E., Blonce, A., Frayssignes, L.: Portable document format (PDF) security analysis and malware threats. J. Comput. Virol. **3**, 75–86 (2007)

4. Maiorca, D., Giacinto, G., Corona, I.: A pattern recognition system for malicious pdf files detection. In: International Workshop on Machine Learning and Data Mining in Pattern Recognition, pp. 510–524 (2012)
5. Esparza, J.M.: Obfuscation and (non-)detection of malicious pdf files. In: S21Sec e-crime (2011)
6. Laskov, P., Srndić, N.: Static detection of malicious javascript-bearing pdf documents. In: Proceedings of the 27th Annual Computer Security Applications Conference, pp. 373–382, December 2011
7. Tzermias, Z., Sykiotakis, G., Polychronakis, M., Markatos, E.P.: Combining static and dynamic analysis for the detection of malicious documents. In: Proceedings of the Fourth European Workshop on System Security, p. 4 (2011)
8. Tiwari, A., Prakash, A.: Improving classification of J48 algorithm using bagging, boosting and blending ensemble methods on SONAR dataset using WEKA. Int. J. Eng. Tech. Res. **2**, 207–209 (2014)
9. Mila: Contagio Malware Dump. http://contagiodump.blogspot.in/2010/08/Malicious-documents-archive-for.html. Accessed 10 Oct 2014
10. Maiorca, D., Corona, I., Giacinto, G.: Looking at the bag is not enough to find the bomb: an evasion of structural methods for malicious pdf files detection. In: Proceedings of the 8th ACM SIGSAC Symposium on Information, Computer and Communications Security, pp. 119–130 (2013)
11. Corona, I., Maiorca, D., Ariu, D., Giacinto, G.: Lux0r: detection of malicious pdf-embedded javascript code through discriminant analysis of API references. In: Proceedings of the 2014 Workshop on Artificial Intelligent and Security Workshop, pp. 47–57. ACM, November 2014
12. Li, W.-J., Stolfo, S., Stavrou, A., Androulaki, E., Keromytis, A.D.: A study of malcode-bearing documents. In: Proceedings of the 4th International Conference on Detection of Intrusions and Malware, and Vulnerability Assessment (2007)
13. Shafiq, M.Zubair, Khayam, S.A., Farooq, M.: Embedded malware detection using Markov n-Grams. In: Zamboni, D. (ed.) DIMVA 2008. LNCS, vol. 5137, pp. 88–107. Springer, Heidelberg (2008). doi:10.1007/978-3-540-70542-0_5
14. Snow, K.Z., Krishnan, S., Monrose, F., Provos, N.: SHELLOS: enabling fast detection and forensic analysis of code injection attacks. In: USENIX Security Symposium, pp. 183–200, August 2011
15. Schmitt, F., Gassen, J., Gerhards-Padilla, E.: PDF SCRUTINIZER: detecting javascript-based attacks in PDF documents. In: 10th Annual International Conference on Privacy, Security and Trust (PST), pp. 104–111. IEEE, July 2012
16. Liu, D., Wang, H., Stavrou, A.: Detecting malicious javascript in pdf through document instrumentation. In: 44th IFIP International Conference on Dependable Systems and Networks (DSN), pp. 100–111. IEEE (2014)
17. Stevens, D.: PDF Tool. http://blog.didierstevens.com/programs/pdf-tools/
18. Stevens, D.: Malicious pdf analysis ebook, September 2010. http://didierstevens.com/files/data/malicious-pdf-analysis-ebook.zip. Accessed 22 Sep 2015
19. Kittilsen, J.: Detecting malicious PDF documents. Master thesis, Gjovik, Norway, pp. 1–112, December 2011
20. Cova, M., Kruege, C., Vigna, G.: Detection and analysis of drive-by-download attacks and malicious JavaScript code. In: Proceedings of International Conference on World Wide Web, pp. 281–290, July 2010

A System Architecture for Mapping Application Data into Complex Graph

Sonal Tuteja[(✉)] [ID] and Rajeev Kumar [ID]

School of Computer and Systems Sciences, JNU, New Delhi, India
sonalt9@gmail.com, rajeevkumar.cse@gmail.com

Abstract. Abundance of interrelated data from heterogeneous sources in different formats is generated by applications which can be unified and modeled using complex graphs. Complex graphs provide a natural way of modeling relationships among entities which is an important aspect for today's applications like social network, biological network etc. Therefore, we have proposed an architecture which can be used for transforming application data to graph and subsequently utilized by various subsystems of the application. We have also incorporated various software engineering properties like maintainability, trustworthiness, robustness etc. in the architecture. In addition, architecture prototype for student course management system has been implemented using academic data set.

Keywords: Data modeling · Data mapping · Complex graph · System architecture · Social network · E-commerce

1 Introduction

Every fraction of second, huge amount of unstructured data having heterogeneous sources and formats is generated by today's applications. Using this data, different queries need to be answered with accurate, fast and contextual results which is infeasible without modeling data in appropriate form. Considering an e-commerce application for example, some of the data can be present in relational model, e.g.; product catalog, customer information, order information etc. and other can be in log files, e.g.; customer search history, browsing patterns etc. For personalized recommendations to the customer, data from log files and relational model need to be unified into appropriate form.

Relationships among entities play an important role to produce fast, accurate and contextual results for the users. Considering again the scenario of an e-commerce application, relationships among products can be used to recommend products to customers according to his preferences. For such applications, graph provides a natural way of modeling, querying and updating the data of applications, hence called as *Complex Graph* or *Complex Network* [1, 2].

Complex graphs have successfully been applied in many *relationship* centric applications by transforming application data to complex graphs. Various techniques like property graph, hypergraph, triple store can be used to represent complex graphs [5, 6, 11] out of which property graphs are used most frequently. Property graphs model data in the form of nodes representing entities and edges representing

S. Kaushik et al. (Eds.): ICICCT 2017, CCIS 750, pp. 148–155, 2017.
https://doi.org/10.1007/978-981-10-6544-6_15

relationships among different entities. In addition, properties of nodes and edges are represented in the form of key-value pairs.

Depending on requirements of application, different mapping criteria like communication, co-relation, citation etc. can be used to create relationships among nodes [4]. Considering again the scenario of an e-commerce application, co-relation among products as well as co-existence of products in same orders can be used to create relationships among them. Complex graphs have been successfully applied for different subtasks like information diffusion, data analysis, contextual searching and recommendation etc. [8, 10].

Many applications like social network, e-commerce, transportation network etc. have been using complex graphs for data representation as well as data analysis [4]. As application data can be generated in various forms, different mapping techniques to convert data into complex graph have been discussed by L. Costa et al. [4]. In the research carried out by C. Chen et al. [3], citation mapping has been used to create relationships among articles. Z. Wang et al. [13] have associated social mapping with their existing transactional data to transform into complex graph. In the research carried out by Q. Wang [12], a conceptual modeling framework for network analytics has been discussed. The framework helps to model data based on analytics requirements of application but does not provide complete architecture to transform existing data to complex graph.

The goal of this article is to propose a system architecture for transforming application data into complex graph and subsequently utilized by various subsystems of the application. We have also incorporated various software engineering properties like maintainability, trustworthiness, robustness etc. in the architecture. Also, architecture prototype for student course management system for academic data set has been implemented.

The rest of paper is organized as follows. Section 2 describes proposed system architecture which can be used for modeling application data into complex graph based on application requirements. In Sect. 3, case study of online course management system using proposed architecture has been discussed. Implementation details with desirable software engineering principles has been discussed in Sect. 4. In Sect. 5, the paper has been summarized with possible future work.

2 System Architecture

Application data in various forms can be generated as well imported from external sources. We have defined an architecture which can be used to transform heterogeneous data into a unified structure in the form of complex graph. The generated graph can be further utilized by various subsystems of the application. The proposed architecture mainly consists of two components (1) Data Management, and (2) Data Analysis. Data management component deals with unifying the data from multiple heterogeneous sources into complex graph whereas data analysis component utilizes complex graph for performing various subtasks. The architecture can be represented using three layers as (Fig. 1):

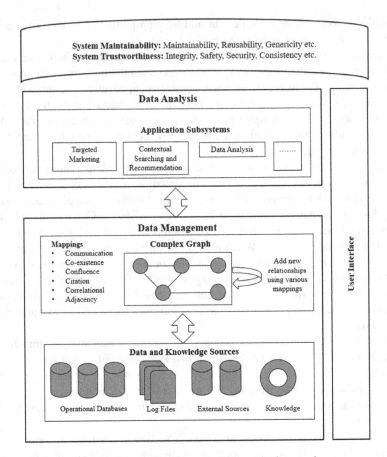

Fig. 1. A system architecture using complex graph

- **Data and Knowledge Sources:** There can be various data and knowledge sources for an application which can be used to generate complex graph. Considering the scenario of e-commerce application for example, some of the data can be present in relational model, e.g.; product catalog, customer information, order information etc. and other can be in log files, e.g.; customer search history, browsing patterns etc. The data need to be processed before converting to complex graph which consists of the following steps:

  – **Extract and Clean:** It consists of extracting data from multiple sources to a single place. For example, data may be available in relational tables, log files, flat files etc. which needs to be brought together. After extraction, data is cleaned to remove noisy and irrelevant attribute which may not be required for generating complex graph.

  – **Transform:** It consists of transforming data from one format to another. For example, date format in flat file and relational file can be different which need to be transformed into one before sending data to target system.

- **Load:** It consists of loading data from source to target system after completion of extracting, cleaning and transformation process.
- **Refresh:** It consists of periodically updating changes from data and knowledge sources to complex graph.

- **Complex Graph:** After extraction, transformation and loading from data and knowledge sources, data is converted into complex graph with nodes representing entities and edges representing relationships among entities. Moreover, the properties of nodes and edges can be represented using key-value pairs. Based on application requirements, different mapping techniques can be used to create relationships among nodes as [4]:
  - **Communication mapping:** Different entities are represented as nodes and communications among them are mapped as relationships. For example, social network, email network etc.
  - **Citation mapping:** Different entities are represented as nodes and citation among them are mapped as directed edges from cited object to citing object. For example, publication network, WWW etc.
  - **Coexistence mapping:** Different entities are represented as nodes and coexistence of objects in same containers are mapped as edges. For example, movie network, publication network etc.
  - **Confluence mapping:** Different pathways are represented as edges and their confluence are represented as nodes. For example, power grids, street maps etc.
  - **Correlation mapping:** Different entities are represented as nodes and metrics like *Pearson Correlation* can be used to find edges among them. For example, Financial Market, E-Commerce etc.
  - **Adjacency mapping:** Different entities are represented as nodes and adjacencies (spatial or temporal) among them are represented as edges. For example, restaurant network, earthquake network etc.

Different subsystems of the applications require different types of nodes and edges for query processing. Considering again the scenario of E-Commerce application, co-relation mapping among products is required to recommend products which are similar to the products purchased by customer in the past. Therefore, nodes and edges of complex graph are created based on requirements of application subsystems.

- **Application Subsystems:** The generated complex graph can be utilized by different subsystem of the application as follows:
  - **Targeted Marketing:** It involves concentrated marketing effort on few segments of users which may be closely related to the product or service to be marketed. In applications like social network, users are influenced by other users who are close to him in his social network. Hence for marketing specific set of users, community detection in the graph can be applied and influential spreaders in that community can be used for spreading information [9].
  - **Contextual Searching and Recommendation:** In many applications like social network, e-commerce, transportation network etc., traditional searching is very time-consuming and can give many irrelevant results. Therefore, contextual searching and recommendation provide result specific to the user considering his

relationships with other users, products, services etc. Graph properties like path and path length can be used for contextual searching and recommendations [10].

- **Data Analysis:** It can be defined as analyzing large data sources and finding relevant and useful information from it. Considering the scenario of e-commerce application, analyzing the degree of product nodes can be used to find most popular as well as obsolete products. Various graph properties like degree, centrality, and community detection can be used for analyzing data from the graph.

Using different mappings, the discussed architecture can be adapted to any application but the subsystems may vary from one application to another. For example, path navigation can be used in transportation systems for determining the path from one location to another.

3   Case Study of Online Course Management System

The abundance of course related information makes it difficult for students to find, organize and use resources to match their goals and interests [7]. Therefore, we have taken a case study of online course management and discussed how proposed architecture can help students to find relevant content. We have discussed how three layers of the system function together to find relevant courses for the students as:

- **Data and Knowledge Sources:** There can be various data sources for course management system as:

  - **Transactional Data:** Assuming transactional data is stored using relational model, various relations for storing and accessing data about courses, students, faculty etc. have been shown in Fig. 2.
  - **Log Files:** It can be used to find students' search history and browsing patterns which can help understanding their behavior.
  - **Student Social Network Information:** The system can be linked with social network which can be used to find students' social network information.
  - **Domain Knowledge:** There can be some domain specific knowledge which discusses about pre-requisite and/or allocation policy for assigning a course to the student.

The data from these sources is extracted, transformed and loaded into the next phase to generate complex graph from it.

- **Complex Graph:** It can be generated from the data loaded from data and knowledge sources taking into consideration which subsystems require which types of data and queries. For student job management system, the nodes chosen for creating complex graph are: (1) Student, (2) Faculty, (3) Institute, and (4) Course as shown in Fig. 2. The relationships among nodes are created using transactional data as: (1) student enrollment in courses, (2) faculty supervision in courses, (3) student and faculty affiliation to institution etc. In addition, different mappings to create relationships among nodes are: (1) co-existence mappings among students who are from same institutions or enrolled in same courses, (2) co-relation mappings among courses which are highly co-related to each other etc. as shown in Fig. 2.

- **Application Subsystems:** There can be different subsystems in Online Course Management as follows:
  - **Contextual Searching and Recommendation:** It helps in searching the relevant courses based on (1) popularity of courses, (2) previous courses enrolled, and (3) courses enrolled by peers etc. Graph properties like centrality, path and path length can be used for contextual searching and recommendation For example, searching of courses by student 'S2' can results in course 'C3' using path 'S2-C2-C3' and 'C1' using course with highest popularity among all courses.
  - **Data Analysis:** It helps in understanding the behavior of the system which can be further utilized for various decision purposes. Different types of analysis queries for course management system can be (1) identifying faculty with maximum number of students enrolled in his courses, (2) identifying course with maximum number of students, and (3) analyzing trends for enrollment in various courses etc.

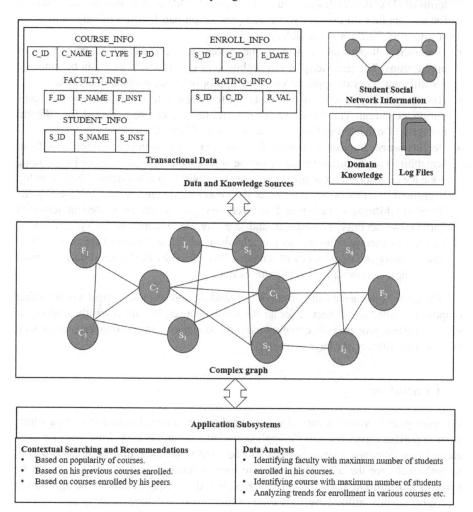

Fig. 2. System architecture of online course management system using complex graph

4 Implementation Details

For realizing an application using system architecture discussed in Sect. 2, software engineering principles like maintainability, trustworthiness etc. are highly desirable. We have partially addressed there principles as follows:

- **Maintainability:** It measures how easy and fast is to make the system functional when it is (1) ported to another platform called portability, (2) extended in functionality called extendibility, and (3) corrected for a bug called correctability. The maintainability in the system architecture is ensured using data abstraction at different layers. Therefore, one layer can be modified as well as corrected without affecting other layers.
- **Reusability:** It measures how well the system can be reused by other systems in terms of (1) code, (2) design, and (3) binaries. Our architecture design can be reused for any application as well as the complex graph can be used by any number of subsystems, hence it is reusable.
- **Genericity:** It measures how well the system is applicable to different types of applications. The genericity of our architecture is conformed as it can be modeled for different types of applications using appropriate mappings and subsystems.
- **Robustness:** It measures how well the system cope with errors and adverse inputs during execution. The robustness of our architecture can be achieved for different subsystems considering their possible errors and inputs.
- **Performance:** It measures how well the system performs in terms of response time, scalability etc. To improve the response time of the system, relationships among node are customized according to the need of application subsystems. The scalability is ensured in terms of any number of data and knowledge sources, subsystems etc.
- **Trustworthiness:** It measures how well the system can be trusted in terms of correctness, security, consistency and integrity etc. Security in the system can be ensured by incorporating security mechanisms at different layer of the architecture. The integrity and consistency of data can be ensured by the backend database used for storage, access and manipulation of data.

We have implemented the prototype of student course management system using proposed architecture in Sect. 2 for an academic data set. We are currently working to validate system properties like maintainability, robustness, trustworthiness etc. as well as to test its efficacy for larger dataset.

5 Conclusion

Complex graphs provide a natural way of modeling relationships among entities which is an important aspect for today's applications like social network, biological network etc. Also, relationships among nodes can be used to produce fast, accurate and contextual results for the user. Therefore, we have defined an architecture which can be used for transforming data to complex graph based on requirements of the application and subsequently utilized by its various subsystems. We have incorporated various software engineering properties like maintainability, trustworthiness, robustness etc. in the architecture. In addition, we have implemented architecture prototype for student course management system using for an academic data set. We are currently working to validate system properties like maintainability, robustness, trustworthiness etc. as well as to test its efficacy for larger dataset.

References

1. Angles, R.: A comparison of current graph database models. In: Proceedings of the 2012 IEEE 28th International Conference on Data Engineering Workshops, pp. 171–177. IEEE Computer Society (2012)
2. Angles, R., Gutierrez, C.: Survey of graph database models. ACM Comput. Surv. **40**, 1–39 (2008)
3. Chen, C., Song, I.-Y., Zhu, W.: Trends in conceptual modeling: citation analysis of the er conference papers (1979–2005). In: Proceedings of the 11th International Conference on the International Society for Scientometrics and Informetrics, pp. 189–200 (2007)
4. Costa, L.D.F., Oliveira Jr., O.N., Travieso, G., Rodrigues, F.A., Villas Boas, P.R., Antiqueira, L., Viana, M.P., Correa Rocha, L.E.: Analyzing and modeling real-world phenomena with complex neworks: a survey of applications. Adv. Phys. **60**, 329–412 (2011)
5. Mariethoz, J., Alocci, D., Horlacher, O., Bolleman, J.T., Campbell, M.P., Lisacek, F.: Property graph vs RDF triple store: a comparison on glycan substructure search. PLoS ONE **10**, 1–17 (2015)
6. Das, S., Srinivasan, J., Perry, M., Chong, E.I., Banerjee, J.: A tale of two graphs: property graphs as RDF in oracle. In: Proceedings of the 17th International Conference on Extending Database Technology, pp. 762–773 (2014)
7. Farzan, R., Brusilovsky, P.: Social Navigation Support in a Course Recommendation System. In: Wade, V.P., Ashman, H., Smyth, B. (eds.) AH 2006. LNCS, vol. 4018, pp. 91–100. Springer, Heidelberg (2006). doi:10.1007/11768012_11
8. Guille, A., Hacid, H., Favre, C., Zighed, D.A.: Information diffusion in online social networks: a survey. SIGMOD Rec. **42**, 17–28 (2013)
9. Lin, L.-F., Li, Y.-M., Wu, W.-H.: A social endorsing mechanism for target advertisement diffusion. Inf. Manag. **52**, 982–997 (2015)
10. Ma, S., Li, J., Hu, C., Lin, X., Huai, J.: Big graph search: challenges and techniques. Front. Comput. Sci. **10**, 387–398 (2016)
11. Riaz, F., Ali, K.M.: Applications of graph theory in computer science. In: 2011 Third International Conference on Computational Intelligence, Communication Systems and Networks (CICSyN), pp. 142–145. IEEE (2011)
12. Wang, Q.: A conceptual modeling framework for network analytics. Data Knowl. Eng. **99**, 59–71 (2015)
13. Wang, Z., Tan, Y., Zhang, M.: Graph-based recommendation on social networks. In: Web Conference (APWEB), 2010 12th International Asia-Pacific, pp. 116–122. IEEE (2010)

Ontology-Driven Shopping Cart and Its Comparative Analysis

Aditya Vardhan$^{(\boxtimes)}$ ⓘ and Amrita Chaturvedi ⓘ

Department of Information Technology,
Indian Institute of Information Technology, Allahabad, India
IIT2013044@iiita.ac.in, amritaiitk@gmil.com

Abstract. Design Patterns are formal solutions to commonly occurring design problems in software development. Compound Patterns are amalgamation of two or more individual Design Patterns. In spite of having advantages, they have certain limitations in the form of coupling, increased dependency between class hierarchies and several others. In this paper we present a comparative analysis between the ontology driven Compound Pattern and their classical GOF (Gang of Four) version. We have implemented a shopping cart application based on a compound pattern comprising visitor, observer and strategy Patterns. We, then implemented the same application based on ontology driven version of the compound pattern and then compared the two designs. We found that the ontological approach has certain edges over the former one in terms of modifiability and maintainability. The application based on ontology driven design pattern even adapts to some changes made during the runtime. The end users can make changes in the ontology driven application and thus change its behavior altogether during the run time. We conducted some modifications during non-runtime conditioned in both applications and got convincing results. We noted that the time and effort required to extend the application is much less in ontology version than in the GOF version.

Keywords: Ontology · GOF (Gang of Four) design pattern · Compound design pattern · Visitor pattern · Observer pattern · Reflection · Maintainability · Adaptability · Modifiability

1   Introduction

Design Patterns are solutions to recurring problems in software design [1]. Compound Patterns comprise two or more individual design patterns that work together synergistically to solve a recurring design problem. The compound pattern that we have used in our shopping cart application comprises visitor, observer and strategy patterns.

The visitor pattern is used where an operation needs to be implemented differently on different concrete classes. It consists of two main classes namely visitor and visitable. A visitor (the feature class) is accepted by a concrete user class (which uses the feature) which then visits or performs operations on the visitable class. Visitor class mainly differentiates between the different visitable classes using function overloading in its visit method by accepting different argument(s).

© Springer Nature Singapore Pte Ltd. 2017
S. Kaushik et al. (Eds.): ICICCT 2017, CCIS 750, pp. 156–167, 2017.
https://doi.org/10.1007/978-981-10-6544-6_16

The observer Pattern is used where a class needs to be notified about any state changes occurring in the observed class(s). It consists of two main classes namely Observer and Observable. The observer class 'observes' (subscribes to) the observable class and is notified whenever the state of the observable class changes. Consequently the observer classes update themselves according to the state of the observable.

We have implemented a basic shopping cart in which we use the visitor pattern to define operations such as calculation of taxes, Shipping Costs and Discount Costs for the available items. Observer Pattern in our application is used to notify the registered customers about the offers and sales on different items. Any change in the availability of the items is also notified to the concerned registered customer. Here, the registered clients are the observers. The taxes, shipping and discount costs are the visitors. The items to be sold serve the purpose of both the visitables and observables.

Usage of design patterns in software applications in traditional way gives rise to several problems and limitations (described in Sect. 3). Absence of run time changes, intermixing of pattern and application logic, huge coupling and dependency between the component classes are to be named a few. For example, for every concrete visitable, a visit method needs to be defined in the visitor even if the concerned visitor does not need to visit all the visitables. Similarly, in the observer pattern, if the observable state changes, all the observers need to update themselves even if they are not interested in the observable property changed. Ontology based patterns provide more convenient approach by mitigating some of the limitations of the classical patterns.

An Ontology is a formal specification of any system, which consists of entities and rules. The rules define the relationships between the entities. It is one of the most used semantic technologies. The ontology driven compound pattern that we have used is based on the ontology driven technique that is described in [6–9] that uses reflection technique to use ontology as a runtime component. They include an intermediate entity called the ontology manager that reduces the direct dependency between the component classes, uses reflection to accommodate run time changes. These runtime changes can be done by both programmers and non-programmers alike. The pattern logic is embedded in a separate entity in the ontology. The observer and visitor ontology contain the pattern logic at the schema level. This in turn improves over the maintainability, modifiability of the application. Detailed aspects of ontology driven observer and visitor pattern can be found in [6, 7].

2 Related Research

2.1 Compound Design Patterns

Riehle [2] presented a work that introduced the concept of composite design pattern more than just the composition of different design pattern. His paper presented an analysis and composition technique to better cope with complexity of composite patterns. Shalloway and Trott [3] in their book titled 'Design Pattern Explained' also stated a work on compound design pattern and difference between compound and composite design pattern. Yueping et al. [12] introduced a compound pattern consisting of chain of responsibility and observer pattern. The observer pattern was merged in the handler of the chain of responsibility which in turn strengthens the latter's ability. The handler actually provides various services to the user, and when there is no object for any handler, next handler in the chain is used. This arrangement provided an upper hand for both the patterns and the application.

2.2 Ontologies in Software Systems and Design Patterns

Alnusair and Zhao [4, 5] presented a paper that utilizes ontological modeling for understanding complex software systems. They focused their discussion on retrieving design pattern information from the source code. In another paper they use model driven engineering to capture design pattern logic from source code as reverse engineering using the semantic technologies. Mai and Champlain [11] presented a paper on reflective visitor pattern that uses reflection technique, to perform runtime dispatch on itself. It removes cyclic dependency between the visitor and the element structure, but increases the overall complexity of the pattern. Ontology driven technique to implement design patterns has been proposed in [6–10]. These papers discuss several limitations of design patterns because of the design decisions made in patterns to observe pattern intent and also because of their traditional usage in software applications. Some of these limitations pertaining to observer and visitor pattern are discussed in Sect. 3. To mitigate these limitations, ontology driven technique was proposed and described in [6–10]. Detailed aspects of ontology driven observer pattern can be found in [7] and of visitor pattern can be found in [6]. We complement the above mentioned works by implementing a shopping cart application based on compound pattern comprising observer and visitor pattern. We also provide a comparative analysis of the above applications based on GOF compound pattern as well as its ontology driven version.

3 Limitations of the GOF Approach

Since the proposed compound pattern comprises observer and visitor patterns so it has the drawbacks existing in these patterns. Considering the classical approach of the pattern representation, there is no explicit method to present the pattern logic other than the application itself. Because of this, the pattern logic gets somewhat lost in the application code and thus for any new programmer it becomes very difficult to understand the code. Implicit coupling, mutual dependency are other two big disadvantages of the classical implementations of the GOF version. This in turn reduces the modifiability of the application.

Also in case of visitor pattern, addition of a new visitor implies its implementation for every listed visitables, even if there is no necessity. Similarly, in observer pattern, sometimes unnecessary notifications are sent to the observers. Also, partial subscription rules of observers are hard to define in the application code. Also in the traditional implementation of design patterns, the design pattern logic is embedded in the application code so any changes in the pattern logic require a programmer's intervention in non-runtime conditions.

4   Design of the Compound Pattern

Our shopping cart application consists some of the basic features such as displaying details about the items, displaying the customer details, adding new customers and items, notification of any new offers or sales to the registered customer, etc. The compound pattern used by us, includes visitor and observer pattern. The visitor pattern is used to provide features for calculation of taxes, shipping costs and discount costs. The items listed in the cart serve as the concrete visitables and the listed costs are the concrete visitors. So whenever any such relevant information needs to be calculated by the application, the double dispatch mechanism of the visitor pattern is used to calculate the final values. The observer pattern is used for the notification purposes to the registered customers. Since the list of all the registered customers is maintained, arrival of any new offer is shown to them using the 'notify' method of the observer pattern. Also, if any item desired by the customer is not available in the product list, the customer is subscribed to the product list and whenever the status of this product changes, the customers in the list are automatically notified. Here one thing to notice is that the items serve both as visitables and the observables. The clients are observers. Hence, the visitor and observer pattern overlap in the application to work together. The class diagram of the shopping cart application with GoF versions of patterns used is shown in Fig. 1.

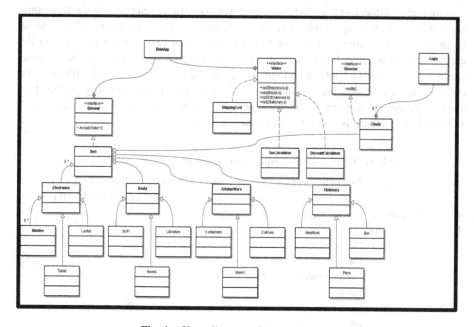

Fig. 1. Class diagram of the application

This is the basic working of the GOF pattern based application. The working of ontology driven application is altogether different. Pattern logic is enclosed in a non programming entity i.e. the pattern ontology which in turn separates the pattern and application logic. An intermediate entity between the constituent classes called 'ontology manager' is introduced which reduces mutual dependency and cyclic dependency between the classes. Also, this approach makes the pattern a plug and play component which facilitates an easy extension and modification of the original application.

5 Analysis and Observations

In this section we present a comparative analysis of the shopping cart application based on the classical GOF version of the patterns and that based on the ontology driven patterns. Our experiment is conducted in two dimensions. In one, we recorded the time and effort (lines of code written and/or modified) required to design and develop both the applications and then implement changes in them. In the other dimension, we measure and compare the mutual dependency between the elements of the two applications. We have used JArchitect tool [13] for comparing them on the basis of mutual dependency. And code metrics are measured using LOC Metrics tool [14].

Table 1 shows the initial measurements obtained for both the applications. It has three visitor classes namely, tax calculation, discount calculation and shipping calculation. There were a number of different visitable classes such as shirts, mobiles, laptops etc. Since, the observables were the same as the visitable classes so they were equal in number. LOC metrics defines number of lines we wrote for application development. Time taken defines the time we took to develop the fully functional application. Since the application structure was same for both the versions, hence some initial metrics are same. Time taken to develop the ontology version is less than the classic version because former included time to design and develop the whole application writing both the application logic as well as the design pattern code. While in the ontology driven version, we just need to hook in the pattern functionality provided by the ontological component in the skeleton code of the application. Also, the overall LOC in latter version is less owing to stated advantages.

Table 1. Time and effort required to design and develop applications

Design pattern type	Parameters/metrics	Values obtained for GoF pattern	Values obtained for ontology driven pattern
Compound pattern (visitor + observer)	No. of visitor classes	3	3
	No. of visitable classes	20	20
	No. of observer classes	1	1
	No. of observable classes	20	20
	LOC* written by developers	16,612	16,438
	Time taken to design and develop (h)	3 (requirement analysis and design time) + 14 (development time) = 17	2 (learning time) + 1 (Ontology component hook in time) = 3

[a]LOC (Lines of Code)

Table 2 shows the measurements obtained to make changes in the existing application by adding classes. First change included addition of an observable/visitable hierarchy to the application which included three subclasses and their abstract base class (total 4). As shown in Table 2 the LOC and time metrics for ontology version are less than the classical version. We observed that considerably lesser time is required to implement changes in the ontology driven application. This happens because no class is required to be modified to implement the desired changes. Just the entries in the pattern ontology are changed to establish the relationship of the newly added class with the existing classes. While in case of the GoF version of patterns, the application code needs to be scanned and modified and then the classes need to be recompiled to implement the changes.

Table 2. Adding classes non-run time

Changes made in the applications	Parameters/metrics	Values obtained for GoF design patterns	Values obtained for ontology driven design patterns
Add: 1 visitable/observable class hierarchy (1 parent class and 3 children classes)	No. of visitor classes	3	3
	No. of visitable classes	20 + 4 = 24	20 + 4 = 24
	No. of observer classes	1	1
	No. of observable classes	20 + 4 = 24	20 + 4 = 24
	LOC added by developers	2507	2462
	Time taken to add classes (min)	30	10
	No. of classes added	4	4
	No. of existing classes modified	3	1
Add: 1 concrete visitable/observable class	No. of visitor classes	3	3
	No. of visitable classes	24 + 1 = 25	24 + 1 = 25
	No. of observer classes	1	1
	No. of observable classes	24 + 1 = 25	24 + 1 = 25
	LOC added by developers	843	810
	Time taken to add classes (min)	15	5
	No. of classes added	1	1
	No. of existing classes modified	3	1

(continued)

Table 2. (*continued*)

Changes made in the applications	Parameters/metrics	Values obtained for GoF design patterns	Values obtained for ontology driven design patterns
Add: 1 concrete observer class	No. of visitor classes	3	3
	No. of visitable classes	20	20
	No. of observer classes	2	2
	No. of observable classes	20	20
	LOC added by developers	154	154
	Time taken to add classes (min)	10	3
	No. of classes added	1	1
	No. of existing classes modified	20	0

Second change included adding a single concrete observable/visitable. Similar to first observation, concerned metrics were better for ontology version than GOF version.

Third and final change included adding an additional observer. We accommodated this by making two types of clients (Regular and Premium). Similar to above LOC, time and modified class metrics were better as compared to the GOF version. Also, the changes that we made were non-runtime i.e. the application was stopped, changes made, classes recompiled and then it was re-started. Table 3 shows the measurements obtained to change the relationships between the classes during non-runtime environment in both the applications. Since, adding runtime changes to a classical pattern based application is not possible, hence for classical version it was non-runtime operation. Number of relationship modified means making changes to the application code. For ontology case we just removed the relation between the component classes in the pattern ontology and then re-run the same functionality. Therefore the time taken to reflect such changes are way less in ontology driven case. Metrics measured included the number of lines of code added/removed, number of existing classes modified and time taken to make that change For all the cases, the measurements obtained are much better for the ontology case than the classical Pattern based Application.

Table 3. Changing relationships between the classes non-run time

Situation	Parameters/metrics	Values obtained for GoF design patterns	Values obtained for ontology driven design patterns
Number of relationships modified = 1 (1 visitor removed)	LOC modified by developers	139	0
	Time taken to make modifications (min)	10	0.05
	No. of classes added/removed	1	0
	No. of existing classes modified (GUI related classes modified)	3	0
Number of relationships modified = 2 (2 visitors removed)	LOC modified by developers	266	0
	Time taken to make modifications (min)	15	0.1
	No. of classes added/removed	2	0
	No. of existing classes modified (GUI related classes modified)	3	0
Number of relationships modified = 3 (3 visitors removed)	LOC modified by developers	405	0
	Time taken to make modifications (min)	25	0.5
	No. of classes added/removed	3	0
	No. of existing classes modified (GUI related classes modified)	3	0
Number of relationships modified = 4 (4 visitables removed)	LOC modified by developers	857	0
	Time taken to make modifications (min)	40	1
	No. of classes added/removed	4	0
	No. of existing classes modified (concrete visitors modified)	3	0
Number of relationships modified = 1 (1 observer removed)	LOC modified by developers	154	0
	Time taken to make modifications (min)	5	0.5
	No. of classes added/removed	1	0
	No. of existing classes modified	20	0
		275	0

(*continued*)

Table 3. (*continued*)

Situation	Parameters/metrics	Values obtained for GoF design patterns	Values obtained for ontology driven design patterns
Number of relationships modified = 2 (2 observers removed)	LOC modified by developers		
	Time taken to make modifications (min)	7	0.5
	No. of classes added/removed	2	0
	No. of existing classes modified	20	0

Figure 2 shows a graph showing the lines of codes modified to include the number of relations modified in the existing application. The graph has somewhat an exponential curve.

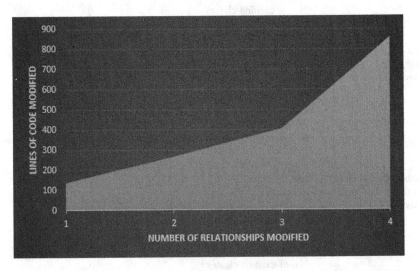

Fig. 2. Plot between lines of code modified to the number of relations modified

Figures 3 and 4 shows the dependency relationship between the components in the classical Pattern driven and ontology driven application. The measurements were done using the JArchitect tool. The blue and green boxes represent the dependencies between the modules/classes of the application. The black boxes designate the cyclic dependencies between the member classes, thereby increasing coupling in the application. Found cyclic dependencies are included in a bigger red box across all the member classes. Therefore lesser the number of such boxes, better the application. In Classical version of the application, the number of cyclic dependencies are much more than the ontology driven application.

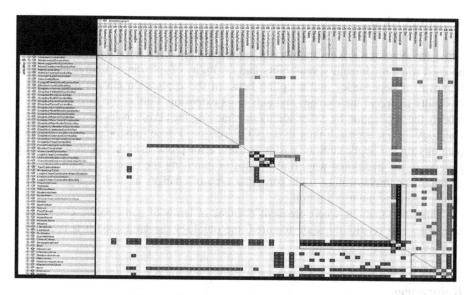

Fig. 3. Dependency Matrix(GOF Version)

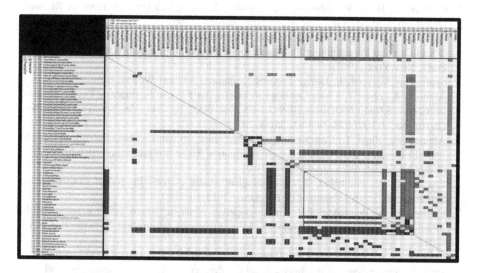

Fig. 4. Dependency matrix (Ontology version)

Thus, it is clear that cyclic dependencies are much more in the Classical version of the application than its ontology driven counterpart. This is evident from the metrics reflected in Tables 1 and 2.

Therefore making additional and frequent changes in classical pattern driven applications is a time and labor intensive task as compared to ontology driven application. Also, the case of intensive and complicated dependencies between the classes is better handled in the latter case.

6 Conclusion

Thus, the ontology driven approach to implement patterns is better and should be adopted when modifiability, reusability and flexibility of software system is important. Removal of dependency and coupling between the application classes increases its flexibility to accept the changes and aids in its extension. Further the time required to modify the application by either adding or removing the classes is lesser in the case of Ontology-driven approach than in the GOF version. Hence, modifications in case of ontology driven application are easier and less error prone than the application using patterns in the traditional way. It also helps in removing the dependency on the programmer for implementing some particular type of changes as such changes can be implemented by the user himself.

Thus for situations where frequent changes in terms of participating classes and their roles and relationships are required, the ontology driven approach is preferable because of its stated advantages.

References

1. Gamma, E., Helm, R., Johnson, R., Vlissides, J.: Design Patterns Elements of Reusable Object-Oriented Software. Addison-Wesley, Boston (1995)
2. Riehle, D.: Composite design patterns. In: Proceedings of the 1997 Conference on Object-Oriented Programming Systems, Languages, and Applications (OOPSLA '97). ACM Press, New York (1997)
3. Shalloway, A., Trott, J.: Design Patterns Explained. Addison Wesley, Boston (2001)
4. Alnusair, A., Zhao, T.: Using Ontology Reasoning for Reverse Engineering Design Patterns. In: Ghosh, S. (ed.) MODELS 2009. LNCS, vol. 6002, pp. 344–358. Springer, Heidelberg (2010). doi:10.1007/978-3-642-12261-3_32
5. Alnusair, A., Zhao, T.: Component search and reuse: an ontology-based approach. In: The 11th IEEE International Conference on Information Reuse and Integration (IRI-2010). IEEE Computer Society Press, Las Vegas (2010)
6. Chaturvedi, A., Prabhakar, T.V.: Ontological visitor pattern. In: Indian Conference on Patterns and Pattern Languages of Programs (2013)
7. Chaturvedi, A., Prabhakar, T.V.: Ontology-driven observer pattern. In: Proceedings of the International Workshop on Ontologies Meet Advanced Information Systems (OAIS'13) (2013)
8. Chaturvedi, A., Prabhakar, T.V.: Ontology-driven MVC: a variant of MVC architectural style. In: Proceedings of the International Conference on Software Engineering and New Technologies (2012)
9. Chaturvedi, A., Prabhakar, T.V.: Ontology driven creational design patterns creating objects on the fly. In: Proceedings of International Conference on Reliable and Convergent Systems (2012)
10. Chaturvedi, A., Prabhakar, T.V.: Ontology driven builder pattern a plug and play component. In: The 29th ACM Symposium on Applied Computing (ACM SAC 2014)
11. Mai, Y., Champlain, M.: Reflective Visitor Pattern, Department of Electrical and Computer Engineering Concordia University (2001)

12. Yueping, Z., Yuefan, L., Keshang, X.: The compound pattern on the chain of responsibility and observer, 2009. In: International Forum on Computer Science-Technology and Applications (2009)
13. JArchitect Tool: http://www.jarchitect.com/
14. LOC Metrics Tool: http://www.locmetrics.com/

Security of Web Application: State of the Art

Research Theories and Industrial Practices

Habib ur Rehman[1,2(✉)] [ID], Mohammed Nazir[1], and Khurram Mustafa[1]

[1] Department of Computer Science, Jamia Millia Islamia, New Delhi, India
way2habibmca@gmail.com, {mnazir,kmustafa}@jmi.ac.in
[2] DXC Technology, Noida, India

Abstract. As complexity inherent in web application is growing rapidly. Testing web applications with more sophisticated approaches is essentially needed. Several approaches for security testing are available, but only a few of them are appreciated in common IT industries and hence in practice. The paper recapitulates the current approaches, considering the limitations of real world applications. An effort has been made in the direction of bridging the gaps with the study of foremost web security concerns and the current web testing techniques, including their strengths and weaknesses. The paper highlights the security issues pertinent to web applications, along with actual practices in industries related to these issues. It also includes gap between practices and theories in the industry.

Keywords: Web application security · Web testing · Security testing approaches · Testing techniques · Testing in industrial practices · Security testing limitations

1 Introduction

Web applications are one of the most ubiquitous platforms for information and services delivery over Internet. These applications are increasingly used to deliver security critical services, such as financial transactions, commercial business, and cyber community services. When web applications are developed and tested considering little or no security in mind, the possibility of security holes increases dramatically. It becomes a viable target for security attacks that may lead to severe economic losses [15]. The security problems are becoming serious with increasing complexity of applications and the sophisticated techniques of attackers to exploit the vulnerabilities. The heterogeneous nature with growing complexity of web applications raise security issues and emphasize on the need to make them more secure and robust.

A number of web application development technologies and frameworks are proposed and actively maintained [2]. Their fast evolving nature requires testing techniques to be most effective that is still course of investigation, not merely a matter of creating and following the routine process. An industrial tester should be aware that there are – and possibly more – different testing approaches exist. The author have rich background of web security industrial practices and also pursuing research in the domain

© Springer Nature Singapore Pte Ltd. 2017
S. Kaushik et al. (Eds.): ICICCT 2017, CCIS 750, pp. 168–180, 2017.
https://doi.org/10.1007/978-981-10-6544-6_17

of web application's security testing, with the objective of industrial academic research collaboration and coordination.

The review of available approaches and comparative studies of theories and current industrial practices have been done. It highlights severity of web application security, threats and testing challenges, strength and weakness of existing testing approaches and suggestions for the direction of improvements. Section 2 provides brief introduction of web applications and their security concerns. Section 3 outlines testing approaches, their applicability and issues. Section 4 discusses Industrial trends and practices. Section 5 concludes the paper with future research directions.

2   Web Application Security: Needs and Concerns

Web applications are unique and different with respect to traditional desktop applications. This uniqueness leads to new challenges for testing and quality assurance domain.

- Open operating environment of typical web applications makes it wide visible and susceptible to various attacks, such as denial-of-service (DoS) and distributed denial-of-service (DDoS) attacks [24]. This creates difficulty in predicting and simulating the realistic workload. The differences in implementation and levels of standards compliance adds further complexity on and across the browsers while delivering coherent user experiences. The proliferation of numerous popular browsers and inadequate compatibility testing creates innumerable challenge [26].
- The multilingual feature of backend and frontend, numerous components under different programming languages creates an additional challenge for a fully automated continuous integration (CI) practices. The heterogeneous nature of application development frameworks and different encoding standards further enhances the trials [17].
- Real time multi-user environment along with multi-threaded nature creates difficulty in detecting and reproducing resource contention issues. The effective management of resources such as HTTP, files or database connections, threads are crucial concerns for security, scalability, usability and functionality of web applications and their associated challenges [17] (Fig. 1).

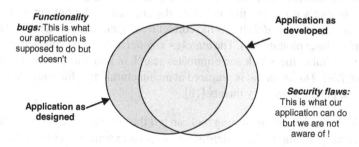

Fig. 1. Any deviation in design and development is the platform for flaws.

For a popular e-commerce web application, exploitation of vulnerabilities may result loss of company reputation. Hence, detection of security bugs will improve the quality and reliability of web application along with preventing economic losses [15]. The threat landscape for web applications is consistently changing. Key factors for this evolution are the advancements made by attackers, deployment of increasingly complex systems as well as the release of new technologies [9]. All this proclamations needs to identify the risk associated with web application; categorize the typical risk severity, risk consequences and detection accuracy during testing [30].

3   Brief Description on Testing Approaches

In fact, web application testing in general and web application security testing in particular, are the active research areas. Several algorithms have been proposed for detecting security vulnerabilities [15]. Paths have been enlighten using various approaches from fault injection based security testing approach to vulnerability scanning approach to mutant injection approach to fuzzy testing approach, but web application security still does not have a comprehensive solution [6, 13]. On the basis of controlled environment laboratory results the formal methods promises about the security but the real-world situations, miss their stipulation. On the other hand hackers apply artistic approaches right at real world application, fight with numerous obstacles and challenge the security of web application. Security is still one of the holy grails of web applications [13]. Following sections precisely describe testing approaches. A single generic approach is not available that can be applied to catch all types of security vulnerabilities.

3.1   Model Based Testing

The basic model based testing approach applies in graph based techniques [25]. It suggests creating web application's model then deriving test cases based on covered test statements, paths and branches. To drive test cases, it is further enhanced with finite state model of the system [4]. Considering the state transition uncertainties, the probable finite state machines model is proposed where the transitions are associated with probabilities and the shortest length message is inferred from the data [23]. While *fault-based model* tries to find a transition that exists on the original model but not on the faulty model. *Implementation model* checks the correct refinement of specification. The error sub-state might be exploitable [5]. The *attacker's model* focuses the knowledge, requirements for performing the attack and eliminates search in scenarios, where the attack is not possible [29]. *Threat model* is prepared at architectural level for understanding and managing the potential security threats [18].

Applicability: A model-based testing tool can test the system based on available information in corresponding model. It depends on manual expertise to construct the model of overall system, then driving regular expression and choosing input randomly. The manual dependency creates difficulty for automation of this approach. The scalability issue with complex model causes state-space exploration paradigm to process the models and miss the accuracy. Tools do not have much contextual knowledge; difference arises with the experience of product testers. Future work should focus on combining various model based testing approaches and automating the process to make it more accurate and reliable for industrial usage [6].

Indications: Getting contextual knowledge and incorporating fault models into model-based testing tools is active research area and there are still plenty of unknown territories to apply the knowledge base [23]. For example FSM-based testing has limited support for URL rewriting, unanticipated back and forward navigation, i.e. user-controlled operational transitions. User goes directly on an internal web page with a book mark. In order to test such transactions, more exploration is needed to develop a method to model operational transitions in a tractable manner and avoid space explosion problems in a test sequence from the list of potential operational transitions.

3.2 User Session-Based Testing

A large number of user sessions are created when a user interacts with a web site that results in the creation of huge list of URLs, hence the name–value pairs of different attributes, their security apprehension are also required to be tested [10]. For instance, client sends most of the requests to server that logged down all GET requests received (with minimal configuration changes) [17]. This provides high level abstraction about the heterogeneous nature of different components when concerned with session data. This testing approach is not much appreciated during recurrent changes of application components. It is only done by keeping track of user sessions.

Indications: Several techniques are present for reducing the number of sessions to test, such as lattice construction [30], incremental reduced test suite update [16], batch test suite reduction [10], and the test case reduction through examining the URL traces [22]. These testing techniques could not detect faults for rare data. Their effectiveness increases with more number of user sessions though increases the time and cost [31]. They have limitations in revealing faults that arises under complex run-time behavior of rich modern web applications of real world.

3.3 Mutation Testing

It has ambition to detect the most common errors that typically exist in web application. Some lines of source code are randomly alter in the program, to check whether the test case is able to perceive the change or not, e.g. on HTML form, at client side the desti-nation address may be replaced with an invalid address or at server side of the program, an invalid file may be included [16]. If the test suite can detect such errors, then an error message will be displayed, i.e. a modified version of program P' (called mutants [8] is created in place of the given input program P. The test case has to kill the mutant, by detecting the change (i.e., LOC where mutation operator has been applied). Otherwise the mutant stays live. The input variables are mutated one by one, the process continues until all branches have been traversed or there is no further possibility of improvements in the fitness function [3].

Applicability: This approach exposes security flaws and ensures safer and more robust web applications [21]. There is still need to improve the quality of mutation testing, to address high execution, a vast number of mutants, realism of faults and equivalent mutant problem [19].

Indications: This type of testing is primarily intended to ensure that testing has been done accurately and covering additional faults, which may exist in a web site, and might be uncovered later in normal testing [6]. The main advantage of this approach is to test errors that are more probable and most crucial such as server errors due to invalid form attribute, missing files or user input not validated properly. Similarly at client side errors due to broken links, invalid HTML, etc.

3.4   Search-Based Software Testing

It is based on *search based software engineering* (SBSE) where problems are treated as optimization problems and solutions require searching through the state space [3]. The probable solutions encoded in the way based on similar solutions proximate in the search space. A defined fitness function is used to compare with probable solutions [16]. An iterative incremental algorithm (e.g., Hill climbing) follows SBSE found to be effective for testing [3]. Execution starts with an aim for finding a solution that maximizes the heuristic of fitness function. For example in hill climbing, a randomly chosen solution is evaluated at first then the nearest neighbors are evaluated (e.g., determined by distance heuristic).

Applicability: Thorough testing is the prime aim of this approach, which improves through branch coverage in iterations. It is slow as compared to other simple testing techniques such as (random testing, mutation testing), but for complex real world applications it promises the possibility of exhaustive testing [6].

Indications: It starts with a static analysis phase and collects static information to aid subsequent SB phase [3]. However, there are several limitations that affects search based techniques e.g. dynamic typing (e.g., in Ruby, PHP variables are dynamically typed). The type of variables used is hard to determine the fitness function. There is no method to know, how many inputs are required for an application to execute. It becomes harder to determine the interface in different JSP or PHP applications [27]. Other problem occurs in simulating client-side dynamic web pages and server-side dynamic include statements. The major limitation of SBST is insufficiently informed fitness function that guide search for test target within nested constraints (predicates).

3.5   Scanning and Crawling Based Testing

Scanners are tools that detect errors which are injected by invalid inputs into the web application. They determine the type of errors as per the behavior of application. Crawlers are the tools, which browse the web application and gather information in a predefined and automated manner. Scanner helps in detecting the bugs, which programmer typically does not think of testing during the design phase [16] e.g., excessive 'reads from' and 'writes to' database. If they are not addressed properly, might result in the breach of susceptible private information [17].

Applicability: Scanners works on the principle of injecting unsanitised input into HTML forms, they are then sent to the server, e.g. to check web applications security by injecting unsanitised input. If undetected it may result in malicious modifications of database. The testing based on this approach, improves overall security of a web site [17]. If the application have proper user data validations and execute proper input sanitation, then it would behave normally, else severe implications might breach the security e.g. breaching of privatized data by writing unsafe values in the database.

Indications: Scanners can be a black-box or a white-box. The tools based on these approach launch attacks against web application and observes the response [6]. The white-box vulnerability scanners are less popular due to heterogeneous programming environments and complexities in web applications incorporated with business logic, databases, and user interface components. The black-box scanners are effective in detecting simpler XSS vulnerabilities but poor in detecting "stored" vulnerabilities (e.g. second-order SQL injection vulnerabilities) [16].

3.6   Randomness Based Testing and Boundary Value Fuzz Testing

Providing random input to the application and checking its functional behavior while handling the invalid input is random testing. Unlike classical testing techniques, it did not follow the usual practice of generating the set of test cases ahead of following their execution on the system.

Applicability: Several web applications involve logical dependencies between its operations, that could be invoked independently or in sequence i.e. result of particular operation may depend on data of previous operation. So test cases should take into account the states of service, operation dependencies and the data to simulate user inputs. Automatically generate test cases on-the-fly would lower the overall effort to create a test suite, and deals with more specific and appropriately observed test cases.

Indications: The test case generation, execution, and assessment happen in lockstep. Hence reduces the state space explosion problems that are limitation of conventional model-based testing techniques [12] and achieves adequate validation coverage. Frantzen et al. proposed a Java based on-the-fly approach tool called Jambition [12]. Random testing is not appropriate to generate the input values to drive the program through all its execution paths [16]. Special form of random testing is *fuzz testing*, where the boundary values are chosen as inputs to test that application is performing appropriately, when passed rare input combinations [16]. It is combined with symbolic execution that attempts to cover maximum possible branches to make the testing complete [28]. This could be categories as white-box fuzz testing and black-box fuzz testing. Fuzz testing helps in detecting serious, exploitable bugs which probably couldn't be detected in model-based approaches for complex applications. It is effective for finding invalid values, boundary values or values that are rarely used.

3.7 Usability Testing

Security that is not usable should be avoided or circumvented. Usability testing balances the web application *security* and *usability*. It is intended to test how users use an application, realize inaccuracy and finding areas of improvement (in order to make the artifact more intuitive and user-friendly). It evaluates efficiency, accuracy, recall and emotional response of users in context of application usage, hence, primarily a black-box testing technique. The first test results are the baseline, to compare all subsequent tests and that becomes the indicator of improvements [16].

Applicability: It is more significant for complex applications where product is difficult to plan, build and test. Hence might introduce security challenges and causes end-user frustration. Application usage shouldn't become harder for security [26]. Usability testing is not 100% representative of real situation; rather categorical.

Indications: Firstly, it tests *appearance and layout* of application, on different devices such as mobile, tablets, laptop and desktop systems. Secondly, it tests *ease of using the application*, and finally, it tests if different messages displayed during application testing are appropriate and sufficient [17]. Usability testing does not provide large samples of feedback that a questionnaire might provide, but it is the approximation. Some common security usability issues arise in web development that cannot be resolved adequately without manual intervention of security specialist.

3.8 Biometrics and Behavior Biometrics Security Approach

Biometrics security system is a lock and biometrics is the key to open that lock [1, 16]. Systems just need to verify user's identity by the unique characteristics that are always with user, hence reducing the chances of losing other identifying accessories, behavior is a combination of observable actions of an Internet user; together the most frequent of these actions summarizes the habit. This offers a ways to recognizing the user and harder to change or make copy. Behavior biometrics is passive monitoring of characteristic is relatively a new research direction, e.g. web application authentication for a user basis on his web browsing behavior [1].

Applicability: It is addressing the biggest problem for network security, i.e. the authentication of *system identify* by verifying the *person's identity* [11]. It has been implemented in public for short period of time and has shown effectiveness, reduced frauds and password administrator costs. The biometrics technologies in various aspects have several weaknesses such as: adaptability to rate of change in life, scalability, information and physical privacy accuracy and religious objections.

The different testing techniques have different goals. Some of the techniques were found effective for fault findings (scanning and crawling), fuzz testing, and mutation testing, where as others might be more effective to ensure that application is exhaustively tested. None of these techniques could give full assurance that all test cases have covered and addressed all possible security challenges. Every technique differs for its inputs, outputs, stopping criteria, test logic and mere purpose. It depends on the nature and performance of application that can influence to club the technique for more adequate coverage.

4   Security Testing: Industry Needs and Limitations

The web application security is its ability to provide required functioning during attack instances [14]. Web application security testing ensures that it would continue working under attack [24]. The real-world tester hardly encounters the ideal conditions for security testing that are generally assumed in theories [33]. For an approach the class of faults detection may varies and might be complimentary with others. Selection of right approach at right time will make security testing more effective and efficient. Security team need to make explicit connection with business strategies to meet safe and secure customer demands (Fig. 2).

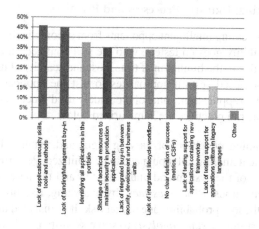

Fig. 2. Various challenges in web application security [32].

A security tester faces number of constraints, i.e. besides on common resource limits—time, money, processing power, network bandwidth, and memory [16]. There is shortage of application security expertise/skills in the market. Developers generally leave subtle vulnerabilities in the application. In recent attacks, intruders were trying to breach system security by understanding the logic behind the coding [26], rather than capitalizing on an evident vulnerability [20]. Such types of issues are likely to be fueled nearby in future, which would not trap under conventional routine defense mechanisms. There are parallel fights with incomplete system information for a particular issue. Organizations uses multiple practices and services in their security programs e.g. static analysis testing, dynamic analysis testing, penetration testing, third-party assessments, virtual patching and application firewalls to detect or block attacks etc. But they are not getting as much value as it should come out of it [6] (Fig. 3).

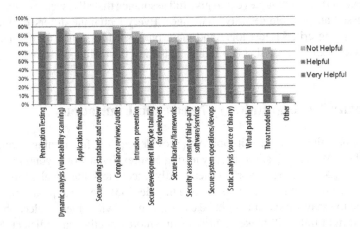

Fig. 3. Web application security testing techniques used in industry and its effectiveness [32].

4.1   Security Testing: Industry Processes and Practices

Security is about preventing intelligent opponents from accomplishing their nasty objective; major responsibility goes on testers, who are still confined on manual process or on automated tools due to the limitation of time, cost and scarcity of mentors. However, researchers have proposed several approaches to test the application. In context of security testing of web application, some of the widely used processes, methods, testing techniques and industrial practices are summarized below.

Processes: Maintaining *checklists* of varying vigor and feature. They may contain specific or unspecific items, e.g. all input need to be sanitized. Performing *security audit* for direct inspection of the system and underling OS and the network, to find out the weaknesses of applications. *Risk assessment* by analyzing, risk involvement with the system along with the loss probability due to that risk. It is analyzed through interviews, discussions, etc. Performing *static analysis* to solve security problems (SAST) in early phase of development by scanning source code or binaries for frequent security vulnerabilities & identifying bug patterns. Commercial analysis tools are expensive, sometime beyond reach of the organizations.

Practices: Vulnerability scanning for all known vulnerability. Applying *virtual patching* as an Instant action of temporary solution until the development team can fix the code for use, but it's difficult to scale and needs extra efforts. Action Involved in virtual patching are, setting up of application firewall in blocking mode, testing and finding vulnerabilities of online application, intriguing the testing results and creating rules or signatures for the firewall. Implementation of these rules in production and blocks the possibility of attacks against these vulnerabilities [6].

Techniques: Use of *penetration testing* to find the potential web application loopholes by forcibly entering into the system with the help of combination of open loopholes left unknowingly. It is highly automated testing technique that covers numerous boundary cases by providing invalid data input (from API calls, network protocols, files, etc.) and relies on tool which uses fuzzing or fault injection approaches [28]. It executes in three phases, during *crawling* it sneaks web pages that contain vulnerable inputs, at *fuzzing* actual penetration testing is performed while executing the fuzz data with the fuzzer and sends input to the vulnerable spots [16]. Finally *analyzing* the data, e.g. monitoring SQL injection vulnerabilities is by analyzing SQL errors. The result depends on fuzzed data, similarly monitoring for XSS vulnerabilities consist of crawling the web application and searching for pages that contain input which could be injected during execution of fuzzed data. This is followed by manual check to determine exploitability of discovered vulner- abilities.

Testing Tactics: Usually perform *ethical hacking* that engrosses large number of pene- tration testing on complete system to test forced entry through external elements. *Posture assessment* is to understand complete system security with combined features of security scanning, risk assessment and ethical hacking. *Functional test cases* are reuse with slight modification in terms of security test cases, e.g. by changing test inputs in such a way that might trigger further error conditions.

Threat Modeling: It is partial realization of *model based* approach, still under improve- ment. To understand and manage security threats, developers and security experts needs to be committed with true team spirit, to work together starting from the architecture phase and design a structured process [18]. Threat modeling is a formal, document-heavy security walkthrough of system design artifacts. It does not work well for teams following the agile development practices, where the design is always in flux and the details are worked out iteratively and incrementally [32]. Exploring the possible threat actors which are targeting the organization and which applications are likely to be the targets of attack. Web applications are under biggest security risks [7, 32]. Organizations are in search of less-expensive alternatives to threat modeling in order to identify and manage application security risks up front [6]. Attackers constantly modify their tech- niques, update with innovations to bypass these security systems; researchers in turn, update their approaches to handle new attacks.

5   Observations and Indications

Theories are significant if they are used to cater better tools for betterment of testing, in terms of processes and techniques. The useful tools will promisingly support human testers rather than replacement. There are various approaches to test security aspects of application, but effective testing of complex web application is not merely a matter of creating and following the routine process. This comparative study argues that the impact of research upon industrial practices seems less prominent and not recognized so far. Hence, researchers in academics, working in the area of security testing essentially requires to consider real-world exploits and organizations' constraints. Which are still relying tool based dynamic testing; vulnerability scanning and penetration testing or on less expensive alternatives of threat modeling (Fig. 4).

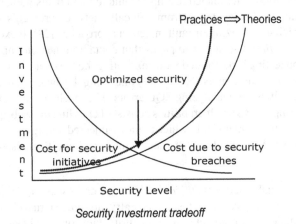

Security investment tradeoff

Fig. 4. Gap between practices and theories in the industry.

Typical challenges in the field of security are emerging. Hence, industrial and academic collaboration is highly desirable in order to strengthen and improve the security methods, to develop new testing techniques, to address the evolving and emerging security challenges. It is an obvious fact that organizations in today's scenario need more holistic approaches to tackle threats of security breaches. Therefore, academic efforts are needed in parallel to clearly understand, define and deliver more reliable testing models, methods, tools and techniques that can syndicate traditional testing approaches. On the other hand, industry should open its doors to cooperate and collaborate with academics and vice versa. It should be promoted at least through panel discussion, lecture series of experts, key note addresses both from academia and industry experts.

References

1. Abramson, M., Aha, D.W.: User Authentication from web browsing behavior. In: Proceedings of the Twenty-Sixth International Florida Artificial Intelligence Research Society Conference, pp. 268–273. Naval Research Lab, Washington DC (2013)
2. Alalfi, M.H., Cordy, J.R., Dean, T.R.: Modelling methods for web application verification and testing: state of the art. Softw. Test Verif. Reliab. **19**, 265–296 (2009)
3. Alshahwan, N., Harman, M.: Automated web application testing using search based software engineering. In: 26th IEEE/ACM International Conference on Automated Software Engineering pp. 3–12. IEEE Computer Society, Washington DC (2011)

4. Andrews, A.A., Offutt, J., Alexander, R.T.: Testing Web applications by modeling with FSMs. Softw. Syst. Model. **4**, 32–345 (2005)
5. Anwer, F., Nazir, M., Mustafa, K.: Automatic testing of inconsistency caused by improper error handling: a safety and security perspective. In: 2014 International Conference On Information and Communication Technology For Competitive Strategies, pp. 43–49. ACM, New York (2014)
6. Anwer, F., Nazir, M., Mustafa, K.: Security Testing, pp. 35–66. Springer, Singapore (2017)
7. OWASP Top 10–2013.: The ten most critical web application security risks (2013)
8. Chevalley, P., Thenod-Fosse, P.: A mutation analysis tool for Java programs. Int. J. Softw. Tools Technol. Transfer **5**, 90–103 (2003)
9. Dukes, L., Yuan, X., Akowuah, F.: A case study on web application security testing with tools and manual testing. In: IEEE Computer Society Southeastcon Proceedings, pp. 1–6 (2013)
10. Elbaum S., Karre S., Rothermel G.: Improving web application testing with user session data. In: 25th International Conference on Software Engineering, vol. 03. pp. 49–59. IEEE Computer Society, Washington DC (2003)
11. Evans, M., Maglaras, L.A., He, Y., Janicke, H.: Human behaviour as an aspect of cybersecurity assurance. Secur. Commun. Netw. **9**, 4667–4679 (2016)
12. Frantzen, L., de las Nieves Huerta, M., Kiss, Z.G., Wallet, T.: On-the-fly model-based testing of web services with jambition. In: International Workshop on Web Services and Formal Methods. pp. 143–157, Springer, Heidelberg (2008)
13. Tian-Yang, G., Yin-Sheng, S., You-Yuan, F.: Research on software security testing. World Acad. Sci. Eng. Technol. Issue **69**, 647–651 (2010)
14. Hope, P., Walther, B.: Web Security Testing Cookbook™: Systematic Techniques to Find Problems Fast, O'Reilly Media, Inc. (2009). ISBN: 978-0-596-51483-9
15. Li, X., Xue, Y.: A survey on web application security. Technical Report, Vanderbilt University (2011)
16. Li, Y.F., Das, P.K., Dowe, D.L.: Two decades of web application testing—a survey of recent advances. Inf. Syst. **43**, 20–54 (2014)
17. Mayhew, D. J.: The usability engineering lifecycle. In: 98th Conference Summary on Human Factors in Computing Systems. pp. 127–128. ACM, New York (1998)
18. Myagmar, S., Lee, A.J., Yurcik, W.: Threat modeling as a basis for security requirements. In: Symposium on Requirements Engineering for Information Security, Symposium SREIS, pp. 1–8 (2005)
19. Nguyen, Q.V., Madeyski, L.: Problems of mutation testing and higher order mutation testing. In: Advanced Computational Methods For Knowledge Engineering, pp. 157–172, Springer International Publishing, New York (2014)
20. OWASP AppSec Europe 2009. HTTP Parameter pollution, May 2009. http://www.owasp.org/images/b/ba/AppsecEU09_CarettoniDiPaola_v0.8.pdf
21. Praphamontripong U., Offutt J.: Applying mutation testing to web applications. In: ICST Workshops, pp. 132–141 (2010)
22. Qian, Z.: Test case generation and optimization for user session-based web application testing. J. Comput. **5**, 1655–1662 (2010)
23. Qian, Z., Miao, H.: Towards testing web applications: a PFSM-based approach. Adv. Mater. Res. **1**, 220–224 (2011)
24. Raghavan, S.V., Dawson, E.: An Investigation into the detection and mitigation of denial of service (Dos) Attacks: Critical Information Infrastructure Protection. Springer Science & Business Media, New York (2011)

25. Ricca F., Tonella P.: Analysis and testing of web applications. In: 23rd International Conference on Software Engineering, ICSE, vol. 01, pp. 25–34. IEEE Computer Society, Washington, DC (2001)
26. Robert S., Philip S.: Client-side attacks and defense. In: Syngress (2012). ISBN: 978-1-59749-590-5
27. Sakti, A., Guéhéneuc, Y.G., Pesant, G.: Constraint-based fitness function for search-based software testing. In: Integration of AI and OR Techniques in Constraint Programming for Combinatorial Optimization Problems, pp. 378–385. Springer, Heidelberg (2013)
28. Salas, M.I.P., Martins, E.: Security testing methodology for vulnerabilities detection of XSS in web services and WS-security. Elec. Notes Theor. Comput. Sci **302**, 133–154 (2014)
29. Salas, P.A.P., Krishnan, P., Ross, K.J.: Model-based security vulnerability testing. In: IEEE Computer Society 18th Australian Software Engineering Conference, vol. 07, pp. 284–296 (2007)
30. Sampath S., Mihaylov V., Souter A., Pollock L.: A scalable approach to user-session based testing of Web applications through concept analysis. In: 19th International Conference on Automated Software Engineering, pp. 132–141 (2004)
31. Sampath S., Souter A., Pollock L.: Towards defining and exploiting similarities in web application use cases through user session analysis, pp. 17–24. IEEE Seminar Digests (2004)
32. SANS: Application Security Programs & Practices Survey (2014) https://www.qualys.com/docs/sans-enterprise-application-security-policy-survey-report.pdf
33. Turpe, S.: Security testing: turning practice into theory. In: IEEE International Conference Software Testing Verification and Validation Workshop, vol. 08, pp. 294–302 (2008)

Ring Segmented and Block Analysis Based Multi-feature Evaluation Model for Contrast Balancing

Kapil Juneja[✉] [iD]

Department of Computer Science and Engineering, University Institute of
Engineering and Technology, Maharshi Dayanand University,
Rohtak, Haryana 124001, India
kapil.juneja81@gmail.com, kapil.juneja.1981@ieee.org

Abstract. Image capturing in different indoor and outdoor environment requires high quality and sensing camera devices. Image capture in fog, night, rainy atmosphere, etc., can face an unequal contrast problem. Visibility is the primary concern for any image processing application to extract the content information and features accurately. In this paper, a ring segment based block feature evaluation method is provided to setup the enhancement individually in each segmented region. In this model, an intelligent method is applied to raw image to locate the regions with extreme visibility difference. The ring specific geographical mapping is applied to locate these regions. Three blocks from the region are evaluated based on visibility, entropy and frequency parameters. The comparative evaluation on block content strength is applied to get the referenced block blocks with maximum containment. Finally, each region block is mapped to this reference block to stabilize the contrast unbalancing. The proposed method is applied in real time captured images with different lighting effects. The comparative evaluation against histogram equalization method is applied for the PSNR and MSE parameters. The evaluation results show that the proposed method enhanced the visible quality and error robustness of dark, dull and faded images.

Keywords: Image representations · Appearance and texture representations · Feature selection · Image processing · Visibility · Image manipulation · Design and analysis of algorithms

1 Introduction

The photo-capturing in a photo studio can only provide the noise free, color balanced and contrast adjusted image. In real time, there are many of complex environment that cannot ensure the quality photo capturing. These regions can be challenging environment areas such as dusty regions, high mountain regions, forests, etc. The photo

© Springer Nature Singapore Pte Ltd. 2017
S. Kaushik et al. (Eds.): ICICCT 2017, CCIS 750, pp. 181–193, 2017.
https://doi.org/10.1007/978-981-10-6544-6_18

capturing in the night through surveillance cameras or hidden cameras also capture the dull and dark photos. The content recovery from such images is the requirement for any image processing application to better image aspect representation. In more challenging condition, a single image can have multiple contrast variation [1–5]. The content recovery from such unbalanced image is quite difficult. In this paper, a ring segmented and block specific feature evaluation method is provided for adaptive regional balancing. The method is effective for situational contrast unbalanced images captured in different environments [16–19]. The characterization and requirements of contrast enhancement are shown in Table 1.

Table 1. Contrast enhancement characterization

Characterization	Values
Factors affects contrast	Bad light, foggy environment, dark and mix light, snow, camera quality, camera configuration, device mishandling, lack of experience
Impact of contrast unbalancing	Dark images, dull image, bright image, shadowing, illuminance
Technical impact	Histogram unbalancing, poor visibility ratio, larger entropy difference, intensity difference
Application	Biometric authentication, medical image capturing, surveillance image analysis
Contrast balancing methods	Histogram balancing, convolution filters, morphological operators, non-linear filters

Table 1 shows the characteristics of problem, application and available solutions to the contrast unbalancing. The contrast variation is the common problem that can occur because of individual mistake, image capturing environment or the device quality problem. Histogram balancing, conventional filters, etc. are the available methods that can preserve the image information adaptively [6–11].

In this paper, a ring segmented and block adaptive multi-featured analysis method is provided to recover the contrast damaged information. The region specific featured evaluation is applied to adjust the contrast based on referenced region block. In this section, the behaviour, impact and problems associated to the contrast unbalancing are discussed. In Sect. 2, the work provided by earlier researchers is discussed in contrast balancing. In Sect. 3, the proposed ring segmented and block feature analysis method is presented with algorithmic formulation. In Sect. 4, the comparative evaluation of the proposed method is provided on multiple real time contrast unbalanced images. In Sect. 5, the conclusion obtained from work is explained.

2 Related Work

The images captures in a bad environment suffer from low contrast, bad light and darkness situations. The reliability and integrity of any image processing application depend on the quality of the image. To enhance the image quality, a preprocessing stage is always integrated to each algorithmic approach. Balanced Contrast is one such essential aspect that represents the quality of the image. In this paper, an improved reference adaptive model is provided to balance the contrast feature of real time images. The qualitative [11] methods are available to enhance the bad feature image without any reference image or metrics. The method is acceptable for complex real images.

One of common reason of contrast unbalancing is the night captured images. An image structure [1] preserved method was provided to enhance the contrast for night captured images. Dithering [4] based complex wavelets were applied to balance the variance and directionality. The diffusion weight assignment method improved the contrast feature at each wavelet level. Parihar et al. [5] applied the fuzzy based contextual estimation to enhance the contrast feature. The statistical evaluation based fuzzy decision was taken to achieve contrast balancing. Jabeen et al. [12] has provided a weighted transformation method to enhance the contrast based on dynamic bin and sight contribution. A fuzzy integrated histogram [13] based method was provided to enhance the clustered region. The neighbour histogram was formed to enhance the local region. A symmetric histogram [16] based method was applied dynamically to enhance the generalized real images.

Contrast unbalancing is common in medical applications. The indoor images captured through specialized sensor need contrast enhancement to present the disease features effectively. Gandhamal et al. [2] provided S-curve based local gray transformation method to enhance the contrast feature. A work on contrast enhancement for Mammogram [3] images was provided using artifact suppression based wavelet transformation method. Before enhancing the image, the labels and artifacts were removed to achieve the better content enhancement. A tone [7] preserved contrast enhancement method was provided to reduce the conflicts. A comparative [10] evaluation of contrast balancing was provided using average filter, bilateral ratinex and sigmoid function. The contrast enhancement of CT [15] images was provided by locating the region of interest. The selective region enhancement had improved the medical information and features.

Remote Sensing images are the satellite captured images which suffer from environmental disturbance. This results the noisy, low contrast and bad contrast capturing. Mehta et al. [6] applied the Cuckoo Search based Dual Tree Complex Wavelet transformation method to balance the contrast feature of images.

Various methods are measures are available to evaluate [8] the quality of contrast enhancement. The error based and rank based metrics were defined to characterize the image quality. Mamoria et al. [9] has provided an analytical study on fuzzy based contrast enhancement methods. The membership function was provided to quantize the darkness and brightness factors. A comparative study on various contrast enhancements was provided by Yadav et al. [14].

3   Ring Segmented and Multi-featured Block Referenced Model

In this paper, an intelligent model is model is presented to improve the contrast features of real time images. The functionality is divided into two main work stages to recover the dull features from images. The first stage is the wider evaluation stages to measure the problem existence, criticality and the referenced region block. In this stage, the regional division, featured evaluation on blocks is done to identify the reference block. After generating the block features and reference block features, the image contrast balancing is done in the second stage. The feature adaptive formula is prescribed in this stage to recover the image information. The model is effective to provide a solution against partial blur, pixel lever occlusion, highly dark and highly bright images. The visibility preserved method is provided to equalize the image features with symmetric contrast adjustment. Figure 1 shows the proposed model with integrated sub stages.

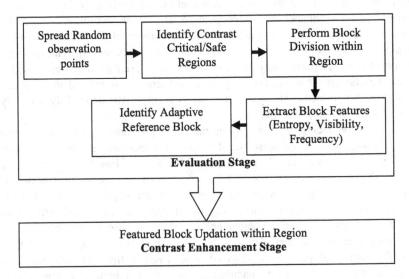

Fig. 1. Ring segmented and multi-featured block referenced contrast enhancement model

The contrast enhancement of dull and dark images is proposed using two stage models. These integrated process stages are feature evaluation stage and the contrast enhancement stage as depicted in Fig. 1. The proposed contrast enhancement approach is an intelligent, non-linear and multi-aspect driven evaluation method. To increase the robustness and scope of this method, a wider evaluation module is defined. This module divided the image in multiple geometric regions to recognize the partial unbalancing over the image. The regional division based on contrast difference observation is provided at this stage. After regenerating the regions. The sequential block driven observation based on multiple parameters is applied. The parameters considered in this work are visibility, frequency and the entropy. In each region, the ideal reference block with high visibility is identified. In the contrast enhancement stage, the evaluation of each region block is done respective to identify the referenced block. Based on the comparative measure, the identification of the low featured blocks is done. Finally, the featured updation based on the feature of reference block is applied to reconstruct the image. In this section, the algorithmic formulation with functionality description for each stage is provided.

3.1   Evaluation Stage

The quality of the proposed contrast enhancement model depends on the integrated evaluation stage. This is the wider process stage with multiple sub-stages. This stage is responsible to tackle various contrast level deficiencies. The partial information occlusion, regional visibility variations and pixel level information loss. The quality of the evaluation process and reference image generated directly affects the visibility and contrast balancing of the image. To perform this evaluation, and number of random seed points are distributed over the image. These seed points capture the information from nearest pixels of r radius and identify the m control points. The random placement of seeds and seed count depends on the full image coverage. After setting up the seed points, the evaluation on region points and control points is done as shown in Fig. 2.

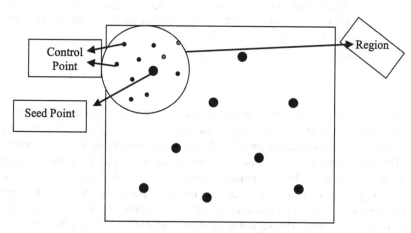

Fig. 2. Seed point based region separation

For each region, the seed point is considered as the central point and m control points are observed under intensity parameter. The Intensity variation and frequency count is done for these regional control points. The frequency, distance and magnitude based analysis is taken to identify the variation. The min, max and average feature constraints are observed to identify the requirement of contrast enhancement over the block. The inter-region strength is evaluated based on control-to-seed point feature evaluation. The algorithmic formation of this stage is shown in Algorithm 1.

Algorithm 1 : RegionalEvaluationAlgorithm

```
RegionalEvaluationAlgorithm(UBImage)
/*UBImage is the unbalanced contrast image*/
Begin
1.        Seeds=GenerateSeed(N, UBImage.Dimension, r)
          /*Generate  N  control  points  under  redial
          coverage r to cover complete*/
2.        For i=1 to Seed.Length /*Analyze Each Region*/
          Begin
3.        CPoints=GetControls(Seed(i)  ,  r  )/*Generate
          Control Points within Region*/
4.        Freq=GetFrequency(CPoints)    /*Identify    the
          Intensity class frequency  over the region*/
5.        [Max Min Avg]=GetStatistics(CPoints)  /*Obtain
          the Intensity driven statistics*/
6.        Feasibility(i)=EvaluateVariation(Freq,Max,Min,
          Average)/*Evaluate  the  variation  within  the
          region  based  on  the  frequency  elements  of
          different intensities*/
          End
End
```

Algorithm 1 has provided the regional division of the image by placing the random seeds and evaluates each region based on the random control points surrounding the seed points. The corresponding intensity based evaluation through control points is done. The max intensity, min intensity, average intensity and frequency of varied intensity control points in the seed point coverage are provided. A number of variations within the region and distance evaluation from seed point are taken. This internal aggregate region analysis is performed to identify the feasible blocks on which contrast enhancement is required. The region criticality is identified between 0 and 1. After selecting the effective blocks, each selective region (SReg) is divided into smaller blocks. These blocks are processed sequentially under statistical featured observation. The block specific regional evaluation is listed in Algorithm 2.

Algorithm 2 : BlockAdaptiveRegionAnalysis

BlockAdaptiveRegionAnalysis (SReg)

/*SReg is any of the selected regional block on which featured observation is applied for contrast enhancement*/

Begin

1.   Blks = GetBlocks(SReg) /*Obtain Region Specific Block over the Selected Region*/

2.   For i=1 to Blks.Length /*Extract and process the region blocks*/

        Begin

3.   Ent(i)=EvalEntropy(Blks(i))

        Vis(i)=EvalVisibility(Blks(i))

        Freq(i)=EvalFreq(Blks(i)) /*Evaluate the Block level evaluation for contrast criticality*/

4.   Ratio1(i)= Visibity(i)/Freq(i)+Ent(i)/Freq(i)

        Ratio2(i)=Visibility(i)/Ent(i) /*Estimate the content and visibility ratio based on visibility,frequency and entropy observation*/

5.   Weight   (i)=Ratio1(i)*.5+Ratio2(i)*.5 /*Generate the Featured weight for each region block*/

        End

6.   Index=Max(Weight)/*Indentify the Index of most effective block*/

7.   Return Blks(Index)/*Return the Reference block over the region*/

End

Algorithm 2 has provided the featured evaluation on blocks of each region. For this evaluation, the region is divided into smaller blocks of size n × n. The featured evaluation within the block is done using Entropy, visibility and frequency parameters. A ratio based evaluation method is to recognize the visibility strength within region. The region values are combined significantly to generate the overall weight of regional block. The maximum weight block is obtained and considered as reference block. It is the high visibility feature based block on enhancing the contrast feature relatively over the region. The contrast enhancement within the region is applied based on this captured reference block.

3.2   Contrast Enhancement Stage

After processing each of the generations unbalanced or low contrast region, the most visible region block is identified. These reference blocks are measured again collaboratively, under ratio weight. This mapping has identified the most effective reference block over the image. Now the comparative analysis on region block and aggregate block is done to finalize the reference block. The featured improvement on each block is done based on final reference block. The contrast enhancement method is shown in Algorithm 3.

Algorithm 3: ContrastEnhancementStage

ContrastEnhancementStage (Regions)

/*Regions are the feasible regions for which contrast enhancement is required*/

Begin

1.   RBlk(1)=BlockAdaptiveRegionAnalysis(Regions(i)
)/*Identify reference block for first region*/

2.   For i=2 to Regions.Lengths /*Each of region is
           evaluated for contrast enhancement*/

           Begin

3.   RBlk(i)=BlockAdaptiveRegionAnalysis(Regions(i)
) /*Identify region Reference Block*/

4.   ARef=Evaluate(RBlk(i-1),RBlk(i),Weights)
           /*Identify Aggregate Reference Block*/

           End

5.   For i=1 to Regions.Lengths /*Enhance Each of
           Region*/

           Begin

6.   Blks=GetBlocks(Region(i))   /*Obtain   Region
           Blocks*/

7.   Ref= GetQuality(ARef,RBlk(i)) /*Compare the
           Visibility and Weight of Aggregate and Region
           Reference Block and Identify Max Mapped
           Block*/

8.   ForEach Blk in Blks /*Enhance Each Region
           Block*/

           Begin

9.   Blk=Average(Blk,Ref,ARef)

           Blk.Visibilty=Ref.Visibility   /*Update   the
           Contrast Feature for Region Blocks*/

10.   UImg.Add(Blk)

           End

           End

11.   Return UImg

End

Algorithm 3 has provided the procedure for contrast enhancement based on local and aggregate reference block. To perform this enhancement, the reference block for each region is identified. The reference blocks of each region are evaluated under visibility and entropy parameters. The collaborative reference block analysis is applied to identify the aggregate reference block (ARef). At the enhancement stage, each of the reference blocks is compared to aggregate reference block and identifies the quality content constraint from the block. An average value of visibility features of input block, local reference block and aggregate block is taken to quantify the feature of region block. The average feature map based on local and global constraints is applied to achieve the smoothness and enhancement in contrast. The implementation of this method is applied real time images. The evaluation results are shown in the next section.

4 Results and Discussions

The paper has presented a ring segmented and blocks analysis method to enhance the contrast of dull and dark images. The proposed method is applied to a random set of 30 images. The collected poor contrast images are of random size. The sample images from this set are shown in Fig. 3. The proposed model is implemented in matlab 7.8 environment. The comparative analysis of proposed contrast adjustment method is done against the histogram equalization technique. The analytical evaluation is done under MSE (Mean Square Error) and PSNR (Peak Signal to Noise Ratio) parameters. In this section, the comparative results are derived to validate the significance of the proposed model

Fig. 3. Low contrast sample images

Figure 3 shows the different forms of bad contrast images. This smaller sample set includes the images from different environments and situations. The bad light, dark light, snow based, night captured and the fog affected images are shown in this sample set. Rest of the real images considered are also belongs to such complex environments and conditions. The proposed method first applied the ring segmentation to divide the image in smaller regions. The region is analyzed by placing the seed points and control points. Once the bad regions are identified, the region is divided into smaller rectangular blocks. Each of the blocks is analyzed under visibility, entropy and frequency parameters. Based on this evaluation, the reference block is obtained. The local and aggregate reference images are obtained from the work. Finally, the block level region enhancement is done by identifying the features of effective referenced block. As the proposed method is applied on the randomly captured bad contrast images, the improved balanced images are reformed. The contrast level reformed sample set images obtained from the proposed model are shown in Fig. 4.

Fig. 4. Contrast adjusted images (sampleset)

Figure 4 shows the outcome of the proposed regional segmentation assisted block feature analysis model. The figure clearly highlighted the image contents by preserving the image features. The regional map has improved the features based on the requirement. The featured analysis in each region and block is applied to identify the need of contrast enhancement. Figure 3 showed the features in real images complexly invisible and overridden. The proposed model not only enhances the contrast, but also maintained the structural features. The visible results clearly showing the strength of the proposed model. To valid the results quantitatively, the MSE and PSNR evaluation are performed on these results. The comparative results are also taken against the histogram equalization method. Figure 5 shows the MSE based comparative analysis on these 6 images.

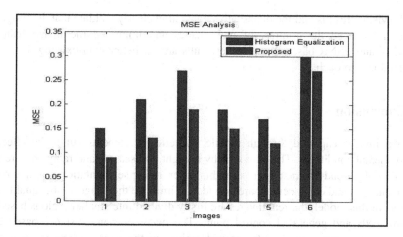

Fig. 5. MSE analysis (histogram equalization vs. proposed)

Figure 5 shows the MSE based comparative analysis of the proposed method against the histogram equalization technique. The evaluation is taken for 6 sample set images. The evaluation result shows that the error robustness of result images obtained from proposed model is higher. Another evaluation based on PSNR parameter is shown in Fig. 6.

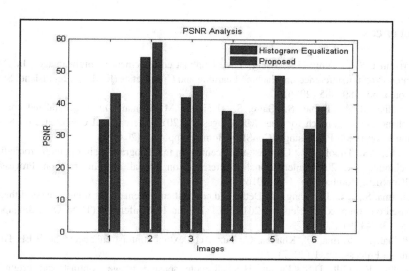

Fig. 6. PSNR analysis (histogram equalization vs. proposed)

Figure 6 shows the evaluation of proposed method against existing histogram equalization approach using PSNR parameter. This parameter defines the noise robustness of an image. The figure shows that the noise robustness of image taken from the proposed model will be higher.

The visible results and the quantitative evaluation clearly validate that the proposed approach balanced the contrast of real images and improved the image features. The MSE and PSNR based quantitative results are far better than existing histogram equalization approach.

5   Conclusion

The real images captured through mobile, surveillance cameras suffer the effect of environmental conditions. The photography in night, fog season, and rainy areas results the dark, dull or bad contrast images. In this paper, a ring segmentation adaptive block feature analysis and enhancement are provided to improve the image visible quality and features. In this model, the real images are firstly divided into smaller regions based on random seeds and generated control point. The magnitude and distance based estimation was performed to identify the bad regions of the image. These regions were divided into smaller blocks and the featured evaluation is performed on these blocks under visibility, entropy and frequency parameters. Based on the feature analysis, the local referenced block for each region is recognized. The local and aggregate reference image block based features updation is applied to enhance the quality of poor contrast image. The method is implemented on randomly captured bad contrast images. The comparative evaluation shows that the proposed method enhanced the images with better visibility and error robustness.

References

1. Priyanka, S.A., Tung, H.J., Wang, Y.K.: Contrast enhancement of night images. In: 2016 International Conference on Machine Learning and Cybernetics (ICMLC), Jeju Island, South Korea, pp. 380–385 (2016)
2. Gandhamal, A., Talbar, S., Gajre, S., Hani, A.F.M., Kumar, D.: A generalized contrast enhancement approach for knee MR images. In: 2016 International Conference on Signal and Information Processing (IConSIP), Bombay, pp. 1–6 (2016)
3. Vikhe, P.S., Thool, V.R.: Contrast enhancement in mammograms using homomorphic filter technique. In: 2016 International Conference on Signal and Information Processing (IConSIP), Bombay, pp. 1–5 (2016)
4. Sharma, S., Zou, J.J., Fang, G.: Detail and contrast enhancement for images using dithering based on complex wavelets. In: 2016 IEEE Region 10 Conference (TENCON), Singapore, pp. 1388–1391 (2016)
5. Parihar, A., Verma, O., Khanna, C.: Fuzzy-contextual contrast enhancement. IEEE Trans. Image Process. **99**, 1 (2017)
6. Mehta, R., Gill, D.S., Pannu, H.S.: Remote sensing image contrast and brightness enhancement based on Cuckoo search and DTCWT-SVD. In: 2016 International Conference on Inventive Computation Technologies (ICICT), Coimbatore, pp. 1–6 (2016)
7. Wang, L., Jung, C.: Tone-preserving contrast enhancement in images using rational tone mapping and constrained optimization. In: 2016 Visual Communications and Image Processing (VCIP), Chengdu, pp. 1–4 (2016)

8. Qureshi, M.A., Beghdadi, A., Sdiri, B., Deriche, M., Alaya-Cheikh, F.: A comprehensive performance evaluation of objective quality metrics for contrast enhancement techniques. In: 2016 6th European Workshop on Visual Information Processing (EUVIP), Marseille, pp. 1–5 (2016)

9. Mamoria, P., Raj, D.: An analysis of images using fuzzy contrast enhancement techniques. In: 2016 3rd International Conference on Computing for Sustainable Global Development (INDIACom), New Delhi, pp. 288–291 (2016)

10. Kaur, R., Kaur, S.: Comparison of contrast enhancement techniques for medical image. In: 2016 Conference on Emerging Devices and Smart Systems (ICEDSS), Namakkal, pp. 155–159 (2016)

11. Yelmanova, E.: Automatic image contrast enhancement based on the generalized contrast. In: 2016 IEEE First International Conference on Data Stream Mining & Processing (DSMP), Lviv, pp. 203–208 (2016)

12. Jabeen, A., Riaz, M.M., Iltaf, N., Ghafoor, A.: Image contrast enhancement using weighted transformation function. IEEE Sens. J. 16(20), 7534–7536 (2016)

13. Devi, G.S., Rabbani, M.M.A.: Image contrast enhancement using Histogram equalization with Fuzzy Approach on the Neighbourhood Metrics (FANMHE). In: 2016 International Conference on Wireless Communications, Signal Processing and Networking (WiSPNET), Chennai, pp. 774–777 (2016)

14. Yadav, V., Verma, M, Kaushik, V.D.: Comparative analysis of contrast enhancement techniques of different image. In: 2016 Second International Conference on Computational Intelligence & Communication Technology (CICT), Ghaziabad, pp. 76–81 (2016)

15. Kaur, A., Girdhar, A., Kanwal, N.: Region of Interest Based Contrast Enhancement Techniques for CT Images. In: 2016 Second International Conference on Computational Intelligence & Communication Technology (CICT), Ghaziabad, pp. 60–63 (2016)

16. Rajpoot, P.S, Chouksey, A.: A systematic study of well known histogram equalization based image contrast enhancement methods. In: 2015 International Conference on Computational Intelligence and Communication Networks (CICN), Jabalpur, pp. 242–245 (2015)

17. Juneja, K.: Multiple feature descriptors based model for individual identification in group photos. J. King Saud Univ. Comput. Inf. Sci. (2017) (**Available online 23 February 2017**)

18. Juneja, K.: Generalized and constraint specific composite facial search model for effective web image mining. In: 2015 International Conference on Computing and Network Communications (CoCoNet), Trivandrum, pp. 353–361 (2015)

19. Juneja, Kapil: MFAST Processing Model for Occlusion and Illumination Invariant Facial Recognition. In: Choudhary, Ramesh K., Mandal, Jyotsna Kumar, Auluck, Nitin, Nagarajaram, H.A. (eds.) Advanced Computing and Communication Technologies. AISC, vol. 452, pp. 161–170. Springer, Singapore (2016). doi:10.1007/978-981-10-1023-1_16

A Scheme of Visual Object Tracking for Human Activity Recognition in Social Media Analytics

Naresh Kumar[✉] [iD]

Department of Mathematics, Indian Institute of Technology Roorkee, Roorkee 247667, India
`atrindma@iitr.ac.in`

Abstract. Human action recognition is an open challenge in computer vision area. It means recognizing the action of human in a video. It can be divided into two steps, first step is extracting feature from video and second step is to use a classifier to find tag for the action like jump, walk, sit, hand waving etc. It is very challenging task due noise, occlusion, motion blur, and camera movement. Actions are performed by a single person or more than one person at a time. Activity recognition now a days is having a lot importance due to its many of the advantages like surveillance systems at airport, patient monitoring system, care of elderly people etc. are very few to mention. In this work we proposed Ohta color space along with RGB channel which used with LBP texture. We are extracting texture feature with the help of local binary pattern. It is used five major non uniform rotational invariant LBP and Ohta along with RGB color for the representation of the target. This scheme successfully extract the color, edge and corner information. Our proposed method maintains a trade-off between exactness of object detection and ensure that it is faster. The fusion of rotationally invariant LBP and Ohta color features make this scheme useful in object tracking for specific human activity recognition. The fused features are tested by mean shift tracker.

Keywords: Human Activity Recognition (HAR) · PCA · Local Binary Pattern (LBP) · Local Extrema Pattern (LEP) · GMM · HOG · Mean shift tracking · Social media analytics

1 Introduction

Human activities may be categorized in various sub categories which can be listed as gestural interaction, group activity. Gesture is a kind of human activity in which any particular part of human moves e.g. stretching hand, weaving hands, moving one leg, nodding etc. Action is a combination of gestures like it is the activity like walking, swimming, jumping etc. which is a combination of various gestures. Interaction is where more than one person are involved or at least one person and some other object is involved. Example of interaction can be two person sitting, one person sitting and other person standing and both are talking. Group activity is performed in the group by multiple person and object in combination. Like playing a cricket match, watching movie in a movie hall etc. are few examples of group activity. Actions are performed by a single

© Springer Nature Singapore Pte Ltd. 2017
S. Kaushik et al. (Eds.): ICICCT 2017, CCIS 750, pp. 194–204, 2017.
https://doi.org/10.1007/978-981-10-6544-6_19

person or more than one person at a time. Activity recognition now a days is having a lot importance due to its many of the advantages like surveillance systems at airport, patient monitoring system, care of elderly people etc. are very few to mention. So overall the objective is to develop a frame reference for recognition of human activities and to understand the advantages of all these things which is generally not possible to achieve through the normal video frames of human activities. Now in the market cameras are available for collecting depth information e.g. Kinect SDK launched by Microsoft in year 2011.

Now our problem definition is formulated as to recognizing the ongoing human activities with for social media in complex environment. So, it may be a single person activity like gesture or action performed or two person interaction or it may also be a group activity as per the context. Our goal is to recognize these all ongoing activities with the help of depth image frames taken from a depth camera or depth images created by some other means.

1.1 Motivation

The ability to identify and track human activity has always been very critical to variety of problems in computer vision. With the advancements in technologies of interactive multimedia devices, it has attracted researchers from the different domains for solving problems in varied fields like secure communication and surveillance for suspicious activities, smart homes, clinical and financial applications. It is not last but it never ends due to listing changed parameters that may be belongs from human biometric of human to weather forecasting. It may range from problems dealing with different scales and dealing with different scenarios like monitoring the footage of a commercial building, crowded areas like surveillance at airports, malls etc. where people will not mind watching them for monitoring cameras at doctor's clinic etc. whose information leakage to the outside world may be an issue of leakage of privacy information. Intelligent video surveillance systems aim to minimize malfunctions caused by human operators that may be due to the limited ability to monitor scenes simultaneously or lack of concentration at all times (Fig. 1).

Hence, such systems are very much demanded to boost up performance and overcome the limitations existing in the systems that involve human activity recognition and behavior analysis. Many suspicious activities and losses caused to resources as well as man power could be avoided by proper human activity monitoring systems.

Fig. 1. Activities of humanoid object

1.2   Feature Reduction for Big Data

The data consisting of only color information of any human activity through a normal camera requires a large dataset of features to get a high accuracy. This create a room for developing a robust low dimensional feature extraction technique. Overall computational complexity of recognizing activities becomes high, which is more cost effective way of recognition of activities. This problem can be resolved by depth information data. This create a room for developing a robust low dimensional feature extraction technique. Overall computational complexity of recognizing activities becomes high, which is more cost effective way of recognition of activities. This problem can be resolved by depth information data.

1.3   Representation of Objects for Tracking

Object is anything that can be used for further analysis. We can represent object by their shape and look. Based on the need of algorithm we have to represent object. Object can be point, primitive geometric shape, silhouette, articulated shape and skeleton etc. various representation as given in [1]. We can represent object by point that is centroid, or with set of points. This representation is suitable for small object which favors means to occupy small place in an image. Figure 2 represents the point, shape, silhouette, contour, skeleton and articulated object of human body.

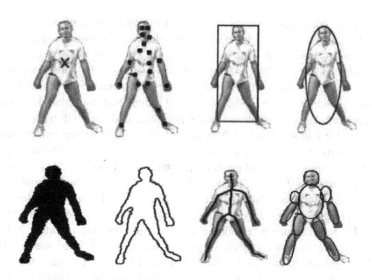

Fig. 2. Representation of object in visual tracking

2 Related Work

Object detection based on learning class models directly from the images has been proposed that utilized the intra-class variations, scale variations, boundary changes, cluttered backgrounds etc. to accurately find the object boundaries rather than just the bounding boxes [10, 11]. The exact identification of the objects was addressed based on incorporating stopping thresholds which enhanced the efficiency of the scheme [12]. The utilization of Hough transform and trained Gaussian mixture model (GMM) as well as a discriminative histogram computation further improved the efficiency of the approach [13]. Kernel based object tracking by mean shift algorithms are also considerably important for tracking the objects in multimedia analytics [1]. However, to track objects in large data models, robust template based approach has been proposed [14]. Histogram information could also be employed for object tracking. Combining the background histogram information with mean shift algorithm result in more robust object tracking [15].

Human activity recognition is one of the very active ongoing research area as it has a lot of potential applications like military, surveillance, robotics, sports and entertainment [16]. The human activities need to be assessed at atomic levels and thereafter combined to interpret the human behavior with an elaborate description [18]. Optical flow estimation relaxing the constraints via employing multiple levels of warping schemes has also been proposed to recognize human activity [18]. Usage of random forests to enhance the efficiency of performing generalized Hough transform has also been adopted where activity recognition on done on categorical basis [19]. To handle multiple activities in the same scene, unsegmented image sequences were also used [20]. For safety purposes, non-invasive techniques are applied to process videos for analysis of human behavior [21]. Automatic recognition and classification of human activities in different categories has been done in [22]. Many wavelet based algorithms have been employed for image and video processing tasks with varied mother wavelets and filters like real valued wavelet transform are efficient for detecting the isotropic objects at different scales but not well for anisotropic objects in images (e.g. lines, contours, etc.). It has many drawbacks like shift-sensitivity, poor directional selectivity, and no phase information. Hence, to tackle the translated and rotated frames of the video, complex wavelet transform has been explored. In the proposed study, we will try to explore the potential of it for human analytics. Tracking of object in video sequence is meant to estimate the position of the object in frames to meet some specific goal which is possible exactly by computing special and temporal parameters. Yilmaz et al. [1] presented literature of visual tracking. Tracking by mean shift algorithms on the basis kernel functions is very popular tool for this objective. Recently Shen et al. [14] works for developing a model which handles a huge dataset. This technique is robust for kernel tracking methodology. The mode common techniques for objective tracking literature is listed as histograms computation. Considering this as a bases, it was fused mean shift with weighted background histogram by Ning et al. in [15] which proved a robust object tracking. Recently developed techniques for object tracking are highlighted as transformation based methods. Hare et al. [23] efficiently used Daubechies complex wavelet transform for object tracking in video sequences.

Recognizing human activities from video sequences data related to social media is one of the most promising applications of computer vision. Recognition of human action from video streams has many applications in the field of surveillance, robotics, sports, military and entertainment [16]. In recent years, this problem has caught the attention of researchers from academic, industry, security agencies and consumer agencies [24]. Most of these applications require an automated recognition of high-level activities, composed of multiple simple (or atomic) actions of persons. The task of human activity recognition is to analyze human activities and produce a high level description of them [17]. Aggarwal et al. [25] provided a broad overview of several state-of-the-art methods on human activity recognition just as a base of object tracking. Brox et al. [18] used classical optical flow estimation technique and relaxed the constraints by incorporating coarse-to-fine warping schemes. Gall et al. [20] introduced Hough forests which are random forests adapted to perform a generalized Hough transform in an efficient way. In comparison to earlier Hough-based methods such as implicit shape models, their method improved the performance of the generalized Hough transform for activity recognition on a categorical level. Oikonomopoulos et al. [21] addressed the problem of object localization and their tracking in unsegmented domain for activity recognition. Their methods are robust to deal multiple activities analysis in the same scene.

3   Proposed Methodology

In the literature, several methodologies are found in the application of object tracking like in video surveillance and human action recognition. The exactness of the object tracking can be effective by selecting good features and improving the performance of tracking algorithm. We propose a joint feature descriptor of uniform rotational invariant

LBP and Ohta color features, finally mean shift algorithms is used for tracking object of our specific activity.

3.1 Feature Selection

Instead of RGB color information we can use many other uniform color scheme like L * u * v *, L * a * b * etc. but the problem is that they are sensitive to noise, change in illumination etc. RGB color feature due high dimension and non-uniformity of perception are ignored. Ohta color features (3.1), (3.2) and (3.3) are uniform and de-correlated which color is nothing but a linear transformation of the Red Green Blue channel.

$$I_1 = 1/3 * (R + G + B) \tag{3.1}$$

$$I_2 = (R - B) \tag{3.2}$$

$$I_3 = 1/2 * (2 * G - R - B) \tag{3.3}$$

3.2 Texture Feature

In this section, LBP and its variants are discussed, which is a grey-scale texture operator computes features vector based on neighboring pixel values. In the pixel value in (3.4) is non-zero for s(x) is greater or zero otherwise pixel values is zero. For $N \times M$ texture image the histogram value in (3.6) and f(x,y) in (3.5) is one for x and y having same values otherwise zero.

$$LBP_{P,R} = \sum_{p=0}^{p-1} s(g_p - g_c)2^p \tag{3.4}$$

$$s(x) = \begin{cases} 1, x \geq 0 \\ 0, otherwise \end{cases} \tag{3.5}$$

$$H(k) = \sum_{i=1}^{N} \sum_{i=1}^{M} f(LBP_{P,R})((i,j), k), k \in [0.K] \tag{3.6}$$

K is maximum pattern values corresponding to the pixel. Uniform pattern is defined in (3.7) which is a specific pattern for fixing the value of local texture of an image. The uniformity in rotational invariant LBP is shown by (3.8). If this condition is not justified the values of LBP is P + 1.

$$U(LBP_{P,R}) = \left| s(g_{p-1} - g_c) - s(g_0 - g_c) \right| + \sum_{p=1}^{p-1} \left| s(g_p - g_c) - s(g_{p-1} - g_c) \right| \tag{3.7}$$

$$LBP_{P,R}^{riu2} = \begin{cases} \sum_{p=0}^{p-1} s(g_p - g_c), & if \ U(LBP_{P,R}) \ll 2 \\ P+1, & otherwise \end{cases} \quad (3.8)$$

3.3 Mean Shift Tracking

Tracking process is performed by mean shift algorithms according which the center of origin is denoted the normalize pixel location in target region. We keep on adding the frame to the tracker till the exactness in the object detection is justified. The iteration of mean shift tracker for specified object is shown in Fig. 3.

Fig. 3. Frame wise location updates using mean shift iterations

3.4 Proposed System Frame Work

Object tracking method [7] is proposed by fusing the histogram of color information with texture information for feature representation and mean shift for tracking. Local binary pattern is applied to extract texture features of the target and after that joint features of color texture are used for more descriptive, effective, informative representation of the specified target. The uniform local binary pattern forms a mask by testing the key point in target domain. Our proposed method utilizes rotational invariant LBP and Ohta color along with RGB color. Ohta color channel and LBP fusion represent the target domain. Then we applied these features on mean shift tracker for tracking our specified region. We use 8 * 8 * 8 and 5 histogram bin for storing color and texture distribution respectively. First bin represent ohta color and last represent LBP texture. The complete system for propose work in shown in Fig. 4 in which a sequence of video from which local uniform rotational invariant LBP and color features histogram are computed. The fused features are fed up to mean shift tracker.

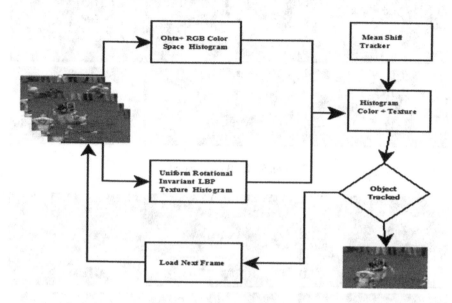

Fig. 4. System frame work of proposed methodology

4   Results and Evaluations

In this work, we illustrate the result of proposed method by performing extensive and representative experiment. We compare our result with covariance technique of color information, joint color texture histogram and joint color LEP histogram. Two different videos are used in evaluating our proposed method represented in Figs. 5 and 6 respectively. In first case there are total 58 frames while second case, we have taken 87 frames. This experiment is carried out in MATLAB 2015b and runs on a laptop with Intel core i5, 2.3 GHz processor with 8 GB RAM. The tracking speed and accuracy is shown for both the experimental videos. Tracking speed and accuracy matters for the object of interest and outer environment also. In first experiment, we computed for face tracking of tennis player and in second experiment, the face of a rugby player is tracked (Table 1) (Figs. 7, 8).

Table 1. Comparison of tracking speed on two videos

No. of frames in video sequence	Joint color LBP (tracking speed), s	Joint color LEP (tracking speed), s	Proposed (tracking speed) method, s
58	9.38	9	8.8
87	17.8	16.61	17

Fig. 5. RGB color based

Fig. 6. Joint color LBP texture

Fig. 7. Joint color LEP texture

Fig. 8. Proposed method

5 Conclusion and Future Scope

In this research work we have proposed Ohta color space along with RGB channel which used with LBP texture. We are extracting texture feature with the help of local binary pattern. The local binary pattern is a very effective tool for the spatial structure of the local image pattern. We used five major non uniform rotational invariant LBP and Ohta along with RGB color for the representation of the target. This scheme successfully extract the color, edge and corner information. Our proposed method maintain a trade-off between accuracy and speed.

Our experimental result shows that proposed method is more accurate than others and also can handle occlusion, appearance change, complex background, camera motion and illumination change. Real time processing of data is still difficult because of the complexity of the algorithm, so in future we can further optimize our algorithm so that we can make our algorithm to handle the real time processing more easily. This work is still open for multiple camera and multiple object tracking to recognize human activity in complex environment. Depth information gives recognition rate is higher as compared to non-depth map based recognition. Less computational complexity in terms of feature extraction. There is lot to improve on single person, two person activity recognition and work can be done on group activity recognition which is yet to be explored using depth maps.

References

1. Yilmaz, A., Javed, O., Shah, M.: Object tracking: a survey. ACM Comput. Surv. (2006)
2. Ojala, T., Pietikainen, M., Harwood, D.: A comparative study of texture measure with classification based on feature distribution. Pattern Recognit. (1995)
3. Ojala, T., Pietikainen, M., Maenpaa, T.: Multiresolution gray-scale and rotation invariant texture classification with local binary patterns. IEEE Trans. Pattern Anal. Mach. Intell. (2002)
4. Tan, X., Triggs, B.: Enhanced local texture feature sets for face recognition under difficult lighting conditions. IEEE Trans. (2010)

5. Gauglitz, S., Höllerer, T., Turk, M.: Evaluation of interest point detectors and feature descriptors for visual tracking. Int. J. Comput. Vis. **94**(3), 335 (2011)

6. Calonder, M., Lepetit, V., Ozuysal, M., Trzcinski, T., Strecha, C., Fua, P.: BRIEF: computing a local binary descriptor very fast. IEEE Trans. Pattern Anal. Mach. Intell. **34**(7), 1281–1298 (2012)

7. Ning, J., Zhang, L., Zhang, D., Wu, C.: Robust object tracking using joint color-texture histogram. Int. J. Pattern Recognit. Artif. Intell. (2009)

8. Comaniciu, D., Ramesh, V., Meer, P.: Kernel-based object tracking. IEEE Trans. Pattern Anal. Mach. Intell. (2003)

9. Sonka, M., Hlavac, V., Boyle, R.: Image Processing, Analysis and Machine Vision. Thomson Asia Pvt. Ltd., Singapore (2001)

10. Ferrari, V., Jurie, F., Schmid, C.: From images to shape models for object detection. Int. J. Comput. Vis. **87**(3), 284–303 (2010)

11. Ferrari, V., Fevrier, L., Jurie, F., Schmid, C.: Groups of adjacent contour segments for object detection. IEEE Trans. Pattern Anal. Mach. Intell. **30**(1), 36–51 (2008)

12. Ferencz, A., Learned-Miller, E.G., Malik, J.: Learning to locate informative features for visual identification. Int. J. Comput. Vis. **77**(1), 3–24 (2008)

13. Lehmann, A., Leibe, B., Van Gool, L.: Fast PRISM: branch and bound hough transform for object class detection. Int. J. Comput. Vis. **94**(2), 175–197 (2011)

14. Shen, C., Kim, J., Wang, H.: Generalized kernel-based visual tracking. IEEE Trans. Circuits Syst. Video Technol. **20**(1), 119–130 (2010)

15. Ning, J., Zhang, L., Zhang, D., Wu, C.: Robust mean shift tracking with corrected background - weighted histogram. IEEE Comput. Vis. **6**(1), 62–69 (2012)

16. Weiming, H., Tan, T.: A survey on visual surveillance of object motion and behaviors. IEEE Trans. Syst. Man Cybern. C Appl. Rev. **34**(3), 334–351 (2004)

17. Poppe, R.: A survey on vision based human action recognition. Image Vis. Comput. **28**, 976–990 (2010)

18. Brox, T., Malik, J.: Large displacement optical flow: descriptor matching in variational motion estimation. IEEE Trans. Pattern Anal. Mach. Intell. **33**(3), 500–513 (2011)

19. Gall, J., Yao, A., Razavi, N., Van Gool, L.: Hough forests for object detection, tracking, and action recognition. IEEE Trans. Pattern Anal. Mach. Intell. **33**(11), 2188–2202 (2011). doi: 10.1109/TPAMI.2011.70

20. Oikonomopoulos, A., Patras, I., Pantic, M.: Spatiotemporal localization and categorization of human actions in unsegmented image sequences. IEEE Trans. Image Process. **20**(4), 1126–1140 (2011)

21. Cucchiara, R., Grana, C., Prati, A., Vezzani, R.: Probabilistic posture classification for human-behavior analysis. IEEE Trans. Man Cybern. A Syst. Hum. **35**(1), 42–54 (2005)

22. Turaga, P., Chellappa, R., Subrahmanian, V.S., Udrea, O.: Machine recognition of human activities: a survey. IEEE Trans. Circuits Syst. Video Technol. **18**(11), 1473–1488 (2008)

23. Khare, A., Tiwary, U.S.: Daubechies complex wavelet transform based moving object tracking. In: IEEE Symposium on Computational Intelligence in Image and Signal Processing, pp. 36–40 (2007)

24. Masoud, O., Papanikolopoulos, N.: A method for human action recognition. Image Vis. Comput. **21**, 729–743 (2003)

25. Aggarwal, J.K., Ryoo, M.S.: Human activity analysis: a review. ACM Comput. Surv. **43**(3) (2011)

DNA Based Cryptography

Archana Gahlaut$^{(\boxtimes)}$ ⓘ, Amit Bharti ⓘ, Yash Dogra ⓘ,
and Puneet Singh ⓘ

Department of Computer Science, Atma Ram Sanatan Dharma College,
University of Delhi, New Delhi, India
archana.gahlaut@gmail.com, amitbharti43@gmail.com,
yashdogra31@gmail.com, puneet.singh0902@gmail.com

Abstract. A new emerging research topic in the field of Information storage, security and cryptography is DNA based cryptography. DNA is known to carry information from one generation to other and is turning out to be very promising for cryptography. The storage capacity, vast parallelism of DNA are used for cryptographic purposes. In this paper, we will talk about progress of DNA cryptography, discuss DNA computing, and propose a method for DNA based cryptography through 3 phases where we will first encrypt the plaintext through our proposed encryption algorithm and then prepare a desired DNA sequence ready to send.

Keywords: DNA based cryptography · DNA computing · AYP algorithm

1 Introduction

As the security threats are increasing day by day, information security is a major concern today. Data needs to be encrypted while transmitting in order to ensure the security of data. Cryptography is the practice of hiding information. Cryptographic techniques help in ensuring the security of such sensitive information. DNA cryptography is a new and promising technique in the field of cryptography. In DNA cryptography, information carriers are the DNA nucleotides (denoted by the letters A, C, G and T). The main advantage of DNA cryptography is high storage capacity of DNA, vast parallelism, lower power consumption with extraordinary performance.

1.1 DNA (Deoxyribonucleic Acid)

DNA is a molecule which is present nearly in all living organisms. It transmits the genetic information required for the growth, development, and functioning of all living organisms (including viruses). DNA is found mostly in the nucleus of the cell (Nuclear DNA) but a small proportion of it is also located in the mitochondria (Mitochondrial DNA). The genetic information stored in DNA molecule is in the form of code which consists of four chemical bases namely Adenine (A), Guanine (G), Cytosine (C), and Thymine (T). The above mentioned chemical bases pair up with each other in a way

© Springer Nature Singapore Pte Ltd. 2017
S. Kaushik et al. (Eds.): ICICCT 2017, CCIS 750, pp. 205–215, 2017.
https://doi.org/10.1007/978-981-10-6544-6_20

such that each base is having a specific partner. So overall we have two pairs which are as follows:

1. 'A' always pair up with 'T' and vice versa.
2. 'C' always pair up with 'G' and vice versa.

And they form units which are known as Base Pairs. Each base is also linked to two other molecules namely Sugar molecule, Phosphate molecule. Unitedly a base along with the sugar and the phosphate molecule are known as Nucleotide.

1.2   Structure of DNA

Nucleotides are organized in two long strands which form the spiral known as Double Helix. Thus the structure of DNA is commonly known as the Double Helix Structure. The Double Helix is somewhat similar to a ladder in which the sugar and phosphate molecules are forming the vertical side pipes and the base pair forming the steps of the ladder (Fig. 1).

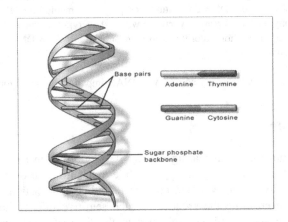

Fig. 1. Double Helix Structure of DNA

1.3   DNA Computing

DNA computing is an emergent field of the computing in which we use the concept of biochemistry, molecular biology hardware along with DNA in place of conventional silicon based computer technology. Leonard Adleman of the University of Southern California in 1994 was the first one known for the creation and initiation of this field. Adleman exhibits a proof-of-concept to solve the Seven-Point Hamiltonian path problem which is using DNA molecule as a means of computation [1].

In the year 2002, researchers of the Weizmann Institute of Science in Rehovot, Israel, uncovers a programmable molecular computing device made up of DNA molecules and enzymes in place of Silicon Microchips [2]. On April 28, 2004, Yaakov Benenson, Ehud Shapiro, Uri Ben-Dor, Binyamin Gil, and Rivka Adar at the Weizmann Institute declared in the journal Nature that they had developed a DNA computer attached to an input and output module which would be theoretically efficient of identifying cancerous activity in a cell, and delivering an anti-cancer drug upon recognition [3]. In January 2013, researchers were able to store a set of Shakespearean sonnets, an audio file of Martin Luther King, Jr.'s speech "I Have a Dream" and a JPEG picture on DNA digital data storage [4]. In March 2013, researchers bring into existence a transcriptor (a biological transistor) [5].

2 DNA Cryptography (Related Work)

In 1994, Adleman used molecular computation to solve the combinatorial problems such as "Hamiltonian path" problem and laid the foundation of DNA computing [1].

In 2003, Jie Chen used DNA cryptographic approach which included one-time pad, molecular theory, and performed encryption and decryption of a 2-dimensional image [6].

In 2004, Ashish Gehani used molecular approach and one-time pad and laid the foundation of DNA cryptography [7]. According to Vernam and Shannon, who are the inventor of one-time pad, it has perfect secrecy. They proposed a method which uses DNA chip and one-time pad for encryption and decryption. Hence it is very difficult to guess any encrypted message for the adversary.

In 2013, Monica Borda and Olga Tornea proposed a DNA based cipher based on DNA indexing [8].

3 Experimental Work

3.1 AYP Algorithm

Input: Plaintext, Key String
Output: Cipher text
Rule to be followed to encrypt the given plaintext using AYP – algorithm

(a) First create the key matrix
The key matrix here is of 5×5 order therefore we can accommodate only 25 alphabets of English letters (as a convention i and j are considered the same while encrypting).

- To create the key matrix first both ALICE and BOB needs to agree on a secret key string.
- After agreeing on a secret key string start writing the key diagonally in the matrix. (Starting from the main diagonal and filling the diagonals of lower triangle and then filling the diagonal of the upper triangle if key length is more than the length of the main diagonal. Also keep in mind that only distinct characters of the key string needs to be filled in the matrix.)
- After filling the secret key sting the key matrix fill the remaining cell of the matrix (if any) in the alphabetical order starting form the first empty cell in the matrix.

We can use any pattern while filling the key Matrix but both sender and receiver must use the same pattern while creating the key matrix.

(b) Locate the character of the plaintext in the key matrix one by one. And for each plaintext character we have to select 2 character from the matrix and these 2 character are the encrypted character for that particular plaintext character.

Here we have a total of 2 cases and further each case have sub-cases also.

Case 1. (Single diagonal possible) plaintext character is at one of the 4 corner position of the matrix (Fig. 2).

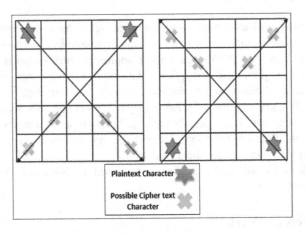

Fig. 2. Case 1

Case 2. (2 diagonals are possible)

Always move in one step away from the plaintext character on the diagonal.

2.1 Two diagonals are possible and both the diagonal are intersecting at the cell containing the plaintext character itself (Fig. 3).

Odd occurrence of the plaintext character means if the plaintext character comes for the

$$\text{1st 3rd 5th.........................}(2n+1)\text{th}$$

Then we need to follow the 1st diagram

Even occurrence of the plaintext character means if the plaintext character comes for the

$$\text{2nd 4th 6th...............................}(2n)\text{th}$$

Then we need to follow the 2nd diagram.

Remark 1. 0th occurrence here has no meaning.

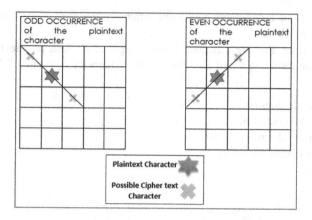

Fig. 3. Case 2.1

2.2 Two diagonal are still possible but one of the diagonals have only one character for that particular plaintext character.

Also we can say that here both the diagonal form right angle with the plain text character at the vertex of the right angle (Fig. 4).

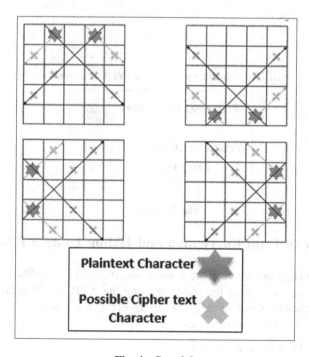

Fig. 4. Case 2.2

2.3 Exactly same case as above with one difference that here any one out of the two Diagonals can be chosen.

Also we can say that both diagonals form a right angle with plaintext character at the vertex of the right angle and also the plaintext character is in one of the following positions

- 1st row middle column.
- 5th row middle column.
- 1st column middle row.
- 5th column middle row (Fig. 5).

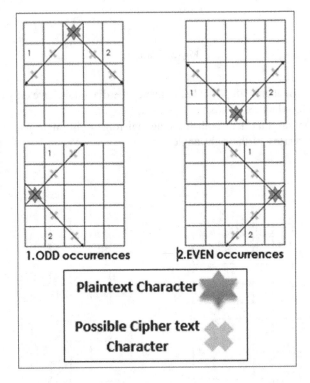

Fig. 5. Case 2.3

4   DNA Based Data Encryption and Hiding Using 3 Phases

Phase I. Encrypting the data using the above specified AYP algorithm.

In this we are encrypting the plaintext using the AYP algorithm to produce the intermediate text that is further encrypted in the upcoming phases.

For this we need following things

(a) Plaintext: Data to be encrypted.
(b) Secret key String: Both sender and receiver need to agree upon a secret string that is known only to them and this string is used to create the Key matrix.

So the basic idea or Aim of this phase is to encrypt the plaintext using the AYP algorithm thereby creating the intermediate text ready to be used in the upcoming phases.

Phase II. Increasing security (making resistant to statistical attack).

Basic idea behind introducing this phase is to disturb frequency of 2 letter string (digrams) and 3 letter string (trigrams) thereby making it resistant to statistical attacks.

Let's say we have a plaintext string as "eeste" and suppose that the letter "e" happens to be in one of the position marked in the Fig. 6.

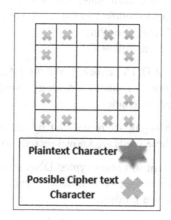

Fig. 6. If the plaintext character is in one of the positions marked above

Then doesn't matter - how many times the letter "e" comes OR whether it is the odd occurrence or even occurrence of letter same 2 letter will be used to encrypt the letter "e".

This happens so because in these cases we don't have any choice to choose from we have either only one diagonal OR two diagonals with one containing only one letter (character).

So if we don't apply phase II it will be very easy for the attacker to guess at least that the letter in the plaintext at these position must be same.

So we recommend applying well known traditional ciphers such as double-transposition/transposition cipher to the intermediate text produced after the Phase I just to jumble the intermediate text characters so that guessing won't be that easy.

Phase III. Hiding the encrypted data into the reference dna sequence using and insertion technique [9]

For this phase we will first convert the encrypted text obtained after the phase 2 to the Binary form. Then by using the Binary coding rule this binary form of data in converted into a DNA sequence (Table 1).

Table 1. Binary Coding Rule

BASE	BINARY CODE
A	00
C	01
G	10
T	11

Now we will use the above encrypted DNA sequence and the reference DNA sequence as input to the insertion technique. This insertion technique was originally introduced in [10] and was also modified in [9]. Now we have further modified this technique in accordance with our algorithm.

This technique is explained as follows.

1. First divide both encrypted DNA sequence and the reference DNA sequence into segments where each segments contains a random number of DNA nucleotides so the segments are not fixed in length.

   (Random length of each segments is decided by the random number generator which seeds are passed and these seeds are known secretly to both sender and receiver.)

2. Next we insert each segment of the encrypted DNA sequence before the segments of reference DNA sequence respectively finally we get a faked DNA sequence with the encrypted DNA sequence hidden.

   Finally we present our algorithm and we call this as AYP- Insertion algorithm

   The proposed AYP-Insertion algorithm can be summarized in the following steps and figure below is the block diagram that illustrates this algorithm in a better way.

Input: Plaintext P, Secret key string for AYP key matrix, Secret seeds, Key for Double Transposition cipher, Reference DNA sequence.

Output: Faked DNA sequence with hidden plaintext in it.

1. First make the key matrix using the method described in the AYP Algorithm using the secret key string.
2. Encrypt the plaintext using the AYP algorithm to produce the intermediate text to be further encrypted by the Phase II of the AYP-Insertion Algorithm.
3. Now apply the Double transposition cipher to further encrypt the intermediate text. After this step we finally get out cipher text.
4. Convert the cipher text obtained from above in binary form using 4 - bits coding (*By first converting the whole cipher text in ASCII and then converting it into the binary from where each of the digits is converted to 4 bit binary number.*
   Ex. 6 is converted to 0110
   1 is converted to 0001).
5. After converting the cipher text into binary from use binary coding scheme to convert the same into a DNA sequence. For simplicity let's call this encrypted DNA sequence be DS and length of DNA sequence be represented as [DS].

6. Now generate the Random number sequence $r_1, r_2, r_3, r_4\ldots\ldots\ldots\ldots$ using the random number generator seed R and another random number sequence $k_1, k_2, k_3, k_4\ldots\ldots\ldots\ldots$ using the random number generator seed K

7. Then find the smallest integer "t" such that ......

$$\sum_{i=1}^{t} r_i > [DS]$$

8. Now divide the DS into segments with length $r_1, r_2, r_3, r_4\ldots\ldots\ldots\ldots\ldots\ldots\ldots\ldots\ldots r_{t-1}$ for the simplicity we denote these segment by the $DS_1, DS_2, DS_3, DS_4\ldots\ldots\ldots\ldots DS_{t-1}$ and let the residual part be DS_t

9. Now divide the reference DNA sequence into segments of length $k_1, k_2, k_3, k_4\ldots\ldots\ldots\ldots\ldots\ldots k_{t-1}$ and truncate the residual part of theREF. For simplicity we denote these segments by the $REF_1, REF_2, REF_3, REF_4\ldots\ldots\ldots\ldots\ldots REF_{t-1}$

10. Insert each DS_i, where $1 \leq i \leq t-1$ of DS before each segment of Reference DNA string i.e., before REF_i.

11. Finally put the DS_t in the end of the sequence to produce the Faked DNA sequence with the encrypted data hidden.

Let's denote this faked DNA sequence be C.

To use this method what we require is

1. Secret Key String for AYP Key Matrix [SK].
2. Key for the Double Transposition cipher [DT].
3. Two random number seeds [R] and [K].

So the Faked DNA sequence C can be send in public channel while [SK], [DT], [R], [K], [T] need to be sent on secure channel between sender and the receiver.

The receiver should follow the following algorithm to recover the hidden data and perform the subsequent decryption:

1. Generate two number sequences
   $r_1, r_2, r_3, r_4\ldots\ldots\ldots\ldots\ldots\ldots$ and $k_1, k_2, k_3, k_4\ldots\ldots\ldots\ldots\ldots\ldots$
   By using the same random number generator and the seeds [R] and [K] respectively.

2. Now find the largest integer "n" such that

$$\sum_{i=1}^{n} r_i + k_i \leq [C]$$

And divide the [C] into segments with lengths

$$r_1 + k_1, r_2 + k_2, r_3 + k_3\ldots\ldots\ldots\ldots\ldots\ldots r_n + k_n$$

And the remaining part of C is denoted as DS_{n+1}

3. For each segment i, $1 \leq i \leq n$ of C extract the first r_i bits called DS_i and concatenate all DS_i where $i \leq j \leq n+1$ to be DS.
4. Convert DS into binary form and group into groups of 4 bits each and convert it into the corresponding decimal digit.

   After this we get a string containing digit only. Now divide this string obtained into groups containing 2 digits only. Now convert each group to its corresponding English alphabet characters.

   Remark 2. Here we are assuming that plaintext consists only uppercase letters just for simplicity. We can also do this encryption decryption process if the plaintext is a mixture of both upper case and lower case with a little bit of manipulation.
5. Now apply decryption process of Double Transposition Cipher.
6. After that to Decrypt further the receiver needs to construct the AYP Key Matrix.
7. Now again group the obtain text into groups contain 2 letters each. And locate the letters of each group in the AYP Key Matrix and just follow reverse of the steps that are followed while selecting the encrypted characters for a particular plaintext character.

5   Conclusion

In this paper, we discussed new chapter in information security. i.e. DNA Based Cryptography. The storage capacity, vast parallelism of DNA are its main advantages for cryptographic purposes. We presented an Encryption algorithm named AYP Algorithm. We then used this algorithm in DNA based cryptography which we discussed through the 3 phases where in phase 1 we are using AYP algorithm and we can clearly see that number of characters in the intermediate text after Phase I is getting double. This helps us to increase the number of possible ways thereby making the brute force attack more difficult.

References

1. Adleman, L.M.: Molecular computation of solutions to combinatorial problems. Science **266** (5187), 1021–1024 (1994)
2. Lovgren, Stefan (2003-02-24). Computer Made from DNA and Enzymes. National Geographic. Retrieved 2009-11-26
3. Benenson, Y., Gil, B., Ben-Dor, U., Adar, R., Shapiro, E.: An autonomous molecular computer for logical control of gene expression. Nature **429**(6990), 423–429 (2004)
4. DNA stores poems, a photo and a speech|Science News
5. Bonnet, Jerome, Yin, Peter, Ortiz, Monica E., Subsoontorn, Pakpoom, Endy, Drew: Amplifying Genetic Logic Gates. Science **340**, 599–603 (2013)
6. Jie, C.: A DNA-based bio molecular cryptography design. Proc. IEEE Int. Symp. **3**, III–822 (2003)
7. A. Gehani, T.H. LaBean, J.H. Reif: DNA-based cryptography. DNA Based Computers V. Providence **54**, 233–249 (2000)

8. O. Tornea, .B.E. Monica: Security and complexity of a DNA-based cipher. In Roedunet International Conference (RoEduNet), 11th IEEE International Conference (2013)

9. Atito, A., Khalifa, A., Rida, S.Z.: DNA-based data encryption and hiding using playfair andinsertion techniques. J. Commun. Comput. Eng. **2**(3), 44–49 (2012)

10. Shiu, H.J., et al.: Data hiding methods based upon DNA sequences. Inf. Sci. **180**, 2196–2208 (2010)

A Noise Robust VDD Composed PCA-LDA Model for Face Recognition

Kapil Juneja(✉)

Department of Computer Science and Engineering,
University Institute of Engineering and Technology,
Maharshi Dayanand University, Rohtak 124001, Haryana, India
kapil.juneja81@gmail.com, kapil.juneja.1981@ieee.org

Abstract. Face recognition is most widely used biometric realization approach implemented as online, offline and mobile services. Noise is one major disturbing factor that misrepresents the image and obscures the facial features. Image reformation aims to fix the noise impact and enhance the recognition rate. In this paper, a dual mode VDD (Vector-Directional-Distance) impainting method is presented to preserve the image content. VDD filter is composition of Vector-Directional and Directional-Distance filter. The rectified image is processed under Gabor filter to generate the robust structural and textural feature. The featured image is mapped under PCA and LDA classifiers. The method is implemented on salt & pepper, Gaussian and Poisson Noise included Utrecht ECVP and Stirling datasets. The comparative observation is taken against the Median filter, Gaussian Filter and Morphological Filter rectified PCA and LDA methods. The comparative observation identified the significance of VDD filter over other face rectification methods considered in this work. The evaluation results show that VDD-composed PCA-LDA method has enhanced the accuracy of face recognition for noise disturbed images.

Keywords: Object recognition · Image segmentation · Object identification · Reconstruction · Matching · Noise reduction · Biometrics · Visual content-based indexing and retrieval · Appearance and texture representations · Interest point · Salient region detection

1 Introduction

Today, most of the online and offline authentication systems are inspired from the biometric recognition system. Face recognition [1–5] is one of the favourite identification systems because of its versatile support for various applications. The wider scope of facial recognition system is because of easy capturing of face image through low cost camera and mobile devices. Such low configuration devices or cameras result the low resolution or the noisy image. Noise is just the variation of the image pixels that disrupt the actual image information. Noise can be generated from the device itself, if the device has poor sensors, film grain, etc. The inclusive noise is categorized as the additive and the multiplicative noise [8–11]. As the name describes the accumulative

S. Kaushik et al. (Eds.): ICICCT 2017, CCIS 750, pp. 216–229, 2017.
https://doi.org/10.1007/978-981-10-6544-6_21

noise add some noisy information to the image pixel intensity and distort the image, given as.

$$\text{NoiseImage(i, j)} = \sum_{w}^{i=1} \sum_{h}^{j=1} (TrueImage(i,j) + Noise(i,j)) \qquad (1)$$

$$i = 1 \quad j = 1$$

Here in Eq. (1) TrueImage is the source image of size w × h. Noise is the additive noise vector added to each pixel within the image. The noise value can be 0 or can be set from the variance. NoiseImage is the infected image obtained after the noise inclusion over the image. The multiplicative noise is another noise form distributed over the image in a nonlinear fashion. Multiplicative noise is distributed under mathematical approach because of this it is difficult to analyze and remove. These different noise forms with relative categories are shown in Fig. 1.

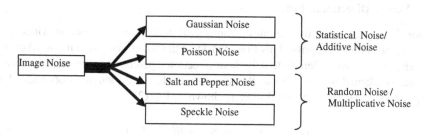

Fig. 1. Different noise types

One of the most common noise types is Gaussian noise or sometimes called Gaussian white noise. It is additive noise that performs the normal distribution of the noise over the image. This noise form is specified by using the mean and the variance of the image. Gaussian noise exists in different forms including film grain noise, photon counting noise and thermal noise [1]. Another kind of noise based on the statistical formula is the Poisson noise [6]. This noise model is based on the Poisson distribution.

Instead of using the statistics based noise model there also exist random noise model such as salt and pepper [7] noise. This noise model basically on-off the arbitrary pixels over the image. This noise is an impulse noise that can be generated because of some internal circuit problem or the light flash, etc. Speckle noise [8] is also the multiplicative noise model as granular noise which affects the gray level of pixels. Speckle noise increase surface roughness of the image and this distortion occur because of electromagnetic effect.

In this paper, VDD-PCA and VDD LDA model are provided to rectify the image and to obtain the effective noise robust face recognition. The paper has proven the significance of both the image rectification method and the face recognition model. In this section, the exploration of serious noise threat to face recognition system is identified. The section explained different noise and their impact on facial recognition system. In Sect. 2, the characterization of various noise rectification methods is provided. In Sect. 3, the VDD-PCA and VDD-LDA method is inspected with algo-rithmic formulation. In Sect. 4, the comparative evaluation of the proposed method against Median, Gaussian and Morphological rectified classification method is pro-vided. In Sect. 5, the conclusion obtained from the proposed model is presented.

2 Noise-Rectification Methods

The reliability of the facial recognition process depends on the transformation of an image to the normalized image. A normalized image is defined as the identical image in brightness, contrast, size and should be noise free. However, the image taken from the primary source can have kind of distortion because of device fault or some other technical factor. In this section, the characterization and process modeling of various noise rectification methods are discussed.

2.1 Vector Directional Filter

Vector directional (Vd) filter applies a directional analysis on processing window to maintain the content integrity. This filter considers the target pixel as centralized object and evaluates the vector length to neighbour directional pixels. The directional ordering statistics is adapted by this filter as the reduction in the vector length is obtained. The computation of vector directional filter is shown in Eq. (2)

$$Vd_i = \left(\sum_{j=1}^{n} FaceImgBlk(f_i, f_j) \right) \tag{2}$$

Where

$$FaceImgBlk(f_i, f_j) = cos^{-1} \left(\frac{f_i f_j}{|f_i|,|f_j|} \right)$$

f_i is the image function
FaceImgBlk is the processing window
n is the number of pixels in the processing window
j is the relative pixels for directional distance evaluation

To preserve the content information in the processing window, the Vd filter shrinks the accumulated angles relative to base pixel. In the proposed VDD inclusive filter, the directional observation is applied at an earlier stage to gain the corrupted contents of face image. The magnitude level processing in the subsequent processing window can revive the image structure integrity.

2.2 Directional-Distance Filter

Directional distance (Dd) filter applies the multiplication based method based on inter-channel correlation and directional distance estimation. To strengthen the corre-lation of processing window pixels, the normalized Euclidean distance is obtained.

The likelihood estimation on neighbouring pixels is obtained and relative correlation update is gained. This correlation (Cr) filter is shown in Eq. (3)

$$C_i = \sum_{j=1}^{n} ||f_i - f_j||, \quad i = 1 \text{ to } n \tag{3}$$

Here, f is the correlation evaluation function within process window
n is the number of pixels in processing window
j is the relative pixels in processing window
C is the correlation preserved filter to maintain the pixel integrity

The Directional-Distance (Dd) filter combines the functionality of the Eqs. (2) and (3) using multiplication operator. The educational representation of this filter is shown in Eq. (4). The filter revives the pixel integrity under correlation normalization and neighbourhood directional consideration.

$$Dd_i = \left(\sum_{j=1}^{n} ||f_i - f_j|| \right) \cdot \left(\sum_{j=1}^{n} FaceImgBlk(f_i, f_j) \right) \tag{4}$$

Dd filter enhances the processing window quality by reducing the distance and the aggregate angle collectively. It can restore the brightness and chrominance information of the pixel. As the brightness and contrast are adjusted and normalized, the information loss is recovered significantly. The multispectral quality of this filter able to provide the significant results against different noise forms.

2.3   Median Filter

Median filter [12] is a low pass filtration tool which is very adaptive to remove the impulse noise from the image such as speckle noise. However, in this work, the comparative evaluation is taken against the median filter for all four kinds of noise defined in this paper earlier. Median filter moves a filter window of defined size over the image as shown in Fig. 2.

Fig. 2. Median filter moving window architecture

The size of the moving window can be of any odd size such as $3 \times 3, 5 \times 5, 7 \times 7$ or more. In Fig. 2, the active window of size 3×3 is shown that will move up-to-down and left-to-right over the image.

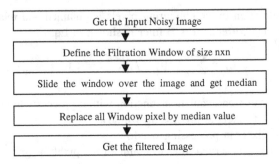

Fig. 3. Median filter for denoising

Each pixel of the image covered by moving window will be multiplied by the value at pixel position. Now the median of these values will be taken, and all the pixels of window area will be replaced by this median value. The basic steps followed by the approach are shown in Fig. 3.

2.4   Morphological Filter

Morphological Filter [13, 14] approach is a mathematical approach defined by the collection of operators. These operators include the closing, opening, erosion and dilation. The morphological filter is a shape oriented nonlinear filter in which the mathematical approach is implemented over the image in small segments. These segments are specified along with segment shape and the size. These operators will perform the structural changes in the image and get the smoothness over the image to reduce the noise. In this present work, three morphological operators in a sequence: Dilation, Opening and Closing. The overall procedure followed by the morphological operator approach is shown in Fig. 4.

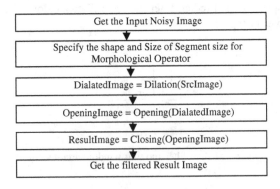

Fig. 4. Morphological operator

Let A is the Image Segment, and B is the component for morphological filter and the size and shape of both A and B is same. Then the dilation operator basically expands the size of connected component over the image. The dilation operator is given by the **A** ⊕ **B**. The erosion operator performs the work just inverse to the dilation operator. The erosion operator shrinks the size of connected component over the image. Other two operators are the composite functions. The opening operator is erosion operator followed by dilation, and the closing operator is defined as the dilation operator followed by the erosion operator.

2.5 Gaussian Filter

Gaussian filter [15] is a convolution filter based approach in which the convolution matrix is defined in the form a moving filtered window. This window is moved over the image, and the matrix values are multiplied with the image pixel under the matrix segment. Now the sum of these values is taken and divided by some value. Straight away this obtained value is placed at the center position in the matrix position in the image. The approach implemented here is shown in the form a flowchart shown in Fig. 5.

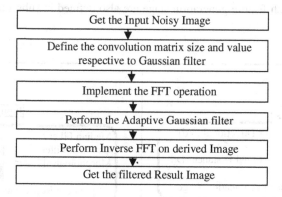

Fig. 5. Gaussian filter

The Gaussian filter is based on the mean or the standard deviation on the matrix segment over the image. In this work, we have used the mean value to replace the center pixel. Because of this, the approach increases the smoothness because of repetitive pixels of the same intensity.

3 Proposed Model

The noise occurred from several means signify that it is difficult to avoid the noise existence. In Face recognition, the presence of noise will definitely degrade the accuracy ratio. It designates the integration of essential noise processing stage in each image processing model. In this paper, the improvement to the traditional face recognition model is provided by hybrid face rectification stage. The proposed VDD composed

PCA-LDA PCA model shown in Fig. 6 has integrated a dual mode face rectification layer to revive the noise impurities and restructure a clean face. VDD is the face rectification stage composed of Vector Directional (Vd) and Directional Distance (Dd). Individual functionality of these methods is already explained in Sects. 2.1 and 2.2. In this proposed model, the sequential mapping of these two rectification methods is applied to generate more revive the face image. Vd first applied the directional observation to rectify the magnitude level deficiencies. This contrast managed image is then evaluated using Directional-Distance (Dd) method. This method applied the distance and directional observation collectively to balance the luminance and the contrast value. This dual phase rectification improves, rectified and balanced the facial features. After obtaining the clean revived face image, the feature extraction stage is applied over it. The Gabor and eigenface feature extraction are performed on this normalized clean face image. A dual map of these two feature aspects is applied to recognize the face accurately. LDA is applied on both PCA featured dataset and Gabor featured dataset. LDA generated a maximum mapped subset for both Eigen featured and Gabor featured set. These subsets are compared internally to identify the maximum matched common image and considered it as the recognized face image. The algorithmic formulation and the exploration of each feature generation stage are also defined in subsections.

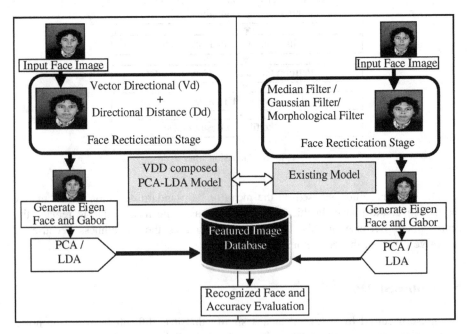

Fig. 6. VDD composed PCA-LDA model

3.1 PCA

The input rectified image is processed by the model under eigenface to generate the feature image. To generate the eigenface at first the mean and the covariance is calculated from the source image. Based on the covariance the eigenface is calculated. Higher the eigenface means; more variation in the face image exists. PCA [16, 17] model it uses the same Eigen faces to perform the identification process. The available data is also presented in the form eigenface images. To generate the eigenface at first the mean and the covariance is calculated from the source image. Based on the covariance the eigenface is calculated. Higher the eigenface means; more variation in the face image exists. To recognize the image, we compare the eigenface value of input normalized image with all images of the dataset. Lower the difference between the inputs featured image and the database image will be elected as the identified image. The procedure of the Eigen value analysis respective of dataset creation is shown in Fig. 7.

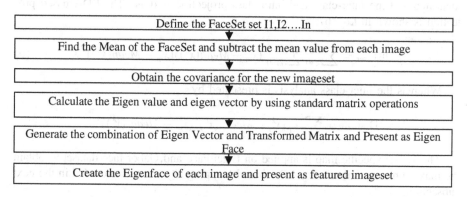

Fig. 7. PCA

3.2 Gabor Feature Generation

Gabor filter is based on orientation and frequency observation on image to identify the structural features. It can be used adaptively to recognize the textural and content information. It is modulated through a kernel function in spatial domain to highlight the features significantly. It is applied as a band pass filter with Gaussian envelope to extract the features. In this work, the symmetric Gabor filter is applied as given in Eq. (5)

$$Gabor_{\theta_k, f_i, \sigma_x, \sigma_y}(x, y) = exp\left(-\left[\frac{x_{\theta_k}^2}{\sigma_x^2} + \frac{y_{\theta_k}^2}{\sigma_y^2}\right]\right) \cdot \cos(2\pi f_i x_{\theta_k} + \varphi) \qquad (5)$$

Where,

$$x_{\theta_k} = x\cos\theta_k + y\sin\theta_k$$
$$y_{\theta_k} = y\cos\theta_k - x\sin\theta_k$$

f_i is central frequency of sinusoidal wave at angle θ_k

σ_x and σ_y Represents the standard deviation of the Gaussian Envelope along x, y axis

The phase φ set is $\pi/2$

The window specific evaluation is taken for box x and y axis. The local orientation, and radial frequency are taken for each window over the face image. The generated Gabor image is finally processed under PCA and LDA methods to perform the effective face recognition.

3.3   LDA

LDA (Linear Discriminant Analysis) extracts the discriminative face information and map them to the particular image class for effective face recognition. The method accepts a set of N image and maps them on c classes. Each of the group images can be processed separately to identify the feature class. The mean for each of the group is identified and the inter-class and intra class projection is done. The LDA based projection is shown in Eq. (6)

$$\text{Dist}_{\text{inter}} = \sum_{k=1}^{K} \sum_{m=1}^{M} (x_m^k - Mean(x^k))(x_m^k - Mean(x^k))^{\mathrm{T}} \tag{6}$$

Whereas the inter-class analysis is presented by

$$\text{Dist}_{\text{inter}} = \sum_{k=1}^{K} (x_m^k - Mean\ (x^k))(x_m^k - Mean\ (x^k))^{\mathrm{T}}$$

The kernel specific map is applied on EigenFace and Gabor face dataset to obtain the maximum map subset. The LDA based mapping algorithm is provided in the next subsection.

3.4   Algorithm

The proposed VDD composed PCA-LDA model is able to provide solution against various noise disturbances occurred because of environment or capturing device. Algorithm 1 has summarized the complete procedure of the proposed model. The face model is applied to the rectified face database and the real time face image. At the earlier stage, the feature generation is applied on the available training set to form feature set. The Gabor process and PCA method are applied separately to training face set and the two separate feature sets are formed. As a real time face is captured, the VDD filter is applied to remove the noise impurities. The directional magnitude balancing is applied using vector directional (Vd) filter. To attain the distance based similarity in composition with directional magnitude balancing is obtained using Directional distance (Dd) filter. After passing through this VDD filtration window, a rectified face image is obtained. To transform the input image compatible with feature face dataset, the eigenface and Gabor features are extracted from the input image. These feature images are separately mapped on an Eigen face dataset (EFaceSet) and Gabor Feature Set (GFaceSet) using the LDA approach. LDA applied a distance measure separately through the mean feature and generated the maximum mapped subset. Each of the subsets is finally compared internally to recognize the commonly and maximum mapped face image. This dual check based on two feature sets adaptively provides the significant results. The implementation results and comparative observations are presented in the next section of this paper.

```
Algorithm 1 : VDD Composed PCA-LDA

Algorithm (NFaceSet, RealFace)

/*NFaceSet is the normalized training set, RealFace is the captured noisy
image*/

Begin

1.      [GFaceSet  MeanFace]=  ApplyGabor(NFaceSet,  wsize,  angles)  /*
        Generate  Gabor  FeatureSet  for  Face  Dataset  with  window,
        orientation and angle  specification, Also  Generate  Mean  Face
        Image */

2.      EFaceSet = PCA (NFaceSet)/*Generate the EigenFaces using PCA
        method defined in figure 7*/

3.      FFFace = Vd(RealFace) /*Apply first level filteration uing Vector
        Directional Filter*/

4.      RFace = Dd (FFFace) /*Generate Rectified Face Image using Second
        level Directional Distance Filter*/

5.      ERFace = EigenFace(RFaceSet,MeanFace) /*Generate Eigen Face by by
        considering mean dataset image*/

6.      GRFace = ApplyGabor (RFace) /*Generate Gabor feature face for
        Filtered face*/

7.      EMapSet = LDAFeatureMap(EFaceSet, ERFace) /*Apply the LDA feature
        formation on Eigen feature set and real Face Eigen Image*/

8.      LMapSet=LDAFeatureMap(GFaceSet,GRFace) /*Apply LDA feature map on
        Gabor real face and faceset*/

9.      Ratio=GetRatio(EMapSet,LMapSet)/*Get  Euclidian  Distance  based
        ratio on Eigen-LDA and Gabor-LDA set*/

10.     Index = MaxMap(Ratio)/*Get Maximum mapped Image over the dataet*/

11.     Return NFaceSet(i)

End
```

4 Results

To validate the proposed VDD composed PCA-LDA model, the experimentation is applied on Utrecht ECVP and Stirling dataset. The images of these datasets are taken in same form as training set and to generate the test set, three different noise are included. These included noises are Gaussian Noise, Poissson Noise and Salt & Pepper Noise. The characterization of dataset, sample images and experimentation features are listed in Table 1. The comparative evaluation is taken against Median Filter, Gaussian Filter and Morphological Filter rectified testset and implication of PCA and LDA classifiers over them. The evaluation is taken in terms of accuracy ratio for each dataset with different noise intensities.

Table 1. Dataset properties

Properties	Dataset I	Dataset II
Dataset Name	Utrecht ECVP	Stirling dataset
Sample Images	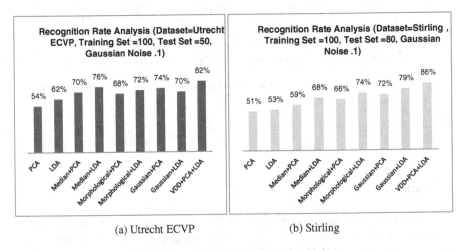	
Dataeset Url	www.pics.psych.stir.ac.uk	www.pics.psych.stir.ac.uk
Number of Images	131	312
Number of Individuals	69	35
Resolution	900x1200	269x269
Number of Viewpoint	2	3
Noise Distortion	Gaussian Noise, Poisson Noise, salt & pepper	
Filteration Method	VDD, Median Filter, Gaussian Filter, Morphological Filter	

Table 1 shows the experimental features for two completely different datasets. Two separate training and testing sets are taken from each dataset and processed on three different noise forms. The comparative evaluation of Guassian infected datasets is shown in Fig. 8.

(a) Utrecht ECVP   (b) Stirling

Fig. 8. Accuracy analysis (Gaussian Noise)

Figure 8 shows that the classification results on noisy image are very poor. The applied filtration methods improved the recognition accuracy. The observations against Gaussian Noise shows that the proposed VDD composed PCA-LDA method improved the accuracy upto 82% for Utrecht ECVP and 86% for Stirling dataset.

Figure 9 shows the recognition accuracy evaluation using different methods for Poisson Noise infected dataset. The proposed method achieved the accuracy of 86% and 92.5% for both considered test sets.

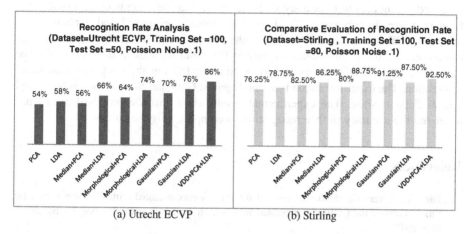

(a) Utrecht ECVP   (b) Stirling

Fig. 9. Accuracy analysis (Poisson Noise)

Figure 10 shows the recognition accuracy evaluation using different methods for Salt & Pepper infected dataset. The proposed method achieved the accuracy of 88% and 92.5% for both considered test sets.

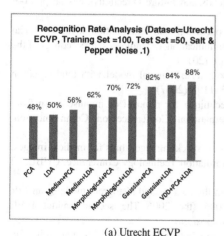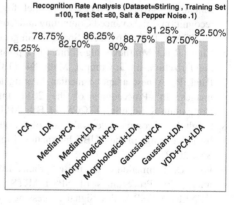

(a) Utrecht ECVP   (b) Stirling

Fig. 10. Accuracy analysis (Salt & Pepper Noise)

5 Conclusion

The accuracy level of the facial recognition process can be degraded if some distortion occurs in the source image. Different kinds of distortions are possible in a source image while extracting data from primary sources. These distortions are here presented in the form of noise. In this paper, the impact of noise is evaluated and explained. An effective VDD composed PCA-LDA method is proposed to rectify the face image extensively by using directional magnitude filter and directional distance filter. The extracted PCA and Gabor filters are processed under LDA method to perform the facial recognition. The experimentation is applied against Gaussian Noise, Poisson Noise and Salt & Pepper Noise. The experimental results show that the proposed model has improved the accuracy of face recognition in complex noisy situations.

References

1. Jain, A.: A versatile denoising method for images contaminated with Gaussian noise. In: Proceedings of the CUBE International Information Technology Conference, CUBE 2012, Sept 2012
2. Juneja, K.: Multiple feature descriptors based model for individual identification in group photos. J. King Saud Univ. Comput. Inform. Sci. Available online 23 Feb 2017
3. Juneja, K.: Generalized and constraint specific composite facial search model for effective web image mining. In: 2015 International Conference on Computing and Network Communications (CoCoNet), Trivandrum, pp. 353–361 (2015)
4. Juneja, K., Gill, N.S.: A hybrid mathematical model for face localization over multi-person images and videos. In: 2015 4th International Conference on Reliability, Infocom Technologies and Optimization (ICRITO) (Trends and Future Directions), Noida, pp. 1–6 (2015)
5. Juneja, K.: MFAST processing model for occlusion and illumination invariant facial recognition. In: Advanced Computing and Communication Technologies: Proceedings of the 9th ICACCT, pp. 161–170, Springer, Singapore (2015)
6. Chan, R.H.: Multilevel algorithm for a poisson noise removal model with total-variation regularization. Int. J. Comput. Math. **84**, 1183–1198 (2007)
7. Patel, P.: A new adaptive median filtering technique for removal of impulse noise from images. In: Proceedings of the 2011 International Conference on Communication, Computing & Security, ICCCS, 11 Feb 2011
8. Singh, S.: A comparative evaluation of various de-speckling algorithms for medical images. In: Proceedings of the CUBE International Information Technology Conference, CUBE, 12 Sept 2012
9. Poot, D.: Estimation of the noise variance from the background histogram mode of an MR image. In: Proceedings of SPS-DARTS 2006 (the 2006 The second annual IEEE BENELUX/DSP Valley Signal Processing Symposium)
10. Jain, A.: A versatile denoising method for images contaminated with Gaussian Noise. In: Proceedings of the CUBE International Information Technology Conference, CUBE 2012, Sept 2012
11. Kornatowski, E.: Probabilistic measure of colour image processing fidelity. J. Electr. Eng. **59** (1), 29–33 (2008)

12. Dhanasekaran, D.: High speed pipeline architecture for adaptive median filter. In: Proceedings of the International Conference on Advances in Computing, Communication and Control, Jan 2009
13. Wang, J., Tan, Y.: Morphological image enhancement procedure design by using genetic programming. In: Proceedings of the 13th Annual Conference on Genetic and Evolutionary Computation, July 2011
14. Peters, R.A., : A new algorithm for image noise reduction using mathematical morphology. IEEE Trans. Image Process. 4(3), 554–568 (1995)
15. Wang, L.: Adaptive approach to fingerprint image enhancement. In: Mobile Multimedia Security, MoMM2010 Proceedings, Nov 2010
16. Gottumukkal, R.: System level design of real time face recognition architecture based on composite PCA. In: Proceedings of the 13th ACM Great Lakes Symposium on VLSI, April 2003
17. Barahate, S.R.: Face recognition using PCA based algorithm and neural network. In: International Conference and Workshop on Emerging Trends in Technology (ICWET 2010), TCET, Mumbai, India (2010)

Software Engineering

Extending AHP_GORE_PSR by Generating Different Patterns of Pairwise Comparison Matrix

Mohd. Sadiq[1(✉)] and Arashiya Afrin[2]

[1] Computer Engineering Section, UPFET, Jamia Millia Islamia, A Central University, New Delhi 110025, India
serg.bsoft@gmail.com, Sadiq.jmi@gmail.com,
msadiq@jmi.ac.in
[2] Department of Computer Science and Engineering, Al-Falah University,
A NAAC- UGC 'A' Grade University, Dhauj, Faridabad, Haryana, India
afrin47@gmail.com

Abstract. Software requirements selection and prioritization (SRSP) is an important process of software requirements elicitation and analysis methods like AGORA, PRFGORE process, GOASREP, AHP_GORE_PSR, etc. In these methods, pairwise comparison matrices (PCM) are constructed by the decision makers (DM) for the selection and prioritization of the software requirements. In these methods, consistency of the PCM plays an important role to decide whether the preferences given by the DM for the software requirements are consistent or not. If the PCM will not be consistent then it may lead to failure of software system. Based on our literature review, we identify that, less attention is given in SRSP methods to check the consistency of the PCM. Therefore, in order to address this issue, we extend the AHP_GORE_PSR by generating different patterns of PCM. Finally, we explain the proposed method by considering the example of Institute Examination System.

Keywords: Analytic hierarchy process (AHP) · Goal oriented requirements engineering (GORE) · Pairwise comparison matrix · Consistency · Software requirements selection and prioritization

1 Introduction

Software requirements selection and prioritization (SRSP) is an important sub-area of software's requirements engineering [12]. SRSP is an important activity of software requirements elicitation methods, for example, goal oriented requirements elicitation methods [10]. The objective of SRSP is to select and prioritize the set of requirements on the basis of different criteria, like security, cost, performance, etc., after the mutual consensus of all the stakeholders [12]. Based on our literature review in the area of SRSP, we identify that SRSP methods are broadly classified into two parts:

- SRSP methods based on search based software engineering (SBSE) [13] like, ant colony optimization, teaching learning based optimization, genetic algorithms, swarm intelligence optimization algorithms, etc.

© Springer Nature Singapore Pte Ltd. 2017
S. Kaushik et al. (Eds.): ICICCT 2017, CCIS 750, pp. 233–245, 2017.
https://doi.org/10.1007/978-981-10-6544-6_22

- SRSP methods based on multi-criteria decision making (MCDM) methods [8, 14] like analytic hierarchy process (AHP), technique for order preference by similarity to ideal solution (TOPSIS), etc.

In our work, we mainly focus on SRSP methods based on MCDM algorithms. Therefore, in this line of interest, different methods have been developed for SRSP like, AHP_GORE_PSR [11], PRFGORE process [10], GOASREP [5], etc. AHP [8], TOPSIS [14], alpha-level weighted preference relation [10, etc., have been used as a mathematical tools to prioritize the software requirements. Based on our review, we identify that in SRSP methods less attention is given to check the consistency of the pairwise comparison matrix (PCM). These matrices are constructed by the decision makers (DMs) [8]. If the PCM will not be consistent then it may lead to failure of software. Therefore, to address this issue, in our work we generate the different patterns the PCM to check the consistency of the SRSP methods based on AHP, i.e., AHP_-GORE_PSR. The objective of AHP_GORE_PSR is to prioritize the software requirements using AHP in goal oriented requirements elicitation process [11]. The remainder of the paper is organized as follows: Sect. 2 presents the related work. Extended AHP_GORE_PSR is given in Sect. 3. Explanation of the proposed method with the help of case study is given in Sect. 4. Finally, conclusions and future work are given in Sect. 5.

2 Related Work

In literature of search based software engineering (SBSE), software requirements selection is referred to as "*Next Release Problem*" (NRP). In SBSE, different methods have been developed for NRP. For example, Cheng et al. [4] proposed an "adaptive memetic algorithm based on multi-objective optimization for software NRP". Chaves-Gonzalez et al. [2] proposed a multi-objective "*teaching learning based optimization*" (TLBO) for the selection of software requirements. In another study, Chaves-Gonzalez et al. [3] optimized the software requirements using swarm intelligence evolutionary algorithm. Multi-objective ant colony optimization was used by Sagrado et al. [12] for requirements selection. Chaves-Gonzalez and Perez-Toledano [1] solve the NRP by using differential evolution with Pareto tournament.

In non-SBSE area, multi-criteria decision making methods like AHP, TOPSIS, etc., have received much attention by research community for SRSP. Different methods have been developed for SRSP like AHP-GORE-PSR [11], PRFGORE process [10], GOASREP [5], etc. Sadiq et al. [11] proposed a method for the prioritization of software requirements using analytic hierarchy process (AHP) in goal oriented requirements elicitation process, i.e., AHP_GORE_PSR. Sadiq and Jain [10] proposed a method for the "*prioritization of requirements using fuzzy based approach in goal oriented requirements elicitation (PRFGORE) process*". Kaiya et al. [6] proposed a method called, "*attributed goal oriented requirements analysis*" (AGORA) method. In these methods, less attention is given to check the consistency of the pairwise comparison matrix. In 2016, Mohammed et al. [7] proposed a "*fuzzy attributed goal oriented requirements analysis method*" by extending the AGORA method. Garg et al. [5]

proposed GOASREP, i.e., *"Goal Oriented Approach for Software Requirements Elicitation and Prioritization using AHP"*. In similar studies, Sadiq et al. [9] proposed the approach for the elicitation of software. In non-SBSE area, less attention is given to check the consistency of the PCM, which is developed by the decision makers during SRSP process using AHP. Therefore, to address this issue, in this paper, we proposed a method to check the consistency before the selection and prioritization of software requirements in AHP_GORE_PSR.

3   Proposed Method

In this section, we extend AHP_GORE_PSR, proposed by Sadiq et al. [11], by considering the different set of pairwise comparison matrices before software requirements selection and prioritization. The extended AHP_GORE_PSR is given below:

- **Step 1:** Elicitation of different types of software requirements using goal oriented method
- **Step 2:** Construct pairwise comparison matrix (PCM)
- **Step 3:** Match the PCM with the patterns and sub-patterns of the database of PCM
- **Step 4:** Check the consistency of all the PCM
- **Step 5:** Find out the ranking values of the software requirements

Step 1: Elicitation of different types of software requirements using goal oriented method

Elicitation is an important sub-process of requirements engineering. The objective of requirements elicitation is to identify the different types of goals/requirements like functional goals (FG), non-functional goals (NFG), etc. There are different methods for the elicitation of software requirements like traditional method, cognitive method, contextual method, goal oriented methods, etc. [10]. In our work, we employed goal oriented method for the elicitation of software goals/requirements because these methods visualize the software requirements using AND/OR graph. Visualization of software requirements using AND/OR graph helps requirements analyst to identify those requirements that are logical AND connective or logical OR connective [10].

Step 2: Construct pairwise comparison matrix

Pairwise comparison matrices are constructed to compare the different FG by considering different NFG. In our method, we use the following rating scale, as shown in Table 1, to construct the pairwise comparison matrix (PCM), proposed by Saaty in 1972. The detail discussion about the construction of PCM is given in Sect. 4.

Step 3: Match the PCM with the patterns and sub-patterns of the database of PCM
The objective of this step is to decide whether the PCM is valid or not. If the PCM would be valid it means that definitely the results of the ranking values of the FG would be consistent. Otherwise, non-consistency will arise and it may lead to wrong ranking values of the FG. If the FG ranking value will not be evaluated by using the consistent PCM then it may lead to the failure of software. Therefore, in our method we generate the patterns of the PCM. Here, we are considering the case of three FG and one NFG. The initial pairwise comparison matrix for three different FG is given in Fig. 1.

Table 1. Rating scale

Intensity of importance	Meaning
1	*"Equal important"*
3	*"Somewhat more important"*
5	*"Much more important"*
7	*"Very much important"*
9	*"Absolutely more important"*
2, 4, 6, 8	*"Intermediate values (when compromise is needed)"*

FGs	FG1	FG2	FG3
FG1	1		
FG2		1	
FG3			1

Fig. 1. Initial pairwise comparison matrix

Diagonal entries in Fig. 1 are one; it means that FGs are equally important For three different goals/requirements, the different cases of generalized set of PCM would be as follows:

- **Case 1:** When FG1 is preferable over FG2, when FG1 is preferable over FG3, and when FG2 is preferable over FG3
- **Case 2:** When FG1 is preferable over FG2, when FG1 is preferable over FG3, and when FG3 is preferable over FG2
- **Case 3:** When FG1 is preferable over FG2, when FG3 is preferable over FG1, and when FG2 is preferable over FG3
- **Case 4:** When FG1 is preferable over FG2, when FG3 is preferable over FG1, and when FG3 is preferable over FG2
- **Case 5:** When FG2 is preferable over FG1, when FG1 is preferable over FG3, and when FG2 is preferable over FG3
- **Case 6:** When FG1 is preferable over FG2, when FG1 is preferable over FG3, and when FG3 is preferable over FG2
- **Case 7:** When FG2 is preferable over FG1, when FG3 is preferable over FG1, and when FG2 is preferable over FG3
- **Case 8:** When FG2 is preferable over FG1, when FG3 is preferable over FG1, and when FG3 is preferable over FG2

Step 4: Check the consistency of all the PCM

Once the PCM of the software requirements will match with the patterns and sub-patterns of the PCM requirements, then the ranking value of all the FG would be computed.

Step 5: Find out the ranking values of the software requirements

Here, we calculate the ranking values of the software goals/requirements depending on the different criteria like, cost, performance, reliability, etc.

In the next section, we explain the proposed method with the help of a case study. In our case study, we apply the extended AHP_GORE_PSR on Institute Examination System (Figs. 2 and 6).

4 Case Study

Here, we apply the proposed method for the selection and prioritization of software requirements when the PCM is consistent. We apply the proposed method on the software requirements of Institute Examination System (IES).

Step 1: In this step, we identify the FG and NFG of IES using goal oriented method, as discussed in our previous work [10]. After applying the "goal oriented method" we identify the following set of requirements: login module, student module, faculty module, and administration module. The AND/OR graph of IES is given below:

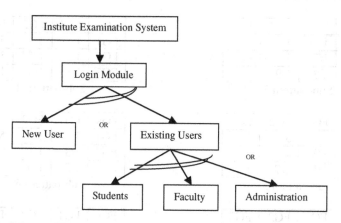

Fig. 2. AND/OR graph of IES (a partial view) [11]

Finally, we have identified the following set of FG and NFG: FG1-Student module; FG2-Faculty module; FG3-Administrative module. After refinement and decomposition of FGs, we have identified the following set of sub-goals: FG1-1: Submission of examination form; FG1-2: Examination fee submission; FG1-3: Generate hall tickets; FG1-4: View semester results; FG1-5: Notices related to examinations; FG1-6: Providing information of students to their family members; FG2-1: Compilation of student's attendance record; FG2-2: Prepare the list of detained students; FG2-3: Entry of internal and external marks of theory and practical papers; FG3-1: Generate mark-sheet; FG3-2: Tabulators; FG3-3: Seating Plan of the students; NFG1: Cost.

Step 2: In our case study, we consider the Case 1, when FG1 is preferable over FG2 (i.e. FG1 > FG2), when FG1 is preferable over FG3 (i.e. FG1 > FG3), and when FG2 is preferable over FG3 (i.e. FG2 > FG3). In this case, we generate the pattern of the PCM for the possible values that could be provided by the requirements analysts. The possible patterns of the PCM are given as below:

Pattern 1: when (FG1 > FG2) = (FG1 > FG3) = (FG2 > FG3); **Pattern 2:** when (FG1 > FG2) = (FG1 > FG3) ≠ (FG2 > FG3); **Pattern 3:** when (FG1 > FG2) ≠ (FG1 > FG3) = (FG2 > FG3); **Pattern 4:** when (FG1 > FG2) = (FG2 > FG3) ≠ (FG1 > FG3); **Pattern 5:** when (FG1 > FG2) ≠ (FG2 > FG3) = (FG1 > FG3); **Pattern 6:** when (FG1 > FG2) ≠ FG1 > FG3) ≠ (FG2 > FG3).

To generate the sub-pattern on the basis of the above patterns, we use the following intensity of importance for the ranking of the software requirements, as proposed by Saaty in [8], i.e., 3, 5, 7, and 9. As a result, we have generated the following possible sub-patterns based on pattern 5, which are represented in the form of PCM:

FGs	FG1	FG2	FG3
FG1	1	3	3
FG2	1/3	1	5
FG3	1/3	1/5	1

Sub-pattern 1

FGs	FG1	FG2	FG3
FG1	1	3	3
FG2	1/3	1	7
FG3	1/3	1/7	1

Sub-pattern 2

FGs	FG1	FG2	FG3
FG1	1	3	3
FG2	1/3	1	9
FG3	1/3	1/9	1

Sub-pattern 3

FGs	FG1	FG2	FG3
FG1	1	3	5
FG2	1/3	1	5
FG3	1/5	1/5	1

Sub-pattern 4

FGs	FG1	FG2	FG3
FG1	1	3	5
FG2	1/3	1	7
FG3	1/5	1/7	1

Sub-pattern 5

FGs	FG1	FG2	FG3
FG1	1	3	5
FG2	1/3	1	9
FG3	1/5	1/9	1

Sub-pattern 6

FGs	FG1	FG2	FG3
FG1	1	3	7
FG2	1/3	1	5
FG3	1/7	1/5	1

Sub-pattern 7

FGs	FG1	FG2	FG3
FG1	1	3	7
FG2	1/3	1	7
FG3	1/7	1/7	1

Sub-pattern 8

FGs	FG1	FG2	FG3
FG1	1	3	7
FG2	1/3	1	9
FG3	1/7	1/9	1

Sub-pattern 9

FGs	FG1	FG2	FG3
FG1	1	3	9
FG2	1/3	1	5
FG3	1/9	1/5	1

Sub-pattern 10

FGs	FG1	FG2	FG3
FG1	1	3	9
FG2	1/3	1	7
FG3	1/9	1/7	1

Sub-pattern 11

FGs	FG1	FG2	FG3
FG1	1	3	9
FG2	1/3	1	9
FG3	1/9	1/9	1

Sub-pattern 12

Fig. 3. Sub-patterns for pattern 5

FGs	FG1	FG2	FG3
FG1	1	5	3
FG2	1/5	1	3
FG3	1/3	1/3	1

Sub-pattern 13

FGs	FG1	FG2	FG3
FG1	1	5	3
FG2	1/5	1	7
FG3	1/3	1/7	1

Sub-pattern 14

FGs	FG1	FG2	FG3
FG1	1	5	3
FG2	1/5	1	9
FG3	1/3	1/9	1

Sub-pattern 15

FGs	FG1	FG2	FG3
FG1	1	5	5
FG2	1/5	1	3
FG3	1/5	1/3	1

Sub-pattern 16

FGs	FG1	FG2	FG3
FG1	1	5	5
FG2	1/5	1	7
FG3	1/5	1/7	1

Sub-pattern 17

FGs	FG1	FG2	FG3
FG1	1	5	5
FG2	1/5	1	9
FG3	1/5	1/9	1

Sub-pattern 18

FGs	FG1	FG2	FG3
FG1	1	5	7
FG2	1/5	1	3
FG3	1/7	1/3	1

Sub-pattern 19

FGs	FG1	FG2	FG3
FG1	1	5	7
FG2	1/5	1	7
FG3	1/7	1/7	1

Sub-pattern 20

FGs	FG1	FG2	FG3
FG1	1	5	7
FG2	1/5	1	9
FG3	1/7	1/9	1

Sub-pattern 21

FGs	FG1	FG2	FG3
FG1	1	5	9
FG2	1/5	1	3
FG3	1/9	1/3	1

Sub-pattern 22

FGs	FG1	FG2	FG3
FG1	1	5	9
FG2	1/3	1	7
FG3	1/9	1/3	1

Sub-pattern 23

FGs	FG1	FG2	FG3
FG1	1	5	9
FG2	1/5	1	9
FG3	1/9	1/9	1

Sub-pattern 24

FGs	FG1	FG2	FG3
FG1	1	7	3
FG2	1/7	1	3
FG3	1/3	1/3	1

Sub-pattern 25

FGs	FG1	FG2	FG3
FG1	1	7	3
FG2	1/7	1	5
FG3	1/3	1/5	1

Sub-pattern 26

Fig. 3. (*continued*)

FGs	FG1	FG2	FG3
FG1	1	7	3
FG2	1/7	1	9
FG3	1/3	1/9	1

Sub-pattern 27

FGs	FG1	FG2	FG3
FG1	1	7	5
FG2	1/7	1	3
FG3	1/5	1/3	1

Sub-pattern 28

FGs	FG1	FG2	FG3
FG1	1	7	5
FG2	1/7	1	5
FG3	1/5	1/5	1

Sub-pattern 29

FGs	FG1	FG2	FG3
FG1	1	7	5
FG2	1/7	1	9
FG3	1/5	1/9	1

Sub-pattern 30

FGs	FG1	FG2	FG3
FG1	1	7	7
FG2	1/7	1	3
FG3	1/7	1/3	1

Sub-pattern 31

FGs	FG1	FG2	FG3
FG1	1	7	7
FG2	1/7	1	5
FG3	1/7	1/5	1

Sub-pattern 32

FGs	FG1	FG2	FG3
FG1	1	7	7
FG2	1/7	1	9
FG3	1/7	1/9	1

Sub-pattern 33

FGs	FG1	FG2	FG3
FG1	1	7	9
FG2	1/7	1	3
FG3	1/9	1/3	1

Sub-pattern 34

FGs	FG1	FG2	FG3
FG1	1	7	9
FG2	1/7	1	5
FG3	1/9	1/5	1

Sub-pattern 35

FGs	FG1	FG2	FG3
FG1	1	7	9
FG2	1/7	1	9
FG3	1/9	1/9	1

Sub-pattern 36

FGs	FG1	FG2	FG3
FG1	1	9	3
FG2	1/9	1	3
FG3	1/3	1/3	1

Sub-pattern 37

FGs	FG1	FG2	FG3
FG1	1	9	3
FG2	1/9	1	5
FG3	1/3	1/5	1

Sub-pattern 38

FGs	FG1	FG2	FG3
FG1	1	9	3
FG2	1/9	1	7
FG3	1/3	1/7	1

Sub-pattern 39

FGs	FG1	FG2	FG3
FG1	1	9	5
FG2	1/9	1	3
FG3	1/5	1/3	1

Sub-pattern 40

Fig. 3. (*continued*)

FGs	FG1	FG2	FG3
FG1	1	9	5
FG2	1/9	1	5
FG3	1/5	1/5	1

Sub-pattern 41

FGs	FG1	FG2	FG3
FG1	1	9	5
FG2	1/9	1	7
FG3	1/5	1/7	1

Sub-pattern 42

FGs	FG1	FG2	FG3
FG1	1	9	7
FG2	1/9	1	3
FG3	1/7	1/3	1

Sub-pattern 43

FGs	FG1	FG2	FG3
FG1	1	9	7
FG2	1/9	1	5
FG3	1/7	1/5	1

Sub-pattern 44

FGs	FG1	FG2	FG3
FG1	1	9	7
FG2	1/9	1	7
FG3	1/7	1/7	1

Sub-pattern 45

FGs	FG1	FG2	FG3
FG1	1	9	9
FG2	1/9	1	3
FG3	1/9	1/3	1

Sub-pattern 46

FGs	FG1	FG2	FG3
FG1	1	9	9
FG2	1/9	1	5
FG3	1/9	1/5	1

Sub-pattern 47

FGs	FG1	FG2	FG3
FG1	1	9	9
FG2	1/9	1	7
FG3	1/9	1/7	1

Sub-pattern 48

Fig. 3. (*continued*)

The objective of this step construct the PCM for the given set of FG and NFG by comparing the FGs with each other on the basis of NFG, i.e., cost. Let us assume that requirements analysts compare the FG and construct the PCM, as shown in Fig. 4. The contents of the PCM matrix, as shown in Fig. 4, matches with the pattern 5 of case 1, because FG1 is somewhat more important than FG2 (see Table 1). Therefore, we put 3 in the FG1-row and FG2-column in Fig. 4. Similarly, FG1 is much more important than FG3, so in this case we put 9 in the FG1-row and FG3-column; and finally, we put 5 in the FG2-row and FG3-column because FG2 is somewhat more important than FG3. The PCM matches with the sub-pattern 10 of Fig. 3. This PCM is consistent because the consistency ratio (CR) of the PCM is 2%, see Table 2. According to the Saaty [8], for better decision making process the value of CR should be less than 10%.

FGs	FG1	FG2	FG3
FG1	1	3	9
FG2	1/3	1	5
FG3	1/9	1/5	1

Fig. 4. Pairwise comparison matrix

Consider another PCM; let us assume the requirements analyst construct the following PCM after evaluating the three FGs on the basis of the cost:

FGs	FG1	FG2	FG3
FG1	1	9	3
FG2	1/9	1	7
FG3	1/3	1/7	1

Fig. 5. Pairwise comparison matrix

The above PCM matches with the sub-pattern 39 of Fig. 3; and this PCM will not produce the consistent results because its CR is more than 10%, i.e., 96%, as shown in Table 2. Proposed method will generate the raking values of those FG whose CR is less than 10%. If the PCM is not generating the CR less than 10% then such type of PCM will not produce the consistent ranking value of the FG. In Table 2 we have stored the CR for all the sub-patterns of the Fig. 3 as a database of the CR. When the requirements analyst will generate the PCM then it would be checked with the database, as shown in Table 2. If the CR of the given PCM would be less than 10% then only that PCM would be used for the ranking purpose. Such type of analysis will save the time of the decision makers at the time of the selection and prioritization of the software requirements.

Table 2. Database of CR of the sub-patterns given in Fig. 5

Sub-Patterns	CR	Sub-Patterns	CR	Sub-Patterns	CR
Sub-pattern 1	25.39%	Sub-pattern 17	37.55%	Sub-pattern 33	48.34%
Sub-pattern 2	37.52%	Sub-pattern 18	48.27%	Sub-pattern 34	**6.9%**
Sub-pattern 3	48.34%	Sub-pattern 19	**5.5%**	Sub-pattern 35	17.96%
Sub-pattern 4	11.68%	Sub-pattern 20	25.39%	Sub-pattern 36	37.55%
Sub-pattern 5	20.10%	Sub-pattern 21	19.86%	Sub-pattern 37	48.34%
Sub-pattern 6	27.96%	Sub-pattern 22	**2.5%**	Sub-pattern 38	75.13%
Sub-pattern 7	**5.5%**	Sub-pattern 23	17.96%	Sub-pattern 39	96.65%
Sub-pattern 8	11.68%	Sub-pattern 24	25.39%	Sub-pattern 40	27.96%
Sub-pattern 9	17.74%	Sub-pattern 25	37.0%	Sub-pattern 41	48.34%
Sub-pattern 10	**2.48%**	Sub-pattern 26	61.10%	Sub-pattern 42	65.22%
Sub-pattern 11	**6.96%**	Sub-pattern 27	96.65%	Sub-pattern 43	17.74%
Sub-pattern 12	11.68%	Sub-pattern 28	20.10%	Sub-pattern 44	34.24%
Sub-pattern 13	25.34%	Sub-pattern 29	37.55%	Sub-pattern 45	48.34%
Sub-pattern 14	95.70%	Sub-pattern 30	65.22%	Sub-pattern 46	11.68%
Sub-pattern 15	37.90%	Sub-pattern 31	11.55%	Sub-pattern 47	25.39%
Sub-pattern 16	11.68%	Sub-pattern 32	25.39%	Sub-pattern 48	37.55%

Step 4: To compute the ranking value of FG, we first calculate the Eigen vector by using the following steps: (i) take the product of each row of the PCM and then compute the nth root of the product values

FGs	FG1	FG2	FG3	Nth root of the product values	Eigen vector
FG1	1	3	9	3	0.6716
FG2	1/3	1	5	1.1856	0.2654
FG3	1/9	1/5	1	0.2811	0.0629
Total				4.4667	≈ 1

Fig. 6. Normalized PCM

The Eigen Vector of the given FG is (0.6716, 0.2654, 0.0629). Thus, FG1 is most valuable goal. (ii) The next stage is to calculate the λ_{max}, the Consistency Index (CI) and CR. We first multiply on the right matrix of judgements by the Eigen vector, obtaining a new vector. The calculation for the first, second, and third row of the matrix is given below:

$$1 * 0.6716 + 3 * 0.2654 + 9 * 0.0629 = 2.0334$$

$$\frac{1}{3} * 0.6716 + 1 * 0.2654 + 5 * 0.0629 = 0.8037$$

$$\frac{1}{9} * 0.6716 + \frac{1}{5} * 0.2654 + 1 * 0.0629 = 0.1906$$

Divide 2.0334, 0.8037, and 0.1906 by the 0.6716, 0.2654, and 0.0629, respectively. As a result, we get the following vector for the first, second, and third row, i.e., (3.0284, 3.0282, 3.0302). The mean of these values would be 3.0289. This is the value of λ_{max}. So, $\lambda_{max} = 3.0289$. Now, we check the consistency, whether the results are consistent or not. To check the consistency, we use the following equation:

$$Consistency\,ratio(CR) = \frac{Consistency\,Index(CI)}{Random\,Index(RI)} \qquad (1)$$

Here, we first calculate the CI as [8]:

$$CI = \frac{\lambda_{max-n}}{n-1} \qquad (2)$$

$$CI = \frac{\lambda_{max-n}}{n-1} = \frac{3.0289 - 3}{2} = 0.0144$$

To compute the value of *CR*, we will have to calculate the value of random index (*RI*). Saaty proposed the following Table to find out the value of (*RI*) depending on the value of n [8].

Table 3. Values of *RI* [8]

N	1	2	3	4	5	6	7	8	9	10
RI	0	0	0.58	0.9	1.12	1.24	1.32	1.41	1.45	1.49

From the Table 3, it is clear that the value of *RI* for n = 3 is 0.58. Finally, the value of the CR can be calculated as:

$$CR = \frac{CI}{RI} = \frac{0.0144}{0.58} = 0.0248$$

Here, the value of *CR* is less than 10%. It means that the entries of the PCM are consistent. Now step 5 would be used to compute the ranking values of the requirements [10].

5 Conclusions and Future Work

In this paper, we proposed a method to extend the AHP_GORE_PSR by generating different patterns of the pairwise comparison matrix (PCM). In the proposed method, we have the following steps: (i) elicitation of different types of software requirements using goal oriented method, (ii) construct PCM, (iii) match the PCM with different patterns of PCM, (iv) check the consistency of all the PCM, and (v) find out the ranking values of the software requirements. In the proposed method, we generate 48 different sub-patterns of the PCM and store the values of each pattern in database along with its CR. When the requirements analyst will generate the PCM for different types of goals then that PCM would be checked with the database. If CR of the PCM is found to be less than 10% then PCM would be considered for the ranking of the functional goal (FG), otherwise decision makers will generate the other PCM. In future, we will generate the patterns for different set of requirements, i.e. when there are 4 requirements/goals or 5 requirements/goals, etc.

Acknowledgement. This work has been carried out in collaboration with the Software Engineering Research Group of *Bakewarr Software Solutions* (BSS), New Delhi-110025, India.

References

1. Chaves-Gonzalez, J.M., Perez-Toledano, M.A.: Differential evolution with Pareto tournament for the multi-objective next release problem. Appl. Math. Comput. **252**, 1–13 (2015)
2. Chaves-Gonzalez, J.M., Perez-Toledano, M.A., Navasa, A.: Teaching learning based optimization with pareto tournament for the multi-objective software requirements selection. Eng. Appl. Artif. Intell. **43**, 89–101 (2015)
3. Chaves-Gonzalez, J.M., Perez-Toledano, M.A., Navasa, A.: Software requirements optimization using a multi-objective swarm intelligence evolutionary algorithm. Knowl. Based Syst. **83**, 105–115 (2015)
4. Cheng, X., Huang, Y., Cai, X., Wei, O.: An Adaptive memetic algorithm based on multi-objective optimization for software next release problem. In: GECCO (2014)
5. Garg, N., Sadiq, M., Agarwal, P.: GOASREP: Goal Oriented Approach for Software Requirements Elicitation and Prioritization Using Analytic Hierarchy Process. In: Satapathy, S.C., Bhateja, V., Udgata, S.K., Pattnaik, P.K. (eds.) Proceedings of the 5th International Conference on Frontiers in Intelligent Computing: Theory and Applications. AISC, vol. 516, pp. 281–287. Springer, Singapore (2017). doi:10.1007/978-981-10-3156-4_28
6. Kaiya, H., Horai, H, Saeki, M.: AGORA: attributed goal-oriented requirements analysis method. In: IEEE Joint International Conference on Requirements Engineering (2002)
7. Mohammad, C.W., Shahid, M., Husain, S.Z.: FAGOSRA: fuzzy attributed goal oriented software requirements analysis method. In: 9th International Conference on Contemporary Computing, pp. 11–13 (2016)
8. Saaty, T.L.: Decision making with the analytic hierarchy process. Int. J. Serv. Sci. **1**(1), 83–98 (2008)
9. Sadiq, M., Ahmad, J., Asim, M., Qureshi, A., Suman, R.: More on elicitation of software requirements and prioritization using AHP. In: IEEE International Conference on Data Storage and Data Engineering, Bangalore, pp. 232–236 (2010)
10. Sadiq, M., Jain, S.K.: Applying fuzzy preference relation for requirements prioritization in goal oriented requirements elicitation process. Int. J. Syst. Assur. Eng. Maint. **5**(4), 711–723 (2014)
11. Sadiq, M., Hassan, T., Nazneen, S.: AHP_GORE_PSR: applying analytic hierarchy process in goal oriented requirements elicitation method for the prioritization of software requirements. In: 3rd IEEE International Conference on Computational Intelligence and Communication Technology (CICT), Organized by ABES College, pp. 9–10 (2017)
12. Sagrado, J.D., Aguila, I.M., Orellana, F.J.: Multi-objective ant colony optimization for requirements selection. Empir. Softw. Eng. **20**(3), 577–610 (2015)
13. Pitangueira, A.M., Macial, R.S.P., Barros, M.: Software requirements selection and prioritization using SBSE approaches: a systematic review and mapping of the literature. J. Syst. Softw. **103**, 267–280 (2015)
14. Behzadian, M., Otaghsara, S.K., Yazdani, M., Ignatius, J.: Review: a state of the–art-survey of TOPSIS applications. Expert Syst. Appl. **39**(17), 13051–13069 (2012)

Analysis of Errors in Safety Critical Embedded System Software in Aerial Vehicle

Lakshmi K.V.N.S.$^{(\boxtimes)}$ (ID) and Sanjeev Kumar (ID)

Advanced Systems Laboratory, DRDO, Hyderabad, India
{lakshmikvns, sanjeevkumars}@asl.drdo.in

Abstract. A study and analysis of software errors has been carried out. The present study analyzed approximately 400 errors of safety critical Navigation system software in 10 project variants. Framework used was: (i) Identification of types and severity of errors (ii) Gathering errors from error database and categorizing them according to the type and severity (iii) Recognition of the pattern and deriving the relation to software change rationale (iv) Proposing the error prevention guidelines for software requirements specification and code implementation for future software projects as a part of Software Quality Assurance (SQA) process. The main aim is to propose the error prevention guidelines that are practical to be implemented despite the project schedules. This is considered valuable outcome of the Independent Verification and Validation (IV&V) effort carried out for this safety critical embedded software.

Keywords: Embedded software · Real-time systems software · Software verification and validation · Requirements analysis · Software functional properties: correctness · Functionality · Consistency · Completeness · Software testing · Logic and verification · Software defect analysis

1 Introduction

In safety critical embedded systems, removal of sources of software errors is mandated for success of the project. In this context, effective Independent Verification and Validation process and Quality Assurance process plays a major role for detection and prevention of errors in software. The benefits of IV&V and SQA processes is to see that the system works as intended and provide additional confidence that requirements are satisfied. To reap these benefits efficiently, guidelines are required for the prevention of errors rather than detection. Need for guidelines that are practical to implement is identified, especially in tight project schedules. This motivated us to recognize trends in software errors detected across multiple variants of project and propose error prevention guidelines addressing software specifications and code implementation for future software projects. Software change rationale and errors are of technical nature and are not related to human, since human related errors cannot be completely avoided in tight project deadlines. Guidelines related to software process are not addressed in this paper.

We identified the need for research on error analysis methodologies for software. Many approaches are available but they differ in types of errors and their relationship to causes of errors. [1] specifies various types of errors and their relationship to human

© Springer Nature Singapore Pte Ltd. 2017
S. Kaushik et al. (Eds.): ICICCT 2017, CCIS 750, pp. 246–257, 2017.
https://doi.org/10.1007/978-981-10-6544-6_23

error and process flaws. [2] focuses on the types of errors but not in detail and their relationship to root causes and process flaws. [3] considers software structure in terms of cyclomatic complexity and its relation to software error. [4] presents an overview of different practices in different countries with software error data collection and analysis. [5] specify the mapping of software errors and causes to ISO 26262 requirements only. Software process improvements have been proposed in [6]. [7] addresses design and code inspections to reduce errors. After due research, it has been identified that these methodologies and approaches are not addressing the relation between types and severity of errors accumulated from past projects and their relation with software change rationale. Practical guidelines related to software specifications and code implementation which are technical in nature are not addressed by above references. These are highly essential in the scenario of tight project schedules.

In this paper, we propose the framework for error analysis and thereby proposing guidelines for prevention of errors related to software specifications and code implementation. This paper is organized as follows. Section 2 presents the brief overview of the approach being followed right from definition of types and severity of errors till the guidelines recognition. Section 3 presents the overview of the embedded Navigation system software requirements and analysis techniques used for software requirements and code implementation. Identification of various types and severity of errors is discussed in Sect. 4. Section 5 presents the error data collection mechanism and analysis of errors with respect to various aspects. Section 6 proposes the guidelines for software error prevention, which in turn improve the quality of software. Section 7 summarizes and concludes the paper.

2 Approach

We defined and followed a unified framework for error analysis and proposing guidelines. This comprises of sequence of steps for identification of types of errors, categorizing and utilizing them to observe the pattern of errors. This fits within the IV&V activities and is given below.

1. Identify the types and severity of errors.
2. Analyze the error database and observe the trend of errors.
3. Propose the error prevention guidelines for improving the quality of software.

This approach is unique for this embedded system. Each step is decomposed progressively in greater level of detail in the next subsections.

3 Software Requirements and Analysis Techniques

An aerial vehicle's Navigation System provides present state vectors of the vehicle to Flight Guidance and Control System. This provides the capability to guide, stabilize, control and steer the vehicle in desired flight path. The safety critical Navigation system is an embedded system composed of sensor blocks and associated processing electronics. The software embedded in it is of real time nature and is inherently complex.

This is highly algorithm intensive and complexity is enhanced by many folds by introducing fault tolerance features in hardware and so its handling in software. This complex software and redundancy requirements must be verified and validated to assure that it works as intended and that unintended interactions do not arise during its operation. Following analysis techniques have been used during software specifications review and code inspection:

- Formal analysis techniques - [8] specifies these techniques for software implementation
  - Data flow analysis
  - Control Flow analysis
  - Fault Tolerance analysis – [9] provides the complete details of this analysis carried out
- Semi-formal analysis techniques - These were identified and performed across various artifacts carried out as per the software requirements. These were especially beneficial to correlate and analyze the requirements.
  - Interface analysis with hardware and software
  - Timing analysis
  - Algorithm analysis
  - Inter system dependency
  - Inter project (variants) dependency
  - Change and Impact analysis
  - Reuse analysis.

4 Identification of Types and Severity of Errors

The errors that have been found out in software artefacts i.e. software requirements specification, interface requirements and source code by the above mentioned analysis techniques are logged in error database on regular basis. This helped to determine the extent and nature of software errors. On analyzing the specifications and implementation aspects, two parameters have been identified that characterize the errors. One parameter is type of error and the other is severity of error.

4.1 Types of Errors

The types of errors that have been identified are determined as per the functionalities and performance requirements of this software. Even, they were chosen to reflect commonly found defects.

4.1.1 Functional Errors
These types of errors effect the basic functional and performance requirements of the software and system.

- Operational - These errors which affect the core functional requirements w.r.t. execution sequence, are addressed as incorrect or incomplete requirements.

- Algorithm or computation - Following type of errors are related to algorithm requirements and implementation aspects.
  - Effect on accuracy
  - Incorrect equation
  - Incorrect parameters
  - Sign conventions – specific to project requirements
- Timing – Effect of these errors result into following cases
  - Incorrect instant of access or processing
  - Inadequate processing time
  - Inadequate waiting time
- Logic checking condition– Errors related to decision logics that are related to parameters or operators within the conditional statements. They can be of following types
  - Inappropriate
  - Incorrect
  - Inadequate or missing
- Data – The errors related to data being used in execution of software and are encountered in following aspects
  - Assignment
  - Access
  - Overflow
  - Incorrect parameter
  - Clearance for next run
  - Accuracy
- Monitor – The errors related to monitoring requirements of system (incorrect/missing) in terms of
  - Bits of status words
  - Condition flags
  - Data parameters.

4.1.2   Errors Related to Maintainability and Other Quality Factors

The errors that do not effect the functionality of the software but effect the maintainability and understandability of the software are considered as errors related to maintainability and other quality factors types and are given below:

- Redundant – These types of errors are characterized for following operations which result in no change in output of the execution of software. These types of errors cannot be detected by static analysis tools since these are specific to requirements implementation and are considered as dead code. Unused code variables and function prototypes are not considered in this study.
  - Checks
  - Assignments
  - Computations
  - Bits clearances
  - Bits checking
  - Duplicate flags

- Logical bit operators
- Data sent and received
- Arguments to functions
- Initializations
- Parameters in structures
- operations

- Nomenclature – These errors are related to nomenclature of variables implemented in software
  - Inappropriate
  - Incorrect
- Storage and access – The errors related to data variables are identified under this type and cannot be detected by static analysis tool
  - Excess data type (for example- double instead of float)
  - Local instead of global
  - Excess array sizes
  - Array overflow but no impact
  - Uninitialized element of array accessed but not used
- Comments – Incorrect comments incorporated in the software code
- Document anomalies
  - Reference documents submission – Overview of functionalities mentioned in requirements documents/changes mentioned in change notes, but details are not submitted for reference
  - Incomplete – Details mentioned in requirements documents/change notes are incomplete for understanding/reference
  - Incorrect and inconsistent across multiple documents
- Unauthorized changes - Changes carried out in code implementation without approval by the change control board
- Clarifications – Types of errors that need clarification from developers which result in enhancement of clarity of software in terms of
  - Explanation
  - Future requirements
  - Missing information
- Recommendations – These are related to coding or requirements enhancements for better understandability or maintainability of the software or system.

4.2 Severity of Errors

On carrying out impact analysis of errors on software, severity of the errors are designated as given below:

1. Catastrophic - These are the errors that would result in system failure
2. Major – These are the errors that affect the core functional capabilities of the system significantly and would result in system failure in simulation modes of operation
3. Minor – These errors effect the functional requirements of the software in negligible manner
4. Normal – These errors don't effect the operational capability or software execution at all

An error matrix relating the type and severity of errors is generated and is shown in Table 1.

Table 1. Error matrix

Severity type	Catastrophic	Major	Minor	Normal
Operational	X	X	X	
Algorithm or computation	X	X	X	
Timing	X	X	X	
Logic checking condition	X	X	X	
Data	X	X	X	
Monitor	X	X	X	X
Redundant				X
Nomenclature				X
Storage and access				X
Comments				X
Document				X
Unauthorized changes				X
Clarifications				X
Recommendations				X

5   Analysis of Errors

After identification of types and severity of errors, 400 errors found for Navigation system software covering 10 variants of projects from the database have been categorized with respect to its characteristics and impact as per the error matrix shown in Table 1. Review and analysis has been carried out to observe the pattern of errors for different variants of projects. Each variant of project consists of multiple versions of software. This analysis provides different views of errors in the software.

5.1   Analysis of Types and Severity of Errors

The classification results of error database w.r.t. type and severity are presented in Figs. 1, 2 and 3 as shown below. These are used to infer the data in better way.

1. Following are the inferences from Fig. 1:
   a. It indicates that operational, logic checking condition and monitor errors are of significant proportion in functional errors category.
   b. It demonstrates that document, clarifications and redundant type of errors in maintainability category are highly significant compared to functional errors. Documentation of artifacts is not matured enough for understanding the software requirements.

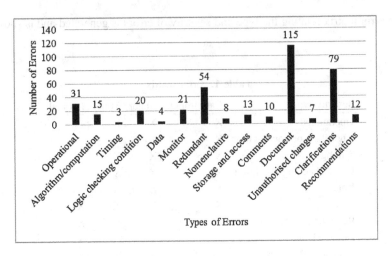

Fig. 1. Error categorization w.r.t. type

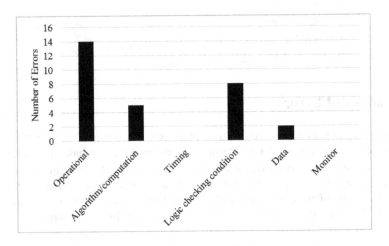

Fig. 2. Catastrophic errors categorization w.r.t. type

2. From the analysis of "what type" and "which severity" errors as depicted in Fig. 2 and Fig. 3, following are the inferences made:

   a. Data showed that 50% of catastrophic and major errors are related to operational type of errors.

   b. It implies that logic checking condition errors cover more than 25% of catastrophic errors and 25% of major errors.

   c. Algorithm errors also cover 25% of catastrophic errors.

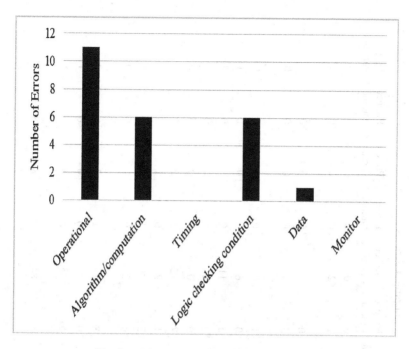

Fig. 3. Major errors categorization w.r.t. type

5.2   Analysis of Types of Errors w.r.t Project Variants

Table 2 gives the enumeration of types of errors found in 10 variants of projects. Figure 4 depicts the instances of major changes in hardware. This effects the relative size of software modification at each instance.

5.2.1   Inferences from Enumeration of Errors w.r.t. Hardware Change

Table 2 and Fig. 4 exhibits that there is strong correlation between number of software errors and proportion of major hardware modifications. It is implied by the significant proportion of software architecture and design change w.r.t. hardware change. In this process of revising the software for multiple configurations, new errors have been added unexpectedly. Occurrence of significant number of functional and maintainability errors become apparent w.r.t. hardware change.

5.2.2   Inferences from Types of Errors w.r.t. Hardware Change

Evaluation of each of the errors resulted in correlation that there is strong association between frequencies of occurrence of certain types of errors with change in hardware. Existence of such patterns lead to following conclusions.

1. Most of the operational errors due to hardware change are observed in initial variants.
2. Sign conventions are not properly taken care as part of algorithm errors.

Table 2. Enumeration of types of errors w.r.t project variants

		Project variant 1	Project variant 2	Project variant 3	Project variant 4	Project variant 5	Project variant 6	Project variant 7	Project variant 8	Project variant 9	Project variant 10
Functional errors	Operational	13	16	1	1	0	0	0	0	0	0
	Algorithm/computation	5	5	0	1	1	2	0	0	0	1
	Timing	0	1	0	2	0	0	0	0	0	0
	Logic checking condition	4	10	0	0	3	3	0	0	0	0
	Data	0	2	0	1	1	0	0	0	0	0
	Monitor	5	5	1	3	0	6	0	0	0	1
A-Total number of functional errors		27	39	2	8	5	11	0	0	0	2
Errors related to maintainability	Nomenclature	1	2	1	2	0	2	0	0	0	0
	Storage and access	1	7	1	1	0	0	0	0	3	0
	Redundant	18	5	6	1	7	12	1	2	2	0
	Comments	0	6	0	0	1	2	0	1	0	0
	Document	13	32	0	2	31	26	1	2	3	5
	Unauthorized changes	0	0	1	0	4	2	0	0	0	0
	Clarifications	8	25	3	8	8	21	1	3	0	2
	Recommendations	0	3	0	0	0	8	0	0	0	1
B-Total number of errors related to maintainability		41	80	12	14	51	73	3	8	8	8
Total number of errors (A + B)		68	119	14	22	56	84	3	8	8	10

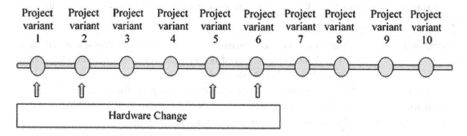

Fig. 4. Instances of major hardware changes

3. Significant proportion of errors related to missing and incorrect parameters are observed in logic checking conditions.
4. Many a monitoring parameters and status bits are missing and not adequate in the specifications and henceforth in code implementation. These new parameters are addressed by the hardware changes. Complete list of parameters are not monitored.
5. Incorrect implementation is demonstrated by the code related to monitoring parameters in most of the cases.
6. Redundant parameters in structures and pointers pointing the obsolete hardware addresses are observed in many a cases.
7. Comments related to hardware parameters are not updated at all in the code implementation.
8. Most of the clarifications are sought for clarity and missing information corresponding to hardware change.
9. Reference documents giving details of hardware changes are not submitted in almost all of the cases.
10. In almost all of the cases, updations are not reflected in existing documents to address the parameters details of changed hardware.

6 Quality Improvement - Error Prevention Guidelines

Nearly 400 errors of Navigation system software of 10 variants of project are evaluated. These are adequate to establish the stability of observed error trend. On evaluation and pattern recognition, the need for proposing the guidelines to prevent the errors is triggered. This analysis results are being used to identify the areas in specifications, implementation and documentation that need improvement. Guidelines are proposed to target the improvement of software quality addressing the software requirements specification and code implementation.

6.1 Guidelines for Software Requirements Specification and Code Implementation

After analyzing the trend of errors as elaborated in Sect. 5, guidelines for software requirements specification and code implementation are provided in Table 3.

Table 3. Guidelines for software requirements specification and code implementation

Types of errors	Guidelines
Operational	The operational sequences are to be tested in simulation test beds and by code instrumentation (if not feasible to test in simulation test beds) for all the modes of operation
Algorithm or computation	Sign conventions are to be taken care properly for all requirements and appropriate parameters are to be considered in all algorithms
Timing	Timing requirements are to be addressed properly
Logic checking condition	Review of all parameters (range and type) required for logic checking conditions is to be carried out for requirements identification. They are to be tested in simulation test beds and by code instrumentation (if not feasible to test in simulation test beds) for all the modes of operation
Data	Type of data and instants of assignments are to be addressed properly
Monitor	Carry out review of all monitoring parameters for completeness and are to be tested in all modes of operation
Redundant	Redundant parameters and operations are to be removed
Nomenclature	Consistent and appropriate nomenclatures for variable parameters are to be identified and followed
Storage and access	Manual analysis is to be carried out for appropriateness
Comments	Comments should be made appropriate when there is change in software requirements or hardware
Document	Complete details of software and system requirements are to be updated correctly and should be in line with the identified requirements and code implementation. All the reference documents are to be archived along with the source code. This assures that all artefacts are of appropriate maturity.
Clarifications	Concrete reasons are to be specified for each of the change mentioned in the change note. Clarity is to be maintained in the documentation

6.2   General Guidelines

General guidelines specific to this type of characteristics of project are provided as below:

1. All the details of errors trend observed should be taken care in eliciting software requirements.
2. Requirements of previous variants of projects are to be addressed, wherever applicable.
3. Complete list of changes carried out in code implementation are to be reflected in change notes, approved and authorized by change control board.

   These guidelines encourage and help the designers and developers to look at the specifications and code implementation effectively to expend every possible effort to eliminate the above mentioned types of errors. These eliminate the rework during regression and serve as cost and effort saving advantage relative to code inspection and testing which require quantum amount of times and resources.

7 Conclusion

A methodology for the identification of various types of errors that are likely to occur and severity of errors is demonstrated. Error database across 10 variants of projects for Navigation system software are categorized. Analysis w.r.t identified types and severity leads to observation of pattern of errors. The objective of proposing the guidelines aimed at elimination of these types of errors and thereby enhancing the quality of the software is met. This methodology can be applied to any other project with appropriate modifications and derive the benefits of error preventive guidelines.

It is worth learning from errors encountered from previous variants of project, when we start a new project. Guidelines are proposed and implementation of these guidelines are to be monitored for future variants of project to develop robust embedded systems. This enables us to observe the effectiveness of these guidelines and thereby identification of new guidelines can be carried out. Further results will be presented in future.

References

1. Nakajo, T., Kume, H.: A case history analysis of software error cause-effect relationships. IEEE Trans. Software Eng. **17**(8), 830–838 (1991)
2. Lutz, R.R.: Analyzing Software Requirements Errors in Safety-Critical, Embedded Systems. IEEE (1992). ISBN: 0-8186-3120-1/92
3. Schneidewind, N.F., Hoffmann, H.-M.: An experiment in software error data collection and analysis. IEEE Trans. Software Eng. **SE-5**(3), 276–286 (1979)
4. Ohba, M.: Software Error Data Collection and Analysis in Industry. IEEE (1995). ISBN:1071-9458/95
5. Carvalho, P.V.: Mapping the Software Errors and Effects Analysis to ISO26262 Requirements for Software Architecture Analysis. IEEE (2014). ISBN:978-1-4799-7377-4/14
6. Haugh, J.M.: Never Make the Same Mistake Twice-Using Configuration Control and Error Analysis to Improve Software Quality. IEEE AES Systems Magazine, January 1992
7. Fagan, M.E.: Design and code inspections to reduce errors in program development. IBM Syst. J. **15**(3), 219–248 (1976)
8. Beizer, B.: Software Testing Techniques Second Edition. International Thomson Computer Press (1990). ISBN 1-8503-2880-3
9. Lakshmi, K.V.N.S, Ranjana, N.: Verification & Validation of Fault Tolerant Features of Dual Redundant Navigation Systems Software Using Reliability Analysis Methods, Workshop on Scientific Women and DRDO Harnessing Research and Management, NSTL, DRDO, March 11–12, 2016

Method to Resolve Software Product Line Errors

Megha[1(✉)], Arun Negi[2], and Karamjit Kaur[1]

[1] Computer Science and Engineering Department, Thapar University Patiala,
Patiala, India
mb.meghabhushan@gmail.com, karamjit.kaur@thapar.edu
[2] Government of India, Delhi, India
arun98765@gmail.com

Abstract. Feature models (FMs) are of utmost importance when representing variability in Software Product Line (SPL) by focusing on the set of valid combinations of features that a software product can have. FMs quality is one of the factors that impacts the quality of SPL. There are several types of errors in FMs that reduces the benefits of SPL. Although FM errors is a mature topic but it has not been completely achieved yet. In this paper, disparate studies for the FM errors in SPL are summarized and a method based on rules to fix these errors is proposed and explained with the help of case studies. The results of evaluation with FMs up to 1000 features show the scalability and accuracy of the given method which improves the SPL quality.

Keywords: Software product line · Feature model · Error

1 Introduction

A comprehensive interpretation of the domain, targeted by the Product Line (PL) is required for developing a Software Product Line (SPL). SPL is described as a family of associated software systems by means of common and variable functions which reduces the development time and cost while improving the products quality. The commonalities and variabilities of a PL are represented by the various existing approaches in the literature. One of the possible approach is to do it using Feature Models (FMs). FM describes variability in PL through documentation of features and their correct combinations which further specify a product in SPL [1]. A feature is described as a system quality which is of concern to a stakeholder [2]. FM is a tree like structure consists of nodes that represent features of modeled SPL and their interrelationships (as shown in Fig. 1). The root of the tree represents whole PL and therefore, it is a part of all valid products of the PL. However, constructing a FM is a laborious and time-consuming manual process. Building a FM may inject errors in it, as features are connected to each other via relations. There are many types of errors in FMs e.g., dead feature, inconsistency, false optional feature, void model and so on which drastically diminish the benefits of the PL strategy.

Manually dealing with errors in large sized models is a cumbersome job. Therefore, this key technical issue must be solved by analyzing and fixing errors in FMs. In this

S. Kaushik et al. (Eds.): ICICCT 2017, CCIS 750, pp. 258–268, 2017.
https://doi.org/10.1007/978-981-10-6544-6_24

Notation	Type of dependency
A —● B	**Mandatory:** Child feature B must be included in all valid products containing the parent feature A and vice versa. A feature is a full mandatory feature if the feature and all its ancestors are also mandatory.
A —○ B	**Optional:** Child feature B may or may not be included in valid products containing parent feature A.
A <m..n> B C D	**Group Cardinality:** Represents the minimum (m) and the maximum (n) number of child features (B...C) grouped in a cardinality (<m..n>) that a product can have when its parent feature A is included in the product.
A ·······◄ B	**Requires:** Feature B should be included in valid products with feature A.
A ·······◄ B	**Excludes:** Both features A and B cannot be in valid products at same time.

Fig. 1. Types of dependencies in feature models.

paper, we summarize the disparate studies for FM errors in SPL and proposed a method based on rules to identify and fix errors. This information is useful for PL modelers to produce error free FMs. The proposed method is validated using 20 FMs and the results exhibits the scalability and accuracy with models up to 1000 features which leads to the overall improvement in the SPL quality. The skeleton of paper includes: Sect. 2 provides an overview of various types of FM errors, as well as discusses and summarizes the related research works. The proposed method and its evaluation details are discussed in Sect. 3. Finally, the conclusion and future research directions are presented in Sect. 4.

2 Background

2.1 Types of Feature Model Errors

In case of PLMs, errors are the undesirable properties that adversely affect the quality of the model [3]. In general, these errors arise when the FM has a misuse among the dependencies that relate its features or a group cardinality is defined wrongly [4]. Various types of FM errors along with their descriptions are shown in Fig. 2.

2.2 Review of Feature Model Errors

The identification of errors in FMs and explanations that provide the information about the cause of errors are of paramount importance. Errors are also known as defects or deficiencies by some authors [5, 6]. The works related to this area have been discussed by various researchers as follows:

Domain analysis and its products are described using a method called as Feature Oriented Domain Analysis (FODA) [1]. FM can be expressed using ontologies for analyzing their variabilities and commonalities based on semantic analysis criteria [7]. Web ontology language (OWL) is used to represent FMs and their constraints. The study identified invalid FM configurations and explains the reason why that

Type of error	Description
	Void Model: A feature model is void if it defines no product at all.
	Dead Feature: A feature that despite of being defined in a feature model, it appears in no product in the Software Product Line.
	False Optional Feature: A feature is declared as optional in the FM, but it is present in all products of the Software Product Line.
	Inconsistency: The contradictory information in the model is defined as an inconsistency. It will hinder the derivation of valid products from the model.
	Conditional Dead Feature: A conditional dead feature is a feature that becomes dead under a specific condition (e.g., while selecting another feature).

Fig. 2. Types of errors in feature models.

configuration is invalid using ontological terms [8]. FMs are translated to OWL-DL ontology [9]. FM has been constructed in ontology and evaluates the consistency of the feature configuration with an appropriate example [10]. Descriptive Logic (DL) is used to (i) identify inconsistencies in FMs represented in SXFM (XML standard for representing a FM); (ii) identify inconsistencies in products configured from the PL; and (iii) propose possible corrections [11]. A technique based on propositional logic connectives and calculus is used for PLM validation [12]. A logical expression has been developed to represent PLM. The selection of requirements from the model can be validated by satisfying the logical expression. It can validate the entire model. An approach is used to identify numerous cases of redundancies, inconsistencies and anomalies in FMs [13]. FMs are verified at different binding times using a propositional logic-based method, and a tool that supports the analysis of propositional formulas [14]. FMs are simplified by grouping features into atomic sets, later explored by [15] for detecting dead features. The constraints in cardinality-based FMs are captured using the Object-Constraint Language (OCL) [16].

An explanation is provided for the isolated features and the path to follow to treat them [17]. The calculation of feature commonality is used for detecting them and automate the detection with the help of three different implementations. There is a gap to cover for detecting the relationships that causes isolated features to emerge and providing solutions for them. Four kinds of dependencies between features are identified and these can be analysed and used to design high-level software architecture [18]. The previous work [18] is used to detect 17 types of anomalies and inconsistencies [13, 14]. A framework Feature Model Analyser (FAMA) has been presented for the automated analysis of SPLs in general and FMs in particular [19]. A run-time approach is used to find contradictions in FMs [20]. It explored the possibility of efficiently finding contradictions by statically using model checking. The experimental results showed that a static analysis to find contradictions in FMs with large number of features is very difficult. A Knowledge-Based (KB) method is used to validate FMs. FMs are represented as a KB containing predicates and rules defined using First Order Logic (FOL) [21]. The inconsistencies and redundancies have been identified by looking for particular cause of errors. Later, KB method is used to detect an inconsistency, explores the existing relations and prevents future inconsistency in FM [22].

A literature review for verifying variability models is presented and a table for the verification criteria is build to systematize PLM verification [23]. A prototype tool is developed that implemented some of these criteria [24]. FMs are transformed to generalised feature trees for their analyses and for determining a few of their properties [25]. A few algorithms and an executable specification are provided in a functional programming language known as Miranda. A comprehensive literature review for the automated analysis of FMs is provided in [26]. DOPLER variability models are converted into Constraint Programs (CPs) for supporting verification of variability models [27]. It identified dead errors, assets and decisions in already existing variability models. The non-conformance in the extended FMs is detected by using 9 conformance checking rules [28]. PLMs are transformed into constraint (logic) programs, then a typology of verification criteria is used for the automatic verification of PLMs [4]. The typology of verification criteria is presented for the case of single-view and multiview PLMs [3].

Few researchers have also used tools for dealing with errors like RequiLine is a tool used for detecting inconsistencies in the domain and product configuration level [29]. An approach is used to transform FMs with attributes and feature cardinalities into CPs using the tool VariaMos and the CP solver GNU-Prolog [30, 31]. VariaMos is a tool used for the variability modeling, model analysis, verification, integration and configuration of PLMs [32]. FMs are automatically analysed using automated tools like RACER [33]. An open-source framework FeatureIDE is proposed for Feature-Oriented Software Development (FOSD) [33]. All the phases of implementation techniques of FOSD are supported by FeatureIDE. The results showed that implementation tools require low efforts for integrating new SPL. Logic Truth Maintenance Systems (LTMS) and SAT solvers algorithms are used for translating FMs to propositional formulas [34]. The automated analysis of FMs is done using LTMS. It showed fundamental connection between feature diagrams, propositional formulas and grammars. It allows arbitrary propositional constraints to be defined between features and to debug FMs by enabling off-the-shelf solvers. A direct mapping is proposed from a FM to Constraint Satisfaction Problem (CSP) that represents attributes [35]. An approach used formal engineering to formalize and verify FMs by Z and Alloy Analyzer [36, 37].

A framework organized in three levels: a FM, a diagnosis and an implementation levels are used for providing an automatic support to FM error analysis [5]. Dead features, false optional features, the set of dependencies and explanation in FM have been identified by automating their approach [5] in FAMA [38]. Abductive reasoning is used to identify dead features and their causes [39]. An approach uses ontologies for the identification of dead features in FMs and explain their causes in natural language [40]. An ontological rule-based approach is used to identify false optional features, dead features, and their causes in natural language [41]. A consistency-based approach is used for the explanation of anomalies in FMs [42]. Explanation algorithms are applied for the anomaly detection in FMs. The quality of FM is evaluated by using a framework FODA maturity model [43]. Rincón et al. [6] have identified defects along with solutions to fix them using a minimal subset of relationships (i.e. minimal correction subsets) and CPs. A method based on FOL rules is used to identify and prevent inconsistencies in domain engineering process [44]. The method was validated using their own data sets. An approach based on ontology and FOL rules is used to identify dead features and false optional features in FMs [45].

The studies related to the FM errors in SPL have been summarized in Table 1. There are three groups: Basic FMs, Cardinality-based FMs which include FMs extended with cardinalities [46, 47] and Extended FMs include feature attributes which are used to represent additional information about features [16, 34, 35, 46, 48–50]. The rows of the table provides support to the various errors and explanation in FMs. The studies discussed above provides the information of errors in FMs by formalizing FMs to ontology, providing methods for the error identification in FMs and finally provides information of error explanation in FMs. Correction of errors in FMs is a mature topic which needs to involve additional operations to resolve errors. But, only few researchers have focused on providing corrective explanations [6, 24, 40, 41, 44] to help modelers to correct found errors.

Table 1. Summary of proposals for errors in feature models.

Operations	Basic FMs	Cardinality-based FMs	Extended FMs
Void FM	[1, 5, 6, 8, 9, 11, 12, 14, 18, 25–27, 30, 34–36, 42, 49]	[15, 16, 21, 22, 26, 30, 39]	[1, 21, 22, 26, 30, 35, 39, 45]
Dead feature	[1, 5, 6, 11, 13, 14, 17, 18, 25–27, 30, 40–43]	[21, 22, 26, 30, 39]	[1, 13, 21, 22, 26, 30, 39]
False optional feature	[5, 6, 11, 26, 27, 30, 41, 43]	[26, 30, 39]	[1, 26, 30, 39]
Inconsistency	[8, 20, 42]	[21]	[21]
Conditional dead feature	[26, 42, 43]	[26]	[26]
Explanation	[1, 5, 8, 9, 25, 26, 34, 36, 40–43]	[14, 23, 36, 39, 45]	[22, 26, 39]

3 Proposed Method and Its Evaluation

This section presents a method based on rules to identify FM errors and their causes using case studies as shown in Figs. 3 and 4.

3.1   Proposed Method

FM is converted into Feature Model Ontology (FMO) using predicates to represent model features and the dependencies among them. Prolog [51] is used to develop FOL rules and these rules are implemented on FMO to identify errors and their causes. Further, this information supports modelers to resolve errors. Rules for errors identification and their causes are as follow:

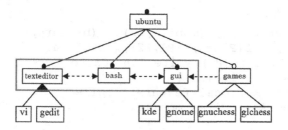

Fig. 3. A feature model.

Rule1 (see Fig. 3)

FMO:f(texteditor,m).f(bash,m).f(gui,m).e(texteditor,bash).
e(bash,gui).
rule1:f(P1,m),f(P2,m),f(P3,m),e(P1,P2),e(P2,P3),write('Er
ror: void model'),write('\n Causes:'), write(' excludes
'),write('between   (i)'),   write(P1),write(' and '),
write(P2),write(' and '),write('\n(ii)'), write(P2),write
(' and '),write(P3).
Result: Error: void model
Causes: excludes between (i)texteditor and bash   and
(ii)bash and gui

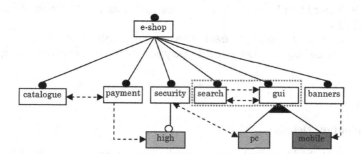

Fig. 4. Green feature is conditionally dead, grey feature is dead, and blue feature is false-optional. (Color figure online)

Rule 2 (see Fig. 4)

FMO: f(security,m). f(pc,o). e(security,pc).
rule2:-f(P1,m),f(P2,o),e(P1,P2),write('Dead feature: '),
write(P2), write('\nCause:'), write(P1), write(' excludes
'), write(P2).
Result: Dead feature: pc
Cause: security excludes pc

Rule 3 (see Fig. 4)

FMO: f(banners,m2). f(mobile,o2). r(banners,mobile).
rule3:-f(P1,m),f(P3,o),r(P1,P2),write('False   optional
feature: '),write(P2),write('\n Cause:'),write(P1),write
(' requires '),write(P2).
Result: False optional feature: mobile
Cause: banners requires mobile

Rule 4 (see Fig. 4)

FMO: f(search,m). f(gui,m). r(search,gui). e(gui,search).
rule4:-f(P1,m),f(P2,m),r(P1,P2),e(P2,P1),write('Error:
Inconsistency '),   write('\n Causes:'),write(' require
and exclude '),write('between '),write(P1),write(' and ')
,write(P2).
Result: Error: Inconsistency
Causes: require and exclude between search and gui

Rule 5 (see Fig. 4)

FMO:f(catalogue,m).f(payment,m).f(high,o).   e(catalogue,
payment). r(payment,high).
rule5:f(P1,m),f(P2,m),f(P3,o),e(P1,P2),r(P2,P3),write('Co
nditionally   dead   feature: '),write(P3),
write('\nCauses:'),   write(P1),   write(' excludes   '),
write(P2),write(' and '), write(P2),write(' requires '),
write(P3).
Result: Conditionally dead feature: high
Causes: catalogue excludes payment and payment requires
high

3.2   Evaluation Details

The proposed method was evaluated by conducting experiments on 20 FMs.

Evaluation Environment

The environment for conducting experiments included a Dell workstation with Windows 8.1 of 64 bits, RAM of 8.00 GB, CPU 2.40 GHz, Intel(R) Core(TM) i7-3630QM processor, SWI-Prolog 7.2.3 and FeatureIDE 2.7.2.

Accuracy

The proposed method identified 100% of the errors along with their causes with 0% false positive. The method was evaluated and verified using 20 FMs with wide-ranging sizes from 10 to 1000 features. The proposed method was validated with 100% accuracy as each rule identified the expected errors along with their causes.

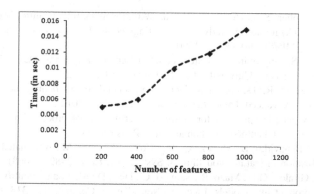

Fig. 5. Execution time required by all rules, per number of features

Scalability

The execution times (in seconds) required by all rules to identify errors and their causes in all FMs with wide-ranging sizes from 10 to 1000 features are shown in Fig. 5. All rules have been executed 50 times to obtain the accurate values of execution time for each of the model. The results show that the method can handle large sized models up to 1000 features in 0.02 s. Thus, it concludes the scalability of the proposed method.

4   Conclusion

SPL based development of software intensive systems is a promising area with emphasis on reusability. The variability in SPL is modeled using FMs. We have presented a review on the proposals related to the errors in FMs e.g., dead feature, void model, conditional dead feature, inconsistency and false optional feature, and summarized that once the error has been identified then explanation can be used to identify the cause. The proposed method based on rules is used to handle FM errors. Feature Model Ontology (FMO) is constructed from FM using predicates. The rules are developed using FOL to identify errors along with their causes. The given method has been validated with 20 FMs up to 1000 features which leads to the scalability and accuracy of the method. This information is useful for PL modelers to produce error free FMs by modifying the dependencies. Therefore, it improves the overall SPL quality.

As future work, though the tools exist but they do not explore all the cases of errors so there is a need for developing a tool which can support all the cases. The set of proposed rules can be extended by adding new rules in other FM notations also.

Acknowledgments. One of the authors, Megha, gratefully acknowledges the University Grants Commission (UGC), New Delhi, Government of India, for awarding her the Rajiv Gandhi National Fellowship (Grant no. F117.1/201415/RGNF 201415SCJAM66324) to carry out this research work.

References

1. Kang, K.C., Cohen, S.G., Hess, J.A., Novak, W.E., Peterson, S.P.: Feature-Oriented Domain Analysis (FODA) feasibility study. Software Engineering Institute, Carnegie Mellon Univ., Tech. report CMU/SEI-90-TR-21 (1990)
2. Megha, Goel, S.: Improving software product line engineering using AOP, LEL and UML. M. Eng. thesis, Thapar University, Patiala, Punjab, India (2012)
3. Salinesi, C., Mazo, R.: Defects in product line model and how to identify them. In: Software Product Line - Advanced Topic, InTech edn., pp. 97–122 (2012)
4. Mazo, R.: A generic approach for automated verification of product line models. Ph.D. dissertation, Paris 1 Panthéon Sorbonne Univ., Paris (2011)
5. Trinidad, P., Benavides, D., Duran, A., Ruiz-Cortes, A., Toro, M.: Automated error analysis for the agilization of feature modelling. J. Syst. Softw. **81**, 883–896 (2008)
6. Rincón, L., Giraldo, G.L., Mazo, R., Salinesi, C., Diaz, D.: Method to identify corrections of defects on product line models. Electron. Notes Theor. Comput. Sci. **314**, 61–81 (2015). doi:10.1016/j.entcs.2015.05.005
7. Lee, S., Kim, J., Song, C., Baik, D.: An approach to analyzing commonality and variability of features using ontology in a Software product line engineering. In: Proceedings of 5th International Conference on Software Engineering Research, Management and Applications, pp. 727–734 (2007)
8. Wang, H., Li, Y., Sun, J., Zhang, H., Pan, J.: Verifying feature models using OWL. Web Semant. Sci. Serv. Agents World Wide Web **5**, 117–129 (2007)
9. Wang, H., Li, Y., Sun, J., Zhang, H., Pan, J.: A semantic web approach to feature modeling and verification. In: Proceedings of Workshop on Semantic Web Enabled Software Engineering (SWESE 2005) (2005)
10. Matcha, V.B., Reddy, P.V.G.D.P., Hari, C.V.M.K., Srinivas, S., Rao, G., Jayachand, B., Swarup kumar, J.N.V.R., SriRamGanesh, G., Vamsi Krishna, N.V.R.V., Pradeep, I.K., Ramesh, C.: Software reuse: ontological approach to feature modeling. Int. J. Comput. Sci. Netw. Secur. **9**(8), 262–268 (2009)
11. Noorian, M., Ensan, A., Bagheri, E., Boley, H., Biletskiy, Y.: Feature model debugging based on description logic reasoning. In: Proceedings of 17th International Conference on Distributed Multimedia Systems (DMS 2011), pp. 158–164. KSI (2011)
12. Mannion, M.: Using first-order logic for product line model validation. In: Chastek, Gary J. (ed.) SPLC 2002. LNCS, vol. 2379, pp. 176–187. Springer, Heidelberg (2002). doi:10.1007/3-540-45652-X_11
13. Von der Massen, T., Lichter, H.: Deficiencies in feature models. In: Proceedings of Workshop on Software Variability Management for Product Derivation - Towards Tool Support, SPLC 2004, Boston, MA, USA (2004)
14. Zhang, W., Zhao, H., Mei, H.: A propositional logic-based method for verification of feature models. In: Proceedings of 6th International Conference on Formal Engineering Methods, ICFEM 2004, pp. 115–130 (2004)
15. Segura, S.: Automated analysis of feature models using atomic sets. In: Proceedings of 12th International Conference of Software Product Line, SPLC 2008, Limerick, Ireland, pp. 201–207 (2008)

16. Czarnecki, K., Kim, C.H.P.: Cardinality-based feature modeling and constraints: a progress report. In: Proceedings of International Workshop on Software Factories, San Diego-California (2005)
17. Trinidad, P., Benavides, D., Ruiz-Corts, A.: Isolated features detection in feature models. In: Proceedings of Conference on Advanced Information Systems Engineering (CAiSE 2006), pp. 1–4 (2006)
18. Zhang, W., Mei, H., Zhao, H.: Feature-driven requirement dependency analysis and high-level software design. Requirements Eng. **11**(3), 205–220 (2006)
19. Benavides, D.: On the automated analysis of software product lines using feature models. A framework for developing automated tool support. Ph.D. dissertation, The Dept. of Comput. Languages and Systems, Univ. of Seville, Spain (2007)
20. Hemakumar, A.: Finding contradictions in feature models. In: Proceedings of 1st International Workshop on Analyses of Software Product Lines (ASPL 2008), pp. 183–190 (2008)
21. Osman, A., Phon-Amnuaisuk, S., Ho, C.K.: Knowledge based method to validate feature models. In: Proceedings of 1st International Workshop on Analyses of Software Product Lines, pp. 217–225 (2008)
22. Elfaki, A.O., Phon-Amnuaisuk, S., Ho, C.K.: Using first order logic to validate feature model. In: Proceedings of 3rd International Workshop VaMoS, pp. 169–172 (2009)
23. Salinesi, A., Rolland, C., Diaz, D., Mazo, R.: Looking for product line feature models defects: towards a systematic classification of verification criteria. In: Proceedings of 17th IEEE International Requirements Engineering Conference, RE 2009, Atlanta, USA, pp. 385–386 (2009)
24. Mazo, R., Salinesi, C.: Methods, techniques and tools for product line model verification, Centre Recherche en Informatique, Universite Paris, Research report (2008)
25. Van den Broek, P., Galvao, I.: Analysis of feature models using generalised feature trees. In: Proceedings of 3rd International Workshop on Variability Modelling of Software-Intensive Systems, number 29 in ICB-Research Rep., Universit'at Duisburg, Essen, pp. 29–35 (2009)
26. Benavides, D., Segura, S., Ruiz-Cortes, A.: Automated analysis of feature models 20 years later: a literature review. Inform. Syst. **35**(6), 615–636 (2010)
27. Mazo, R., Grnbacher, P., Heider, W., Rabiser, R., Salinesi, C., Diaz, D.: Using constraint programming to verify Dopler variability models. In: Proceedings of 5th Workshop on Variability Modeling of Software-Intensive System (VaMos 2011), Namur-Belgium, pp. 97–103 (2011)
28. Mazo, R., Lopez-Herrejon, R., Salinesi, C., Diaz, D., Egyed, A.: Conformance checking with constraint logic programming: the case of feature models. In: Proceedings of 35th IEEE Annual International Computer Software and Applications Conference (COMPSAC), Munich, Germany, pp. 456–465 (2011)
29. Von der Massen, T., Lichter, H.: RequiLine: a requirements engineering tool for software product lines. In: Proceedings of 5th International Workshop on Product Family Engineering (PFE), pp. 168–180 (2003)
30. Mazo, R., Salinesi, C., Diaz, D., Michiels, A.L.: Transforming attribute and clone-enabled feature models into constraint programs over finite domains. In: Proceedings of International Conference on Evaluation of Novel Approaches to Software Engineering (ENASE 2011), pp. 188–199 (2011)
31. Diaz, D., Codognet, P.: Design and implementation of the GNU prolog system. J. Funct. Logic Program. **6**(2001), 542 (2001)
32. Mazo, R., Salinesi, C., Diaz, D.: Variamos: a tool for product line driven systems. In: Proceedings of 24th International Conference on Advanced Information Systems Engineering (CAiSE Forum 2012), pp. 25–29. Springer Press, Gdansk (2012)

33. Thum, T., Kastner, C., Benduhn, F., Meinicke, J., Saake, G., Leich, T.: Feature IDE: an extensible framework for feature-oriented software development. Sci. Comput. Program. **79**, 70–85 (2012)
34. Batory, D.: Feature models, grammars, and propositional formulas. In: Obbink, H., Pohl, K. (eds.) SPLC 2005. LNCS, vol. 3714, pp. 7–20. Springer, Heidelberg (2005). doi:10.1007/11554844_3
35. Benavides, D., Ruiz-Cortes, A., Trinidad, P.: Automated reasoning on feature models. In: Proceedings of 17th International Conference on Advanced Information Systems Engineering, CAiSE 2005, pp. 491–503 (2005)
36. Sun, J., Zhang, H., Li, Y., Wang, H.: Formal semantics and verification for feature modelling. In: Proceedings of 10th IEEE International Conference on Engineering of Complex Computer Systems, ICECSS 2005, pp. 303–312 (2005)
37. Jackson, D.: Alloy: a lightweight object modelling notation. ACM Trans. Softw. Eng. Methodol. **11**, 256–290 (2002)
38. Trinidad, P., Benavides, D., Ruiz-Cortes, A., Segura, S., Jimenez, A.: FAMA framework. In: Proceedings of 12th International Software Product Line Conference (SPLC 2012), Washington, DC, USA, p. 359 (2008)
39. Trinidad, P., Ruiz-Cortes, A.: Abductive reasoning and automated analysis of feature models: how are they connected, In: Proceedings of 3rd International Workshop on Variability Modelling of Software-Intensive Systems, pp. 145–153 (2009)
40. Lucia, G.G.G., Luisa, R.P., Raul, M.: Identifying dead features and their causes in product line models: an ontological approach. Rev. DYNA **81**, 68–77 (2014)
41. Rincon, L.F., Giraldo, G.L., Mazo, R., Salinesi, C.: An ontological rule-based approach for analyzing dead and false optional features in feature models. Electron. Notes Theor. Comput. Sci. **302**, 111–132 (2014)
42. Felfernig, A., Benavides, D., Galindo, J., Reinfrank, F.: Towards anomaly explanation in feature models. In: Proceedings of Workshop on Configuration, Vienna, pp. 117–124 (2013)
43. Javed, M., Naeem, M., Wahab, H.A.: Towards the maturity model for feature oriented domain analysis. Comput. Ecol. Softw. **4**(3), 170–182 (2014)
44. Elfaki, A.O.: A rule-based approach to detect and prevent inconsistency in the domain-engineering process. Exp. Syst. **33**, 3–13 (2016). doi:10.1111/exsy.12116
45. Bhushan, M., Goel, S.: Improving software product line using an ontological approach. Sadhana **41**(12), 1381–1391 (2016). doi:10.1007/s12046-016-0571-y
46. Czarnecki, K., Helsen, S., Eisenecker, U.W.: Formalizing cardinality-based feature models and their specialization. Softw. Process. **10**(1), 7–29 (2005)
47. Riebisch, M., Bollert, K., Streitferdt, D., Philippow, I.: Extending feature diagrams with UML multiplicities. In: Proceedings of 6th World Conference on Integrated Design and Process Technology (IDPT 2002), Pasadena, California, USA (2002)
48. Batory, D., Benavides, D., Ruiz-Cortes, A.: Automated analysis of feature models: challenges ahead. Commun. ACM (CACM) **49**(12), 45–47 (2006)
49. Benavides, D., Trinidad, P., Ruiz-Cortes, A.: Using constraint programming to reason on feature models. In: Proceedings of 17th International Conference on Software Engineering and Knowledge Engineering, SEKE 2005, pp. 677–682 (2005)
50. Streitferdt, D., Riebisch, M., Philippow, I.: Details of formalized relations in feature models using OCL. In: Proceedings of 10th IEEE International Conference on Engineering of Computer-Based Systems (ECBS 2003), pp. 45–54. IEEE Computer Society, Huntsville (2003)
51. Wielemaker, J.: SWI-Prolog (Version 7.2.3), Free Software. University of Amsterdam, Amsterdam (2015)

Test Case Prioritization Based on Dissimilarity Clustering Using Historical Data Analysis

Md. Abu Hasan[1(✉)] [iD], Md. Abdur Rahman[2], and Md. Saeed Siddik[1]

[1] Institute of Information Technology, University of Dhaka, Dhaka, Bangladesh
hasandubits@gmail.com, siddik.saeed@gmail.com
[2] Centre for Advanced Research in Sciences, University of Dhaka,
Dhaka, Bangladesh
mukul.arahman@gmail.com

Abstract. Test case prioritization reorders test cases based on their fault detection capability. In regression testing when new version is released, previous versions' test cases are also executed to cross check the desired functionality. Historical data ensures the previous fault information, which would lead the potential faults in new version. Faults are not uniformed in all software versions, where similar test cases may stack in same faults. Most of the prioritization techniques are either similar coverage based or requirements clustering, where some used historical data. However, no one incorporate dissimilarity and historical data together, which ensure the coverage of various un-uniformed faults. This paper presents a prioritization approach based on dissimilarity test case clustering using historical data analysis to detect various faults in minimum test case execution. Proposed scheme is evaluated using well established Defects4j dataset, and it has reported that dissimilarity algorithm performs better than untreated, random and similarity based prioritization.

Keywords: Software testing · Test case prioritization · Historical data · Similarity · Dissimilarity

1 Introduction

Test case prioritization reorders test case execution sequence to enhance fault detecting rate. In regression testing earlier versions of test cases are considered for testing new functionalities. Regression testing involves revalidating the software when new component is included to meet the modified requirements which may badly impact on existing software system [1]. This revalidating process executes both existing and newly added test cases, which is very expensive and time consuming [2].

It has been experimented that more than 50 days are required to test 20,000 lines of code [1].

Hence, diverse techniques are proposed in order to improve regression testing performance on the basis of cost effectiveness [1, 3, 4], which are categorized into three different techniques namely test suite reduction, test case selection, and test case prioritization [3]. Test case prioritization reorders test cases in such a way so that it meets testing objectives, for example fault detection rate and code coverage or quick feedback [4].

S. Kaushik et al. (Eds.): ICICCT 2017, CCIS 750, pp. 269–281, 2017.
https://doi.org/10.1007/978-981-10-6544-6_25

Faults are not uniformed in previous version of software, which is difficult to detect in regression testing [5].

Researchers introduced several prioritization methods of test cases to increase the rate of fault detection, which are categorized in several domains, such as code coverage [4, 6, 7], requirement coverage [8, 9], historical data analysis based [10, 11], etc. Based on historical execution data, dynamic regression test case prioritization using requirement priority was proposed by Wang et al. [10]. While, Rothermel et al. described several code coverage based prioritization strategies to improve the rate of fault detection [3]. A modified genetic algorithm for prioritizing test cases to improve code coverage was proposed by Patipat et al. [6]. Xiaobin et al. proposed Bayesian Network based test case prioritization technique, where test cases are clustered depend on their method level coverage [12].

On the other hand, Clustering based test case prioritization introduced by [8, 9], where test cases are clustered based on their code coverage to improve earlier fault detection in testing phase. However, clustering test cases based on their coverage information contain threat to detect similar fault consecutively as each cluster contains similar type of test cases. Accordingly, those test cases in each cluster share similar attribute have similar fault detection ability and consequently get similar precedence which may lead to reduce the effectiveness of fault detection rate.

This problem can be illustrated with the following example, where nine test cases cover nine faults of a program as shown in following Table.

F/T	F1	F2	F3	F4	F5	F6	F7	F8	F9
TC1	1	0	0	1	1	1	1	0	0
TC2	0	1	1	1	1	1	0	0	0
TC3	0	1	1	1	0	0	1	1	0
TC4	0	1	1	0	0	0	1	1	1
TC5	1	0	0	0	0	1	1	0	1
TC6	1	0	0	0	1	1	1	0	1
TC7	1	1	1	1	0	0	0	1	0
TC8	1	0	0	0	0	1	0	0	0
TC9	1	1	1	1	0	1	0	0	0

Cluster-1: TC1, TC5, TC6, TC8
Cluster-2: TC2, TC3, TC4
Cluster-3: TC7, TC9

Most of the test cases of cluster-1 cover faults F1, F6 and F7 where none of the test case covers F2, F3 and F8 faults. In case of cluster-2, faults F2 and F3 covered by all test cases but no one covers fault F1. In cluster-3, both test cases cover faults F1, F3, F4 and F9, however, faults F5 and F7 do not covered by any single test case. In this scenario, any single cluster can't cover all or maximum faults, which is the problem of clustered based test case prioritization which shares same properties.

To overcome those limitations, dissimilarity based test case prioritization scheme is proposed in this research, where test case's similarity and historical failure data are incorporated. In this proposed scheme, all the previous and new versions test cases are considered to detect the similar function call graph. Several clusters are formed from this graph based on their degree of connectivity. Inter cluster test cases are ordered based on the preceding version failure history. Finally, the top test cases of each similar cluster are picked to generate the dissimilar test suite to cover maximum varieties of un-uniformed faults.

Proposed method has been experimented with Defects4j dataset [13], and results are compared to several prominent prioritization techniques. It has been discovered that the dissimilarity based test suite using historical data performs better than untreated, random and similarity based prioritization approaches.

The rest of this paper is organized as follows, where Sect. 2 denotes the literature review. Sections 3 and 4 described the proposed method and result analysis respectively. Finally Sect. 5 concludes this paper with future research direction.

2 Literature Review

Test case prioritization technique rearranges test case execution sequence to maximize testing objective functions, like fault detection rate improvement, reducing execution time etc. Because of significance in practice, many academicians, researchers and testers have demonstrated varieties methods of test case prioritization, which are categorized in several domains, such as code coverage [4, 6, 7], requirement coverage [8, 9], historical data analysis based [10, 11], etc. Some of the most prominent prioritization approaches are discussed in this section.

Rothermel et al. demonstrated a number of prioritization strategies to improve fault detection rate [4]. The proposed method uses most advantageous prioritization for finest test case orders to increase fault detection rate. They performed empirical studies to evaluate quality, importance and quantity of the rate of fault detection of different techniques. Empirical studies and results indicate that their proposed approach can efficiently detect the fault early of the execution.

To improve testing efficiency, history based dynamic regression test case prioritization using requirement priority was proposed by Wang et al. [10]. In this research work, test cases are prioritized with the priority of requirements assigned by customers and developers. The initially prioritized test cases are executed and numbers of faults detected by test cases are recorded to be used for next version requirement priority. The differences of requirement priority between two adjacent test cases reorder the execution sequence dynamically. An industrial experimentation has been performed in order to evaluate the technique, and result analysis shows that the proposed history based prioritization method improves testing effectiveness and fault detection ability than random and other methods. However, the efficiency of this technique depends on how accurately requirement priority has been assigned by customers and developers. Biased requirement priority assignment may affect the deserved prioritization effectiveness.

Patipat et al. implemented a modified genetic algorithm for prioritizing test cases to improve code coverage [6]. A control flow graph has been generated based on the selected program, which was derived to get decision graph. Test cases are randomly generated from the decision graph according to the population size (number of test cases). Test cases are preprocessed before feed as chromosome in genetic algorithm, to overcome the unwanted and dislocated desired path. Test suites are formed using selected test cases measuring conditions covered by each test case. The fitness value of every test case has been determined based on the coverage information, which are used to rank the suites. Finally, using fitness value, test suites have been ranked which is measured counting total coverage. After applying the genetic algorithm on test suite, the experimental result shows that modified genetic algorithm performs better than Bee Colony and random approach. However, generating complex decision graph for large scale software may overhead of this approach.

A Bayesian Network (BN) based novel prioritization framework has been proposed to improve fault detection rate by Siavash et al. [7]. The framework takes program modification, tendency of fault occurrence and test case coverage information as a single input and produces the probability of test case as output. The different evidence sets have been extracted from the source code, which are integrated to single BN model. The experimental result shows that proposed method performs better than other implemented techniques, if the available faults are remarkable. However, in this proposed approach, several test cases may indicate similar faults in execution.

Xiaobin et al. proposed an enhanced Bayesian Network (BN) based technique for prioritization, where test cases are clustered using method level coverage matrix [12]. Inter cluster test cases are prioritized based on their fault detection probability by BN approach. Source code change information, and class level coverage matrix are fed as input of BN model to get failure probability as output. The result shows that the improved BN scheme is more effective than normal BN model for test case prioritization. However, failure history which is effective to detect fault in regression testing [5], has not been considered for test case prioritization in the proposed strategy. Furthermore, clustering based on similar code coverage has similar fault detection capability, which may detect similar faults by multiple test cases.

Arafeen et al. introduced prioritization approach using requirement similarity clustering to investigate regression testing efficiency [8]. Distinct terms from software requirements are identified to generate term-document matrix, which lead to k-means cluster. Clusters of test cases have been formed using requirements-test case mapping traceability matrix. Inter cluster test cases has been prioritized based the source code coverage information. Execution sequence of clusters is ordered using code modification information and client's requirement priority. Results denoted that the applied strategy which incorporates requirement information to prioritization improves the effectiveness of prioritization process. However, previous version test case failure history has not been considered for prioritization, which may affect the effectiveness of proposed technique.

Saeed et al. presented test case prioritization technique named as RDCC, which collaborates different software artifacts such as requirements, design diagrams and source code [9]. Their scheme overcomes the limitation of traditional single SDLC phase consideration in software testing. In RDCC approach, requirements connectivity, design inter-dependency and code metrics are collected, and multiplied by their weight for measuring final priority of test case. An academic case study has been used as the experimental analysis and results figure out that use of collaborative information in test case prioritization was significant. However, significant direction was undeclared for assigning weight to SDLC phases, and the result would be more effective by incorporating historical failure data.

Yiting et al. proposed a prioritization approach on the basis of fault severity to overcome random selection problem when multiple test cases have same coverage rate [14]. In this approach, test cases are selected based on the measurement of fault severity of each test case. The detected fault history of selected test cases has been recorded to update the test case priority for next execution. Considering consistent coverage rate, experimental result shows that the proposed technique improves the efficiency of regression testing. However, the fault severity has been assigned based on assumption rather than analysis of faults failed in previous testing execution, which may lead a biased prioritization. Consideration of consistent code coverage may have negative impact on their proposed approach.

Dusica et al. proposed a multi-perspective test case prioritization framework in time-constrained environments for faster fault detection [15]. This scheme considers test execution time, inter dependence functionality, failure impact and frequency factors for selecting the multi-perspective values. When time is limited for test suite execution, this technique selects test cases which are cost effective to execute. This approach prioritizes test cases to detect fault early and maximizes test cases having maximum inter dependence functional coverage, failure impact and frequency. Even though, this strategy used multiple factors for prioritizing test cases, dissimilar based test suite selection has not been considered to detect different types of fault at early execution.

Tanzeem et al. implemented a similarity based prioritization approach using historical failure data to rank new test cases matching with the failed test cases of previous execution [5]. Sequence of method call by previously failed and new test cases are generated to measure distance value from each other, which are used to form similarity matrix in descending order. The new test cases ranked higher whose distance value is less in the matrix. The experimental result shows that this similarity based approach is more effective in test case prioritization compared to other traditional strategies.

Regression test case selection approach has been evaluated in order to investigate the effect of time and resource constraint in testing process by [11]. In this strategy, based on historical data an empirical study has been conducted to prioritize test case in a time limit environment. The cost-benefit analysis of this strategy has been conducted under different software evaluation models to provide directions for further research on this field. The experimentation shows that regression testing for constrained environment has to be conducted differently from non-constraint environment and historical data has significant impact on regression testing. However, dissimilar test cases based on historical data is not considered for prioritization in order to detect various types of fault at the early of testing execution.

The analysis of existing approaches shows different prioritization strategies have been implemented for regression testing such as code coverage, requirement clustering, historical data analysis etc. Very few researchers incorporate the historical data and similarity clusters, where similar test cases are pointing the uniform faults together, which are imperfect in varieties of fault detection. However, no direction has been found yet to detect dissimilar faults using historical data analysis, which may increase fault detection rate in regression testing.

3 Proposed Methodology

Based on historical data, dissimilar based clustering framework is proposed to implement test case prioritization with intent to cover different region of code to detect variance faults at early. In this technique functions between two subsequent test suites version have been listed based on the function call similarity among them. Figure 1 presents the activity flow of proposed prioritization framework. A dependency matrix or graph has been generated based on the similar function of all test cases version. Test cases are clustered considering their function call similarities which are denoted by several circle in Fig. 1. Inter cluster test cases are ordered using the previous version fault detection matrix and degree of connectivity. Finally, the top test cases are picked from every cluster to form a dissimilar test suite, is iterated until all the test cases are picked. This order is the desired prioritization sequence of this proposed approach. The whole proposed method can be divided into five distinct steps which are described below.

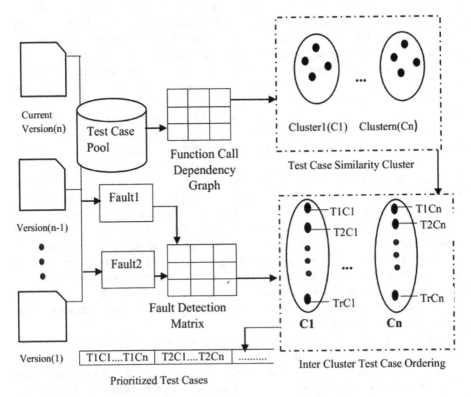

Fig. 1. Activity flow of dissimilar test case prioritization

Step 1: Generating Test Cases Dependency Graph

In this approach one old version and one new version of test suite are taken as input to generate similar functions list. Similarity between old version functions with new version is measured, based on the number of function called. Total number of called function by old and new version program function is calculated to generate similarity score [16]. An example of function called by old and new test cases is given below.

@*Test_ Old_ TestCase*
public void testCaseOld()
{ M1(); M2(); M3(); M4(); }

@*Test_ New_TestCase*
public void testCaseNew()
{ M2(); M4(); M5(); }

In the above example, function *testCaseOld()* called *m1()*, *m2()*, *m3()*, and *m4()*, where function *testCaseNew()* of new Test Case called *m2()*, *m4()*, and *m5()*. Even though, the name of old and new test cases is not same. However, *m2()* and *m4()* are called by both functions. In this example, similarity score is 2, which is calculated by the number of same called functions. Execution function call graph $G (V, E)$ has been generated, where test cases are the vertex (V), and the similarity scores are the edges (E) between two vertices. Degree of connection for each test case is computed on the basis of dependency graph. The square root ceiling value of total test cases is used to find the number of clusters.

Step 2: Forming Similar Test Case Clusters

In this step, the distance among cluster headers and test cases degree of connections calculated from dependency graph. The measuring score is used to assign test cases to the cluster with whose distance is less. The test cases those are not connected with any cluster header (whose similarity score is zero) have been assigned in a cluster named as an orphan cluster.

To assign the members of orphan cluster, first degree of connection of each member inside orphan cluster is measured. This is then compared with each cluster header value and their member's value. If any comparison value found closest to any cluster header, the member is assigned to that cluster. The remaining test cases whose connectivity degree with cluster header or members is zero are assigned to a cluster named as isolated cluster. Also test case pairs those are connected only with each other are assigned to isolated cluster.

Step 3: Prioritizing Inter Cluster Test Cases

In this step, total number of faults detected by similar test cases in previous execution and degree of connection is calculated in order to assign priority. Test cases failed in previous execution are listed in descending order based on the number of faults detected. Degree of connection is considered to assign priority for test cases those are shared same number of fault detection score. The remaining test cases those have only connection degree will be prioritized in a descending ordering based on their degree of connectivity. Total number of faults detected by similar test cases and degree of connection is measured for each clusters test cases. After then, clusters are prioritized based on their previously calculated total score.

Step 4: Dissimilar Test Suite Formation
Top test cases from each cluster have been picked one by one to form dissimilar test suites. This dissimilar test case cluster process is continued until all the test case is picked.

Step 5: Prioritizing and Executing Test Cases
The internal prioritization of dissimilar test suite has been given based on total number of faults detected by similar test cases in previous execution and degree of connectivity of each test case.

4 Result Analysis and Discussion

The implementation of proposed dissimilarity based prioritization approach with their comparative prominent test case prioritization is presented in this section. The result analysis with experimental setup and dataset are also described here.

Dataset
Two versions of three different projects named as JodaTime, Closure, and Chart from well reputed Defects4j datasets are used for experimental analysis in this paper [13]. Defects4j dataset contains 20,109 tests and 357 bugs in each individual projects. Each version of project contains buggy and fixed code segments with corresponding test cases. All the test cases are written in Junit test method. Projects which are used as dataset for this paper experimentation from Defects4j are shown in below Table 1.

Table 1. Dataset details

Identifier	Project name	Number of bugs	Number of test cases
Chart	Jfreechart	26	2,205
Closure	Closure compiler	133	7,927
Time	Joda-Time	27	2,245

Environment Setup
The research work evaluation has been performed on a single personal computer having 2.5 GHz core i5 CPU and 4 GB memory running the Ubuntu 14.04 LTS version operating system. To run Defects4j java 1.7, perl 5.0.10, git 2.10.1, and SVN 1.9.5 have been installed. LAMPP server has been installed in order to execute php scripts, which are used to generate dissimilar test suites.

Measurement Metric

In test case prioritization technique, standard measurement metric named as APFD (Average Percentage of Faults Detection) is used to calculate the average fault detection percentage for the test suite [17]. The limit of APFD result is 0 to 100, where higher number indicates faster fault detection rate. Let a test suite T containing n test cases; F denotes a set having m faults which is revealed by test suite T. *TFi* is the position number of earliest test case of test suite *T* which detects fault *i*. The APFD is calculated using the following Eq. (1).

$$APFD = 1 - \frac{TF_1 + TF_2 + TF_3 + \ldots + TF_m}{n * m} + \frac{1}{2n} \tag{1}$$

Experimental Prioritization Method

Four different test case prioritization schemes are experimented to validate the result of proposed technique on same Defects4j datasets, which are explained below.

1. **Untreated Test Case Prioritization (UTP)**

   In UTP method, executions of test cases are performed on the basis of normal test case ordering without any prioritization. APFD of UTP method was measured by considering normal ordering of whole test suite and the position of test case that detect the faults at first.

2. **Random Test Case Prioritization (RTP)**

   In RTP method, APFD is measured using random test case ordering of a test suite. In this approach random execution sequence of test case is generated twenty (20) times, and APFD is calculated based on the average of all execution.

3. **Similar Test Case Prioritization (STP)**

   In STP, test cases are clustered on the basis of similar function call. Internal ordering of a single test cluster is calculated based on the faults detection of previous version. The connection degrees of test cases are considered for internal test case ordering, when fault detection is absent.

4. **Dissimilar Test Case Prioritization (DTP)**

   In DTP method, test cases are prioritized as dissimilar test suite, which is formed by picking up the top test case of each ordered test similarity cluster. Internal ordering of each test case within a dissimilar test suite is calculated based on their connection degree, and total number of faults they detected.

Results Analysis

The comparative results of proposed Dissimilar Test case Prioritization (DTP) with three prominent prioritization methods named as UTP, RTP and STP are listed below.

   i. **UTP vs DTP:**

   In the experiment, for every project of two versions, DTP performs better than UTP which is shown in the above Table 2. For example in Chart v3 dataset DTP APFD values for different input size are 79%, 79%, 79%, 96% &100% where UTP APFD

Table 2. APFD based on various percentage of test execution

Project	Prioritization technique	APFD based on various percentage of test execution				
		20%	40%	60%	80%	100%
Closure v2	UTP	36.53%	36.53%	42.30%	100%	100%
	RTP	19.61%	45.38%	57.69%	78.07%	100%
	STP	98.07%	98.07%	98.07%	100%	100%
	DTP	100%	100%	100%	100%	100%
Closure v3	UTP	34.61%	40.38%	46.15%	100%	100%
	RTP	28.84%	56.92%	68.07%	97.69%	100%
	STP	86.53%	96.15%	100%	100%	100%
	DTP	94%	100%	100%	100%	100%
Chart v2	UTP	10.52%	10.52%	42.10%	100%	100%
	RTP	13.68%	32.63%	64.21%	88.37%	100%
	STP	26.31%	26.31%	57.89%	100%	100%
	DTP	100%	100%	100%	100%	100%
Chart v3	UTP	0%	0%	29.16%	83%	100%
	RTP	20%	36.65%	62.50%	73.32%	100%
	STP	54.16%	87.50%	100%	100%	100%
	DTP	79%	79%	79%	96%	100%
Joda time v2	UTP	0%	20%	20%	100%	100%
	RTP	10%	18%	64%	94%	100%
	STP	80%	90%	100%	100%	100%
	DTP	80%	100%	100%	100%	100%
Joda time v3	UTP	0%	28%	28%	100%	100%
	RTP	17%	45.60%	63%	91%	100%
	STP	72%	88%	92%	100%	100%
	DTP	80%	90%	100%	100%	100%

values are 0%, 0%, 29.16%, 83%, 100% respectively. The various APFD results for UTP and DTP are averaged and figured out at Fig. 2(a) and (d) subsequently. According to Fig. 2(a) and (d) the area under the curve represents the APFD, and it shows that our DTP method APFD 88.54%, which is higher than UTP APFD 40.77%.

ii. RTP vs DTP:

According to the Table 2 RTP APFD is lower than proposed method DTP. In the experimental analysis for dataset Jodatime v3 the DTP APFD values for different input sizes are 80%, 90%, 100%, 100% and 100% which are always higher than RTP APFD values 17%, 45.60%, 63%, 91% and 100% respectively. The various APFD results for RTP and DTP are averaged and figured out at Fig. 2(b) and (d) correspondingly. According to Fig. 2(b) and (d) the area under the curve represents the APFD, and it shows that our DTP method APFD is 88.54%, which is higher than RTP APFD 51.50%.

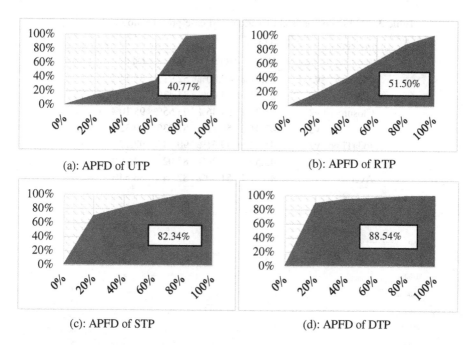

Fig. 2. Average APFD of various prioritization schemes

iii. STP vs DTP:

In this paper the proposed method DTP detects faults earlier than STP in 66.67% cases which is measure according to the APFD metric. According to the Table 2 for dataset Jodatime v3, the calculative APFD for proposed DTP method for various input size are 80%, 90%, 100%, 100%, 100% where STP APFD is 72%, 88%, 92%, 100% and 100% respectively. The various APFD results for STP and DTP are averaged and figured out at Fig. 2(c) and (d) respectively. According to Fig. 2(c) and (d) the area under the curve represents the APFD, and it shows that our DTP method APFD is 88.54%, which is higher than STP APFD 82.34%.

5 Result Discussion

Table 3 and Fig. 3 show the experimental results of three Dataset JodaTime, Closure and Chart. Table 3 shows that the performance ranking of four different test case prioritization technique is UTP < RTP < STP < DTP in terms of APFD metric calculation. According to Table 3, UTP and RTP test case prioritization techniques APFD value is always lower than our proposed DTP technique where 66.67% cases DTP has higher APFD value than STP. The box-plot of Fig. 3 represents the average APFD value of each test case prioritization method of three projects where DTP has higher value 88.54% compare to UTP, RTP and STP 40.77%, 51.50%, 82.34% value respectively. That means the dissimilar test suite selection can reduce the test execution time and maximize the fault detection rate.

Table 3. APFD comparison of various test case prioritization techniques

Project	Version	APFD			
		UTP	RTP	STP	DTP
Chart	v2	36.91%	49.00%	52.98%	87.74%
	v3	28.24%	45.90%	84.43%	81.19%
Closure	v2	46.73%	54.46%	95.55%	95.10%
	v3	47.91%	59.77%	87.23%	90.32%
JodaTime	v2	41.32%	49.61%	90.84%	92.12%
	v3	43.52%	50.26%	83.02%	84.79%
Average		40.77%	51.50%	82.34%	88.54%

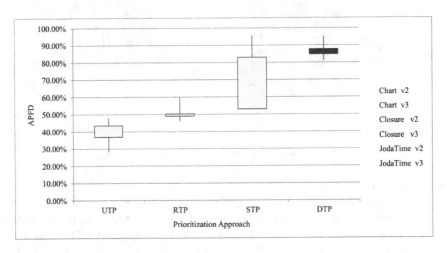

Fig. 3. Box plot of several test case prioritization techniques

6 Conclusion

This paper presents a dissimilarity based test case prioritization based on historical failure data analysis. This method considers both old and new version of test cases for prioritization. It calculates the similarity between two test cases and generates several clusters based on those similarity values. Inter cluster test cases ordered using the failure information form old version of test cases. Finally, test cases selected from every distinct cluster create the new dissimilar test suite. This technique has been experimented on Defects4j dataset, and it performs better than untreated, random ad similarity based approaches in terms of early fault detection. Incorporating time constraints or requirement prioritization would be the future direction of this research.

References

1. Rothermel, G., Untch, R.H., Chu, C., Harrold, M.J.: Prioritizing test cases for regression testing. IEEE Trans. Softw. Eng. **27**(10), 929–948 (2001)
2. Nguyen, C.D., Marchetto, A., Tonella, P.: Test case prioritization for audit testing of evolving web services using information retrieval techniques. In: 2011 IEEE International Conference on Web Services (ICWS). IEEE (2011)
3. Catal, C.: The ten best practices for test case prioritization. In: Skersys, T., Butleris, R., Butkiene, R. (eds.) ICIST 2012. CCIS, vol. 319, pp. 452–459. Springer, Heidelberg (2012). doi:10.1007/978-3-642-33308-8_37
4. Rothermel, G., Untch, R.H., Chu, C., Harrold, M.J.: Test case prioritization: an empirical study. In: Proceedings of IEEE International Conference on Software Maintenance (ICSM 1999), 30 Aug – 3 Sept 1999 (1999)
5. Noor, T.B., Hemmati, H.: Test Case analytics: mining test case traces to improve risk-driven testing. In: SWAN 2015, Montréal, Canada, IEEE (2015)
6. Konsaard, P., Ramingwong L.: Total coverage based regression test case prioritization using genetic algorithm, IEEE (2015)
7. Mirarab, S., Tahvildari, L.: A prioritization approach for software test cases based on Bayesian networks. In: Dwyer, M.B., Lopes, A. (eds.) FASE 2007. LNCS, vol. 4422, pp. 276–290. Springer, Heidelberg (2007). doi:10.1007/978-3-540-71289-3_22
8. Arafeen, M.J., Do, H.: Test case prioritization using requirements-based clustering, In: 2013 IEEE Sixth International Conference (2013)
9. Siddik, M.S., Sakib, K.: RDCC: an effective test case prioritization framework using software requirements, design and source code collaboration. In: 17th International Conference on Computer and Information Technology (ICCIT), pp. 75–80. IEEE, (2014)
10. Wang, X., Zeng, H.: History-based dynamic test case prioritization for requirement properties in regression testing. In: IEEE/ACM International Workshop on Continuous Software Evolution and Delivery (CSED), pp. 41–47, 14 May 2016. IEEE (2016)
11. Kim, J.-M., Porter, A.: A history-based test prioritization technique for regression testing in resource constrained environments. In: International Conference of Software Engineering, ICSE (2002)
12. Zhao, X., Wang, Z., Fan, X., Wang, Z.: A clustering – Bayesian network based approach for test case prioritization, In: 2015 IEEE 39th Annual International Computers, Software and Applications Conference (2015)
13. Just, R., Jalali, D., Ernst, M.D.: Defects4J: a database of existing faults to enable controlled testing studies for Java programs. In: Proceedings of the 2014 International Symposium on Software Testing and Analysis. ACM, (2014)
14. Wang Y., Zhao X., Ding X.: An effective test case prioritization method based on fault severity. In: IEEE (2015)
15. Marijan, D.: Multi-perspective regression test prioritization for time-constrained environments, In: IEEE International Conference on Software Quality, Reliability and Security (2015)
16. Siddik, S., Gias, A.U., Khaled, S.M.: Optimizing software design migration from structured programming to object oriented paradigm. In: 16th International Conference on Computer and Information Technology (ICCIT), pp. 1–6. IEEE (2013)
17. Gao, D., Guo, X., Zhao, L.: Test case prioritization for regression testing based on ant colony optimization. In: 2015 6th IEEE International Conference on Software Engineering and Service Science (ICSESS). IEEE (2015)

Algorithm and High Performance Computing

A Fast GPU Based Implementation of Optimal Binary Search Tree Using Dynamic Programming

Mohsin Altaf Wani[1]([⊠])[ID] and Manzoor Ahmad[2]

[1] Faculty of the Department of Computer Science, University of Kashmir,
South Campus, Srinagar, J&K, India
mohsin.strx@gmail.com
[2] Department of Computer Science, University of Kashmir, Srinagar, J&K, India

Abstract. Modern GPUs (Graphics processing units) can perform computation at a very high rate as compared to CPU's; as a result they are increasingly used for general purpose parallel computation. Parallel algorithms can be developed for GPUs using different computing architectures like CUDA (compute unified device architecture) and OpenCL (Open Computing Language). Determining Optimal Binary Search Tree is an optimization problem to find the optimal arrangement of nodes in a binary search tree so that average search time is minimized. A Dynamic programming algorithm can solve this problem within $O(n^3)$-time complexity and a workspace of size $O(n^2)$. We have developed a fast parallel implementation of this $O(n^3)$-time algorithm on a GPU. For achieving the required goal we need to provide data structures suitable for parallel computation of this algorithm, besides we need to efficiently utilize the cache memory available and to minimize thread divergence. Our implementation executes this algorithm within 114.4 s for an instance containing 16384 keys on an NVidia GTX 570, while a conventional CPU based implementation takes 48166 s to execute. Thus, a speed up factor of 422 compared to a conventional CPU based implementation is obtained.

Keywords: Optimal binary search tree · CUDA · GPU · Dynamic programming

1 Introduction

Graphics Processing Units are the mainstay of many-core parallel computing platforms. Today GPU's are fully programmable parallel processing units having massive data processing capability. This data processing capability drives the use of GPU's for general purpose programming GPGPU. GPGPU's are particularly suited for data parallel tasks since they are based on SIMD (single instruction multiple data) and SPMD (single program multiple data) paradigms [3]. GPU's are even used for algorithms which have highly irregular data access patterns like the branch and bound algorithms, with large gains in performance [11–13]. Dynamic programming being an algorithm design technique where usually the same computing process is applied to multiple data items should be able to use maximum data processing potential of a GPU.

© Springer Nature Singapore Pte Ltd. 2017
S. Kaushik et al. (Eds.): ICICCT 2017, CCIS 750, pp. 285–295, 2017.
https://doi.org/10.1007/978-981-10-6544-6_26

In this paper, we will provide an optimized parallel implementation of a dynamic programming algorithm for computing optimal binary search tree using a GPU. We will modify and adapt data-structures used by this algorithm so that they are optimized for parallel access by the GPU. The primary contribution of this paper is optimized parallelization of the dynamic programming algorithm so that maximum possible speed up is achieved.

The rest of this paper is organized as follows. Section 2 provides a brief introduction to Dynamic programming algorithm as applied to computing optimal binary search tree. Section 3 presents GPU architecture. Section 4 presents related work. Section 5 discusses the parallel implementation at length. Section 6 presents the results of our experiments. Section 7 gives concluding remark and performance issues of each approach used.

2 Dynamic Programming Algorithm for Optimal Binary Search Tree

This section defines the optimal binary search tree problem and reviews a dynamic programming algorithm that solves this problem.

Ordinarily, a binary search tree contains records that are retrieved according to the values of the keys. Our goal is to organize the keys in a binary search tree so that the average time it takes to locate a key is minimized. A tree that is organized in this fashion is called optimal. A tree in which all the keys have an equal probability of being the search key is said to be balanced if the difference between the height of left and right sub-trees is kept to a minimum e.g. 1 or 2. However, we are concerned with the case where the keys do not have the same probability.

The number of comparisons done by the searching procedure to locate a key is called the search time. We will determine a tree for which the average search time is minimal. Let Key_1, Key_2... Key_n be the n keys in order, and let P_i be the probability that Key_i is the search key. If C_i is the number of comparisons needed to find Key_i in a given tree, the average search time for that tree is.

$$\sum (C_i \cdot P_i) \text{ where } 1 \leq i \leq n$$

This value is to be minimized.

The Dynamic programming algorithm for the solution of this problem proceeds as follows. Suppose that keys Key_i through Key_j are arranged in a tree that minimizes

$$\sum (C_k P_k) \text{ where } i \leq k \leq j$$

where C_k is the number of comparisons needed to locate Key_k in the tree.

Let tree 1 be an optimal tree given the restriction that Key_1 is at the root, tree 2 be an optimal tree given the restriction that Key_2 is at the root... tree n be an optimal tree given the restriction that Key_n is at the root.

It has been established that the average search time for tree k is given by the equation below.

$$\underbrace{A[1][k\text{-}1]}_{\substack{\text{Average}\\ \text{time in left}\\ \text{subtree}}} + \underbrace{p_1+p_2+...+p_{k\text{-}1}}_{\substack{\text{Time spent}\\ \text{comparing at the}\\ \text{root}}} + \underbrace{p_k}_{\substack{\text{Average}\\ \text{time}\\ \text{searching}\\ \text{for root}}} + \underbrace{A[k+1][n]}_{\substack{\text{Average time}\\ \text{in right subtree}}} + \underbrace{p_{k+1}+...+p_n}_{\substack{\text{Time spent}\\ \text{comparing at}\\ \text{the root}}}$$

Equation 1. Average time to search in a sub-tree having k^{th} node as root

$$A[i][j] = \min_{i \le k \le j}(A[i][k-1] + A[k+1][j]) + \sum p_m \quad \text{where } i \le m \le j \quad i < j$$

Equation 2. Recurrence to compute an optimal binary search tree

$$A[i][i] = p_i$$

$$A[i][i-1] = 0, \ A[j+1][j] = 0$$

Using Eq. 2, we can write an algorithm that determines an optimal binary search tree. Because $A[i][j]$ is computed from entries in the ith row but to the left of $A[i][j]$ and from entries in the jth column but beneath $A[i][j]$, we proceed by computing in sequence the values on each diagonal. Stage 1 being computed first, then stage 2 and so-on.

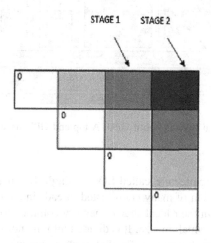

Fig. 1. Stages of computation

3 GPU Architecture

NVIDIA Fermi GPU includes up to 16 Streaming Multiprocessors (SM) on a single die, each one is composed of 32 Streaming Processors (SP). Several types of memories are provided on the GPU, differing in size, latency and access type (read-only or read/write). Device memory which is basically off-chip DRAM is relatively large in size but slow in access time. Fermi based GPU's have six 64-bit memory partitions, a total of 384-bit memory interface Fig. 2.

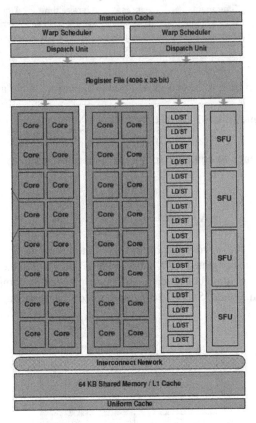

Fig. 2. An SM in a typical NVidia Fermi GPU. A top end GPU usually has 15 to 16 of these SM's

Each SM uses an architecture called SIMT (Single Instruction, Multiple Thread) which allows the execution of many coordinated threads in a data-parallel fashion. All SPs can read and write in their local shared memory common to all SPs in an SM, this is fast in access time but small in size. It is divided into memory banks of 32-bit words that can be accessed simultaneously. Parallel requests for memory addresses that fall into the same memory bank cause the serialization of accesses [3]. Registers are the fastest memories available on a GPU but involve the use of slow local memory when number of registers used is more than what is available. Moreover, accesses may be delayed due to register read-after-write dependences and register memory bank conflicts.

4 Related Work

A number of research articles have been published on parallel GPU based implementation of dynamic programming algorithms. Some of the well cited being [7–10]. Parallel implementation discussed by [7] is for optimal polygon triangulation and the one discussed by [8] is for optimal matrix chain multiplication both of which are non-serial polyadic dynamic programming problems. However none of them provides an actual parallel implementation of the algorithms used neither have they achieved the performance achieved by our implementation on GPU against both single core and multicore CPU based implementations. Similarly a few research articles related to parallel implementation of optimal binary search trees using parallel architectures other than GPU's have also been published [16, 17]. The implementation provided in [16] is based on 48 core Intel Xeon cluster, this paper provides results of three parallel implementations with significant performance gains, however lacks a detailed discussion of these implementations and how the algorithm has been adapted for parallel execution. None of the mentioned approaches provides a GPU based implementation neither addresses the requirements of such an implementation.

5 Parallel GPU Based Implementation

We have divided the dynamic programming algorithm into two separate parts. One part pre-computes sums of probabilities and stores them in required locations. The second part then proceeds with performing rest of the computations. Both the parts are computed using a parallel GPU-based implementation. The first part is computed separately before executing the second portion.

Each stage of given algorithm consists of computing $A_{i,j}$'s in a diagonal where each $A_{i,j}$ is computed as minimum of the sums given by $(A[i][k-1] + A[k+1][j]) + \sum pm$ where $i \leq m \leq j$ and $i \leq k \leq j$. Thus, each entry is calculated using entries in the same row but preceding the element being computed and entries in the same column but below the element being computed. Each stage 'p' computes N-p-1 elements where N is the total number of keys and p is the stage (diagonal) being computed. At each stage 'p' an $A_{i, i+p}$ is computed for $1 \leq i \leq$ N-p-1. A total of N − 2 stages are to be computed to reach the desired solution.

5.1 Granularity Issues on GPU

The manner in which we parallelize a given dynamic programming algorithm can have a significant effect on the execution speed of that algorithm on a GPU. Different implementations cited in Sect. 4 use different types of implementations, for different phases of computation [7, 8]. In certain implementations different levels of granularity have been used in a single implementation [7]. Having fine-grained parallelism during initial phases of execution and going to coarse-grained parallelism during final phases of execution seems natural. However, the performance gains obtained by using fine-grained parallelism initially and coarse-grained parallelism towards final phases of execution also requires a transformation of data structures and shifting to different procedures during different phases of execution [7]. These can more than offset the performance gains obtained by using these transformations in the first place and performance gains obtained if any are very minute, as can be observed from analyzing these.

5.2 Optimizing Data Structures

Data structures used have a huge impact on performance of a GPU-based implementation. A coalesced access to global memory is a key to increasing the speed of computation on the GPU. When threads access contiguous memory locations in the GPU memory; access is coalesced and access to the data in required memory locations is faster. However when the memory locations are not contiguous in the physical memory of the GPU then the memory access is not coalesced and relatively more time is needed to bring in the required data. In case of memory locations in a row of 2d array, access is coalesced as the locations are contiguous while as in case of a column in 2d array the memory locations are not contiguous so access is not coalesced. When the processing cores have to wait for a long duration of time for the required data the utilization of computational resources of the GPU is low. Thus despite having large amount of processing power we are not able to get required performance gains. To get to the desired level of performance, we try to maximize coalesced access in our algorithm.

In our implementation, each thread in a block will be reading an entry preceding the entry being computed but in the same row and an entry in the same column but below the entry being computed. For the purpose of having coalesced access, we need to modify our data structures Fig. 3.

0	A(1,2)	A(1,3)	A(1,4)
	0	A(2,3)	A(2,4)
		0	A(3,4)
			0

0	A(1,2)	A(1,3)	A(1,4)
A(1,2)	0	A(2,3)	A(2,4)
A(1,3)	A(2,3)	0	A(3,4)
A(1,4)	A(2,4)	A(3,4)	0

Fig. 3. Transformation by taking transpose of upper triangular portion and storing it in lower triangular portion

5.3   Modifications to Dynamic Programming Algorithm as Implemented on GPU

The parallel implementation for pre-computing sums of probabilities as discussed in Sect. 5 is given below. These sums are computed in parallel by the GPU before starting the actual computations of the dynamic programming algorithm.

Parallel Algorithm to compute and store sums of probabilities in required memory locations
Input: 2d array A having main diagonal set to 0's and vector D containing probabilities of individual keys. SIZE is the size of vector D.
Output: 2d array A having each entry Ai,j in upper triangular portion set to sums of probabilities of keys from Di to Dj.
1: threadId = (blockDim.x*blockIdx.x) + threadIdx.x;
2: row= col = threadId; // each thread i computes row i of A
3: For SIZE = SizeOf(D) To 1
4:        col++ // Ai,i set to 0, we start computing from Ai,i+1 then Ai,i+2,Ai,i+3...
5:        if(threadId < SIZE)
6:                Lst[row][col] = Lst[row][col-1] + d[col]
7:        End if
8:        __syncthreads();
9: End For
Algorithm 1. Invoked from CPU code with a block size of 32 threads.

Once sums of probabilities are computed and stored in required locations in the 2d array we can proceed to perform our dynamic programming algorithm on that 2d array.

5.4   Parallel Algorithm on GPU

Since the algorithm has to compute optimal binary search tree for n keys in $n - 1$ stages. Here each stage being a diagonal in a 2d array. The diagonals are computed from left to right as shown in Fig. 1. Each stage decreases the size of diagonal to be computed by 1. Each stage (diagonal) of computation is invoked from CPU to avoid synchronization between computations of separate diagonals.

Using this approach, each stage of computation is invoked from CPU. But the actual computation is performed by the GPU. Each block of threads computes one entry in the diagonal. The data (list of probabilities of keys) required for computation is passed from CPU to the GPU but only during the initial invocation, but the remaining invocations need only the stage of computation from CPU.

Parallel algorithm to compute a diagonal in optimal binary search tree
Input: a modified 2d array 'List' containing sums of probabilities required and the stage (diagonal) of computation in 'diagonal', MAX set to ∞
Output: Diagonal containing entries computed according to recurrence i.

```
1:   threadId = blockIdx.x + threadIdx.x + 1
2:        min = MAX
3:        __shared__ temp[BLOCK_SIZE]
4:        temp[threadIdx.x] = MAX
5:        count=0
6:        row = blockIdx.x
7:        col = diagonal + row

8:        For count = 0 to diagonal -1 //while(count < diagonal)
9:                if(threadId <= col)
10:                    value  = List[row][ threadId -1] + List[col+1][threadId]
                           //we are transforming List[row][ threadId -1] + List[threadId
                           +1][col] to  List[row][ threadId -1] + List[col+1][ threadId] to use
                           transposed row instead of column
11:                       if(value < temp[threadIdx.x] )
12:                          temp[threadIdx.x] = value
13:                       End If
14:                End If
15:                threadId += blockDim.x // move ahead by number of threads in a block
16:                count += blockDim.x //repeat the process till  no more entries are left in a row
17:                __syncthreads()
18:        End For
// once block finishes computing and storing minima into shared memory we compute the minimum from the list of minima
using reduction
19:                Min = Reduction(temp)
20:        if(threadIdx.x == 0)
21:                List [row][col] = List[row] [col] + Min
22:                List [col+1][row-1] = List[row][col] // copy to transpose of the location
23:        End If
```

Algorithm 2. Computes a stage (diagonal) in parallel using GPU. Invoked from host code

Our algorithm uses coalesced access during the computation of minimum of the sums and utilizes pre-computed sum of probabilities stored in the same memory location where the computed result is to be stored.

6   Results

We have implemented our dynamic programming algorithms for computing optimal binary search tree using CUDA C. We are using NVidia GTX 570 GPU with 480 processing cores. This GPU has 15 streaming multiprocessors containing 32 cores each running at 1000 MHz and 1.25 GB GDDR5 RAM. The same dynamic programming algorithm has been implemented on a CPU. A parallel algorithm without all the optimizations described in Sect. 5 has been implemented on GPU for comparison with our optimized implementation. We are using an overclocked Intel core i5 760 running at an approximately 3.6 GHz speed and 8 GB RAM to run the CPU based implementations of the dynamic programming algorithm.

Table 1 shows computation time of optimal binary search tree for entries ranging from 4096 to 16384 using GPU. The method explained above is used and the performance of CPU based implementation is also taken into consideration. Time is in milliseconds.

Table 1. Execution times in milliseconds

Size	4096	6144	8192	10240	12288	14336	16384
Optimized GPU	2437	7234	15973	29000	50177	77976	114496
Naïve GPU	22577	89435	385973	782652	1578655	2783569	5007360
CPU	161429	595004	1533123	5627141	13129317	21882777	48166551

For an instance of size 16384, time taken by single core CPU implementation is 48166551 ms while as optimized GPU based approach takes 114496 ms. Thus, a maximum speed-up of 422 is achieved against CPU implementation.

On observing Graph 1, one can see that beyond instances of size 10240 the performance of naive CPU based implementation rapidly deteriorates in the face of GPU based implementations. Even naïve GPU based implementation deteriorates in face of optimized GPU based implementation. However, the performance of CPU based implementation suffers more because the caches both L1 and L2 can't help it in this scenario especially for instances of very large size. Since data once used for computation of an entry in a diagonal will not be reused until computation of this diagonal has not been completed and computation of next diagonal begins.

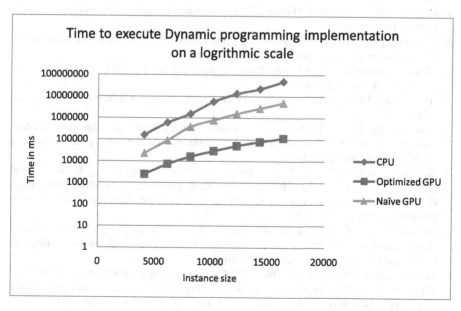

Graph 1. We are using logarithmic scale here since the difference in execution time is very large.

7 Concluding Remarks

In this paper, we have proposed a parallel implementation of the dynamic programming algorithm for finding optimal binary search tree for a given list of keys. We have tried to select optimal parameters for execution, optimal data structures and best implementation to achieve maximum possible speedup. The experimental results show that our parallel implementation on GPU solves an instance of size 16384 keys in 114.4 s while as a naïve CPU based implementation requires 48166 s. Hence, our GPU based implementation achieves a speed up factor of 422 over a single threaded CPU based implementation.

Single threaded CPU based implementation performs badly because of the severe performance penalty imposed by the L1 and L2 cache memories of the CPU. Once the instance size of 10240 entries or more are being solved using this dynamic programming algorithm, the latter stages of algorithm require large number of entries nearly 10000×2 for computing each entry in the diagonal. This means 40 KB of data is to be moved and used to compute a single entry, this severely affects the performance; because more time is spent moving the data than processing it. The cache hit rate also falls drastically which results in CPU spending more cycles waiting for data than processing it.

References

1. Cormen, T.H., Lieserson, C.E., Rivest, R.L.: Introduction to Algorithms, 4th edn. MIT Press, London (1990)
2. Neapolitan, R., Naimipour, K.: Foundations of Algorithms Using C ++ Pseudo Code. Jones & Bartlett, Toronto (2003)
3. NVidia Corporation: CUDA programming guide version 4.1. (2011) http://docs.nvidia.com/cuda/cuda-c-programming-guide/
4. NVidia Corporation: CUDA C Best Practices Guide version 4.1 (2011). http://docs.nvidia.com/cuda/cuda-c-best-practices-guide/
5. Hwu, W.W.: GPU Computing Gems, Emerald edn. Morgan Kaufmann, San Francisco (2011)
6. Man, D., Uda, K., Ito, Y., Nakano, K.: A GPU implementation of computing Euclidean distance map. In: 2011 Second International Conference on Networking and Computing (ICNC), pp. 68–76. IEEE (2011)
7. Nishida, K., Nakano, K., Ito, Y.: Accelerating the Dynamic Programming for the Optimal Polygon Triangulation on the GPU. In: Xiang, Y., Stojmenovic, I., Apduhan, B.O., Wang, G., Nakano, K., Zomaya, A. (eds.) ICA3PP 2012. LNCS, vol. 7439, pp. 1–15. Springer, Heidelberg (2012). doi:10.1007/978-3-642-33078-0_1
8. Nishida, K., Ito, Y., Nakano, K.: Accelerating the dynamic programming for the matrix chain product on the GPU. In: 2011 Second International Conference on Networking and Computing (ICNC), pp. 320–326. IEEE (2011)
9. Liu, Y., Schmidt, B.: GSWABE: faster GPU-accelerated sequence alignment with optimal alignment retrieval for short DNA sequences. In: Fox, G.C., Hey, A.J. (eds.) Concurrency and Computation Practice and Experience, pp. 958–972. Wiley, New York (2014)

10. Li, K., Liu, J., Wan, L., Yin, S., Li, K.: A cost-optimal parallel algorithm for the 0–1 knapsack problem and its performance on multicore CPU and GPU implementations. Parallel Comput. **43**, 27–42 (2015)
11. Chakroun, I., Melab, N.: An adaptative multi-GPU based branch-and-bound. A case study: the flow-shop scheduling problem. In: Proceedings of the 2012 IEEE 14th International Conference, HPCC 2012, pp. 389–395. IEEE Computer Society, Washington, DC (2012)
12. Gmys, J., Mezmaz, M., Melab, N., Tuyttens, D.: A GPU-based Branch-and-Bound algorithm using Integer-Vector-Matrix data structure. Parallel Comput. **59**, 119–139 (2016)
13. Chakroun, I., Melab, N.: Operator-level GPU-accelerated branch and bound algorithms. Proc. Comput. Sci. **18**(2013), 280–289 (2013)
14. Tan, G., Feng, S., Sun, N.: Locality and parallelism optimization for dynamic programming algorithm in bioinformatics. In: Proceedings of the 2006 ACM/IEEE Conference on Supercomputing, p. 41. IEEE (2006)
15. NVidia Corporation, NVIDIA's Next Generation CUDATM Compute Architecture: Fermi (2009). http://www.nvidia.com/content/pdf/fermi_white_papers/nvidia_fermi_compute_architecture_whitepaper.pdf
16. Han, B., Lu, Y.: Research on optimization and parallelization of optimal binary search tree using dynamic programming. In: Advances in Intelligent Systems Research. Atlantis Press, Paris (2012)
17. Myoupo, J.F., Tchendji, V.K.: Parallel dynamic programming for solving the optimal search binary tree problem on CGM. Int. J. High Perform. Comput. Netw. **7**(4), 269–280 (2014)

A Hybridized Evolutionary Algorithm for Bi-objective Bi-dimensional Bin-packing Problem

Neeraj Pathak[(✉)] and Rajeev Kumar

School of Computer and Systems Sciences, Jawaharlal Nehru University,
New Delhi 110067, India
neeraj.bhumcal0@gmail.com, rajeevkumar.cse@gmail.com

Abstract. The bin-packing problem is a widely studied combinatorial optimization problem. In classical bin-packing problem, we are given a set of real numbers in the range (0,1] and the goal is to place them in minimum number of bins so that no bin holds more than one. In this paper we consider a bi-dimensional bin-packing in which we are given a set of rectangular items to be packed into minimum number of fixed size of square bins. Here we consider two objectives applied on a bi-dimensional variant, one is related to minimize number of bins and second is minimize average percentage of wastage/gaps in bins. To solve this problem we incorporate the concept of Pareto's optimality to evolve set of solutions using evolutionary algorithm (EA) tool hybridized with the heuristic operator leading to improve results from existing techniques.

Keywords: Bin-packing · Bi-objective · Bi-dimensional · Evolutionary algorithms · Pareto's optimality

1 Introduction

The bin-packing problem is a special type of cutting stock NP-hard combinatorial problem [1]. In the classical bin-packing problem (BPP) we are given a list L = $\{i_1, i_2, i_3, \ldots, i_n\}$ of real numbers in the range (0,1] and the aim is to place them in minimum number of bins. Initially the primary aim of bin-packing problem focused only concern to minimize number of bins. However various other constraints and objectives such as weights, priority items, center of gravity can also be included depending on our requirements. The problem holds various applications as in cargo airplanes [12], loading of tractor trailer trucks, routing [4], scheduling [16] and resource allocation problems.

First non-trivial results on bin-packing problem were proposed by Ullman [15] in 1971. He studied the problem starting from memory allocation problems that involve table formatting, file allocation and prepaging. He also gave asymptotic analysis of two

© Springer Nature Singapore Pte Ltd. 2017
S. Kaushik et al. (Eds.): ICICCT 2017, CCIS 750, pp. 296–304, 2017.
https://doi.org/10.1007/978-981-10-6544-6_27

heuristics: FirstFit (FF) and BestFit (BF). In the later year 1972, Garay et al. [7] explained more detailed analysis of four heuristics: First Fit (FF), Best Fit (BF), First Fit Decreasing (FFD) and Best Fit Decreasing (BFD).

In bi-dimensional geometric bin-packing, we are given collection of bi-dimensional items list and the aim is to pack them in minimum number of bins. There are various criteria of packing items in a bin. First is concerned to item shape, it may be regular or irregular. Here we consider the rectangle (regular) shape. Second is concerned to orientation of items allowed or not because it affects the number of bins used, % of gaps etc.

Unlike existing classical bin-packing aiming to consider minimum bins, bi-objective bi-dimensional variant model for bin-packing problem is formulated in this paper with multiple constraints applied on it. As it is impossible to solve bi-dimensional bin-packing problems in polynomial time, therefore many heuristics and metaheuristics [3, 5, 8, 9, 11, 13, 14] are formulated to solve in efficient way. Depending on requirements bin-packing problem definition is formulated. Here we consider two objectives, minimize no. of bins and minimize percentage of wastage of bins applied on bi dimensional geometric variant.

The remainder of this paper is organized as follows: Sect. 2 describes problem definition. Section 3 involves the existing heuristics applied on rectangle packing problem. Section 4 discusses proposed algorithms based on evolutionary algorithm as metaheuristic. Section 5 shows computational results on algorithm. Finally, conclusions and future work possibilities are discussed in Sect. 6.

2 Problem Definition

As there is no specific model in literature to design multi-objective variant of bin-packing problem, depending on our requirements mathematical model bi-objective bi-dimensional bin-packing problem is formulated.

We are given unbounded number of bins having fixed height H, width W and J number of rectangle items with dimensions $w_j \leq W, h_j \leq H$, the items are packed into bins such that following objectives are achieved, mathematically formulated as:

Minimize number of bins

$$K = \sum_{i=1}^{I} ceil(\sum_{j=1}^{J} \frac{x_{ij}h_jw_j}{H_iW_i}) \tag{1}$$

Minimize average percentage of wastage/gaps

$$G_{avg} = \frac{1}{K}\sum_{i=1}^{K} \frac{a_i * 100}{W_iH_i} \tag{2}$$

With applying constraints:
For each item j ∈ {1, 2, . . ., J};

- $0 < w_j \leq W_i$; where w_j is width of item j, W_i is width of bin i;
- $0 < h_j \leq H_i$; where h_j is height of item j, H_i is height of bin i;

For all bins i ∈ {1, 2, . . ., I};

- $\sum_{j=1}^{J} x_{ij} w_j h_j \leq W_i H_i$;
- Rotation of any item is allowed through 90°, $w_j \leftarrow h_j; h_j \leftarrow w_j$ if $w_j \leq H_i$ and $h_j \leq W_i$.
- $\sum_{i=1}^{I} \sum_{j=1}^{J} = J$ (for each item should be assigned to only one bin)

Where

- Ceil (x), the smallest integer larger or equal to x
- $x_{ij} \in \{0, 1\}$ for i = {1, 2, ..., I} and j = {1, 2, ..., J}
- $x_{ij} = 1$ if item j is assigned to bin i
- $x_{ij} = 0$ else.

In the formulation of bi-objective bi-dimensional bin-packing problem definition, percentage of gaps G is considered as a second objective to evaluate how balanced or stabilized the bins in packing strategy.

3   Existing Heuristics for Rectangle Packing

In this section, we describe various heuristic algorithms to fill rectangle item in bin. Those algorithms consist of two parts: first part denotes the number of permutation for which we have selected some standard strategy whether order the items in decreasing height, width or area. Second part denotes decoding algorithm for permutations. A level algorithm is a decoding algorithm in which items are placed from left to right in rows forming levels. Three most popular level algorithms are the Next Fit (NF), Best Fit (BF) and First Fit (FF) strategies.

Let we are given n rectangular items and current item i ∈ {1, 2, . . ., n} have to be placed in a bin. The recently created level is s starting from level 1 bottom of the bin in beginning of algorithm.

3.1   Next Fit (NF)

In this strategy item i will be placed at left most feasible position of level s if possible, otherwise goes to next level by creating s := s + 1 and place it left justified as shown in Fig. 1(a).

3.2   Best Fit (BF)

If there are given multiple unused horizontal area for placing an item i, place it in that position minimized unused area among all if possible, otherwise follow NF strategy by creating new level as shown in Fig. 1(b).

3.3   First Fit (FF)

For an item i pack through FF check available space starting from level one to the current level s then place it left justified in first available space if possible, otherwise follow the same procedure as NF by creating next level s: = s+1.

All three procedures are shown in Fig. 1 where we have six rectangle date items of different dimensions {l, m, n, o, p, q}.

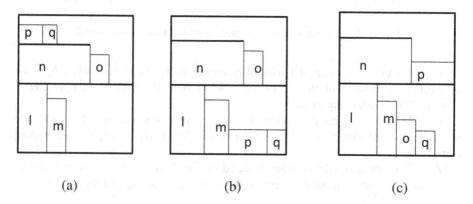

Fig. 1. Strip packing problem of (a) Next Fit, (b) Best Fit and (c) First Fit

3.4   Bottom Left Fill (BLF)

Bottom left strategy is most documented approach given by Baker et al. [2] in 1980. After that many variants have been proposed in successive few decades, but among all the common characteristics is that items are placed at the bottom left stable position one-by-one. Baker et al. used the concept of Bottom Left Fill (BLF) where item is placed at the left most among lowest possible positions. Jakobs [10] proposed another bottom left (BL) method that holds the item at top right first followed by sliding down then left alternately as long as possible.

3.5   Overlapping of Items in Bin

As by definition our aim is to place rectangle items in bin without overlapping fashion. So to avoid this there are two cases as described below:\newline

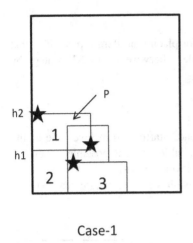 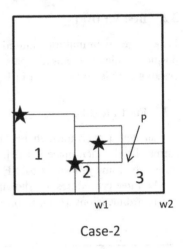

Case-1   Case-2

Fig. 2. Overlapping of new item with point P for case-1 and case-2

Case 1: let (x_i, y_i) is insertion point of incoming item to be placed and h_1, h_2 is the intersection coordinate of item 1 to left side of bin. Therefore mathematically if $h_1 \leq y_j \leq h_2$ overlapping exist.

Case 2: let $(x_i, y_i$ is insertion point of incoming item to be placed and w_1, w_2 is the intersection coordinate of item 3 to bottom side of bin. If $w_1 \leq x_i \leq w_2$ overlapping exit.

All two cases of overlapping are depicted in Fig. 2 where $P(x_i, y_j)$ is the point of overlapping and star represents insertion points for new coming rectangle item.

4 Metaheuristics for 2-D Item Packing

In the last three decades, many local search, heuristics and metaheuristics have been proposed on different variants of bin-packing problem. Dowsland [6] gave meta-heuristics for 2-D item packing using simulated annealing (SA) with results of feasible and infeasible solutions. Jakobs proposed a metaheuristics for strip packing using genetic algorithm (GA) to find good permutation.

Here we have proposed a hybridized evolutionary algorithm to simulate the bottom left fill (BLF) heuristic with genetic algorithm applied on bi-objective bi-dimensional BPP. BLF heuristic is shown in Algorithm 1.

Algorithm 1 BLF: (Bottom Left Fill Heuristic)

> **Input**: set of item I, K number of available bins and archive of insertion points.
> **Output**: updated set of insertion points and number of bins K'
> **for** each rectangle item i∈{1,2,....,I} **do**
> **for** each available bin **do**
> **for** each insertion point of insertion archive **do**
> **if** overlapping then-> insert new insertion point in the insertion archive
> **else**-> insert item i at current insertion point, delete current insertion point and add two new insertion point one at top left and one at bottom right
> **end if**
> **end for**
> **end for**
> **if** no bins to hold item i then-> create new bin with insertion of item i in it and increment K as K'
> **end if**
> **end for**

4.1 Proposed Hybridized Evolutionary BLF Algorithm

In this section we have proposed an hybridized evolutionary algorithm of BLF in Algorithm 2 where K is number of available bins to accommodate J rectangle items with minimum average % gaps (G_{avg}). Here we apply evolutionary algorithm tool as metaheuristic to implement bi-objective bi-dimensional bin-packing problem.

Algorithm 2 Hybridized Evolutionary BLF

> **Input**: set of items J packet through BLF, K number of available bins with average percentage gaps G_{avg}.
> **Output**: (K',G'_{avg}) optimized number of bins with minimum % of gaps.
> **While** it≠iteration **do**
> **Crossover** k'_c=select bins having (% gaps ≤10) from the set k, and k"=k-k' and apply inter-crossover of single item from the set k'
> **Mutation** k'_m=select any bin from the set k' and apply mutation within bin through rotation or interchange of items
> **Merging** k'=merge (k'_m, k'_c) and apply BLF (select item j from the set k" and place it in k')
> Update k=k'+k"
> it=it+1
> **end while**

Selection: Selection criteria depends on fitness function as specified by problem definition. Initially we are given K and G_{avg} as input to selection procedure. As we have taken the percentage of gaps, second objective as fitness function we can break the initial set of K into two different groups one having gaps percentage ≤ 10 as K' and other having percentage >10 as K″. This procedure gives output as K'.

Crossover: For obtained set K' we apply inter flipping of rectangle item between two bins selected randomly from set K' to minimize percentage of gaps G. It gives output k'_c as new updated set.

Mutation: This involves the intra flipping (within bin) of rectangle item to minimize gaps through rotation or exchanging positions of it. Output of mutation procedure is given as k'_m.

Merging and Update: In this procedure we merge solution set k'_m and k'_c to form new K'. Now to reduce set K'' apply BLF on new K' using item i in K''. Output of this procedure gives updated set K with more optimized comparing to previous step.

Termination: Depending on problem definition we have to terminate the algorithm procedure. Here we considered number of iterations as termination condition that control the completion of evolution method.

5 Computational Results

We have implemented the Algorithm 1 for small dataset. Here we have selected random numbers in the range [1, 10] to initialize dimensions (width and height) of 50 rectangle items. The bin's dimension (width, height) is fixed to 10. We show the results in following graphs. Figure 3 shows number of bins used versus the iterations. In Fig. 4 shows average percentage of gaps versus number of iterations.

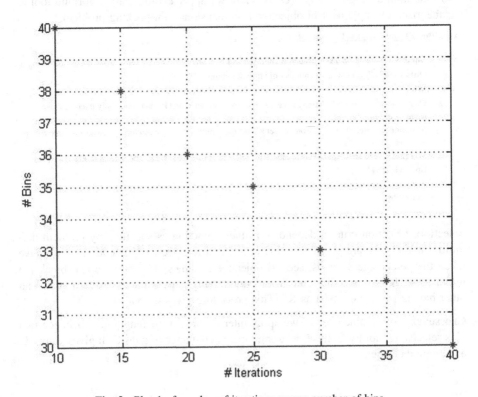

Fig. 3. Plot 1 of number of iterations versus number of bins.

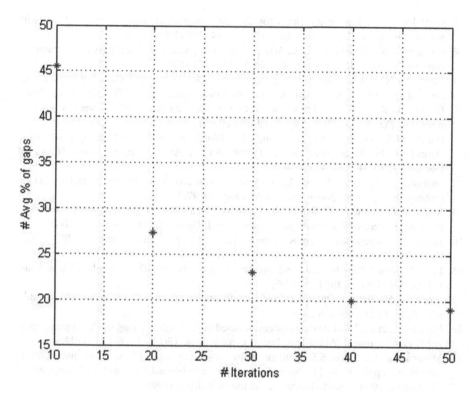

Fig. 4. Plot 2 of number of iterations versus avg % of gaps.

6 Conclusions

In this paper, a hybridized model for bi-objective bi-dimensional BPP is presented and the evolutionary algorithm is proposed to solve the problem. In this algorithm, we have considered bottom left fill (BLF) heuristic as operator to evolve better solutions as per definition of problems. We have implemented it on small data set. We are currently working on large data sets with some challenges to verify the final results as per required for proposed algorithm. The problem could be more complex if we consider irregular item in place of rectangle because finding exact position to minimize space wastage is challenging. We are working to formulate mathematical model to find solution criteria in this regard.

References

1. Anily, S., Bramel, J., Simchi-Levi, D.: Worst-case analysis of heuristics for the bin-packing problem with general cost structures. Oper. Res. **42**(2), 287–298 (1994)
2. Baker, B.S., Coffman Jr., E.G., Rivest, R.L.: Orthogonal packings in two dimensions. SIAM J. Comput. **9**(4), 846–855 (1980)

3. Bortfeldt, A.: A genetic algorithm for the two-dimensional strip packing problem with rectangular pieces. Eur. J. Oper. Res. **172**(3), 814–837 (2006)
4. Chandra, A.K., Hirschberg, D.S., Wong, C.K.: Bin-packing with geometric constraints in computer network design. Oper. Res. **26**(5), 760–772 (1978)
5. Chang, Y.-C., et al.: B*-Trees: a new representation for non-slicing floorplans. In: Proceedings of the 37th Annual Design Automation Conference. ACM, New York (2000)
6. Dowsland, K.A.: Some experiments with simulated annealing techniques for packing problems. Eur. J. Oper. Res. **68**(3), 389–399 (1993)
7. Garey, M.R., Graham, R.L., Ullman, J.D.: Worst-case analysis of memory allocation algorithms. In: Proceedings of the Fourth Annual ACM Symposium on Theory of Computing. ACM, New York (1972)
8. Imahori, S., Yagiura, M., Ibaraki, T.: Local search algorithms for the rectangle packing problem with general spatial costs. Math. Program. **97**(3), 543–569 (2003)
9. Imahori, S., Yagiura, M., Ibaraki, T.: Improved local search algorithms for the rectangle packing problem with general spatial costs. Eur. J. Oper. Res. **167**(1), 48–67 (2005)
10. Jakobs, S.: On genetic algorithms for the packing of polygons. Eur. J. Oper. Res. **88**(1), 165–181 (1996)
11. Lesh, N., et al.: New heuristic and interactive approaches to 2D rectangular strip packing. J. Exp. Algorithmics **10**, 1–2 (2005)
12. Mongeau, M., Bes, C.: Optimization of aircraft container loading. IEEE Trans. Aerosp. Electron. Syst. **39**(1), 140–150 (2003)
13. Murata, H., et al.: VLSI module placement based on rectangle-packing by the sequence-pair. IEEE Trans. Comput. Aided Des. Integr. Circuits Syst. **15**(12), 1518–1524 (1996)
14. Minorikawa, H., Sawa, S.S.: Current status and future trends of electronic packaging in automotive applications. In: Proceedings of the International Congress on Transportation Electronics, 1990. Vehicle Electronics in the 90's. IEEE (1990)
15. Ullman, J.D.: The Performance of a Memory Allocation Algorithm. Computer Science Laboratory, Department of Electrical Engineering, Princeton University, Princeton (1971)
16. Van De Vel, H., Shijie, S.: An application of the bin-packing technique to job scheduling on uniform processors. J. Oper. Res. Soc. **42**, 169–172 (1991)

Protein Features Identification for Machine Learning-Based Prediction of Protein-Protein Interactions

Khalid Raza[✉] [iD]

Department of Computer Science, Jamia Millia Islamia,
Jamia Nagar, New Delhi, India
kraza@jmi.ac.in

Abstract. The long awaited challenge of post-genomic era and systems biology research is computational prediction of protein-protein interactions (PPIs) that ultimately lead to protein functions prediction. The important research questions is how protein complexes with known sequence and structure be used to identify and classify protein binding sites, and how to infer knowledge from these classification such as predicting PPIs of proteins with unknown sequence and structure. Several machine learning techniques have been applied for the prediction of PPIs, but the accuracy of their prediction wholly depends on the number of features being used for training. In this paper, we have performed a survey of protein features used for the prediction of PPIs. The open research challenges and opportunities in the area have also been discussed.

Keywords: Protein-protein interactions · Machine learning · Supervised learning · Feature selection · Protein features

1 Introduction

Proteins are important for functioning of our body. The structure of a protein influences its function by determining the other molecules with which it can interact. The protein interactions can reveal hints about the function of a protein. Protein-protein interactions (PPI) play an important role in living cells that control most of the biological processes, and most essential cellular processes are mediated by these kinds of interactions. Proteins mostly perform their functions with the help of interactions with other proteins. For example, disease-causing mutations that affect protein interactions may lead to disruptions in protein-DNA interactions, misfolding of proteins, new undesired interactions, or enable pathogen-host protein interactions. Similarly, aberrant protein-protein interactions have caused several neurological disorders including Parkinson and Alzheimer's disease. With appropriate knowledge of interaction, scientist can easily predict pathways in the cell, potential novel therapeutic target, and protein functions. Hence, these examples have motivated to map interactions on the proteome-wide scale. The prediction of PPI has emerged as an important research problem in the field of bioinformatics and systems biology.

A PPI network focuses on tracing the dynamic interactions among proteins, thereby illuminating their local and global functional relationships (Rao et al. 2014). Experimentally determined PPI network from high-throughput techniques, such as yeast two

S. Kaushik et al. (Eds.): ICICCT 2017, CCIS 750, pp. 305–317, 2017.
https://doi.org/10.1007/978-981-10-6544-6_28

hybrid (Y2H) screens and Tandem affinity purification coupled to mass spectrometry (TAP-MS), are inherently noisy that contains a large number of false positives. Predicting PPIs using experimental techniques are time-consuming, costly, need manpower, and also unreliable. Therefore, computational methods for the prediction of PPIs have evolved. Among computational techniques, machine learning has been extensively used for several classification and prediction problems, including PPIs. Machine learning is a data-driven approach which requires sufficient number of training sets and features. It has been found that number of protein features play vital role in the accuracy of prediction algorithms. Therefore, it is required that we must identify various protein features that need to be used to train a machine learning algorithm.

This review presents 13 different protein features which can be used for the prediction of PPIs. The paper is organized as follows. Sections 1.1 and 1.2 describes types of PPIs and experimental methods for finding PPIs, respectively. Section 2 presents a brief description of computational approaches for the prediction PPIs. Section 3 covers 13 different proteins features that can be used for training machine learning algorithms. Section 4 describes how protein features are represented so that it can be fed to a learning algorithm. Finally, Sect. 5 concludes the paper and discusses challenges and opportunities in the area.

1.1 Types of Protein–Protein Interaction

It is analyzed and found that determination of PPI by different methods show a low degree of overlap. Hence, researchers have designed computational tools to assess the reliability of data coming out of high-throughput experiments. This low overlapping of interaction data and low reliability of high-throughput experimental techniques show that PPI determined with various approaches explore different types of interactions. De Las Rivas and de Luis (2004) classified the PPI into three level of association with several sublevels, as shown in Fig. 1.

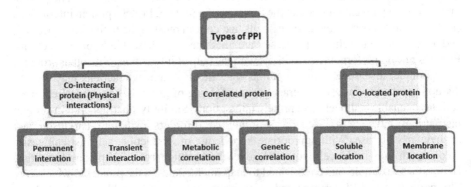

Fig. 1. Classification of protein-protein interaction (Source: De Las Rivas and de Luis 2004)

Physical interactions are that where proteins form a stable protein complex and performs biomolecular role such as structural and functional role. They are protein subunits of the complex that work together. *Correlated proteins interactions* are those which do not interact physically but are involved in the same biomolecular activities. Correlated protein interactions may be metabolic correlation or genetic correlation. *Co-located proteins interactions* are those where proteins are defined to work in the same cellular compartment.

1.2 Experimental Methods

There are two main technologies that determine PPI interactions: binary method and co-complex method. Binary techniques measure direct physical interactions between protein pairs. Yeast Two Hybrid (Y2H) method is one of the mostly used binary method. Co-complex methodmeasures physical interaction among groups of proteins, without finding pairwise interactions. Tandem affinity purification coupled to mass spectrometry (TAP-MS) is most often used Co-Complex method. Generally, Co-complex methods measures both direct and indirect interactions between proteins.

The experimental result of both the methods is totally different from each other. Data obtained from co-complex method cannot be directly mapped to binary interpretation. An algorithm or model is required to map group-based data into pairwise interactions. The 'spoke model' is most widely applied technique to transform data from group-based to pairwise interactions (de Las Rivas and Fontanillo 2010).

2 Computational Predictions

Mostly proteins do their functions by interacting with other proteins. The PPI within a cell may enrich our understanding about protein functions and cellular processes. Over the past few years, due to advancement in computation biology and bioinformatics, an explosion in functional biological data derived from high-throughput technologies to infer PPI has been observed.

Many large-scale experimental techniques have been employed to study PPIs including Y2H screens, X-ray crystallography, NMR and site-directed mutagenesis. But these experimental techniques are costly, tedious, time-consuming, labor-intensive and potentially inaccurate (Browne et al. 2006; Wang et al. 2013). On the other hand, tremendous protein interaction data has been generated out of proteomics research that need to be validated and annotated structural information.

Computational methods play a significant role in the prediction of PPI. They are used to predict potential interactions between proteins, to validate results of high-throughput interaction screens and to analyze the protein networks inferred from interaction data-bases. Several statistical and machine learning based methods have been applied for the prediction of PPI including Bayesian Networks (Jansen et al. 2003; Patil and Nakamura 2005), Simple Naïve Bayesian, Random Forest (Šikić et al. 2009; Zubek et al. 2015), Support Vector Machine (Bock and Gough 2001; Chatterjee et al. 2011; You et al. 2013; You et al. 2014; Zubek et al. 2015), Decision Tree, Logistic Regression, k-Nearest Neighborhood (kNN), Conditional Random Field, Artificial Neural Networks (Fariselli et al. 2002), to name a few. Despite the success of these methods, there is still need for the improvement in terms of prediction accuracy and computational efficiency (Res et al. 2005, Bordner and Abagyan 2005).

PPI predictions can be accomplished broadly in four steps, as shown in Fig. 2. Initially protein features will be extracted from different genomic and proteomic information. These protein features are represented in the form of a vector so that it can be used to train a machine learning classifier. Once a classifier is properly trained with the extracted protein features, it must be compared with the gold standard to assess its performance. A detail description of data-driven approach for prediction of PPIs can be found in Xue et al. (2015).

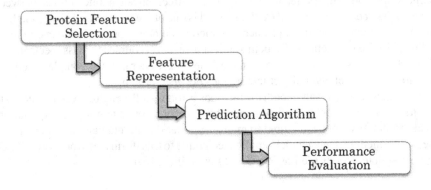

Fig. 2. Generic steps in machine learning-based protein-protein interaction predictions

3   Protein Features Selection

In the literature, various protein features have been used to predict PPI, either individually or in combinations. It has been found that none of the single protein feature is sufficient to predict PPI because single feature alone does not carry adequate information. Hence, a combination of some of these features has been found to be a better way to enhance the performance of machine learning for PPI predictions (Wang et al. 2006; Browne et al. 2006; Šikić et al. 2009). Detail of the protein features are described as follows:

3.1   Primary Sequence

The primary sequence of protein corresponds to linear amino acid sequence. In the literature, initially PPI prediction has been carried out by using sequence information only (Ofran and Rost 2003; Šikić et al. 2009). Ofran and Rost (2003) proposed a neural network based approach to identify PPI interfaces from sequence information. The result shows 94% accuracy for most strongly predicted sites. The results of Ofran and Rost (2003) indicated that PPI sites are possible to be predicted using sequence alone. Šikić and colleagues (2009) have used names of nine consecutive residues in a sequence as input feature vector. The input feature vector was defined on a sliding window of 9 residues. The window was considered as positive, if at least N residues including the central residue were marked as interacting. The data was classified for values of N ranging from 1 to 9 and result was evaluated. The input vector consists of all nine residues' names, and min, max or average value of features. When Random Forest classifier has been applied, the result shows precision of 84% and recall of around 26%. However, accuracy of the method is not good. In this direction, researchers suggested that we cannot predict PPI with acceptable accuracy using sequence information only. We need to incorporate other information, such as evolutionary and structure information, to predict PPI with high accuracy.

3.2 Secondary and 3D Structure

Proteins are polymers comprising of chains of amino acids. The structure of proteins determines their specific function. The structure of the protein can be described at different levels. The first level is the primary structure that corresponds to linear amino acid sequence. At the second level, we have secondary structure that refers to how the amino acid back-bone of the protein is arranged in 3-dimensional space, by forming hydrogen bonds with itself. There are three common secondary structures: alpha helices, beta sheets and random coils. Third level is tertiary structure which is produced when elements of the secondary structure fold up among them. Finally, the quaternary structure is related to the spatial arrangement of several proteins.

Šikić and his colleagues (2009) combined sequence information and 3D structure information to predict PPI using Random Forest classifier. They have used all 3D structure information available from Protein Structure and Interaction Analyzer (PSAIA) developed by Mihel and colleagues (2008), in additional to secondary structure. A total of 26 features have been considered here for training the classifier. Since, Random Forest algorithm is capable to estimate the importance of a particular feature, so they have applied input parameter set reduction. Here, it has been noticed that information acquired from sequence has the highest importance in the prediction. Also, five best structure features has been ranked as: non-polar accessible surface area (ASA), maximum depth index, relative non-polar ASA, average depth index, and minimum protrusion index.

3.3 Sequence Entropy

Variability within related protein sequences has been proved to provide clue about their 3D structure and function. The high variability regions within related proteins groups are linked to the specificity of molecules, while low variability regions are mostly structural or define regions of common function. Shanon entropy can be applied to estimate the diversity among group of protein sequences. For alignment of multiple sequences, the entropy H for each position can be computed as,

$$H = -\sum_{i=1}^{M} P_i \log_2 P_i \qquad (1)$$

where, P_i is fraction of residues of amino acid type i, and M is total number of amino acid type, i.e., 20. The sequence entropy score basically ranks the frequencies of the occurrence of 20 different types of amino acid, where lowest values correspond to the most conserved positions. The HSSP (Homology-derived Structures of Proteins) is a derived database that merges 3D structure and sequence information. This database is a noble resource for extracting sequence entropy (Schneider and Sander 1996).

3.4 Evolutionary Conservation

Conserved sequences are similar or identical sequences that may have been maintained by evolution despite speciation, if it is cross species conservation. More highly conserved sequence may occur in the phylogenetic tree. Since sequence information is normally transmitted from parents to progeny by genes, a conserved sequence implies that there is a conserved gene. There are several methods that use evolutionary conservation as a primary indicator to find location of interface residue in PPI. The main reason for using evolutionary conservation is that it reflects evolutionary selection at the interaction sites to maintain functions of protein families (Lichtarge et al. 1996; Neuvirth et al. 2004; Wang et al. 2013). At the interfaces, evolutionary conservation of residue is observed as higher than general surface residues, and hence has distinct feature of protein interaction sites (Wang et al. 2013).

3.5 Solvent Accessible Surface Area

The accessible surface area (ASA), also known as solvent-accessible surface area (SASA), is the surface area of a biomolecule which is accessible to a solvent (Connolly 1983; Richmond 1984). Measurement of SASA is mostly measured in terms of square angstroms and was initially explained by Lee and Richards (1971). SASA is computed using the 'rolling ball' algorithm proposed by Shrake and Rupley (1973). This algorithm applies a sphere of a particular radius to 'probe' the surface of the molecule. Some of the other methods to calculate SASA are linear combination of pair-wise overlap (LCPO) (Weiser et al. 1999) and Power Diagram method. The relative SASA may be applied to estimate the magnitude of binding-induced conformational changes using structures of either monomeric proteins or bound subunits. When it is applied to a large set of complexes, the result shows large conformational changes due to common binding. The SASA including many other protein features have been used in Šikić et al. (2009) for finding PPI sites.

3.6 Protein Expression

The co-expression of genes may act as an indicator of functional linkage. Hence, Microarray mRNA expression data can be used to predict PPIs. Here, interactions between two proteins are predicted based on similar expression of their coding genes in multiple conditions. There are several methods using which we can compute the similarity among expression profiles of genes in the given gene expression matrix. Pearson's Correlation Coefficient is a popular method to compute similarity since it can distinguish positively and negatively regulated gene pairs. The idea here is to identify set of genes with similar expression patterns.

This microarray mRNA co-expression dataset is based on two assumptions: (i) proteins present in same complex usually interact to each other, and (ii) proteins belong to same complex are co-expressed. One of these datasets has been reported by Cho et al. (1998). The dataset represents time-course gene expression fluctuations during yeast cell cycle and Rosetta compendium, comprises of expression profiles of 300 deletion mutants and cells under various chemical treatments (Cho et al. 1998). Cells have been collected at 17 time points observed at 10 min intervals, covering almost two full cell cycles. Here, pair-wise Pearson's correlation were computed for every gene-pairs, value of which ranges between 0 and 1.

3.7 Marginal Essentiality

At the most basic level, functional significance of genes may be defined by its essentiality, i.e., genes which are knocked out may render the cell unviable. Marginal essentiality is basically based on a hypothesis, called 'marginal benefit', that several non-essential genes make small but significant contributions to fitness of a cell (Browne et al. 2006). Marginal essentiality 'M' can be defined as a quantitative measure of a non-essential gene's importance to a cell (Yu et al. 2004). Yu et al. (2004) described that marginal essentiality measure relates to several topological properties of PPI networks. Particularly, proteins having higher degree of M tend to be hubs of the network, and have a shorter characteristic path length to their neighbors. Yu et al. (2004) obtained marginal essentiality dataset by combining the result of four phenotypic experiments. Two proteins are considered to be interacting, if they have higher combined M.

3.8 Co-essentiality

This feature is based on the hypothesis that proteins are either essential or non-essential, indicating that they belong to the same complex. If this is the case, they may be either essential or non-essential but not both. The reason is that a deletion mutant of either protein would yield same phenotype, and their mutual deletion would harm the function. In Zhang et al. (2012), co-essentiality, along with several proteins features, has been considered for the prediction as well as analysis of Protein Interactome in Pseudomonas aeruginosa. Gene essentiality data were retrieved from Database of Essential Genes (Zhang and Lin 2009). Each gene of PA PAO1 (a pathogen P. aeruginosa which is problematic in chronic airway infections) is considered as either essential (678 genes) or non-essential (4,890 genes). Considering gene essentiality, each gene-pair has a nominal value for co-essentiality: both are essential, both are non-essential, one is essential and other is non-essential.

Browne et al. (2006) has derived co-essentiality dataset from both MIPS complex catalogue and transposon and gene deletion experiments. In this dataset, protein-pairs are assumed to interaction, if both proteins are either essential or non-essential. When there is a combination of essential and non-essential proteins, protein-pair is considered as non-interacting. In Browne et al. (2006), mixture of non-essential and essential protein-pairs is represented by 1 and only non-essential are presented by 0. More detail information about MIPS based co-essentiality data can be found in Mews et al. (2000).

3.9   MIPS Functional Catalogue

It is a hypothesis that protein-pairs acting in same biological processes are more likely to interact to each other. Hence, based on this hypothesis, protein-pairscan be defined as interacting, if they belong to same biological process. Functional similarity between two proteins has been estimated from Gene Ontology (GO) and MIPS functional cata-logue (FunCat). MIPS FunCat is annotation scheme that represents functional descrip-tion of proteins and contains 28 main functional categories covering cellular transport, metabolism and signal transduction. In other words, FunCat is a hierarchically organ-ized, organism independent, flexible, scalable and controlled classification approach that enables functional description of proteins used for manual annotation of prokaryotes, eukaryotes, animals, fungi and plants. The main categories are organized as a hierarch-ical tree-like structure that describes up to 6 levels of increasing specificity. The FunCat version 2.1 includes a total of 1362 functional categories. Here, each protein represents a subtree of overall hierarchical class-tree. Now, it is possible to compute intersection tree of two subtree for two given proteins. This estimation is similarly done for complete list of protein pairs. For example, there are ~18 million interactions in yeast. The FunCat is separate from MIPS complex categories. The functional similarity between protein-pairs can be finally described as frequency at which interaction trees of protein-pair occur in the distribution.

3.10   GO-driven Frequency Based Similarity

By consider the hypothesis, as considered in FunCat, that is, protein-pair involved in same biological process are likely to interact; it is possible to extract participation infor-mation of protein-pairs in specific biological process using Go-driven annotation data-bases such as Saccharomyces Genome Database (Cherry et al. 1998). Browne et al. (2006) applied GO-driven Frequency Based Similarity measures to generate dataset to predict PPIs. This dataset was obtained by computing the similarities between gene products annotated in GO biological process hierarchy. Consider two proteins p_1 and p_2 which has a specific set of lowest common ancestor nodes in hierarchy, then it is possible to count number of proteins pairs having same set of annotation terms. In Browne et al. (2006), for all possible protein pairs in *S. Cerevisiac* (~18 million), they counted how many of these possible pairs share exactly same functional terms resulting a number ranges between 0 and 18 million. A smaller number represents a more specific functional description of a protein pair that suggests higher functional similarity and higher possi-bility to belong to same complex. On the other hand, a larger value of count represents a less functional similarity and there is less possibility for the protein-pair to belong to same complex.

3.11   GO-driven Semantic Similarity

To calculate similarity between Go terms and gene products, Lin's semantic similarity technique (Lin 1998) is mostly applied. The similarity values of gene-pairs can be used for PPI prediction, as used in Browne et al. (2006), to construct GO-driven Semantic Similarity (GOSEM) dataset. The GOSEM method exploits information contents of shared GO terms parents, as well as that of query GO terms applied in annotating gene. This similarity measure is expressed as probability and based on count of each terms occurring in the GO corpus. Lin's method computes similarity between two GO terms x_i and x_j as,

$$sim(x_i, x_j) = \frac{2 \times \max\limits_{x \in S(x_i, x_j)} \left[\log P(x_j)\right]}{\log P(x_i) + \log P(x_j)} \tag{2}$$

Where S is set of parental terms shared by terms x_i and x_j; $P(x)$ is probability of finding terms x or any of its parent in the GO corpus. The similarity between genes can be computed by aggregating similarity values of annotated terms of genes. The similarity between gene products g_k and g_l can be defined as average interest similarity between terms A_i to A_j,

$$SIM(g_k, g_l) = \frac{1}{m \times n} \sum_{x_i \in A_k, x_j \in A_l} sim(x_i, x_j) \tag{3}$$

where, A_k and A_l comprises of m and n terms.

3.12   Position-Specific Scoring Matrices

Position Specific Scoring Matrices (PSSMs), also called Position-Specific Weight Matrix (PSWM), are most commonly applied motifs descriptor in biological sequences. It is often calculated from a set of functionally related and aligned sequences. PSSM attempts to capture intrinsic variability characteristic from multiple sequence alignment (MSA). PSSMs have been used as protein feature vector by many researchers for finding PPIs (Deng et al. 2009). A PSSM has one row for each residue (4 rows for nucleotides or 20 rows for amino acids). Given a set S ($S = \{s_1, s_2, \ldots, s_n\}$) of n aligned sequences having length l, PSSM can be calculated as,

$$M_{ij} = \frac{1}{n} \sum_{k=1}^{n} I_i(s_{kj}) \tag{4}$$

$$where, \quad I_i(q) = f(x) = \begin{cases} 1 & if\, i = q \\ 0 & otherwise \end{cases}$$

where, i = A, C, T, G or amino acid residues; j = 1, 2, ..., l; $s_k = s_{k1}, s_{k2}, ..., s_{kl}$ (s_{ki} being any of the residue). Each coefficient in PSSM indicates count of a residue at a given position.

3.13   Residue Interface Propensity

Residue Interface Propensity (RIP) quantifies preferences of an amino acid to act as interface site of two interacting proteins. It is calculated by using interaction of all the proteins in entire family. For each amino acid i, the propensity is defined as,

$$Propensity_i = \frac{N_{in}(i)/N_{in}}{N_{surf}(i)/N_{surf}} \tag{5}$$

where $N_{in}(i)$ is number of amino acid of type i in interface; N_{in} is total number of amino acids of any type in the family; $N_{surf}(i)$ is number of surface amino acid of type i in all domain; and N_{surf} is total number of amino acids of any type in the family. In general, $Propensity_i > 1.0$ indicates that residue i has high chance for being in interface. The propensity score depends on both, number of interaction inferred from PSIMAP and size of SCOP family. RIP has been applied by Dong et al. (2007) to identify protein binding sites.

4   Protein Feature Representations

There are different proteins features, such as sequence information, co-expression, protein structure information, phylogenetic profiles, and so on, that can be used to predict PPIs computationally. Once protein features has been selected, the next fundamental question is how these protein features are represented so that it can be fed to a classifier for training and prediction. For the representation of sequence information as feature vector, a sliding window is most deployed approach to represent association among neighboring residues. Selecting length of sliding window is a vital issue because it affects the prediction accuracy. There is no thumb rule for the selection of length of sliding window and mostly it is set randomly. In a recently study, Šikić et al. (2009) applied an entropy based method to find out window length, which is given by,

$$-\sum_{i=1}^{L} p_i \times \log_2 p_i - \log_2 L \tag{6}$$

where, L is window length, and p_i represent the appearance frequency of i_{th} interacting residues in window of L residue given a central interaction. Results observed by Šikić et al. (2009) was similar for different window length but window length of 9 shows maximum difference of entropy. You et al. (2014) proposed a novel feature representation technique. It has been assumed here that continuous and discontinuous amino acids segment play a vital role in predicting PPI. The proposed feature representation approach considers interaction between sequentially distant but spatially closed residues. Here, Multiscale Continuous and Discontinuous (MCD) method is deployed for sequence representation to transform protein sequence to feature vector using binary encoding scheme. A multiscale decomposition technique is applied to divide given sequence into chunk of multiple sequences of distinct length. For the extraction of information, entire protein sequence is divided into equal length segments, and further a binary coding scheme is applied to each segment. Each segment is encoded as 4-bit binary sequence of 1's or 0's. For every continuous or discontinuous region, composition (C), transition (T) and distribution (D) – three kinds of descriptors are applied to represent its characteristics. Here, 'C' is ratio of number of amino acids in local region. 'T' specifies frequency (in percent) to which amino acids of a particular property is followed by that other property. 'D' means the length of chain within first 25%, 50%, 75% and 100% of amino acids of particular property are located.

5   Conclusion and Discussion

It has been observed that there are still discrepancies in estimating the number of PPIs even for small size well-studied unicellular organism Saccharomyces cerevisiae (yeast). Different studies estimated different size of complete binary protein interactome of yeast containing ~6,000 proteins. Grigoriev (2003) estimated around 16,000 to 26,000 PPIs, on the other hand Blow (2009) reported more than 30,000 potential interactions in yeast. Some of the databases have only experimental data containing greater than 50,000 binary PPIs in yeast. Thus, this discrepancy in the results indicates that some of the experimentally obtained interactions most probably contain false positives. Machine learning algorithms are playing a pivotal role in several classification and prediction problems including PPIs predictions. Prediction of PPI is a non-trivial problem because there are lots of factors which are involved in binding of amino-acids. Feature selection is an important issue in machine learning techniques, specially protein features in PPI prediction problem. This review covers a maximum of 13 different protein features used in the literation.

In case of incomplete datasets, careful study is required to know the optimal machine learning technique, and optimal protein features. Some of the suggested future directions are as follows:

(i)   Most of the methods proposed earlier consider either single or few protein features for training classifiers. The results show that considering multiple protein features improves the performance of PPI prediction. Hence, we can look forward for integrating more protein features for further improvement in the prediction results.

(ii) Today, several ensembles learning algorithms have been developed, including boosting, bagging and multi-classifier systems, showing better prediction accuracy in various classification and prediction problems. Hence, we can deploy these algorithms to increase the prediction accuracy at the cost of computation.

(iii) Mostly of the studies have been performed on finding PPIs on yeast only. We can look for finding PPIs in *Homo sapiens* in similar way.

Acknowledgments. This work is financially supported by Jamia Millia Islamia, New Delhi, India under innovative research activities.

References

Blow, N.: Systems biology: untangling the protein web. Nature **460**, 415–418 (2009)

Bock, J.R., Gough, D.A.: Predicting protein–protein interactions from primary structure. Bioinformatics **17**, 455–460 (2001)

Bordner, A.J., Abagyan, R.: Statistical analysis and prediction of protein-protein interfaces. Proteins **60**, 353–366 (2005)

Browne, F., Wang, H., Zheng, H., Azuaje, F.: An assessment of machine and statistical learning approaches to inferring networks of protein-protein interactions. J. Integr. Bioinform. **3**, 230–246 (2006)

Chatterjee, P., et al.: PPI_SVM: prediction of protein-protein interactions using machine learning, domain-domain affinities and frequency tables. Cell. Mol. Biol. Lett. **16**, 264–278 (2011)

Cherry, J.M., Adler, C., Ball, C., Chervitz, S.A., Dwight, S.S., Hester, E.T., Jia, Y., Juvik, G., Roe, T., Schroeder, M., et al.: SGD: saccharomyces genome database. Nucleic Acids Res. **26**, 73–79 (1998)

Cho, R., Campbell, M., Winzeler, E., Steinmetz, L., Conway, A., Wodicka, L., Wolfsberg, T., Gabrielian, A., Landsman, D., Lockhart, D., Davis, R.: A genome-wide transcriptional analysis of the mitotic cell cycle. Mol. Cell **2**(1), 65–73 (1998)

Connolly, M.L.: Solvent-accessible surfaces of proteins and nucleic acids. Science **221**(4612), 709–713 (1983)

De Las Rivas, J., de Luis, A.: Interactome data and databases: different types of protein interaction. Comp. Funct. Genomics **5**, 173–178 (2004)

De Las Rivas, J., Fontanillo, C.: Protein-protein interactions essentials: key concepts to building and analyzing interactome networks. PLoS Comput. Biol. **6**(6), e1000807 (2010). doi:10.1371/journal.pcbi.1000807

Deng, L., Guan, J., Dong, Q., Zhou, S.: Prediction of protein-protein interaction sites using an ensemble method. BMC Bioinformatics, **10**, 426 (2009)

Dong, Q., Wang, X., Lin, L., Guan, Y.: Exploiting residue-level and profile-level interface propensities for usage in binding sites prediction of proteins. BMC Bioinformatics **8**, 147 (2007)

Fariselli, P., et al.: Prediction of protein-protein interaction sites in heterocomplexes with neural networks. Eur. J. Biochem. **269**, 1356–1361 (2002)

Grigoriev, A.: On the number of protein- protein interactions in the yeast proteome. Nucleic Acids Res. **31**, 4157–4161 (2003)

Jansen, R., Yu, H., Greenbaum, D., Kluger, Y., Krogan, N.J., Chung, S., Emili, A., Snyder, M., Greenblatt, J.F., Gerstein, M.: A Bayesian networks approach for predicting protein-protein interactions from genomic data. Science **302**(5644), 449–453 (2003). doi:10.1126/science.1087361

Lee, B., Richards, F.M.: The interpretation of protein structures: estimation of static accessibility. J. Mol. Biol. **55**(3), 379–400 (1971)

Lichtarge, O., Bourne, H.R., Cohen, F.E.: An evolutionary trace method defines binding surfaces common to protein families. J Mol. Biol. **257**, 342–358 (1996)

Lin, D.: An information-theoretic definition of similarity. In: ICML, vol. 98, no. 1998, pp. 296–304 (1998)

Mewes, H.W., Frishman, D., Gruber, C., Geier, B., Haase, D., Kaps, A., Lemcke, K., Mannhaupt, G., Pfeiffer, F., Schuller, C., et al.: MIPS: a database for genomes and protein sequences. Nucleic Acids Res. **28**, 37–40 (2000)

Mihel, J., Šikić, M., Tomic, S., Jeren, B., Vlahovicek, K.: PSAIA—protein structure and interaction analyzer. BMC Struct. Biol. **8**, 21 (2008)

Neuvirth, H., Raz, R., Schreiber, G.: a structure based prediction program to identify the location of protein-protein binding sites. J. Mol. Biol. **338**, 181–199 (2004)

Ofran, Y., Rost, B.: Predicted protein–protein interaction sites from local sequence information. FEBS Lett. **544**, 236–239 (2003)

Patil, A., Nakamura, H.: Filtering high-throughput protein-protein interaction data using a combination of genomic features. BMC Bioinform. **6**, 100 (2005)

Rao, V., Srinivas, K., Sujini, G.N., Sunand, G.N.: Protein-protein interaction detection: methods and analysis. J. Proteomics **12**, e0173163 (2014)

Res, I., Mihalek, I., Lichtarge, O.: An evolution based classifier for prediction of protein interfaces without using protein structures. Bioinformatics **21**, 2496–2501 (2005)

Richmond, T.J.: Solvent accessible surface area and excluded volume in proteins: analytical equations for overlapping spheres and implications for the hydrophobic effect. J. Mol. Biol. **178**(1), 63–89 (1984)

Schneider, R., Sander, C.: The HSSP database of protein structure- sequence alignments. Nucleic Acids Res. **24**, 201–205 (1996)

Shrake, A., Rupley, J.A.: Environment and exposure to solvent of protein atoms. Lysozyme and insulin. J. Mol. Biol. **79**(2), 351–371 (1973)

Šikić, M., Tomic, S., Vlahovicek, K.: Prediction of protein-protein interaction sites in sequences and 3D structures by random forests. PLoS Comput. Biol. **5**, e1000278 (2009)

Wang, B., Sun, W., Zhang, J., Chen, P.: Current status of machine learning-based methods for identifying protein-protein interaction sites. Curr. Bioinform. **8**, 177–182 (2013)

Wang, B., Chen, P., Huang, D.-S., Li, J., Lok, T.-M., Lyu, M.R.: Predicting protein interaction sites from residue spatial sequence profile and evolution rate. FEBS Lett. **580**(2), 380–384 (2006)

Weiser, J., Shenkin, P.S., Still, W.C.: Approximate atomic surfaces from linear combinations of pairwise overlaps (LCPO). J. Comput. Chem. **20**(2), 217–230 (1999)

You, Z., Ming, Z., Niu, B., Deng, S., Zhu, Z.: A SVM-based system for predicting protein-protein interactions using a novel representation of protein sequences. In: Huang, D.S., Bevilacqua, V., Figueroa, J.C., Premaratne, P. (eds.) ICIC 2013. LNCS, vol. 7995, pp. 629–637. Springer, Heidelberg (2013). doi:10.1007/978-3-642-39479-9_73

You, Z., Zhu, L., Zheng, C., Yu, H., Deng, S., Ji, Z.: Prediction of protein-protein interactions from amino acid sequences using a novel multi-scale continuous and discontinuous feature set. BMC Bioinform. **15**(Suppl 15), S9 (2014)

Yu, H., Greenbaum, D., Xin, LuH, Zhu, X., Gerstein, M.: Genomic analysis of essentiality within protein networks. Trends Genet. **20**(6), 227–231 (2004)

Xue, L.C., Dobbs, D., Bonvin, A.M., Honavar, V.: Computational prediction of protein interfaces: a review of data driven methods. FEBS Lett. **589**(23), 3516–3526 (2015)

Zhang, R., Lin, Y.: DEG 5.0, a database of essential genes in both prokaryotes and eukaryotes. Nucleic Acids Res **37**, 455–458 (2009)

Zhang, M., Su, S., Bhatnagar, R., Hassett, D., Lu, L.: Prediction and analysis of the protein interactome in Pseudomonas aeruginosa to enable network-based drug target selection. PLoS ONE **7**(7), e41202 (2012)

Zubek, J., Tatjewski, M., Boniecki, A., Mnich, M., Basu, S., Plewczynski, D.: Multi-level machine learning prediction of protein–protein interactions in Saccharomyces cerevisiae. PeerJ. **3**, 1041 (2015)

Load Balancing Task Scheduling Based on Variants of Genetic Algorithms: Review Paper

Ayushi Harkawat[⊠] ⓘ, Shilpa Kumari ⓘ, Poorva Pharkya ⓘ, and Deepak Garg ⓘ

National Institute of Technology, Kurukshetra, Haryana, India
ayushi.h31@gmail.com, erdeepakgarg21@gmail.com

Abstract. In the cloud platform, basic aim of task scheduling based algorithm is to reduce the makespan of the task and to minimize the load on resources. Users are working on large amount and the resources to be used are not up to the requirements. So, to fulfill global performance, cloud computing is used. Stated problem has been improved up to some extent by variant of genetic algorithm like JLGA (Job Spanning Time and Load Balancing and GA) and MPGA. Therefore, here it reviewed variant of genetic algorithm and did comparison among them. Furthermore, this paper proposed HJLGA (Hybridization of good features of JLGA and MPGA) which uses min-min algorithm to initialize population and also brings the concept of hill climbing to find the best fitted value. HJLGA satisfied the requirements of load balancing, least cost and minimum makespan of nodes.

Keywords: Cloud computing · Genetic algorithm · Hill climbing · Load balancing · Task scheduling

1 Introduction

1.1 Cloud Computing

Services those are hosted or delivered via internet is general term for cloud computing. It basically means accessing, maintaining and storing data through the internet rather than hard disk drive. The growth of cloud computing is quick and fast because the communication technologies are extensively enhance [1] and also, in today's world virtualization technologies are used in almost all the system gradually it is imperative [2]. Various companies have given their own cloud services in a regular manner to the client and the client have no idea about how clouds are built without knowing that they work on needful objects. The need of cloud computing is essential and it is increasing even in today's time [2]. Three types of services are used in cloud computing these are Iaas, Paas and Saas using these services the clients work easily on available services given by the companies [2]. Continuously the use of cloud computing services are increasing so the challenges of elevate of performance is increasing day by day. Foremost researches are focus on optimization and balanced the nodes on cloud environment. Pros related to cloud computing includes saving of cost, reliability, maintainability, increased

© Springer Nature Singapore Pte Ltd. 2017
S. Kaushik et al. (Eds.): ICICCT 2017, CCIS 750, pp. 318–325, 2017.
https://doi.org/10.1007/978-981-10-6544-6_29

collaboration and work from anywhere and environmentally friendly. If the spanning of jobs is elongated then surely it will cause unsatisfying condition. The loads between the servers are balanced dynamically on platform of cloud computing and improving utility of resources [3]. Therefore, dynamically the task to be scheduled with time is least wasted and functioning is done in best fitted manner, is the typical problem need to solve it.

1.2 Load Balancing

For solving load balancing variant algorithm are used, most of the cloud hold bulk of solution. NP-complete problem possess the problem of time limit. For balancing the capacity of resources and also to amputate overload of resources the concept of load balancing is use to balance load in equal proportions. Load can be balanced by two ways dynamically and statically. In dynamically load balancing, load is balanced at the time of running state and in the case of static balancing the load is balanced at the stage when scheduling is balanced. Static balancing of load is most preferable because it avoids the virtual machine costs and brings improved time of execution and QOS (quality of services) [4–6].

1.3 Genetic Algorithm

In genetic algorithm, we have a pool or a population of possible solutions to the given problem. These solutions then undergo recombination and mutation, producing new children, and the process is repeated over various generations [1]. Genetic algorithm is the most optimize and powerful algorithm in solving empirical problems and its capability to compute the best fitted individual by observing the generations.

Through this paper the perception is to profess the concept of randomization, virtual machine, for balancing the load and attenuate the minimum makespan of task which is pre-owned in cloud computing.

2 Related Work

2.1 JLGA

GAs are basically used for finding solution in an optimize manner in which it mimic biological expansion. In JLGA, Jobs are divided into tasks and in population initialization a matrix is created where rows represents no. of chromosomes and column represents no. of tasks and matrix value represent node no. on which task i has been assigned by greedy approach. Then it deduce a fitter proximate which is found from every generation. For finding each and every generation, after considering cocksure problem area choosing of individual is dependent on fitness of various individuals. Next combine the individuals and it varies by the use of genetic operators and representing the latest population than the new set of solution in composed. Eliminating the bad solutions and selecting best out of them, ensuring in generation of maturation [1].

2.1.1 Algorithm of JLGA [1]

Input:
MaxVal: maximum iterations
S: Scale of population; N: Node number;
J: jobs
C1, C2: Mass of average spanning of jobs and total planning of jobs C1 + C2 = 1
$\lambda 1, \lambda 2$: Probability of fitness1 and fitness2, $\lambda 1 + \lambda 2 = 1$.

Output:
elite1,N : Ideal solution

```
1:iteration, λ ← 0; fitval←∅
2:elite1,N , temp1,N, p1, p2, Ps,N , Fitval1,S ← ∅
3:p ← Greedy Initialized value
4:while iteration < Maxval do
5:    λ=random(0,1)
6:    if λ < λ2 then
7:           fitval = Fitval2
8:    else
9:           fitval = Fitval1
10: end if
11: for i = 1 to S do
12:        Fitvali ← fitval(i)
13: end for
14: elite1,N ← One by one Ideal fitness
15: p1, p2 ← Roullete wheel selection(Ps,N)
16: calculate pc, pm
17: if random(0, 1) < pc then
18:        temporary 1,N ← crossover(p1, p2)
19: end if
20: if random(0, 1) < pm then
21:        P1,N ← mutation(temporary)
22: end if
23: iteration ← iteration + 1
24:end while
```

2.1.2 Fitness Function

In JLGA Fitness function is categorized into two types fitness1 and fitness2. For first fitness it works on the minimization of inter-nodes load variance [1] and second fitness states that if it consumes less time than it produces better fitness.

The basic need of fitness is to find the need and quality related to individual in population in G.A and to imitate that kind of search procedure that finds the best fitted value for survival. Various operators are performed in fitness process that includes selection then perform crossover and finally mutation. If it holds bigger and finer fitness then better the consummation, vice versa. If fitness is good of individual then there can be multiplication of fitness otherwise it may abolish from one generation to another [1].

2.2 MPGA

Several algorithms for task scheduling can be categorized into algorithm of round robin, minimum algorithm [4], min-min algorithm [4]. If the algorithms mentioned are taken into consideration then performance is acceptable some time, but cannot ignore its drawback as well. When the concept of virtual machine with variant performance is taken into account then the algorithm of round robin and algorithm of minimum link is not acceptable. And there is a problem of balancing load with the algorithm of min-min.

MPGA is a postulate process of global searching mechanism. The main thing in this is fitness function which is combination of cost plus time, use of multipopulation & min-min initialization. It is used for finding method which is optimized which is inspired by the theory of Darwin's evolution [7]. Algorithm used by GA is easy to understand, but there can be convergence and that too premature. It is one of the capacious and efficient today's time algorithm, can get solution for numerous functions that are multi-objective [2] and non-linear [2].

The concept of MPGA can be used to for solving the basic problem of scheduling task in the cloud platform. The solution that is optimal in MPGA can be found by searching parallel population that is multiple [7, 8]. MPGA brings betterment to basic GA, by bringing the poise between the ability of local search and global search. Facilely the problem of convergence of premature can be avoided in MPGA by achieving optimization it in global way.

2.2.1   Algorithm of MPGA [4]

Input:
MaxVal: maximum iteration
Scale S: Population size(scale); Node N: no. of Working node ; Job J: no. of jobs
K1, K2: total job spanning weight and weight of average job spanning, $K1 + K2 = 1$
P1, P2 : consecutively *fitness*1 *and fitness*2 probability
$P1 + P2 = 1$.
iterate:iterator
C:cost
T:time
Output:
*elite*1,*Node*: Best result
```
 1:iterate, P ← 0; fitnessf← Ø
 2:elite1,Node,temp2,N,I1, I2, Pscale,N , Fit1,Scale ← Ø
 3:I ← Min-Min initialization for population
 4:while iterate < MaxIteration do
 5:   P=random(0,1)
 6:   if P < P2 then
 7:        fitnessf = Fit2
 8:   else
 9:        fitnessf = Fit1
10: end if
11: for j = 1 to Scale do
12:        Fitj ← fitnessf(j)
13: end for
14: elite1,Node ← fittest individual among all
15: I1, I2 ← Roullete wheel selection(Ps,N)
16: calculate pcross, pmutat
17: if random(0, 1) < pcross then
18:        temp2,Node ← crossover(I1, I2)
19: end if
20: if random(0, 1) < pmutat then
21:        I1,Node ← mutation(temp1)
22: end if
23: calculate cost Corresponding to time & fitness.
24: iterate ← iterate + 1
25:end while
```

2.3   Comparative Study of JLGA and MPGA

See (Table 1).

Table 1. Comparison of JLGA and MPGA [1, 4, 8]

Method/Parameters	JLGA	MPGA
1. Objective	Minimize the job completion time	Minimize the time and processing cost
2. Algorithm used	Task scheduling using greedy initialization, AGA, JLGA	Task scheduling using Min-Min and Max-Min algorithm
3. Load balancing	Based on Simple GA in cloud computing	Based on Multi-population GA in cloud computing
4. Optimization technique	Local optimization by genetic algorithm	Global optimization by parallel search of multi-population
5. Two fitness functions used	1. To balance the individual with less internodes load variance 2. To balance node utilization time	1. To balance time 2. To balance cost
6. Genetic algorithm virtual machine resources scheduler	Through VM migration load balancing and assignment is done	Here also with the help of VM migration load balancing and assignment is done but it is more efficient

3   Our Proposed HJLGA

In this paper we tried to extract good features of JLGA and MPGA and include properties of hill climbing and bring into light the new algorithm HJLGA which means (Hybridization of JLGA and MPGA). HJLGA combines the goodness of JLGA as well as MPGA and also precedes the important features of hill climbing. By important features of hill climbing we meant that rather than stopping at the first peak value it searches further and try to find the best fitted out of the rest iterations so by this not only we work on cost or time we also work more towards fitness value. JLGA worked on load and time completion and MPGA worked on cost and time completion. And we have mixed these properties to propose hybrid version.

HJLGA Algorithm

Input:
MaxIter: maxium iterations
S: Scale of population; N: Node number; J: Jobs
$C1$, $C2$: Mass of average spanning of jobs and total planning of jobs, $C1 + C2 = 1$
$\lambda1$, $\lambda2$: Probability of *fitval*1 *and fitval*2
$\lambda1 + \lambda2 = 1.$
C:cost
T:time
Output:
*elite*1,N : Ideal solution

```
1:iteration, λ ← 0; fitval← Ø
2:elite1,N , temp1,N, p1, p2, Ps,N , Fitval1,S ← Ø
3:p ← Min-Min initialization for population
  Fitness2=(Minimize Job Completion time + Minimize
  loads per node)
  Fitness1=(Minimize makespan + Minimize cost)
4:while iteration < Maxval do
5:   λ=random(0,1)
6:   if λ < λ2 then
7:       fitval = Fitval2 (Minimize Job Completion time +
                  minimize loads per node)
8:   else
9:       fitval = Fitval1 (Minimize Makespan + minimize
                  cost)
10: end if
11: for i = 1 to S do
12:        Fitvali ← fitval(i)
13: end for
14: elite1,N ← one by one find  fitval
15: p1, p2 ← Roullete wheel selection(Ps,N)
    Optmate1=hill climbing (p1)
    Optmate2=hill climbing (p2)
16: calculate prc, prm
17: if random(0, 1) < prc then
18:        temporary1,N ← cossover(optmate1, optmate2)
19: end if
20: if random(0, 1) < pm then
21:        P1,N ← mutation(temporary)
22: end if
23: iterattion ← iteration + 1
24:end while
```

4 Conclusion

In the paper we have successfully reviewed JLGA and MPGA and also presented a comparison table between these on important parameters like initialization, fitness function, multipopulation, objective etc. Presented a proposed HJLGA algorithm with least cost, minimum makespan and minimum load per node based load balancing. HJLGA takes advantage of JLGA and MPGA. In addition it consists of Hill climbing optimization phase after selection of chromosomes thus improving overall performances. To initialize the population min-min algorithm has been used. Fitness function regarding job completion time, load balancing has been introduced.

5 Future Scope

Possibilities for future, two important terms that needs improvisation is that, we have assumed that when it comes to job management priority is ignored. However while working on cloud platform, it can't be ignored. On scale of population can be adapted that is big enough in preceding generation for management of diversity and then decreases agilely in the later generations. So, to maintain a balanced selection pressure and convergence rate. Next task will be to practically implement this on tool.

References

1. Wang, T., Liu, Z., Chen, Y., Xu, Y.: Load Balancing task scheduling based on genetic algorithm in cloud computing. In: Proceedings of the 12th International Conference on Dependable, Autonomic and Secure Computing, pp. 146–152. IEEE Computer Society (2014)
2. Kruekaew, B., Kimpan, W.: Virtual machine scheduling management on cloud computing using artificial bee colony. In: Proceedings of the International Multi Conference of Engineers and Computer Scientists, vol. 1, pp. 185–189 (2014)
3. Liu, X., Li, K., Min, G., Xiao, B., Shen, Y., Qu, W.: Efficient unknown tag identification protocols in large-scale RFID systems. IEEE Transact. Parallel Distrib. Syst **85**, 190–197 (2014)
4. Bei, W., Jun, L.: Load balancing task scheduling based on multi population genetic algorithm in cloud computing. In: Proceedings of the 35th Chinese Control Conference, IEEE Xplore, pp. 5261–5266 (2016)
5. Ramezani, F., Lu, J., Hussain, F.: Task-based system load balancing in cloud computing using particle swarm optimization. Int. J. Parall. Program. **42**, 739–754 (2013)
6. Aya, A., Salah, F., Mahmoud, S., Sayed, M., Horbaty, E.: Intelligent cloud algorithms for load balancing problems: a survey. In: Proceedings of the Seventh International Conference on Intelligent Computing and Information Systems, pp. 210–216 (2015)
7. Babu, P., Amudha, T.: A novel genetic algorithm for effective job scheduling in grid environment. In: Krishnan, G.S.S., Anitha, R., Lekshmi, R.S., Kumar, M.S., Bonato, A., Graña, M. (eds.) Computational Intelligence, Cyber Security and Computational Models. AISC, vol. 246, pp. 385–393. Springer, New Delhi (2014). doi:10.1007/978-81-322-1680-3_42
8. Pencheva, T., Angelova, M.: Purposeful model parameters genesis in multi-population genetic algorithm. Glob. J. Technol. Optim. **5**, 164–170 (2014)

Deep Learning Model Schemes to Address the Scrutability and In-Memory Purchase Issues in Recommender System

J. Sharon Moses[(✉)] [iD] and L.D. Dhinesh Babu [iD]

School of Information Technology and Engineering,
VIT University, Vellore, India
sharonjmoses@gmail.com, lddhineshbabu@gmail.com

Abstract. Recommender systems are used widely in each and every web services to recommend and suggest user interested information or products. The advancement of digital information era and pain in traversing the vast amount of information made users to realise the importance of intelligent recommender systems. Intelligent recommender system suffers over many issues some among them are scrutability, scalability and in-memory purchase problem. In-memory purchase problem is one of the currently persisting recommender system problems. In this paper the deep learning models based recommendation scheme are framed to address the scrutability and in-memory purchase issue of the recommender system. Initially the working of deep learning models like feed forward and recurrent neural network are discussed. Then the recommendation schemes based on the deep learning models in addressing the issues of the recommender system are detailed.

Keywords: Deep learning models · Recommender system · Scrutability · Recurrent neural networks · Feed forward networks

1 Introduction

Data Science with Big Data techniques revolutionized the IT industry with its futuristic predictions and business analytics. Advancements of Big Data analytics in mining intelligence have changed the perspective of Data science from just being a dataset to a valuable data source. Deep learning appears to be an added advantage to the Big Data analytics in processing unstructured data. 90% of available information is raw and unstructured in nature. Deep learning is a vital big data tool that uses neural network in analyzing and mining the intelligence from unstructured data. Deep learning concepts in implementing the recommender systems are one among the less researched work. The efficiency of deep learning models in mining intelligence can be competently utilized in recommender systems to generate accurate predictions. In this paper possible deep learning schemes are framed to avert the recommender issues like Scrutability, Scalability and prevailing in-memory purchase issue of recommender system. This paper is structured in the following way: Sect. 2 details about the recommender system, its issues and involvement of deep learning models in building recommendation

© Springer Nature Singapore Pte Ltd. 2017
S. Kaushik et al. (Eds.): ICICCT 2017, CCIS 750, pp. 326–335, 2017.
https://doi.org/10.1007/978-981-10-6544-6_30

system. Section 3 details the feed forward network scheme in addressing the scrutability issue. Section 4 elaborates the use of recurrent neural network in addressing the in-memory purchase problem, and Sect. 5 concludes the paper.

2 Recommender Systems

The overwhelming growth of information flooded the World Wide Web with an unimaginable amount of information. The consumers and producers of information needed a specialized mechanism to filter the needed and relevant information. Researchers came up with a recommendation system to suggest users what they need by computing the available history of information associated to the user. In the year 1992, the first recommender system based on collaborative filtering called tapestry came into existence [1]. The successfulness of collaborative filtering algorithm [2] in recommending the personified items to users made the researchers to invent different recommender algorithms. Recommender algorithm takes the user information as input and process to find the similarity between the user and the other users in the system. Based on the similarity, neighbors of the user are found and categorized. Then the neighbor interested, liked item or the item bought by the neighbor is recommended to the user. Also based on user demographical information, item ratings, and other social networking group related information are computed to recommend item to the user. Some of the popular recommender algorithms are collaborative filtering algorithm, knowledge based algorithm, content based recommendation algorithm, computational based techniques, group recommender, and social network based recommender, demographical recommender algorithms and hybrid recommender algorithms [3, 14]. Most of the recommender algorithms are domain specific in nature, association of one algorithm with another forming hybrid algorithm is done to achieve recommendation accuracy and to resolving the factors affecting the efficiency of the system. Even though there is a great development among the recommender algorithm to predict accurate recommendations. The mounting demand for accurateness and the scalability nature of the web applications creates the necessity of intelligent recommender systems.

2.1 Overview of Deep Learning Models Based Recommender System

The study on implementing deep learning models in recommender system is one among the latest research studies. Since, most of the recommendation system works on collaborative filtering algorithm, the development of deep learning based recommender systems is slow paced. In the initial days of recommender system, only one layer is more than enough to predict the outcome. But today, with millions of available data, deep belief models can be employed to perform highly intellectual tasks. Zuo et al. developed a tag aware recommender system based on deep belief network to solve the vagueness, repetitiveness and sparsity problems [4]. In their three phase method, deep belief network acts along with the traditional collaborative filtering algorithm (CF) to derive recommendations. In the first phase, the user profile and tags are modelled as vector model. The second phase consist of three layer sparse autoencoder, this encoder rebuild the input based on the output to minimize the error between them. At last, the CF algorithm is used to recommend the items based on the generated tags. Their method analysis states that the efficiency of recommendations get increased when CF algorithm is collaborated with the sparse autoencoder. Robin and Hugues used CF algorithm along with recurrent neural network to compare and study the item coverage and short term predictions [5]. The objective function of recurrent neural network is modified to maximize the diverseness of the recommendation system without disturbing the accuracy of the system. Though Recurrent neural network needs renewing the structure of CF algorithm, the end results of Robin and Hugues methods shows that better item coverage and predictions are possible by utilizing the recurrent neural network. Zheng lie in his work detailed the possibility of using deep learning methods in recommendation system and concluded that still more detailed study is needed on utilizing deep learning models in recommender system [6]. Cheng et al. [7] used feed forward network and generalized linear models to build a recommender system for Google play store. The proposed wide and deep learning approach by Cheng et al. memorizes the characteristics of the user interaction and feed forward network takes care of generating recommendations.

3 Addressing Scrutability Issue Using Feed Forward Neural Network

The changing patterns in the user behavior and need for the user to adapt the current trend will affect the efficiency of the recommender system. Since the recommender systems are acting on the history of user information, the system would not be able to correct its mistakes resulting in wrong predictions. In recommender system scrutability is defined as the ability of the system to adapt to the changes when corrected by the user [12, 13]. Feed forward neural network can be used to address the growing scrutability issues in recommender system. Back propagation algorithm and feed forward network can educate the system about the current interests of the user.

3.1 Architecture of the Feed Forward Network

Feed forward neural network model is the basic dynamic learning model Feed forward neural network looks like the replica of the human brain bounded within a range. Like neurons in the brain each neuron of the network gets a signal from the other neurons of the layer. Feed forward neural network consist of many layers. Except input and output layer other layer are kept hidden in the network. The inputs in the network are like neurons carrying a weight. The weights of the input layer are passed through the layers by summing up the weights using a fixed range parameter. After input layer, the neurons are passed through the hidden layer until it reaches the output layer of the network. In Fig. 1 the model of feed forward neural network is depicted. Developing the intelligence of the network is totally based on the backward propagation algorithm.

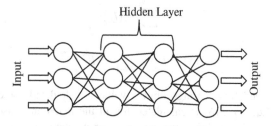

Fig. 1. Feed forward neural network

The work of backward propagation algorithm is to rectify the errors by altering the weight of the neurons until the output becomes expected output. Like an auto encoder that converts input into output by making changes to the circuit back propagation algorithm learns the result by correcting the error. Many data will be given as an input to the network so that the each error will train the neural network to identify and yield the desired output. Training feed forward neural network has its own share of disadvantages [8]. To overcome the disadvantages of feed forward neural network deep belief network came into existence.

3.2   Feed Forward Neural Network Based Recommender

When a user rejects the recommendations, stating that the generated recommendations are wrong. The system will ask the user to correct it. When the user does the correction, the system will correct the input by using the backward propagation algorithm resulting in updating the recommendation system input (Fig. 2).

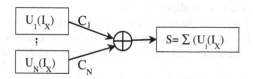

Fig. 2. Calculating value for the function

Consider a recommender system generates the recommendations for user named A based on the S value. S value is calculated using the user rating on that item and correlation value of the neighbor. By updating the input, the system starts to learn the recent interests of the user. Once the system gets the update of the user, the recommender algorithm starts predicting the recommendations based on the updated input. Let the users in the system be $\{U_1, U_2, \ldots, U_N\}$, the user rating on item I_X is given by $\{U_1(I_X), U_2(I_X), \ldots, U_N(I_X)\}$, and the correlation value between the neighbours and the user is denoted as $\{C_1, C_2, \ldots, C_N\}$.

$$S = \sum_{i=0to1} U_i(I_X)C_i \qquad\qquad (1)$$

$$F(S) = f \sum_{i=0to1} U_i(I_X)C_i \qquad\qquad (2)$$

Based on the feed forward algorithm S value is calculated for each item in the system as in the Eq. (1). $F(S)$ is calculated for all the items and based on the higher S value items are recommended to the user A. User A interest on Item I_X is calculated by utilizing the neighbor rating on the item and correlation of the user A with the neighbor as in the Eqs. (1) and (2).

Algorithm : Feed Forward Neural Network Based Recommender

U→list of users in the system{ U_1, U_2, ..., U_N }
U(I_X)→Denotes the rating of user on item I_X
C_i→Correlation value between the user and the neighbors
I_N→Total number of items in the system
1. Let us consider a user A is searching for an item I_X
2. Generate recommendation R based on F(S)

$$\text{where } S = \sum_{i=0to1} U_i\left(I_X\right)C_i$$

3. If S value is generated then calculate F(S)

$$F(S) = f\sum_{i=0to1} U_i\left(I_X\right)C_i$$

4. Consider the item generated by F(S) is IR
5. If User A likes the item IR
    Then the system continues its suggestion
6. If User A dislikes the item
    Then find the recently liked item of the user
    If exist then try to get details of those neighbors
    Based on that start generating the S and F(S) Value.

If user likes the recommended item then the system does not update the system further and tries to generate recommendation normally. If the user dislikes the recommended Item I_X, then by utilizing the back propagation algorithms intimation is sent to the system that the value of $F(S)$ does not interest the user. Once the system gets the update regarding the $F(S)$ the system assumes that the recommendation is wrong and flags the need for new information to generate recommendation for particular user.

For updating the user information for further recommendations, the system finds out the recently liked items of the user. Depending on the user liked item the neighbors of the user is modified. The utilization of feed forward network in calculating $F(S)$ is used in finding the relevant neighbors. The new neighbors will get mapped to the user, based on the new neighbors the system will start generating recommendations. Thus by employing feed forward and back propagation algorithm, better intelligence of the recommender system can be perceived.

4   In-Memory Purchase Issues in Ecommerce Recommender System

Recommendation of products plays a key role in ecommerce industry. Since ecommerce sites are flooded with numerous products every day, every ecommerce websites incorporate recommender system, to help users in finding the needed product. When a user starts to browse for certain product recommender system starts to suggest products that are similar to the user. Though this appears to help the user in getting the relevant product recommender system makes mistake by going on suggesting the similar item despite of user purchasing it. This kind of situation, make user to get confused and can make a user to leave the system without buying any product. Also in other cases, recommender system start suggesting better product to the user after user makes the purchase. By this action recommender system will make user to regret his decision. This kind of scenario makes the user to lose hope in the recommender system. Recurrent neural network can address this issue by monitoring the temporary user behavior and updating the system regarding the user activity.

4.1   Architecture of the Recurrent Neural Network

Recurrent neural network (RNN) is a kind of artificial neural network that displays powerful temporary behavior because of its directed cycle between connected units.

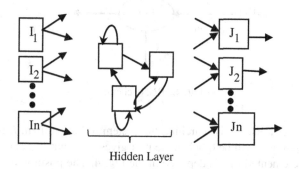

Hidden Layer

Fig. 3. Example of recurrent neural network

Each connection that exists between the units exhibits a cyclic connection. RNN is found to be efficient in recognizing sequence of information since it have the ability to store temporarily and can analyze in a cyclic fashion [9]. Though RNN and Feed forward network uses similar processing unit, there is a difference in their structure [10]. Feed forward network don't have a directed connections and they pass through each layer to process the input and final layer delivers the output. RNN uses directed graph, and they got connected to units like neurons in the brain [11]. Figure 3 represents the example architecture of recurrent neural network where I stand for input layer and J is the final layer. The whole processing of the input information takes place in a hidden layer.

4.2 Recurrent Neural Network Scheme to Address the In-Memory Purchase Issue

The scheme utilizes the efficiency of RNN in identifying the sequence of action. Using recurrent neural network each action of the user is identified and stored. The stored action of the user is analyzed to conclude the state of the user. When the recommender system aware of the user state, it makes meaningful recommendations.

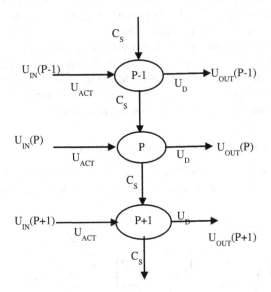

Fig. 4. RNN scheme

Let us consider a user U is searching the system to buy an item I. Initially all the current state C_S of user will be 0, when the user gives the input, the current state of the user will get incremented this is depicted in the Fig. 4. The position of the user in the system P remains as 0 until there is a change is the user current state C_S. User input to the system in searching the item is given as $U_{IN}(P)$. When the input is given by user, the system considers that the user applied some action. So the user action U_{ACT} is considered to be positive and takes the value 1. The position of the user is calculated as depicted in the Eq. (3). In Eq. (3), f is a tangent function that used to determine the position of user in the system. The outcome of the user position in the system is given as $U_{OUT}(P)$ as in Eq. (4). When the user is searching for the product that is considered as the user action, when the user adds the item to the cart change of state C_S is incremented based on the user action and change of state user decision on the item is determined.

Algorithm: Recurrent Neural Network Scheme to address the In-memory purchase issue

---

U→User, U_{IN}→User Input, U_D→User decision
I→Item user may purchase, U_{ACT}→User action
P→Position of the User in the system
C_S→Current state of the user
1. Initially all the user state C_S=0, P=0
2. P+1 denotes the next position of user in system
3. If user gave an input such that
    If $U_{IN}(P)$==True
        Then fetch the User Action U_{ACT}
4. If U_{ACT} is fetched then calculate P
$$P = f(U_{ACT} + C_S(P-1))$$
5. Check whether user added item I
    If the item added then change the
        User position in the system
    Else wait for the user to add the item.
6. If added the item added then P=1
7. Calculate $U_{OUT}(P)$ if position changed
$$U_{OUT}(P) = F(U_D(P))$$
8. If $U_{OUT}(P)$>0
    Assume the user added the item to cart
    Else repeat the steps from step 1.

$$P = f(U_{ACT} + C_S(P-1)) \tag{3}$$

$$U_{OUT}(P) = F(U_D(P)) \tag{4}$$

$$P = f(U_{ACT} + 1(0)) \tag{5}$$

$$U_{OUT}(P) = F(1(f(U_{ACT} + 1(0)))) \tag{6}$$

This is denoted in the Eq. (5), when the position of the system changes, the state value becomes 0. Then the system checks for the U_{ACT} value. The tangent function for the summation of U_{ACT} and the position is found as in Eq. (5). If the $U_{OUT}(P)$ value is greater than 0, then the system is considerers that the user added an item to the cart and updates the recommender about the user decision. Based on the input and user action, the final user decision on the item is calculated as an exponential function as in the Eq. (6). When a user makes the decision in purchasing the product the final outcome will be a positive value that is value greater than else it becomes zero and the system will takes the next input from the user with respect to the change of state value.

Recommending the item that was already bought by the user diminishes the trustworthiness and reliability of the recommendation system. In this scheme by considering the user input and output value the recommender system can change the state of recommendations for the user.

5 Conclusion

The digital information era made general public to depend totally on internet and web services. The vast amount of digital information creates uneasiness among the users to get the needed information at the right time. To improve the chance of user in getting the accurate suggestions there is a need to develop the intelligent recommender systems. The prevailing issues like scrutability and in-memory purchase issue affect the system to produce efficient recommendations. Even though deep learning models were utilized to its fullest in image processing and other fields. Due to the lack of information, the deep learning models cannot be constructed for recommending products. In this paper light weight deep learning models based schemes are framed. These models can be integrated along with the existing recommender algorithm to address the prevailing issues especially scrutability and in-memory purchase problem. The schemes in this paper clearly define the deep learning model architecture, control flow in the architecture and possible implementation of deep learning model in recommender system. Currently, very less research work has been done so for in modelling deep learning algorithm to suggest items. Also, in-memory purchase problem is one of the unattended dominating issues of recommender system. In near future, there will be a significant importance for deep learning based recommender system.

References

1. Goldberg, D., Nichols, D., Oki, B.M., Terry, D.: Using collaborative filtering to weave an information tapestry. Commun. ACM 35(12), 61–70 (1992)
2. Herlocker, J., Konstan, J.A., Borchers, A., Riedl, J.: An algorithmic framework for performing collaborative filtering. In: The 22nd Proceedings of the Annual International ACM SIGIR Conference on Research and Development in Information Retrieval, pp. 230–237. ACM, Berkeley (1999)
3. Burke, R.: Hybrid recommender systems: Survey and experiments. User Model. User-Adap. Inter. 12(4), 331–370 (2002)
4. Zuo, Y., Zeng, J., Gong, M., Jiao, L.: Tag-aware recommender systems based on deep neural networks. Neurocomputing 204(1), 51–60 (2016)
5. Devooght, R., Bersini, H.: Collaborative filtering with recurrent neural networks. arXiv preprint arXiv:1608.07400 (2016)
6. Zheng, L.: A survey and critique of deep learning on recommender systems. Technical report, University of Illinois, Chicago (2016)
7. Cheng, H.-T., Koc, L., Harmsen, J., Shaked, T., Chandra, T., Aradhye, H.: Wide & deep learning for recommender systems. In: The 1st Proceedings of the Workshop on Deep Learning for Recommender Systems, pp. 7–10. ACM, Boston (2016)

8. Glorot, X., Bengio, Y.: Understanding the difficulty of training deep feedforward neural networks. In: International Conference on Artificial Intelligence and Statistics, AISTATS, pp. 249–256 (2010)
9. Evolution of deep learning models. http://www.datasciencecentral.com/profiles/blogs/evolution-of-deep-learning-models
10. Mikolov, T., Stefan, K., Lukáš, B., Jan, Č., Sanjeev, K.: Extensions of recurrent neural network language model. In: IEEE International Conference on Acoustics, Speech and Signal Processing (ICASSP), pp. 5528–5531. IEEE, Prague (2011)
11. A deep dive into recurrent neural nets. http://nikhilbuduma.com/2015/01/11/a-deep-dive-into-recurrent-neural-networks/
12. Moses, J.S, Babu, L.: A scrutable algorithm for enhancing the efficiency of recommender systems using fuzzy decision tree. In: Proceedings of the International Conference on Advances in Information Communication Technology & Computing, pp. 27–29. ACM, India (2016)
13. Moses, J.S., Babu, L.D., Raj, E.D.: Evaluation of similarity based recommender using fuzzy inference system. In: International Conference on Computing and Network Communications (CoCoNet), pp. 576–581. IEEE, Trivandrum (2015)
14. Moses, J.S., Babu, L.: A locality centred recommendation system combining CNM clustering technique with fuzzy preference tree-based ranking algorithm. Int. J. Bus. Intell. Data Min. 11(1), 63–84 (2016)

A Survey of Design Techniques for Conversational Agents

Kiran Ramesh⬤, Surya Ravishankaran$^{(\boxtimes)}$ ⬤, Abhishek Joshi⬤,
and K. Chandrasekaran

Department of Computer Science and Engineering,
National Institute of Technology Karanataka, Surathkal, India
{aditya.kiran1995,surya.rad,joshi.abj13}@gmail.com,
kch@nitk.ac.in

Abstract. A conversational agent also referred to as chatbot is a computer program which tries to generate human like responses during a conversation. Earlier chatbots employed much simpler retrieval based pattern matching design techniques. However, with time a number of new chatbots evolved with an aim to make it more human like and hence to pass the Turing test. Now, most of the chatbots employ generative knowledge based techniques. This paper will discuss about various chatbot design techniques, classification of chatbot and discussion on how the modern chatbots have evolved from simple pattern matching, retrieval based model to modern complex knowledge based models. A table of major conversational agents in chronological order along with their design techniques is also provided at the end of the paper.

Keywords: Pattern matching · Parsing · Markov chains · Ontologies · AIML · Chatscript · Recurrent neural network (RNN) · Long short term memory network (LSTM) · Sequence to sequence model (seq2seq)

1 Introduction

Chatting is a standout amongst the types of correspondence between people. Designing a system that could generate human like response has been an extensively researched topic in the human-machine interaction field. As a result, a lot of approaches have been devised so far with an aim to enhance chat communication between the human and the computer with a specific end goal to reproduce human-human chat interaction.

Chatbot is a computer program that can hold a discussion with human utilizing Natural Language Speech. Chatbots are primarily designed to perform conversation with humans, in such a way that humans can easily communicate with the bot using natural language, so as to make the conversation as humanlike as possible. Chatbots are usually designed to serve some specific task that it is trained for, which includes a wide range of operations such as organizing files on a computer, searching for a keyword on the web, setting up appointments, etc. The biggest challenge that the chatbots currently face is that of keeping up with the context of the conversation and that of understanding the human inputs and the respective responses [1]. The prevalent techniques used in current chatbot development include pattern matching based approach and then

© Springer Nature Singapore Pte Ltd. 2017
S. Kaushik et al. (Eds.): ICICCT 2017, CCIS 750, pp. 336–350, 2017.
https://doi.org/10.1007/978-981-10-6544-6_31

generating predefined outputs that match the given input. The drawback of this approach is that sometimes it cannot produce a satisfactory conversation that will guide conversation towards the desired purpose.

Predefined responses for a given set of questions induces constraint on the conversational agent, in the sense that appropriate context also needs to be considered while generating these responses. Developers and researchers have continued adding new components with improved functionalities to the existing methodologies and in some cases, even proposed a new design architecture. Most of these improvements were mostly based on utilization of some kind of ontologies and recollecting details from the conversation.

Turing test, originally devised in 1950 by Alan Turing, is a test used to identify whether a responder is machine or a human [2]. It is therefore used even now to check a machine's ability to exhibit intelligence as that of humans. This test is used to judge natural language conversations and has become a vital concept in artificial intelligence philosophy. There are two versions of the test. The first known as the original imitation game basically involves a man, a woman and an interrogator who is unaware of the gender of the two people. The role of the interrogator is to determine which of the two is the man and who is the woman through a series of questions while the role of the man is to mislead the interrogator into making the wrong conclusion and the woman is to assist the interrogator. The ability of the computer is determined based on the likelihood of wrong decision by the interrogator when the man is replaced by the computer to the earlier case. In the second version known as the standard implementation, the man and woman are simply replaced by a computer and a human respectively, and the interrogator is to determine which is the computer rather than determining the gender of the person the computer is imitating as seen in the previous version [3]. Loebner Prize is an annual contest that awards the best human like response generating chatbot. The aim of this contest is however to pass the turing test. Once the aim of passing turing test is achieved, the annual contest will be concluded. However, no chatbot till now have achieved this feat. At the end of this paper, a list of Loebner prize winning chatbots is presented along with a short description of their respective design techniques [1].

In this paper, various solutions to building a chatbot are presented at first, followed by general structure of a chatbot and different approaches towards designing them. Then a classification of chatbots is presented. Initially the classical design approaches towards chatbots are discussed and then modern approaches using neural networks and deep learning are presented. The results are well discussed and conclusions are drawn at the end.

2 Classical Solutions

Prior to the advent of machine learning techniques, chatbot development primarily involved specifying rules against which response would be generated. These rules could range from simple pattern matching and extend to include the grammatical structure of the sentence which can be used to understand the context of the conversation. The classical approach to building conversational agents typically use two solutions – AIML and NLP/NLU.

2.1 AIML

Artificial Intelligence Markup Language (AIML) [4, 5] is an XML dialect aimed at creating conversational flows for the bot. It is completely based on pattern-recognition and pattern-matching. AIML is tag-based with three basic tags apart from the opening and closing aiml tag which signifies the beginning and the end of the script.

Category is the fundamental unit of AIML which specifies the stimulus-response, the pattern being the stimulus (pattern can contain regex operators like *) and template being the response (response can contain variables).

Here is a basic example:
<category> defines beginning of category
<pattern>What the User Says</pattern>
<template>What the Bot Responds</template>
</category>

2.2 NLP/NLU

Natural Language Processing (NLP) and Natural Language Understanding (NLU) attempt to solve the problem of chatbot development by parsing language into entities, intents and a few other categories [6]. Agents correspond to applications.

Entities are natural language variables which are associated with certain standard phrases used in daily life. Entities can either be system-defined or developer-defined. For example, the system entity @sys.date corresponds to common date references like 5 January 2017 or the 5th of January.

Intents basically correspond to what actions are to be invoked or triggered as a response to a user input. Actions correspond to the steps the chatbot will take when specific intents are triggered by user inputs. An action may have parameters for specifying detailed information about it.

Contexts are strings that store context of the object the user is referring to/taking about. For example, a user might refer to a previously defined object in a succeeding sentence. A user may input "Switch on the fan". Here the context to be saved is the fan, so that when a user says "Switch it off" as the succeeding input, the intent "switch off" maybe invoked on the context "fan".

3 General Structure

The first step in designing any system is to divide the system into constituent parts according to a standard so that a modular development approach can be followed. This design principle can be extended to chatbot development and as a consequence a typical chatbot can be seen as three parts (Fig. 1): Responder, Classifier and Graphmaster [7]. They are described as follows:

Responder: It acts as an interface between the user and the chatbot's main methods. The responder's functions include - data transfer between the user and the classifier, monitoring the input and output.

Classifier: This component is located in between the graphmaster and the responder. The functionalities of this layer include: normalisation and filtering of input, segmentation of user input into logical parts, transfer of the normalized sentence to the graphmaster, graphmaster output processing and database syntax instructions handling.

Graphmaster: This component is responsible for pattern matching. It is the brain of the bot and its tasks include: organization of the brain's contents, keeping the pattern matching algorithms and storage.

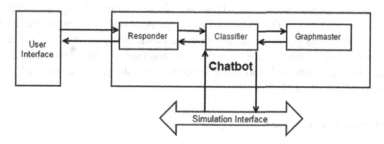

Fig. 1. General Chatbot Structure

4 Approaches

Several approaches have been explored in the development of chatbot since ELIZA. The following section explores each of these approaches in a broad scope.

4.1 Pattern Matching

Pattern matching is the most widely used methodology when it comes to chatbots. Some or the other adaptation of pattern matching algorithms is present in every chatbot system. While the complexity of these algorithms may differ, the fundamental idea behind it remains the same. Simple and basic pattern rules were used in early chatbots like ELIZA [8].

In this technique, the structure of the sentence is identified and a pre-defined response is changed according to the characteristic variables of the sentence and given as a response. Basically, past conversations are made into a generalized form.

This methodology is commonly used in question-answer bots. The disadvantage of this approach is that the responses are quite predictable, repetitive and lack human touch. Also, usually there is no storage of past responses which can lead to looping conversations. As pattern matching algorithms become more complex the responses become very limited, which can lead to uninteresting conversations [9].

4.2 Parsing

Parsing is a methodology which takes text as an input and converts it into a set of strings which are simpler and can be easily stored and manipulated. This is lexical parsing and is used mainly to determine the grammatical structure of the sentence. Once this is done an abstract syntax tree is built and the lexical structure can be then validated if it forms an allowed sentence according to the rules of the language (syntactical parsing).

The primitive parsers were simplistic, only checking if recognizable keywords were present in an allowed order. Example of this type of parsing would parse sentences "please bring the water" and "can you get the water" both into "bring water". With a limited set of patterns, the chatbot will be able to cover a variety of input sentences.

The more complex parsers used in later chatbots perform complete grammatical parsing of the input sentences. This is where Natural Language Processing (NLP) comes into play. The Natural Language Analysis consists of these stages: tokenization followed by syntactic analysis, semantic analysis and finally pragmatic analysis. Syntactic analysis gives an order and structure to each sentence in the input text. The literal meaning is found using semantic analysis and the contextual meaning using pragmatic analysis [10].

4.3 Markov Chain Model

Markov Model is a probabilistic model that based on Markov Property which states that at a given index point i on the state space (say on time t) the decision is just dependent on the last state before i (say time t−1). Therefore, a given decision is just related to the one before decision that was made [11].

The Markov chain seeks to model probabilities of state transitions over time. This helps in building responses that are more suitable probabilistically and as a result, are more correct. The key idea behind Markov Chain Models is that there is a fixed probability of occurrence for every letter in the same textual data. The order of the model determines how many successive occurrences the model takes in as input. For example, if the input text is "bhhhdbhdhhhdh", then the Markov model of order 0 predicts that letter "b" occurs with a probability 2/13, 'd' with probability 3/13, and 'h' with probability 8/13. The following sequence of letters is a typical example generated from this model - b h h d h b h h h b h d h h d b h h h h. A 0-order model makes the assumption that each letter is chosen independently. A model with order 1 would still predict fixed probability of occurrence for every letter, but that the probability depends on the previous letter.

The Markov models are simple to understand and easy to apply, sensitivity calculations (i.e. "what-if" queries) are done with ease. Also, the Markov process provides an insight into changes in the system over time. But Markov model is only a simplified version of a complex decision-making process, thus it does not work well to emulate richer and more complex conversations. In some cases, (HeX) these models were even used to generate incorrect sentence that sounds right, as a failback method [12].

4.4   Ontologies (Semantic Nets)

Ontology can be thought of as a conceptualization of a world model, which in the case of chatbot systems is the concepts used in human interaction. These concepts can be represented as a graph to create a knowledge base. An ontology class describe concepts. A class of cars contains all cars. These classes are also associated with slots (properties that characterize the class). The classes can be arranged in the graph in a superclass-subclass hierarchy if the subclass is referring to concepts that are more specific than the superclass. For example, a subclass of hatchback cars. The classes can also be laterally connected if they share a logical relation between them. The advantage of using an ontology as the knowledge base is that systems can search through the nodes of the knowledge graph to establish relations between concepts that are used in the interaction and also imply new reasoning (Reasoning in the context of dialogue agents, implies new statements). Wordnet and OpenCyc are popular ontologies [13, 14].

4.5   AIML

Artificial Intelligence Markup Language [4, 5] was created during 1995 to 2000 with an aim to define a markup language for encoding the pattern matching rules which are used to create conversational agents. The first chatterbot to be developed in the AIML language and to use the AIML interpreter was the ALICE (Artificial Linguistic Internet Computer Entity) bot. The AIML language, like any XML based dialect can be easily understood by both machines and humans alike and hence a high degree of re-usability has given rise to the development of more bots based on the original ALICE bot.

A fundamental AIML object has the general structure of <tagName>ListOfParameters </tagName>, where the specific opening and closing tagName indicate what the ListofParameters correspond to. The ListofParameters can be simple text which indicate either the stimulus or response or AIML objects themselves. The AIML vocabulary not only consists of tags but also wildcards like '*' or '_' which are used to replace a string. The wildcards have priorities assigned and the order in which they are selected for text matching are based on these priorities. The srai (symbolic reduction artificial intelligence) tag can be used to model a given response template to multiple query strings and the random tag is used to offer a response at random from a given list of respond to a given query.

The user input first undergoes prepossessing in two steps: deperiodization and normalization. The first step involves splitting of the user input into several query strings based on the full stop punctuation. Normalizaion involves conversion to uppercase, removal of other punctuation and replace short forms by their expansions.

The graphmaster in case of AIML is a trie data structure and is a collection of nodes called nodemappers. The branches of the root will either be wildcards or the first words of all the patterns. During searching the last node or the leaf node reached will have the template tag. The number of leaf nodes will be equal to the number of categories. An example graphmaster is given in Fig. 2.

Fig. 2. AIML Graphmaster with 24000 categories with root branching factor about 2000 and average branching pattern of the second pattern word about two

4.6 Chatscript

ChatScript aims to be a successor of the AIML language. While AIML is simple and easy to learn, it has relatively weak pattern matching algorithms and is difficult to maintain. Unlike AIML which is directly based on pattern matching, chatscript is comprised of rules which are associated with topics and the chatscript first finds the best topic that matches the user query string and executes a rule in that topic. Suzette by Brian Wilcox is the first conversational agent based on Chatscript [15].

Chatscript introduces 'concepts' which are sets of similar words with respect to either meaning or any other property like parts of speech. A concept of all nouns or adverbs can be created. There is also an existing database of concepts (concepts are modular) and hence already defined concepts can be used. In case of AIML, separate categories need to be created for each of these words. Chatscript also includes long-term memory in the form of \$ variables which can be used to store specific user information like the name or age of the user. These variables can be later used directly in replies generated by the chatbot or can be used in conjunction with conditionals like set which can used to test whether a variable is set. This may be useful in determining if the user has also mentioned the destination in a conversation pertaining to travel [16].

AIML forgoes flexibility for optimization in the sense that any user input is converted to all uppercase so as to decrease the pattern matching overhead. However, uppercase is typically used in conversations to indicate emphasis. In order to overcome this drawback chatscript is case-sensitive, widening the possible responses that can be given to the same user input based on the intended emotion.

4.7 Recurrent Neural Networks

When it comes to decision making, our minds make use of the previous context and understanding of the conversation to come to a conclusion. Traditional neural networks do not possess this ability to analyze the history of conversation. This is where recurrent neural networks come into picture as these neural networks possess the ability to allow information to persist Table 1.

Table 1. Chatbots and design techniques

Year	Programme name	Designer name	Description
1966	ELIZA [8]	Joseph Weizenbaum	Pattern Matching. The input text is searched for keywords which are assigned a rank and the input is transformed as the rule associated with the highest rank directs. (One of the first chatbots)
1972	PARRY [24]	Kenneth Colby	Design technique very similar to that of ELIZA. Attempted to simulate a person with paranoid schizophrenia
1984	Mark V Shaney [25]	Rob Pike	Markov Chain Model
	Fred [26]	Robby Garner	Minimalistic "ask-reply" approach. Basically, works by storing a database of statements and their responses
1991	PC Therapist [27]	Joseph Weintraub	Predetermined responses (canned) and responses which have no relevance to what preceded it (non-sequitur) along with pattern matching after parsing, and word vocabulary that enable it to recall sentences. (Won Loebner Prize)
1994	TIPS [28]	Thomas Whalen	A database that models one's personal history similar to systems with pattern matching (Won Loebner Prize)
1996	HeX [12]	Jason Hutchens	Uses Markov Chain models, personal history model, pattern matching and a trick sentences database (Won Loebner Prize)
1997	Converse [29]	David Levy	A database with facts, WordNet corpus synonyms, ontology, proper names list, added responsiveness/proactivity, a statistical parser and weighted modules. (Won Loebner Prize)
1998	Albert One	Robby Garner	Emulates the hierarchial structure of past Chatbots, like Eliza and Fred in addition to proactivity and pattern matching. (Won Loebner Prize)
2000	A.L.I.C.E [30]	Richard Wallace	Advance pattern matching, AIML. (Won Loebner Prize)
2001	Eugene Goostman [31]	Vladimir Veselov	Basically, uses a template of canned patterns and responses
2002	Ella	Kevin Copple	WordNet corpus synonyms, pattern matching, trick sentences, normalization of phrases and abbreviation expansion. (Won Loebner Prize)
2003	Jabberwock	Juergen Pirner	Simplistic pattern matching, Markov Chain models, parsing and context free grammar (Won Loebner Prize)
2005	George (Jabberwacky) [32]	Rollo Carpenter	Uses a large database of people's responses which are based on the Chatbot Jabberwacky and no pattern matching or algorithms are used. (Won Loebner Prize)
2007	UltraHAL [33]	Robert Medeksza	Visual basic code along with pattern matching scripts (Won Loebner Prize)
2008	Elbot [34]	Fred Roberts	An NLI (Natural Language Interaction) solution for commercial purposes. (Won Loebner Prize)

(continued)

Table 1. (*continued*)

Year	Programme name	Designer name	Description
2009	CHARLIE [35]	Fernando A. Mikic	Fernando A. Mikic & An AIML chatterbot that works as an interface between Intelligent Education System and humans. CHARLIE knowledge base is the ontology of the INES
2009	Do-Much-More [36]	David Levy	Intelligent Consumer Electronics commercial property providing high entertainment value. (Won Loebner Prize)
2010	VCA [37]	Samira Shaikh	Virtual Chat Agent is one of the first multiparty chat agents. Each chat query is processed by performing stemming, part-of-speech tagging and named entity recognition. This query is enclosed in a frame and is matched with the frames created from clustering the previous training data. The frame with the highest match rate is selected as the output
2011	Rosette [38]	Bruce Wilcox	A chat script based on AIML with database consisting of subject-predicate-objects data entities, variables and concepts. (Won Loebner Prize)
2011	Ontbot [14]	Hadeel Al-Zubaide	Ontology based bot which makes uses of OWL (Web Ontology Language). NLP functionalities such as Tokenization, Filtering, Stemming and Synonym Handling. Rule matching similar to AIML. The ontology used here is Wordnet
2012	Chip-Viviant [39]	Mohan Embar	Chatscript based conversational agent using an ontology based knowledge base (Won Loebner Prize)
2013	Mitsuku [40]	Steve Worswick	AIML based chatbot. (Won Loebner Prize)
2014	Rose [38]	Bruce Wilcox	Primarily based on natural language processing which contains a comprehensive engine to extract the meaning and context of the input text. It is also a Chatscript based dialouge agent. (Won Loebner Prize)

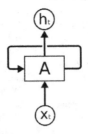

Fig. 3. Recurrent neural networks have loops

In RNN, the neurons are fed with an input (Xt) and information from the previous conversation which forms a loop that allows information to be passed from one step of the network to the next [17]. As seen in the above diagram (Fig. 3) if we unroll the loop in the recurrent neural network it works as shown in the diagram below (Fig. 4):

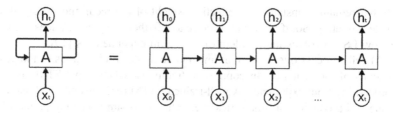

Fig. 4. Unrolled recurrent neural networks

Thus, RNNs can be thought of as multiple copies of the same network each of which passes an information to its successor about the context of the conversation so far. The core of the RNN model is that each cell processes a word and calculates probabilities of the probable words following that word in a sentence. RNNs have achieved incredible success in past few years when they were applied to different problem domains such as image captioning, language modeling, translation, speech recognition, etc.

4.8 Long Short Term Memory Networks

RNN aims to link previous information to the present task so as to derive an output based on the information gathered from all the previous steps and the current input. Sometimes we need recent information to derive the output. In this case the relevant information is quite close to the place where it's required so RNNs can easily deal with this situation to collect the past information. But at times when we need old and more information from past to derive an output the task becomes a bit more difficult. In this case, we need to refer to a distant information which complicates the process a lot. Theoretically RNNs are capable of handling the 'long-term dependencies' but in practice it is very difficult to achieve.

Long Short Term Memory networks (LSTMs), a special kind of RNN, are capable of learning long-term dependencies. LSTMs do so by preventing vanishing gradient problem. Vanishing gradient problem is an obstacle often faced while training an artificial neural network. It is mostly prevalent in gradient based learning methods. In gradient based learning methods, a parameter's value is learned by understanding how a small change in the parameter's value will affect the network's output. Hence, if the change in the network's output is very small, when there is a small change in parameter's value, the network just can't learn the parameter properly [18].

This is exactly the problem that occurs in vanishing gradient problem. As the network grows bigger, the gradients of the network's output with respect to the parameters in the early layers become extremely small. This will cause very minimal effect on the output even if there is a large change in the value of parameters for the early layers. There are two factors that determine the magnitude of gradients: weights and activation functions that the gradient passes through. If either of these factors is smaller than 1, then the gradients may vanish in time leading to the vanishing gradient problem. In the recurrency of the LSTM, the activation function is the identity function with a derivative of 1.0. So, the back-propagated gradient doesn't vanish while passing through, but remains constant. The effective weight of the recurrency is equal to the forget gate activation. So, if activation is close to 1.0, then the gradient does not vanish. This is how LSTM solves the problem of long term dependencies [19].

LSTM cells process one word at a time and computes probabilities of the possible continuations of the sentence. In contrast to traditional RNNs, an LSTM network is ideal for learning from experience. A well-trained LSTM performs better classification, processing and prediction of time series even when there are very long period of gaps of unknown size between significant events. As a result of possessing all these capabilities LSTM performs way better than other available RNNs as well as hidden Markov models and other sequence learning methods that are being used in a number of applications. LSTMs are therefore very useful in designing chatbots where it is required to refer to a distant information in time very frequently [18].

4.9   Sequence to Sequence Neural Network Model

Sequence to Sequence model (seq2seq) is one of the most fundamental machine translation techniques. The general aim is to generate a target sequence by looking at source sequence [20, 21]. It is primarily used in language translation where the source sequence is a sentence in one language (say English) and the target sequence is the translated equivalent in another language (say French). However, this can also be applied to chatbots where the source sequence is the chat message from the user and the target sequence is the corresponding reply from the machine (or another user involved in the chat).

A basic sequence to sequence model consists of two recurrent neural networks, an RNN encoder-decoder which takes a sequence as input and generates another sequence as output. The encoder network is that part of the network that takes the input sequence and maps it to an encoded representation of the sequence. The encoded representation is then used by the decoder network to generate an output sequence. The last state of the encoder is used to provide the additional information to decoder (which is basically a language model) to generate the target sequence element by element (Fig. 5).

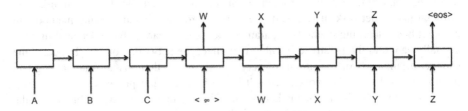

Fig. 5. Sequence to sequence model

5   Classification

Chatbots could be classified into different categories based on several criteria and the design techniques that are typically employed in building these agents depend on the below mentioned criteria. These criteria may include the core design philosophy of the conversational agents or the extent to which context needs to be stored and considered in comprehending the conversation or the type and purpose of the conversation for which the chatbot needs to be designed.

5.1 Retrieval-Based vs. Generative-Based

Retrieval-based chatbots utilize a pool of predefined responses and apply some kind of heuristic in order to choose a proper response that supports both the input and context. A variety of heuristic can be applied in order to choose a proper response. It may be based on fairly simple concept of a rule-based expression match, or may well be as complex as using a combination of Machine Learning classifiers. Systems based on this concept do not produce new responses but just choose one from a pool of predefined responses.

Generative models overcome this reliance on predefined responses by generating new responses that are built from applying a set of techniques. These models are usually based on various machine translation techniques. However, in these models we translate an input to a response, instead of translating from one language to some other language.

The two methods mentioned above have their own advantages and disadvantages. Retrieval based methods do not make grammatical mistakes because they simply pick a response from a set of predefined responses. However, they are not capable of handling unfamiliar conditions for which there is no proper predefined response in the repository of predefined responses. Because of the same reasons, these models are unable to have understanding of previous context. Information such as names of place, person or any other thing mentioned earlier in the conversation cannot be referred to in these models. Generative models on the other hand do possess the capability to refer back to past information and are hence "smarter". This makes the human computer interaction even more human-like. These models are however very hard to train. They are prone to grammatical errors, and usually require huge amounts of training and testing data.

Results of both the retrieval based and the generative based models can be further improved by making use of deep learning techniques. However, the current world of technology is moving towards generative based methods. There are deep learning architectures like Sequence to Sequence that provide various mechanisms for generating text [22].

5.2 Long vs. Short Conversations

As the length of the conversation increases, it becomes more difficult to automate it. Based on the length of the conversation, we have two types of conversation. First are the short-text conversations where a single response is produced in response to a single input. For example, replying with an appropriate response when a specific question is asked by the user. On the other hand, long-text conversations are very lengthy conversations. This means there will be a lot of information exchanged in the past which should be kept track of in present to derive an output. An example of long-text conversation is customer care conversation which are usually very lengthy with multiple questions [23].

5.3 Open Domain vs. Closed Domain

When humans interact, they may initiate discussion in one domain and then switch over to some other domain. Conversations such as these are known as open domain conversations. In these conversation, the domain may change with time. These models are not designed to serve a specific purpose. An example of such conversation is the interaction in social media sites like facebook, twitter etc. Because of the extensive amount of knowledge required to generate a reasonable response, it is quite difficult to emulate such conversations.

While in a closed domain configuration, limited knowledge specific about the domain is required so as to generate an appropriate response to the input. An example that deals with closed domain problem is the customer care system. In systems such as these there is no deviation from the specific purpose that the system is designed to deal with and the conversation mainly focuses on being specific to the domain and generating the response as soon as possible. These systems are usually trained by obtaining domain specific data so as to generate replies based on the context [23].

6 Conclusion

The current world of technology is on a quick transition phase where the goal is to have devices possessing the ability to provide solution with minimal human interference. This survey discusses different approaches towards designing a chatbot and also covers classification and structure of these conversational agents. We have also discussed design techniques that were adopted to design different chatbots in chronological order. From the table, it is understood how design techniques have evolved over the years. We can conclude that chatbots have now come a long way from earlier simple retrieval based pattern matching approaches to deep learning based neural networks.

References

1. Mauldin, M.L.: Chatterbots, tinymuds, and the turing test: entering the Loebner prize competition. In: AAAI, vol. 94 (1994)
2. Turing, A.M.: Computing machinery and intelligence. Mind 59(236), 433–460 (1950)
3. Sterrett, S.G.: Turing's two tests for intelligence. The turing test, pp. 79–97. Springer, Netherlands (2003)
4. Wallace, R.: The elements of AIML style. Alice AI Foundation, (2003)
5. Marietto, M.D.G.B., et al.: Artificial Intelligence Markup Language: a brief tutorial. arXiv preprint arXiv:1307.3091 (2013)
6. Chowdhury, G.G.: Natural language processing. Ann. Rev. Inf. Sci. Technol. 37(1), 51–89 (2003)
7. Stoner, D.J., Louis, F., Mark, R.: Simulating Military Radio Communications Using Speech Recognition and Chat-Bot Technology. The Titan Corporation, Orlando (2004)
8. Weizenbaum, J.: ELIZA—a computer program for the study of natural language communication between man and machine. Commun. ACM 9(1), 36–45 (1966)

9. Meffert, K.: Supporting design patterns with annotations. In: ECBS, vol. 6 (2006)
10. Ahmad, S.: Tutorial on Natural Language Processing. Artificial Intelligence. University of Northern Iowa, Cedar Falls (2007)
11. Bradeško, L., Dunja, M.: A Survey of Chatbot Systems Through a Loebner Prize Competition (2013)
12. Jason, H.: HeX (Conversational Agent) (1996). http://www.simonlaven.com/hex.htm
13. Noy, N.F., Deborah L.M.: Ontology development 101: a guide to creating your first ontology. (2001)
14. Al-Zubaide, H., Ayman A.I.: Ontbot: Ontology based chatbot. In: Proceedings of the 2011 Fourth International Symposium on Innovation in Information and Communication Technology (ISIICT). IEEE (2011)
15. Wilcox, B., et al.: Suzette, the Most Human Computer. (2010)
16. McNeal, M.L., Newyear, D.: Chatbot creation options. Lib. Technol. Rep. **49**(8), 11–17 (2013)
17. Mandic, D.P., Jonathon, C.: Recurrent Neural Networks for Prediction: Learning Algorithms, Architectures and Stability. Wiley, New Jersey (2001)
18. Hochreiter, S., Schmidhuber, J.: Long short-term memory. Neural Comput. **9**(8), 1735–1780 (1997)
19. Bengio, Y., Simard, P., Frasconi, P.: Learning long-term dependencies with gradient descent is difficult. IEEE Trans. Neural Netw. **5**(2), 157–166 (1994)
20. Sutskever, I., Oriol V., Quoc V.L.: Sequence to sequence learning with neural networks. In: Advances in neural information processing systems (2014)
21. Mou, L., et al.: Sequence to backward and forward sequences: A content-introducing approach to generative short-text conversation. arXiv preprint arXiv:1607.00970 (2016)
22. Pavel, S.: Chatbot Architecture (2016). http://pavel.surmenok.com/2016/09/11/chatbot-architecture/
23. Denny, B.: Deep Learning for Chatbots (2016). http://www.wildml.com/2016/04/deep-learning-for-chatbots-part-1-introduction/
24. Colby, K.M.: Ten criticisms of parry. ACM SIGART Bull. **48**, 5–9 (1974)
25. Bruce, E., Yisong, Y.: http://www.yisongyue.com/shaney/
26. Caputo, L., Robby, G., Paco, X.N.: FRED Milton and Barry: the Evolution of Intelligent Agents for the Web. Adv. Intell. Syst. **41**, 400 (1997)
27. Joseph, W.: History of PC Therapist http://www.loebner.net/Prizef/weintraub-bio.html
28. Hutchens, J.L.: How to pass the Turing test by cheating. School of Electrical, Electronic and Computer Engineering research report TR97-05. University of Western Australia, Perth (1996)
29. Batacharia, B., Levy, D., Catizone, R., Krotov, A., Wilks, Y.: Converse: a conversational companion. In: Wilks, Y. (ed.) Machine Conversations. The Springer International Series in Engineering and Computer Science, vol. 511, pp. 205–215. Springer, New York (1999)
30. Wallace, R.S.: The anatomy of ALICE. Parsing the Turing Test, pp. 181–210. Springer, New York (2009)
31. Lance, U.: (2006). http://mashable.com/2014/06/12/eugene-goostman-turing-test/#DiQdlOr7DPqb
32. Fryer, L.K., Rollo, C.: Bots as language learning tools. Lang. Learn. Technol. **10**, 8–14 (2006)
33. Robert, M.: (2007). https://www.zabaware.com/assistant/
34. Fred, R. (2008). http://www.elbot.com/
35. Mikic, F.A., et al.: CHARLIE: An AIML-based Chatterbot which Works as an Interface among INES and Humans. In: Proceedings of the EAEEIE Annual Conference, 2009. IEEE, (2009)

36. David, L.: [Online]. (2009). http://www.worldsbestchatbot.com/Do_Much_More
37. Shaikh, S., Strzalkowski, T., Taylor, S., Webb, N.: VCA: an experiment with a multiparty virtual chat agent. In: Proceedings of the 2010 Workshop on Companionable Dialogue Systems, Association for Computational Linguistics, pp. 43–48 (2010)
38. Wilcox, B.: (2014). http://brilligunderstanding.com/rosedemo.html
39. Embar, M.: (2012) http://www.chipvivant.com/
40. Worswick, S.: [Online]. (2013). http://www.mitsuku.com/

Fault Tolerant Control, Artificial Intelligence and Predictive Analytics for Aerospace Systems: An Overview

Krishna Dev Kumar[(⊠)] [iD] and Venkatesh Muthusamy [iD]

Artificial Intelligence and Predictive Analytics for Aerospace Systems Laboratory (AIPAAS Lab), Ryerson University, 350 Victoria Street, Toronto, ON M5B 2K3, Canada
{kdkumar,vmuthusamy}@ryerson.ca

Abstract. An aircraft or spacecraft represents a highly complex engineering system. The requirements of high performance and increased autonomous capability have necessitated the use of fault tolerant control, artificial intelligence and predictive analytics in aerospace systems. The paper presents an overview of the current state of art in this area with a focus on the work done by the authors. Model-based fault tolerant control methods are considered for spacecraft systems while data driven prognostics is reviewed for fault prediction of aircraft engine failures. The data driven methods including artificial intelligence show promising results for applications to aerospace systems.

Keywords: Fault tolerant control · Artificial intelligence · Predictive analytics · Aerospace systems · Artificial neural networks · Fault diagnosis · Fault isolation · Prognosis

1 Introduction

An aircraft or spacecraft represents a highly complex engineering system; they comprise of several subsystems such as propulsion subsystem, flight control subsystem, environmental control system, and power subsystem. These systems are Multiple Input and Multiple Output (MIMO) systems generally ranging in hundreds of inputs and outputs. In recent years, the complexity of these subsystems has increased more than hundred folds due to high performance requirement and increased autonomous capability. The fault tolerant control, artificial intelligence and predictive analytics can play a significant role in meeting these requirements. Fault Tolerant Control (FTC) has been proposed for developing high performance autonomous aircraft/spacecraft. The FTC includes fault detection and isolation (FDI), robust control, and reconfigurable control (RC). On the other hand, the artificial intelligence and predictive analytics have been proposed for aerospace applications as well. This paper focuses on the current work on the FTC for spacecraft systems while data driven prognostics for aircraft systems.

© Springer Nature Singapore Pte Ltd. 2017
S. Kaushik et al. (Eds.): ICICCT 2017, CCIS 750, pp. 351–362, 2017.
https://doi.org/10.1007/978-981-10-6544-6_32

2   Model Based Fault Tolerant Control

Several methods have been proposed for fault diagnosis; these methods are can be grouped into model based methods and data driven methods (see Figs. 1 and 2).

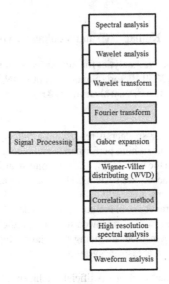

Fig. 1. Fault diagnosis algorithms: data-driven

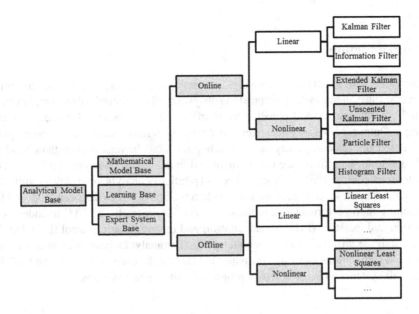

Fig. 2. Fault diagnosis algorithms: analytical model based

The first author and his team have proposed several practical algorithms for Fault Detection and Isolation (FDI), robust control, reconfigurable control, and control of underactuated systems. These are summarized as follows:

2.1 Fault Detection and Isolation

An enhanced adaptive unscented Kalman filter (AUKF) has been proposed for improving the fault detection scheme of reaction wheels (RWs). This filter, based on a generic adaptive Kalman filter combined with a particle swarm optimization, provides superior performance compared with a generic AUKF [1]. Furthermore, an enhanced AUKF is designed based on adapting the covariance matrix to the faulty estimates to significantly improve its tracking speed and accuracy [2]. For fault isolation, the proposed methodology shows faster isolation and superior performance without measurements from RWs [3].

2.2 Robust Control or Reconfigurable Control (Without FDI)

Our proposed control schemes have significantly improved attitude tracking performance under control input magnitude and rate saturations (non-affine) [4]. We were the first to address spacecraft formation and attitude precision in the presence of actuator failures along with system nonlinearities, external disturbances, and control force saturation [5–8].

2.3 Fault Detection and Isolation, Reconfigurable Control, and Control of Underactuated Spacecraft

An integrated FDI and RC algorithm for spacecraft formation flying is proposed; the algorithm results in formation keeping error converge to a small neighbourhood near zero under thruster faults and disturbances [9]. Furthermore, using reduced inputs for spacecraft formation is also examined. Results show robust fault tolerance, and using only radial axis thrust meant a reduction of over 60% in fuel consumption when compared to a fully actuated spacecraft [10]. Furthermore, the use of a single thruster for attitude control is proposed for the first time [11]. Recently, a new control algorithm is proposed; that further improved the spacecraft attitude performance, requiring reduced control efforts [12].

3   Data-Driven Prognostics

This section presents predictive analytics platform followed by sample results on aircraft engine.

3.1   Predictive Analytics Platform

The Predictive Data analytics platform comprising of a 5-node cluster (2 Namenodes and 3 Datanodes) with Hadoop, Spark, Kafka and *R* software installed on each node is used to run queries within the Hadoop data file system (HDFS) to analyse large volume of data (see Figs. 3 and 4)

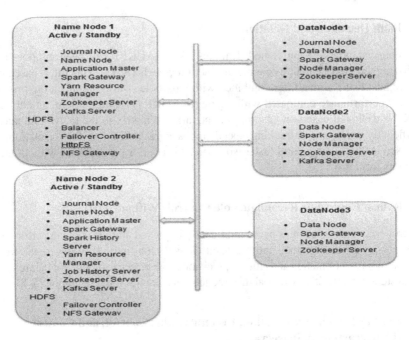

Fig. 3. Predictive data analytics: architecture

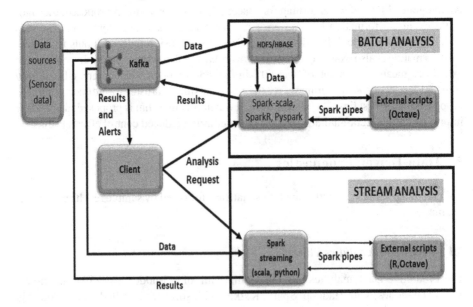

Fig. 4. Predictive data analytics: flow chart

3.2 Predictive Data Analytics for Aircraft Engine

NASA developed a Modular Aero-Propulsion System Simulation (MAPSS) [13] that provides access to health, control, and engine parameters for a turbofan engine. C-MAPSS can simulate a commercial engine model of 90,000 lb. of thrust, altitudes up to 40,000 ft., Mach numbers up to 0.90 and temperatures ranging from −60 to 103 °F. Aircraft performance data was never available to general public due to security reasons. But, NASA made a small set of data of aircraft turbofan engines from their tool.

Data Description. The data provided is for several engines of same type and is a multivariate time series (with cycles as time series unit) that has sensor information from 21 sensors (see Fig. 5) and 3 operational settings. Each engine starts with different degrees of initial wear due to manufacturing variations and while on operation it develops a fault at some unknown point of time that leads to failure. The data has all the sensor information of engine from start to failure. From the plot (see Fig. 6) it is clear that the data is huge and complex in terms of dealing with simple algorithms due to its multivariate nature. Also the data represents only one aircraft engine. What if there are hundreds of aircraft engines and all the data has to be used to get some useful information. This is where some of the machine learning algorithms can make a useful tool.

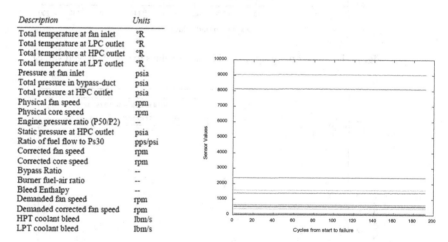

Description	Units
Total temperature at fan inlet	°R
Total temperature at LPC outlet	°R
Total temperature at HPC outlet	°R
Total temperature at LPT outlet	°R
Pressure at fan inlet	psia
Total pressure in bypass-duct	psia
Total pressure at HPC outlet	psia
Physical fan speed	rpm
Physical core speed	rpm
Engine pressure ratio (P50/P2)	--
Static pressure at HPC outlet	psia
Ratio of fuel flow to Ps30	pps/psi
Corrected fan speed	rpm
Corrected core speed	rpm
Bypass Ratio	--
Burner fuel-air ratio	--
Bleed Enthalpy	--
Demanded fan speed	rpm
Demanded corrected fan speed	rpm
HPT coolant bleed	lbm/s
LPT coolant bleed	lbm/s

Fig. 5. Sensor details of turbofan engine [13]   **Fig. 6.** Run to failure data for an engine that fails at 192 cycles

Predictive Algorithm. One of the simple tools to predict the failure of Aircraft systems is developed by Dr. Jamie Coble to predict the failure of aircraft engines based on this data [14]. In first step, kernel regression technique is used, residues are obtained for each sensor data and is weighed for its trendability, monotonicity and prognosability. Using these three metrics on residues, unwanted sensor data was removed and only 6 out of 21 sensor residue information is used further for estimating remaining useful life. Second step involves merging the useful sensor data information into a single parameter (Fig. 7).

Third step is to apply general path model along with Bayesian updating technique to predict the failure. The formulations for this method is provided in [15].

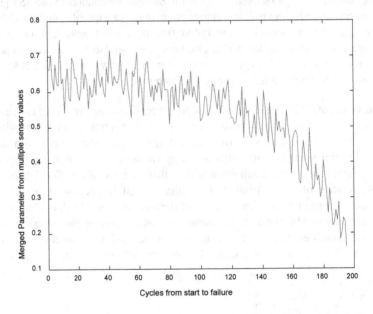

Fig. 7. Parameter merging (from 21 sensor values to single merged value)

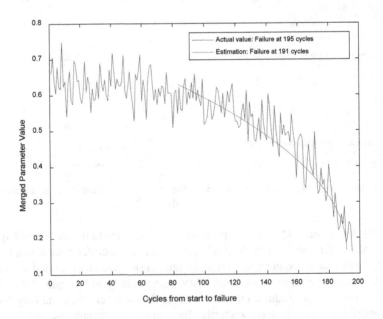

Fig. 8. Prediction of failure using general path model algorithm

Failure predictions for one of the cases is shown in Fig. 8. In this case, data is available only up to 75th cycle. Using this information and the function parameters, an estimation is performed. The estimation for this case is almost accurate predicting that the engine fails at 191st cycle against the actual failure time of 195 cycles.

In general, this algorithm predicts the failure with accuracy of just 75% error. However, as more data becomes available, the prediction accuracy increases proportionally. This algorithm is very light in terms of computational time but the accuracy is not sufficient for real time applications, which will be addresses in Sect. 4.3 using artificial intelligence.

4   Artificial Intelligence Applications to Aerospace Systems

The artificial intelligence has been applied in several areas including aerospace systems. Our research has been focused on applications of artificial intelligence to Spacecraft Orbit and Attitude Control Systems, Fault Diagnosis and Isolation, and Fault Prognosis, as presented next.

4.1   Spacecraft Orbit and Attitude Control Systems

Spacecraft must be controlled for its attitude (orientation) as well as orbit. Orientation control is necessary to point the antenna towards earth for communications. For observatory-based spacecraft such as telescope or remote sensing, it is required to re-orient them towards some distant celestial object under observation. Orbit control is necessary to station the spacecraft in the desired orbit as well as to avoid the orbiting spacecraft from colliding with the primary body that it is orbiting. As discussed in Sect. 2, the reorientation/orbit maneuver is done by developing control algorithms based on the spacecraft dynamics and disturbance torques. The dynamics and disturbance torques on satellites orbiting earth are well understood to develop an accurate control system. However, for other celestial bodies such as asteroids or new planets, the disturbance torques due to gravity is unknown and the gravitational field may be non-linear.

It is highly challenging to develop a robust and an accurate control system for spacecraft to orbit bodies of unknown gravitational field. This is where Artificial Intelligence algorithms assists engineers. A Novel, tracking based sliding mode control scheme is developed using Chebyshev Neural Network [19]. In this case, the fore mentioned neural network function is used to approximate the non-linear functions and the disturbance torques in real time. The controller performance in the presence of unknown mass moment of inertia, external disturbances and control input constraints is shown in Fig. 9.

A neural reinforcement-learning algorithm is used to design an orbit controller to hover around the body efficiently for unknown small bodies. One such example is given in reference [18] where control problem is modelled as a Markov Decision problem and a direct policy search algorithm is used to find the control schemes for orbit station keeping. The performance of the algorithm is shown in Fig. 10.

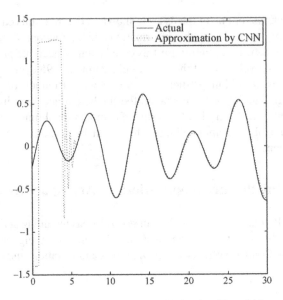

Fig. 9. Capture of unknown function using Chebyshev Neural Network (CNN)

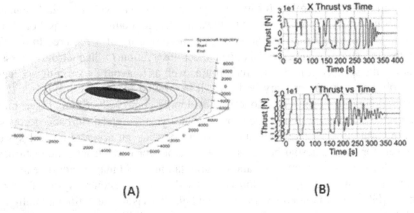

Fig. 10. (A) Simulation of uncontrolled trajectory, (B) reaching steady state after 350 s by using direct policy search algorithm [18]

4.2 Fault Diagnosis and Isolation

There has been an increasing interest in fault diagnosis in recent years, as a result of the growing demand for higher performance, efficiency, reliability and safety in control systems. For a MIMO system like spacecraft, a faulty sensor or actuator may cause process performance degradation, process shut down or even mission failure. An online fault detection and isolation can help identify the fault in advance and take remedial actions. Artificial Intelligence algorithms can be used to train the system performance during nominal and faulty conditions and can be used to identify faults later. Fault diagnosis for One of the highly used actuator, reaction wheel using machine learning algorithms are discussed below.

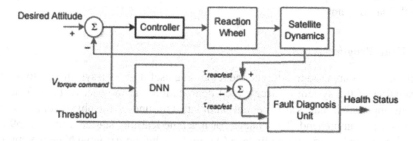

Fig. 11. Satellite fault detection structure using Dynamic Neural Network (DNN) [20]

A data-driven approach proposed in [20] uses a Dynamic Neural Network trained using a EDBP algorithm to capture the nominal Reaction Torque dynamics of the spacecraft with respect to the voltage inputs to the reaction wheel. This trained nominal model is compared with current measurements to generate residues, which are then evaluated for reaction wheel faults based on a threshold level. The fault detection and residual generation plot is shown in Figs. 11 and 12 respectively. Also [20] uses 50,000 samples of data for training and can detect faults due to bus voltage, current and friction. A fuzzy logic based data driven approach mentioned in [21] uses feature extraction technique for satellite measurement data every 512 s and analyze the features to detect fault. A clustering based data-driven method is proposed in [22] where it requires data from all

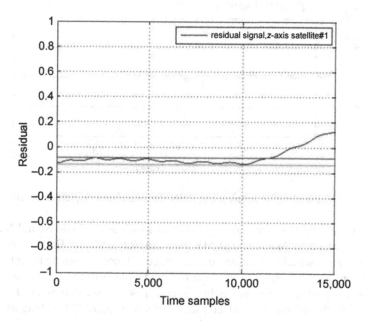

Fig. 12. Residual generation for one of the satellites using Dynamic Neural Network

possible modes of operation. Once the faulty data comes in, fault identification is done based on SPE threshold. In [23], Kernel Fuzzy C-Means clustering technique is used to diagnose different types of fault. This method requires history of data for the types of fault that are diagnosed.

4.3   Fault Prognosis

Prognostic tools are used to estimate the remaining useful life of a system due to normal degradation of the system or accelerated degradation due to onset of fault. Machine learning approaches makes an excellent candidate if the underlying physics of the system is difficult to comprehend. The concept of machine learning started around 1959 and since then several Artificial Intelligence (AI) tools including Artificial Neural Networks (ANN) was developed without having computational power to actually use them. But due to the advancements in processing power of computer technology it is now even possible to apply AI algorithms in our mobile phones.

Heimes [16] developed proprietary a recurrent ANN algorithm for modeling the failure prediction of the aircraft engine data. A recurrent ANN can learn complex non-linear dynamic behaviors of MIMO systems utilizing internal memory and feedback (Fig. 13). The network that was used had 24 inputs, 3 hidden layers of feedforward connections and recurrent connections. The network was trained using several different methods such as back propagation, evolutionary method and Kalman filter training methods. With this algorithm the failure prediction accuracy improved [16].

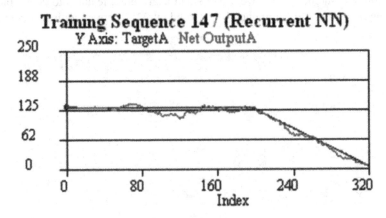

Fig. 13. Prediction of failure using ANN showing actual vs. prediction [16]

There are several machine learning algorithms such as Artificial Neural Networks (ANN), Support Vector Machines (SVM), Bayesian Networks. Etc. Each algorithm will certainly have its own advantages and disadvantages. Hence combining the information from different methods helps to increase the prediction performance to get the best among these algorithms. One such hybrid approach was developed by Dr. Juiping Xu which involves the combination of Dempster-Shafer regression (DSR) along with recurrent ANN/RNN and SVM. These three algorithms were run individually and the results were combined using Cementrophy-based Fusion Prognostics process [17]. This method even performed better than the recurrent RNN method (Figs. 12 and 14).

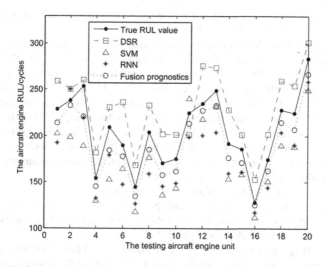

Fig. 14. Performance of hybrid/fusion method with other methods [17]

5   Conclusions

The paper presents an overview of the current work done by the authors in the area of fault tolerant control, artificial intelligence and predictive analytics for aerospace systems. Fault tolerant control algorithms are discussed for the spacecraft systems while the data driven prognostic algorithms are presented for prediction of aircraft engine failures. The data-driven algorithms especially machine learning can be promising methods for aerospace systems.

References

1. David, J.L.: Artificial intelligence in aerospace. In: Arif, T.T. (ed.) Aerospace Technologies Advancements. InTech, Croatia. http://www.intechopen.com/books/aerospacetechnologies-advancements/artificial-intelligence-in-aerospace (2010). ISBN 978-953-7619-96-1
2. Krishnakumar, K.: Intelligent systems for aerospace engineering—an overview. http://ti.arc.nasa.gov/m/pub-archive/364h/0364%20%28Krishna%29.pdf (2003)
3. Rahimi, A., Kumar, K.D., Alighanbari, H.: Enhanced adaptive unscented Kalman filter for reaction wheels. IEEE Trans. Aerosp. Electron. Syst. **51**(2), 1568–1575 (2015)
4. Rahimi, A., Kumar, K.D., Alighanbari, H.: Novel unscented Kalman filter for reaction wheels parameter tracking. IEEE Trans. Aerosp. Electron. Syst. (2016) (under review)
5. Rahimi, A., Kumar, K.D., Alighanbari, H.: Novel hierarchical model-based likelihood fault isolation for satellite attitude. IEEE Trans. Aerosp. Electron. Syst. (2016) (under review)

6. Zou, A., Kumar, K.D., de Ruiter, A.: Robust attitude tracking control of spacecraft under control input magnitude and rate saturations. Int. J. Robust Nonlinear Control **26**(4), 799–815 (2016)

7. Li, J., Kumar, K.D.: Decentralized fault tolerant control for satellite attitude synchronization. IEEE Tran. Fuzzy Syst. **20**(3), 1–15 (2012)

8. Zou, A., Kumar, K.D.: Robust attitude coordination control for spacecraft formation flying under actuator failures. AIAA J. Guidance Control Dyn. **35**(4), 1247–1255 (2012)

9. Godard, G., Kumar, K.D.: Fault tolerant reconfigurable satellite formations using adaptive variable structure techniques. J. Guidance Control Dyn. **33**(3), 969–984 (2010)

10. Lee, D., Kumar, K.D., Sinha, M.: Fault detection and recovery of spacecraft formation using nonlinear observer and reconfigurable controller. Acta Astronaut. **97**, 58–72 (2014)

11. Godard, G., Kumar, K.D., Zou, A.: Robust station-keeping and reconfiguration of underactuated spacecraft formations. Acta Astronaut. **105**(2), 495–510 (2014)

12. Godard, G., Kumar, K.D., Zou, A.: A novel single thruster control strategy for spacecraft attitude stabilization. Acta Astronaut. **86**, 55–67 (2013)

13. https://www.grc.nasa.gov/www/cdtb/software/mapss.html

14. Saxena, A., Goebel, K., Simon, D., Eklund, N.: Damage propagation modeling for aircraft engine run-to-failure simulation. In: International Conference on Prognostics and Health Management, 2008. PHM 2008, pp. 1–9 (2008)

15. Coble, J.B.: Merging data sources to predict remaining useful life—an automated method to identify prognostic parameters. PhD dissertation, University of Tennessee (2010)

16. Heimes, F.O.: Recurrent neural networks for remaining useful life estimation. In: International Conference on Prognostics and Health Management, 2008. PHM 2008, pp. 1–9 (2008)

17. Xu, J., Wang, Y., Xu, L.: PHM-oriented integrated fusion prognostics for aircraft engines based on sensor data. IEEE Sens. J. **14**(4), 1124–1132 (2014)

18. Willis, S., Izzo, D., Hennes, D.: Reinforcement learning for spacecraft maneuvering near small bodies, pp. 16–277. American Institute of Aeronautics and Astronautics, Napa (2016)

19. Zou, A.-M., Kumar, K.D.: Finite-time attitude tracking control for spacecraft using terminal sliding mode and Chebyshev Neural Network. IEEE Trans. Syst. Man Cybern. **41**(4), 950–963 (2016)

20. Khorasani, K., Mousavi, S.: Fault detection of reaction wheels in attitude control subsystem of formation flying satellites: a dynamic neural network-based approach. Int. J. Intell. Unmanned Syst. **2**(1), 2–26 (2014)

21. Baura, A., Khorasani, K.: Hierarchical fault diagnosis and fuzzy rule-based reasoning for satellites formation flight. IEEE Trans. Aerosp. Electron. Syst. **47**(4), 2435–2456 (2011)

22. Wang, R., Gong, X., Xu, M., Li, Y.: Fault detection of flywheel system based on clustering and principal component analysis. Chin. J. Aeronaut. **28**(6), 1676–1688 (2015)

23. Sarosh, A., Dong, Y.F., Hu, D.: A novel KFCM based fault diagnosis method for unknown faults in satellite reaction wheels. ISA Trans. **51**(2), 309–316 (2012)

An Optimal Multi-view Ensemble Learning for High Dimensional Data Classification Using Constrained Particle Swarm Optimization

Vipin Kumar$^{(\boxtimes)}$ and Sonajharia Minz

School of Computer and Systems Sciences, Jawaharlal Nehru University,
New Delhi, India
rt.vipink@gmail.com, sona.minz@gmail.com

Abstract. Multiple views of a dataset are constructed using the Feature Set Partitioning (FSP) methods for Multi-view Ensemble Learning (MEL). The way of partitioning of features influences the classification performance of MEL. The possible numbers of features set partition of the dataset are equal to the Bell number, which is in polynomial nature and a NP-hard problem (Shown in Fig. 1). It is essential to find an optimal classification performance of MEL for a features set partition among all possible features set partition in high dimension scenario. Therefore, an optimal multi-view ensemble learning approach using constrained particle swarm optimization method (OMEL-C-PSO) is proposed for high dimensional data classification. The experiments have been performed on ten high dimensional datasets. Using four exiting features set partitioning methods; the result shows that OMEL-C-PSO approach is feasible and effective for high dimensional data classification.

Keywords: Classification · High dimension · Feature set partitioning · Multi-view ensemble learning · Constrained particle swarm optimization

1 Introduction

Multi-view ensemble learning (MEL) is a process of learning algorithms with multiple source data. The properties of the data provide insight of multiple information sources, such as objects may have many features like colour, size and shape; web pages can be described by texts, hyperlinks and images etc. The information sources are also generated by partitioning of domain features, called views of the dataset. In the literature, many strategies have been proposed for partitioning of the features of the dataset that are categorized by Rokach [13] such as random based partitioning [3–5], collective performance based partitioning [6, 7], reduct based partitioning [8–10], rotation forest based [11] and feature set partitioning [12]. In higher dimension, partitioning of features generates many redundant views that are exploited by MEL to improve learning performance [1, 2]. MEL algorithms are categorized by Xu [1], into three groups, namely, co-training, subspace learning and multiple kernel learning. Mutual agreements between two separate views are maximize in co-training style algorithm. In multiple kernel learning, the views constructed by kernels are exploited. Latent

© Springer Nature Singapore Pte Ltd. 2017
S. Kaushik et al. (Eds.): ICICCT 2017, CCIS 750, pp. 363–378, 2017.
https://doi.org/10.1007/978-981-10-6544-6_33

subspace is utilized for constructing views from the dataset, where latent space is shared by each view.

Total numbers of ways to partition the features into any numbers of blocks (subsets of features) is equal to Bell numbers [59], where it is assume that each feature is appropriate for learning. Each block may consider as view of the dataset. The classification performance of MEL is dependent on the way of partition of features set and ensemble method. Therefore, for fixed ensemble method, it is not necessary that the performance of MEL is optimal for each partition of features set. The Bell number is in polynomial nature. Therefore, it is NP-hard problem to obtain the partition for which the classification performance of MEL is optimal. The problem is in even more difficult in high dimensional environment.

The evolutionary algorithm may be utilized to obtain the optimal classification performance of MEL. Kennedy et al. [20] proposed a Particle Swarm Optimization (PSO) method to optimize continuous multi-dimensional function. It is a stochastic population based evolutionary method that is inspired by flocking of bird. The objective of the PSO is to find optimal solution using a population of particles (called a swarm) [21–23].

Besides, these advantages, PSO lack an explicit mechanism to include constraints. Incorporation of constrains into the objective function suggested by Jordehi [24] for PSO problem, called constrained particle swarm optimization (C-PSO). In this method the diversity of the population is retained and the solutions are maintained both inside and outside feasible region. Constrained PSO can be handled by two approaches. First approachincorporates the constraints in the objective function using penalty function. In second approach, constraints and fitness function are treated separately [21]. Therefore, an OMEL-C-PSO approach has been proposed to obtain the optimal classification performance of MEL within the solution space. In this approach, particles of the swarm are the feature set partitions of the dataset. MEL function F (k) is the fitness function that returns classification performance of MEL for the k -number features set partitions of a given dataset. The proposed approach has been experimented on ten high dimensional datasets. Four features set partitioning methods have been implemented namely Random Feature Set Partitioning (RFSP) [39], Bagging (Ba) [56], Attribute Bagging (AB) [5] and View Construction using Genetic Algorithm (VC-GA) [57]. The results show that the proposed method obtains the optimal classification performance of MEL effectively using AB, RFSP, Ba, and VC-GA feature set partitioning methods.

The rest of this paper is organized as follows: In the Sect. 2, related work of multi-view learning, vertical partitioning methods and constrained particle swarm optimization have been discussed. A brief description of multi-view ensemble learning, constrained particle swarm optimization and the problem are defined in the Sect. 3. In the Sect. 4, experimental setup, results and analysis are described. Conclusion and future work are described in the Sect. 5.

2 Related Work

In literature, MEL is applied many machine learning area such as supervised learning [1, 14, 15], semi-supervised learning [16], ensemble learning [17], clustering [18], dimensionality reduction [19]. Many view construction methods have been proposed that utilize the views for better performance while learning. These methods can be categorized as follows: performance based view construction, feature set partitioning based view construction and random based view construction.

In feature set partitioning based view construction, the original features set are vertically partitioned, which has pair wise disjoint subsets [13]. Kumar and Minz [61] has also find the an optimal feature set partitioning method and utilized non-parametric statistical method for algorithm comparison [60]. The attributes of the data are grouped according to their types such as nominal value features, text value features and numerical value features [31, 32]. Based on the mutual information, Lee and Moody [33] are proposed to group those features that are similar features statistically. In [34], Feature set decomposition has been proposed to group those features that are highly correlated in the same class. For feature set partitioning, genetic algorithm is also applied successfully. The new encoding schema, a new caching mechanism to avoid reformation of the same classifiers and speed up is proposed [35]. Reinforced multi-view ensemble learning (RMEL) has been proposed that include the random feature set partitioning on high dimensional data classification [53]. And another research, feature set partitioning has been done of the poem data classification using MEL [54]. The Bagging (Ba) [48, 56] is the most common method that utilizes a set subsets of samples for ensemble learning.

Objective of performance-based view construction is to find the best collection of features of feature subsets where diversity is the evaluation measure [36, 55]. In another method, the performance of ensemble and diversity of features subsets has been proposed [37]. In [38], accuracy, diversity and compatibility parameters are considered to construct different views for hyperspectral data. View construction using genetic algorithm (VC-GA) [57] has utilized agenetic algorithm to obtain the views of the dataset. In this, features are considered as chromosomes in which 1's represent the feature that is included in the subset otherwise 0's. To obtained feature set automatically, the genetic algorithm is used that creates binary bit string, where if selected the ith bit is denoted by 1, otherwise 0. Each candidate subset of the features is considered as a view of the dataset. To consider the final feature subsets, Zenobiet al. [7] has indicated the association between the error of subset of the features and disagreement among the ensemble members.

In random based view construction, Ho [39] has used merits aggregation and bootstrapping in the feature space, called random subspace method (RSM). In Attribute Bagging (AB) [5], the algorithm finds an appropriate size of the subset of the featuresusing random search and then randomly selects the features to obtain the subsets. Tao et al. [40] have identified and reduced the discrepancy between training size for asmall set of features and feature vector length, where themethod is called random subspace method. Random subspace method also solves the over-fitting problem.

Commonly, two views of data are considered in MEL. But, in [53, 54], it is considered more than two views of the data and tried to find out a suitable number of views for MEL. A maximum number of random features set partitioning of the dataset can be performed equal to the number of domain features. To find the appropriate number of feature set partitioning, the exhaustive search is computationally expensive for thehigh dimensional dataset. Therefore, optimization techniques can be applied to search OFSP. Kennedy et al. [20] proposed Particle Swarm Optimization (PSO) algorithm. Constrained Particle Swarm Optimization (C-PSO) algorithm is proposed [24, 41–44, 47] and applied in many areas in literature, such as Geotechnical engineering [25–27], power system engineering [21, 28], machine learning [29, 30] etc.

Table 1. OMEL-C-PSO algorithm

Begin
1. The position $X_i(t)$ and velocity $V_i(t)$ initialized randomly for $t = 0$ iteration
repeat
2. **for** i=1 to ddo
3. Evaluate the fitness function
$$F(X_i(t)) = f(X_i(t)) + \alpha(t) \times H(X_i(t))$$
4. if$F(X_i(t)) \leq F(X_i(t-1))$then
$$pbest_i(t) = X_i(t)$$
end if
end for
5. if$F(pbest_i(t)) \leq F(pbest_j(t+1))$for all particles j, where, $i \neq j$then
$$gbest(t) = pbest_i(t+1)$$
end if
6. **for**i = 1 to d **do**
7. Update velocity
$$V_i(t+1) = \chi(w(t) \times V_i(t) + c_1 r_{i,1}(t) \times (pbest_i(t) - X_i(t)) + c_2 r_{i,2}(t)$$ $$\times (gbest(t) - X_i(t)))$$
8. Update position
$$X_i(t+1) = X_i(t) + V_i(t+1)$$
end for
until stopping criteria
end begin

3   Basics and Problem Formulation

The difference between single view and MEL algorithm is the requirement of the redundant views of the same dataset. Redundant views have abundant information which is utilized by MEL [1]. If the algorithm is not able to handle the multiple views of the data, then the performance of MEL is decreased. There are mainly three categories of view construction methods namely performance-based view construction, random based view construction and feature set partitioning based view construction [13]. In this research work,

Principle of PSO is a population-based, globalized search algorithm that akin to social behavior of the swarm. It produces better results in multi-peak and complicated problems [41, 42, 45, 46]. Each particle shifts their position according to its velocity.

Let, the search space is d–dimension and $X_i = (x_{i,1}, x_{i,2}, x_{i,3}, \ldots, x_{i,d})$ is the position of the ith particle of the swarm. The best previous position of the ith particle is represented as $pbest_i = (pbest_{i,1}, pbest_{i,2}, pbest_{i,3}, \ldots, pbest_{i,d})$ and the velocity of the ith particle is $V_i = (v_{i,1}, v_{i,2}, v_{i,3}, \ldots, v_{i,d})$. Therefore, for tth iteration, the particle movement is computed as follows:

$$X_i(t+1) = X_i(t) + V_i(t+1) \tag{1}$$

$$V_i(t+1) = \left(w(t) \times V_i(t) + c_1 r_{i,1}(t) \times (pbest_i(t) - X_i(t)) + c_2 r_{i,2}(t) \times (gbest(t) - X_i(t))\right) \tag{2}$$

where, $i = 1, 2, 3, \ldots, N$ and N is the size of the population. $X_i(t)$. and $V_i(t)$ are the position and velocity of the particle i at the time t respectively. $pbest_i(t)$ and $gbest(t)$ are the best position found by particle itself and whole swarm so far respectively. c_1 and c_2 are two positive constant acceleration coefficients, called cognitive and social parameter respectively that influence $pbest_i$ and gbest. The values of $r_{i,1}$ and $r_{i,2}$ are randomly distributed within the range of 0 and 1. $w(t)$ is the inertia weight scaling the previous. w_s and w_e are the starting inertia weight and ending inertia weight respectively. Let a data set D have attributes set $A = \{a_1, a_2, a_3, \ldots, a_n\}$, where, $dom(a_i) = \{v_{i,1}, v_{i,2}, v_{i,3}, \ldots, v_{i,|dom(a_i)|}\}$, is the finite cardinality of the domain. Let attribute set of the dataset D is partitioned into k-views using feature set partitioning method and $A_i \subset A$, that satisfies $A = \cup_{i=1}^{k}(A_i)$ and $A_i \cap A_j = \emptyset$, where $A_i = \{a_{i,1}, a_{i,2}, a_{i,3}, \ldots, a_{i,p}\}, 1 \leq i \leq k, 1 \leq j \leq k$, and $i \neq j$. The data can be represented in multiple views as $D = \{A_1, A_2, A_3, \ldots, A_k\}$. Therefore, for i-th views of the dataset can be written as $D_L^i = dom(a_{i,1}) \times dom(a_{i,2}) \times dom(a_{i,3}) \times \ldots \times dom(a_{i,p}) \times dom(1)$, where, $dom(1) = \{l_1, l_2, l_3, \ldots, l_{|dom(a_i)|}\}$ are the categorical labels.

Let, f is an inducer, which is applied to learn with each i-th view A_i of the dataset D. It is defined $f_i : A_i \rightarrow y$, corresponding to the partitions of π_A, the set of classifiers can be written as $f_{\pi_A} = \{f_1(A_1), f_2(A_2), f_3(A_3), \ldots, f_k(A_k)\}$. The predictions of the classifiers are combined using ensemble method. The classification accuracy for the partition π_D of the dataset can be defined as in Eq. 3:

$$Acc_{\pi_A}^{k}(D_L) = \mathcal{E}_{i=1}^{k}(f_i(A_i)) \tag{3}$$

The total number of ways to partition a feature set of n elements into k–non-empty subsets is denoted by $\begin{Bmatrix} n \\ k \end{Bmatrix}$. These numbers are called the Stirling set numbers of the second kind [58]. The number of ways to divide n features into any number of subsets (partition) can be obtained by the sum of Stirling set numbers, which is called Bell number [59]. The Bell number can be written in recurrence relation as in Eq. (4):

$$B_n = \sum_{j=0}^{n-1} \binom{n-1}{k} B_j \tag{4}$$

The initial some Bell numbers are $B_0 = 1, B_1 = 1, B_2 = 2, B_3 = 5, B_4 = 15$, etc. Each feature subset A_k of the partition π_A^k is called block of partition π_A^k. Let, SetPart(A) is the set of partitions of a feature set A, where total numbers are calculated by Bell number, which can be written as $B_n = |\text{SetPart}(A)|$. The partition that has feature set A itself, is denoted as δ_A and the partition which has all singletons of the form $\{a_i\}$, where $a_i \in A$, denoted as θ_A. Therefore, partition of feature set A must be satisfied $\delta_A \leq |\pi_A^k| \leq \theta_A$, where, the numbers of blocks in the partition π_A^k is $|\pi_A^k|$.

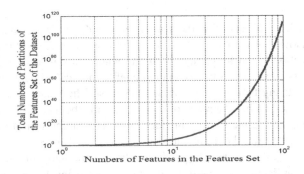

Fig. 1. Graphical representation of log (sequence of Bell numbers).

- **Optimal Multi-view Ensemble Learning Using C-PSO (OMEL-C-PSO)**
  As per the above analysis, the problem belongs to the NP-hard problem. Therefore, an evolutionary algorithm may be applied for optimal solution of the problem. The C-PSO is the evolutionary algorithm which has many advantages than other evolutionary algorithms. Therefore, C-PSO may utilize to find the optimal performance of MEL for feature set partitioning of the dataset, within the solution space.

  Let the set of possible feature set partitioning S is the solution space, where $|S| < |A|$ and search space is d-dimension $X_i = (x_{i,1}, x_{i,2}, x_{i,3}, \ldots, x_{i,d})$ is the ith particles of the swarm, where $x_{i,q} \in X_i \subset S, q = 1, 2, 3, \ldots, d$. Classification performance of MEL for the partition π_A^k is represented as $f(k) = \text{Acc}_{\pi_A}^k(D_L)$. Our objective is to maximize classification accuracy of MEL. Therefore, the objective function can be written as $\max_k f(k)$, subject to constrain $2 < k < |S|$, where k is integer. The $f(k)$ may be maximized by OMEL-C-PSO procedure that is given in Table 1. OMEL-C-PSO algorithm begins with randomly initialization of position $X_i(t)$ and $V_i(t)$ for $t = 0$ iteration. First of all, evaluate the fitness function $F(X_i(t)) = f(X_i(t)) + \alpha(t) \times H(X_i(t))$, where, penalty factor can be written as

$H(k) = \sum_{i=1}^{m} \theta(q_i(k)) \times q_i(k)^{\gamma(q_i(k))}$, where $q_i(x) = \max\{0, g_i(x)\}$ is related to constraint violation function $i = 1, 2, 3, \ldots, m$. $\theta(q_i(x))$ is the multi-stage assignment function [44]. The power of the penalty function is $\gamma(q_i(x))$. Then calculate the personal best (pbest) values of each particle (in step-4). Then, among the pbest values of the particles, find the global best (gbest) in the step-5. The update of particles velocity and position is performed in step-7 and step-8. Repeat the process step-2 to step-8 until stopping criteria is not found. For more illustration of OMEL-C-PSO, a framework of optimal multi-view ensemble learning using C-PSO is shown in the Fig. 2. In this, the partition π_A^k of $A = \{a_1, a_2, a_3, \ldots a_n\}$ features set is obtained for which classification accuracy of MEL is optimal using OMEL-C-PSO algorithm from the training dataset, where $\pi_A^k \in \text{SetPart}(A)$ and $A = \{A_1, A_2, A_3, \ldots, A_k\}, A_i \subseteq A$. Then, the unlabelled instance is classified by each classifier which has learned from corresponding blocks of partition π_A^k. The classifiers prediction is ensemble and predicts the final label of unlabeled instance.

4 Experimental Study

4.1 Datasets and Experimental Setup

Total ten numbers of high dimensional datasets are carefully chosen manually from UCI dataset repository [49], NIPS2003 Feature Selection Challenges [50], and Kent Ridge Bio-medical Dataset [51] for the experiments. The high dimensional datasets (Samples × Features) are Central Nervous System [50] (60 × 7130), Colon Cancer [49] (62 × 2000), Color Tumor [50] (62 × 2000), DLBCL Tumor [50] (77 × 7130), DLBCL_NIH [50] (160 × 7400), Lung Cancer Harvard2 [50] (32 × 12534), Lung Cancer Michigan [50] (93 × 7130), Lung Cancer Ontario [50] (39 × 2881), Prostate Tumor VS Normal [50] (102 × 12601).

Matlab-2012b (64-bit) server version is used for all experiments from the university server. For learning purposed, SVM (linear kernel) classifier of PRtools [52] is used for the classification. Feature set partitioning having k-number of blocks that is $k = 1, 2, 3, 4, \ldots, 100$. The parameter setting of RFSP, Ba, AB and VC-GA partitioning methods are shown as follow: *Random Feature Set Partitioning (RFSP):* The features set A is partitioned such as $U_{i=1}^k A_i = A$; and $A_i \cap A_j = \emptyset$, where $i \neq j$; *Bagging (Ba):* It utilizes random sampling k-times to generate k-training sets with replacement, where obtained test sets are utilized for learning purpose respectively; *Attribute Bagging (AB):* In the first phase of AB method, It obtains the size of the features subset and second phase has classifiers are ensemble for the final prediction; *View Construction using Genetic Algorithm (VC-GA):* In this method, each bit of chromosomes represents the feature of the dataset, where 1 or 0 denote the selection of feature or no selection of the feature respectively.

The SVM classifier learns from each block of partition π_A^k. To ensemble the classifier's decision, performance weighting ensemble method is used. Generalized performance evaluation (accuracy): For generalized performance evaluation, 10-fold cross-validation is performed 10-times with disjoint subset of instances. Each instance

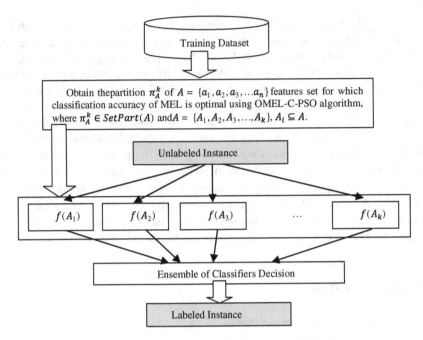

Fig. 2. Optimal multi-view ensemble learningusing C-PSO framework

subsets are used 1-time as a test set and 9-times as training sets. Average classification accuracies of Multi-view ensemble learning are noted for each k-views. The same cross-validation setting are implemented for all datasets. 1000 iterations are performed using OMEL-C-PSO framework and average has been taken for OMEL performance. C-PSO parameter setting: All parameters for the OMEL-C-PSO are Swarm size = 5, Solution = (1,100), $w_s = 0.9$, $w_e = 0.4$, $c_1 = c_2 = 2.0$, $r_{i,1}$ and $r_{i,2}$: range of (0, 1) (randomly distributed), $\chi = 0.729$, $\alpha(t) = \sqrt{t}$, θ = if $q_i < 1$ then $\theta = 10$; else if $q_i < 10$ then $\theta = 20$; else $\theta = 50$.

4.2 Results

Figure 3 shows the OMEL-C-PSO performances on ten high dimensional datasets using RFSP, Ba, AB and VC-GA feature set partitioning methods. In this, X-axis represents feature set partitions $(1 \leq \pi_A \leq 100)$ of the datasets which is considered as the solution space of partitioning and Y-axis represents the classification accuracies of MEL using RFSP, Ba, AB and VC-GA feature set partitioning methods. The average optimal classification accuracies obtained by OMEL-C-PSO approach has shown in Fig. 3 corresponding RFSP, Ba, AB and VC-GA feature set partitioning methods for each dataset as red diamond, blue star, green circle and black triangle respectively. For each feature set partitioning methods, a horizontal line has drawn corresponding OMEL-C-PSO average classification accuracy. Intersection of horizontal line and graph drawn of classification accuracy of MEL for corresponding feature set partitioning are circled for better visualization. Table 2 has shown the minimum, average

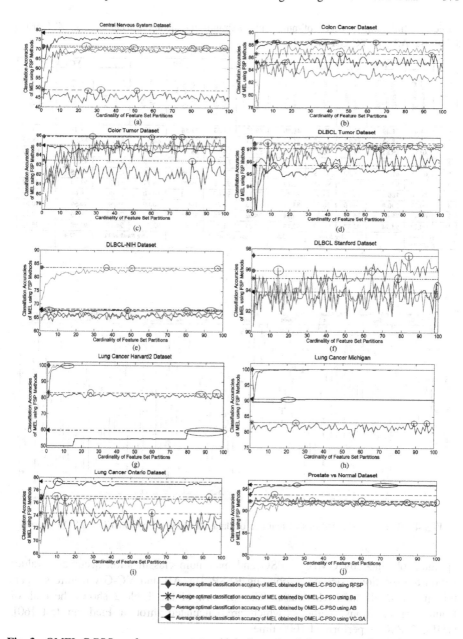

Fig. 3. OMEL-C-PSO performances on ten high dimensional datasets are shown in (a) to (j), where solution space patitions is [1,100].

Table 2. Minimum, average optimum and maximum classification accuracies of MEL using RFSP, Ba, AB and VC-GA methods

S.N.	RFSP			Ba			AB			VC-GA		
	Minimum Accuracy	Average Optimum Accuracy	Maximum Accuracy	Minimum Accuracy	Average Optimum Accuracy	Maximum Accuracy	Minimum Accuracy	Average Optimum Accuracy	Maximum Accuracy	Minimum Accuracy	Average Optimum Accuracy	Maximum Accuracy
1.	44.00	**71.09**	71.17	42.17	**48.88**	49.17	58.33	**71.56**	72.17	64.83	**78.43**	78.50
2.	82.26	**85.24**	85.32	83.39	**86.58**	86.61	78.23	**88.45**	88.55	87.26	**88.55**	88.55
3.	80.16	**85.87**	85.97	80.55	**83.45**	83.71	76.13	**85.91**	85.97	82.90	**84.97**	85.00
4.	62.86	**97.49**	97.66	93.40	**97.08**	97.14	88.05	**97.40**	97.40	92.08	**95.70**	95.71
5.	63.38	**67.92**	68.00	63.79	**67.60**	67.94	71.38	**83.58**	83.75	66.50	**67.95**	68.00
6.	91.70	**97.35**	97.45	90.48	**95.13**	95.32	91.28	**95.89**	96.17	51.06	**93.84**	94.68
7.	80.00	**100.0**	100.0	78.44	**83.04**	83.13	94.69	**100.0**	100.0	50.00	**59.69**	59.69
8.	90.73	**100.0**	100.0	78.44	**83.03**	83.13	97.29	**100.0**	100.0	89.58	**90.59**	90.63
9.	69.49	**76.67**	76.92	70.51	**74.34**	74.62	72.56	**77.04**	77.18	76.67	**79.35**	79.49
10.	90.98	**93.74**	93.82	90.32	**92.15**	92.25	81.76	**92.43**	92.45	94.12	**95.98**	95.98
	Avg Rank of RFSP =	2.3		*Avg Rank of Ba =*	3.6		*Avge Rank of AB =*	1.7		*Avg Rank of VC-GA =*	2.4	

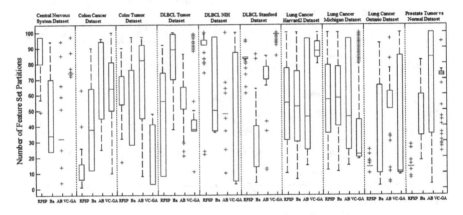

Fig. 4. Box plot of partitions of features of datasets obtained by OMEL-C-PSO method

optimum obtained by OMEL-C-PSO and maximum classification accuracies values within the solution space corresponding RFSP, Ba, AB and VC-GA feature set partitioning methods for each dataset. The last row of the Table 2 shows the rank of feature set partitions methods, which are calculated through Fiedman test [60]. OMEL-C-PSO is performed 1000 times.

The partition π_A^k is obtained the optimal classification accuracy for each iteration. The box plot of partitions corresponding RFSP, Ba, AB and VC-GA feature set partitioning methods are plotted in Fig. 4 for statistical analysis, where X-axis has RFSP, Ba, AB and VC-GA feature set partitioning methods for respective datasets and Y-axis represents the feature set partitions of the datasets.

4.3   Analysis

The features set partition methods effect the MEL classification performance on the datasets. Therefore, the following analysis has done according to the features set petitions RFSP, Ba, AB and VC-GA methods. Within the solution space $k = 1, 2, 3, \ldots, 100$, classification accuracies have obtained and from the graphical representation the behavior according to features set partitions may be analyses. It can also be analyzed that the OMEL-C-PSO method is obtained optimal performance of MEL within the solution space.

- *Random based feature set petitioning (RFSP):* For the datasets Central nervous System, Color tumor, DLBCL tumor, DLBCL-NIH, DLBCL Stanford, Lung cancer harvard2 and Lung cancer Michigan, the performance of MEL according to the partition of the features set are have increasing behavior that can be observed from the Fig. 3. The optimal performances of MEL obtained by the OMEL-C-PSO method are those performances which are optimal within the solution space. Therefore, the performance obtained by OMEL-C-PSO method is optimal for all datasets. It can also be observed from the Table 2 that the optimal accuracy obtained by OMEL-C-PSO using RFSP features set partitioning method are very closed to maximum accuracy within the solution space for all datasets. For the datasets Central nervous System, Color tumor, DLBCL tumor, DLBCL-NIH, DLBCL Stanford, Lung cancer harvard2 and Lung cancer Michigan, the distributions of the features set partitions obtained while optimization process can be observed from the box plot in Fig. 4.

  The boxes have small sizes for those that have continuously increasing performance in nature and have higher median than others. The performance of MEL is increasing in nature but after a partition the behavior is almost constant. In this case, the size of box will be wider that can be observe from the datasets DLBCL tumor, Lung Cancer Harvard2 and Lung Cancer Michigan. On the Colon cancer, Lung Cancer Ontario and Prostate vs. Normal dataset, the performance of the MEL are decreasing, if the partition of features set is increasing (Fig. 3). In this case, optimal performance of MEL is obtained by OMEL-C-PSO method. For the same dataset, the box of distribution is smaller and median is less than the increasing nature performance of MEL. From the above analysis, OMEL-C-PSO method obtains the optimal performance of MEL using RFSP method when the behavior of performance of MEL is in increasing or decreasing nature. The distribution box of partitions is smaller strictly for the continuous increasing and decreasing behavior for the performance of MEL that means, the OMEL-C-PSO method obtains the features set partitions more precisely, which is strictly higher and lower features set partition value respectively.

- *Bagging (Ba):* If the features set partitions increasing, the nature of performances of MEL is increasing and decreasing for the DLBCL tumor and DLBCL Stanford dataset respectively (Fig. 3). The performance of MEL obtained by OMEL-C-PSO method is optimal within the solution space for the increasing and decreasing nature of MEL performances. It can also be observed form the Table 2 that the optimal accuracy obtained by OMEL-C-PSO method using Ba features set partitioning method are very closed to maximum accuracy within the solution space for all datasets. For the other datasets, the performances of MEL are having same behavior throughout the solution space. Form the Fig. 4, it can be observed that features set partition distribution box of DLBCL tumor and DLBCL Stanford dataset are smaller than other datasets and medians have higher and lower than others respectively. The median of features set partition other than DLBCL tumor and DLBCL Stanford dataset, are close to $k = 50$, which is half of the maximum features set partition $k = 100$. From the above analysis, OMEL-C-PSO method obtains the optimal performance of MEL using Ba method when the behavior of performance of MEL is in increasing and decreasing nature. The distribution box of partitions is smaller for the continuous increasing and decreasing behavior for the performance of MEL that means, the OMEL-C-PSO method obtains the features set partitions more precisely, which is strictly higher and lower features set partition value respectively. Other than this, the features set partition is more likely to close to middle value of features set partition solution space.

- *Attribute Bagging (AB):* Other than DLBCL Stanford dataset, it can be clearly observed from the Fig. 3 that the behavior of MEL performances is increasing, if features set partition is increasing. The performance of MEL obtained by OMEL-C-PSO method is optimal in this scenario. The performanceobtained by OMEL-C-PSO method is optimal for all datasets. It can also be observed form the Table 2 that the optimal accuracy obtained by OMEL-C-PSO method using AB features set partitioning method are very closed to maximum accuracy within the solution space for all datasets. The Colon cancer, Color cancer, Lung cancer harvard2, lung cancer Michigan and Prostate tumor vs. normal datasets have not clearly increasing behavior. Therefore, it can be observed from the Fig. 4 that features set partition distribution boxes are bigger and their respective medians are higher than others datasets. For the Central nervous system DLBCL tumor, DLBCL-NIH and Lung cancer Ontario datasets, the features set partition distribution box in Fig. 4 are smaller than others. The above analysis, OMEL-C-PSO method obtains the optimal performance of MEL using AB method when the behavior of performance of MEL is in increasing or not in increasing and decresing nature. The distribution box of partitions is smaller for the continuous increasing behavior for the performance of MEL that means, the OMEL-C-PSO method obtains the features set partitions more precisely. If the dataset has increasing performance of MEL behavior but after features set partition the performance is not strictly increasing then the obtain features set partition is not précised. The case where the performance of MEL is not strictly increasing or decreasing, then the features set partition is more likely to close to middle value of features set partition solution space.

- *View Construction using Genetic Algorithm (VC-GA):* Except from DLBCL-NIH dataset, it can be observed from the Fig. 3 that the behavior of performance of MEL on datasets is increasing, if features set partition is increasing. The performance obtained by OMEL-C-PSO method is optimal for all datasets. It can also be observe form the Table 2 that the optimal accuracy obtained by OMEL-C-PSO method using VC-GA features set partitioning method are very closed to maximum accuracy within the solution space for all datasets. From the Fig. 4, it can be observed that the features set partition distribution box Colon Cancer, Colon Tumor and Lung Cancer Ontario are bigger than the other datasets for increasingbehavior of MEL performance because the performances of MEL are closed to constant behavior. The Central nervous system, DLBCL tumor, DLBCL Stanford, Lung Cancer Harvard2 and Prostate vs. Normal datasets are have strictly continuous increasing performance of MEL, therefore, the features set partitions are more précised (have smaller features set partition distribution box). The above analysis indicates that the OMEL-C-PSO method obtains the optimal performance of MEL using VC-GA method when the behavior of performance of MEL is in increasing nature. The distribution box of partitions is smaller strictly for the continuous increasing for the performance of MEL that means, the OMEL-C-PSO method obtains the features set partitions more precisely, which is strictly higher features set partition value.

As per above analysis according to the features set partitioning methods namely, RFSP, Ba, AB and VC-GA, can be concluded that the OMEL-C-PSO method has obtained optimal performance of MEL for all datasets. The performance of OMEL-C-PSO is not dependent on the behavior of MEL performance within the solution space. Therefore, OMEL-C-PSO may be applied without worrying about the Nature of MEL performance. It can also be concluded that if features set partition π_A^k obtained by OMEL-C-PSO method is closed to δ_A, means that the performance of the MEL on the dataset is in decresing nature when features set partition is increasing. If features set partition π_A^k obtained by OMEL-C-PSO method is closed to θ_A, then the performances of MEL on the dataset is in increasing behavior when features set partitions increases. If the closeness of features set partition π_A^k is not clear then it may conclude that the MEL performance is not strictly increasing and decreasing in behavior. The RFSP, Ba, AB and VC-GA methods has been ranked (shown in Table 2) using Friedman. The OMEL-C-PSO method using AB method has smallest rank among four features set partition that means; OMEL-C-PSO method has performed best for all datasets. Therefore, AB can be utilized for the OMEL-C-PSO method.

5   Conclusion and Future Work

In this work, partitioning of features set problem has been identified theoretically for MEL, which is a NP-hard problem. To solve this problem, OMEL-C-PSO approach has been proposed using C-PSO evolutionary algorithm. Four features set partitioning methods are utilized for partition the features set in high dimensional environment while MEL. The results and their analyses areconcluded that the proposed method is effective and efficient for obtaining the optimal performance of MEL within the solution space. The blocks of partition obtained by OMEL-C-PSO method helps to guess the dataset has increasing and decreasing in nature for MEL, if the blocks of partition of features set increases.

The solution space can be extended till domain of the features and analyzed. The computational time complexity may be discussed according to the increasing number of blocks of partition. Other optimizations techniques and features set partition method may be used to find the optimal performance and compared each other.

References

1. Xu, C., Tao, D., Xu, C.: A survey on multi-view learning. Learning (cs.LG) (2013)
2. Kakade, S.M., Foster, D.P.: Multi-view regression via canonical correlation analysis. In: COLT (2007)
3. Ho, T.K.: Nearest neighbors in random subspaces. In: Proceedings of the Second International Workshop on Statistical Techniques in Pattern Recognition, Sydney, Australia, pp. 640–648 (1998)
4. Bay, S.: Nearestneighbour classification from multiple feature subsets. Intell. Data Anal. 3(3), 191–209 (1999)
5. Bryll, R., Gutierrez-Osunaa, R., Quek, F.: Attribute bagging: improving accuracy of classifier ensembles by using random feature subsets. Pattern Recogn. 36, 1291–1302 (2003)
6. Cunningham, P., Carney, J.: Diversity Versus Quality in Classification Ensembles Based on Feature Selection. In: López de Mántaras, R., Plaza, E. (eds.) ECML 2000. LNCS, vol. 1810, pp. 109–116. Springer, Heidelberg (2000). doi:10.1007/3-540-45164-1_12
7. Zenobi, G., Cunningham, P.: Using diversity in preparing ensembles of classifiers based on different feature subsets to minimize generalization error. In: Proceedings of the European Conference on Machine Learning (2001)
8. Wu, Q.X., Bell, D., McGinnity, M.: Multi-knowledge for decision making. Knowl. Inf. Syst. 7(2005), 246–266 (2005)
9. Hu, Qing-Hua, Yu, Da-Ren, Wang, Ming-Yang: Constructing Rough Decision Forests. In: Ślęzak, Dominik, Yao, JingTao, Peters, James F., Ziarko, Wojciech, Hu, Xiaohua (eds.) RSFDGrC 2005. LNCS, vol. 3642, pp. 147–156. Springer, Heidelberg (2005). doi:10.1007/11548706_16
10. Bao, Y., Ishii, N.: Combining Multiple K-Nearest Neighbor Classifiers for Text Classification by Reducts. In: Lange, S., Satoh, K., Smith, C.H. (eds.) DS 2002. LNCS, vol. 2534, pp. 340–347. Springer, Heidelberg (2002). doi:10.1007/3-540-36182-0_34
11. Rodriguez, J.J.: Rotation forest: a new classifier ensemble method. IEEE Trans. Pattern Anal. Mach. Intell. 20(10), 1619–1630 (2006)
12. Rokach, L., Maimon, O., Arad, O.: Improving supervised learning by sample decomposition. Int. J. Comput. Intell. Appl. 5(1), 37–54 (2005)
13. Rokach, L.: Pattern Classification Using Ensemble Methods. Series in Machine Perception and Artifical Intelligence, vol. 75. World Scientific Publishing Company, Singapore (2010)
14. Kudo, M., Sklansky, J.: A Comparative evaluation of medium and large-scale feature selectors for pattern classifiers. In: Proceedings of the 1st International Workshop on Statistical Techniques in Pattern Recognition, Prague, Czech Republic, pp. 91–96 (1997)
15. Bluma, A.L., Langley, P.: Selection of relevant features and examples in machine learning. In: Greiner, R., Subramanian, D. (eds.) Artificial Intelligence on Relevance, Artificial Intelligence, vol. 97, pp. 245–271 (1997)
16. Brefeld, U., Gartner, C., Scheffe, T.: Multi-view Discriminative sequential learning. Machine Learning. In: ECML 2005, pp. 60–71 (2005)
17. Almuallim, H., Dietterich, T.G.: Learning Boolean concepts in the presence of many irrelevant features. Artif. Intell. 69(1–2), 279–305 (1994)
18. Ben-Bassat, M.: Pattern recognition and reduction of dimensionality. In: Krishnaiah, P.R., Kanal, L.N. (eds.) Handbook of statistics-II, pp. 773–791. Elsevier, Amsterdam (1982)
19. Hall, M.A.: Correlation-based feature selection for discrete and numeric class machine learning. In: Proceedings of the 17th International Conference on Machine Learning, pp. 359–366 (2000)

20. Eberhart, R., Kennedy, J.: Particle swarm optimization. In: Proceedings of the IEEE International Conference on Neural Networks, pp. 1942–1948 (1995)
21. Valle, Y., Venayaganmoorthy, G.K., Mohagheghi, S., Hernandez Ronald, J., Harley, G.: Particle swarm optimization: basic concepts, variants and applications in power system. IEEE Trans. Evolut. Comput. **12**(2), 171–195 (2008)
22. Engelbrecht, A.P.: Particle swarm optimization: Where does it belong? In: Proceedings of the IEEE Swarm Intelligence Symposium, pp. 48–54, May (2006)
23. Bai, Q.: Analysis of particle swarm optimization algorithm. Comput. Inf. Sci. **3**, 180–184 (2010)
24. Jordehi, A.R., Jasni, J.: Heuristic methods for solution of FACTS optimization problem in power systems. IEEE SCRD **2011**, 30–35 (2011)
25. Chen,B., Feng, X.: CSV-PSO and its application in geotechnical engineering. Swarm Intelligence, Focus on Ant and Particle Swarm Optimization (2007)
26. Zhang, Y., Gallipoli, D., Augarde, C.: Parallel Hybrid Particle Swarm Optimization and Applications in Geotechnical Engineering. In: Cai, Z., Li, Z., Kang, Z., Liu, Y. (eds.) ISICA 2009. LNCS, vol. 5821, pp. 466–475. Springer, Heidelberg (2009). doi:10.1007/978-3-642-04843-2_49
27. Hsieh, S., Sun, T., Liu, C., Lin, C.: An improved particle swarm optimizer for placement constraints. J. Artif. Evolut. Appl. **13**, (2008)
28. Al Rashidi, M.R., AlHajri, M.F., Al-Othman, A.K., El-Naggar, K.M.: Particle swarm optimization and its applications in power systems. Comput. Intell. Power Eng. **302**, 295–324 (2010)
29. Singh, N., Arya, R., Agrawal, R.K.: A novel approach to combine features for salient object detection using constrained particle swarm optimization. Pattern Recogn. **47**, 1731–1739 (2014)
30. Sapankevych, N.I., Sankar, R.: Constrained motion particle swarm optimization and support vector regression for non-linear time series regression and prediction applications. In: 12th International Conference on Machine Learning and Applications (ICMLA), vol. 2. IEEE (2013)
31. Gama, João: A Linear-Bayes Classifier. In: Monard, Maria Carolina, Sichman, Jaime Simão (eds.) IBERAMIA/SBIA -2000. LNCS, vol. 1952, pp. 269–279. Springer, Heidelberg (2000). doi:10.1007/3-540-44399-1_28
32. Kusiak, A.: Decomposition in Data Mining: An Industrial Case Study. IEEE Trans. Electron. Packag. Manuf. **23**(4), 345–353 (2000)
33. Liao, Y., Moody, J.: Constructing heterogeneous committees via input feature grouping. In: Solla, S.A., Leen, T.K., Muller, K.-R. (eds.) Advances in neural information processing systems, vol. 12, pp. 921–927. MIT Press, Cambridge (2000)
34. Tumer, K., Ghosh, J.: Error correlation and error reduction in ensemble classifiers. Connect. Sci. **8**(3–4), 385–404 (1996)
35. Rokach, L.: Genetic algorithm-based feature set partitioning for classification problems. Pattern Recogn. **41**(5), 1676–1700 (2008)
36. Tsymbal, A., Pechenizkiy, M., Cunningham, P.: Diversity in search strategies for ensemble feature selection. Inf. Fusion **6**(1), 83–98 (2005)
37. Gunter, S., Bunke, H.: Feature selection algorithms for the generation of multiple classifier systems. Pattern Recogn. Lett. **25**(11), 1323–1336 (2004)
38. Sun, S., Jin, F. Tu, W.: View construction for multi-view semi-supervised learning. Advances in Neural Networks–ISNN 2011, pp. 595–60 (2011)
39. Ho, T.K.: The random subspace method for constructing decision forests. Pattern Anal. Mach. Intell. IEEE Trans. **20**(8), 832–844 (1998)

40. Tao, D., Tang, X., Li, X., Wu, X.: Asymmetric bagging and random subspace for support vector machines-based relevance feedback in image retrieval. Pattern Anal. Mach. Intell. IEEE Trans. **28**(7), 1088–1099 (2006)

41. Floudas, C.A., Pardalos, P.M.: A Collection of Test Problems for Constrained Global Optimization Algorithms. LNCS, vol. 455. Springer, Heidelberg (1990). doi:10.1007/3-540-53032-0

42. Parsopoulos, K., Vrahatis, M.: Particle swarm optimization method for con- strained optimization problems. Intell. Technol. **16**(2002), 214–220 (2002)

43. Yang, Jinn-Moon, Chen, Ying-Ping, Horng, Jorng-Tzong, Kao, Cheng-Yan: Applying family competition to evolution strategies for constrained optimization. In: Angeline, Peter J., Reynolds, Robert G., McDonnell, John R., Eberhart, Russ (eds.) EP 1997. LNCS, vol. 1213, pp. 201–211. Springer, Heidelberg (1997). doi:10.1007/BFb0014812

44. Homaifar, A., Lai, A.H.Y., Qi, X.: Constrained optimization via genetic algorithms. Simulation **2**(4), 242–254 (1994)

45. Ahmed, A., Esmin, A., Coelho, R.A., Matwin, S.: A review on particle swarm optimization algorithm and its variant to clustering high- dimensional data. Artif. Intel. Rev. **44**(1), 23–45 (2013)

46. Kennedy, J.: The behavior of particles. Evol. Progr. **VII**(1998), 581–587 (1998)

47. Clerc, M.: The swarm and the queen: Towards a deterministic and adaptive particle swarm optimization. In: Congress on Evolutionary Computation (CEC 1999), pp. 1951–1957 (1999)

48. Opitz, D.: Feature Selection for Ensembles. In: Proceedings 16th National Conference on Artificial Intelligence. AAAI, pp. 379–384 (1999)

49. http://archive.ics.uci.edu/ml/

50. http://www.nipsfsc.ecs.soton.ac.uk/datasets/

51. http://datam.i2r.a-star.edu.sg/datasets/krbd/index.html

52. http://www.37steps.com/prtools/

53. Minz S., Kumar, V.: reinforced multi-view ensemble learning for high dimensional data classification. In: International Conference on Communication and Computing (ICC 2014), Elsevier (2014)

54. Kumar, V., Minz, S.: Multi-view Ensemble Learning for Poem Data Classification Using SentiWordNet. In: Kumar Kundu, M., Mohapatra, D.P., Konar, A., Chakraborty, A. (eds.) Advanced Computing, Networking and Informatics- Volume 1. SIST, vol. 27, pp. 57–66. Springer, Cham (2014). doi:10.1007/978-3-319-07353-8_8

55. Kumar, V., Minz, S.: Feature selection: a literature review. Smart Comput. Rev. KAIS **4**(3), 211–229 (2014)

56. Breiman, L.: Bagging predictor. Mach. Learn. **24**, 123–140 (1996)

57. Sun, S., Jin, F., Tu, W.: View construction for multi-view semi-supervised learning. Advances in Neural Networks–ISNN 2011, pp. 595–601 (2011)

58. Branson, D.: Stirling numbers and Bell numbers: their role in combinatoricsand probability. Math. Sci. **25**, 1–31 (2000)

59. Pitman, J.: Some probabilistic aspects of set partitions. Amer. Math. Monthly **104**, 201–209 (1997)

60. Garcia, S., Herrera, F.: An extension on statistical comparison of classifiers over multiple datasets for all pair-wise comparisons. Mach. Learn. Res. **09**, 2677–2694 (2008)

61. Kumar, V., Minz, S.: Multi-view ensemble learning: an optimal feature set partitioning for high dimensional data classification. Knowl. Inf. Syst. **49**(01), 1–59 (2015)

Identifying Metaphors Using Fuzzy Conceptual Features

Sunny Rai[1(✉)] [ID], Shampa Chakraverty[1] [ID], and Devendra K. Tayal[2] [ID]

[1] Division of Computer Engineering, NSIT, Delhi, India
post2srai@gmail.com, apmahs.nsit@gmail.com
[2] Department of Computer Science and Engineering, IGDTUW, Delhi, India
dev_tayal2001@yahoo.com

Abstract. Metaphor comprehension is a challenging problem which equally intrigues researchers in linguistics as well as those working in the domain of cognition. The use of psychological features such as *Imageability* and *Concreteness* has been shown to be effective in identifying metaphors. However, there is a certain degree of vagueness and blurring boundaries between the sub-concepts of these features that has hitherto been largely ignored. In this paper, we tackle this issue of vagueness by proposing a fuzzy framework for metaphor detection whereby linguistic variables are employed to express psychological features. We develop a Mamdani Model to extract fuzzy classification rules for detecting metaphors in a text. The results of experiments conducted over a dataset of nominal metaphors reveal encouraging results with an F-score of more than 79%.

Keywords: Metaphor · Computational linguistics · Natural language processing · Fuzzy sets · Psychological features · Metaphoricity

1 Introduction

Metaphorically speaking, a metaphor is a lighted path in a dark tunnel with multiple exits. The *tunnel* represents a collection of different ways in which a concept can be interpreted, an *exit* denotes a particular interpretation and the *lighted path* projects a set of features that guides us towards an appropriate interpretation. A metaphor enables a reader to comprehend a vague concept in a target domain by importing a set of concepts from a known source domain without being verbose. It provides a way to express an idea in an impactful manner that reflects the perception a writer desires to leave. Let us consider a sentence:

An *atom* is a *solar system*. (a)

The above metaphorical expression maps an *atom* (target domain) to the *solar system* (source domain). In this mapping, electrons and protons correspond to planets and the nucleus corresponds to the sun. While comprehending (a), we import our existing knowledge about the domain *solar system* and its well-known concepts such as *planets revolve around the sun* and *a planet has an orbit* to understand the model of an atom in a succinct manner.

In social interactions, metaphors and other figures of speech play a significant role in expressing thoughts and enabling lucid communication. Metaphor processing is a

S. Kaushik et al. (Eds.): ICICCT 2017, CCIS 750, pp. 379–386, 2017.
https://doi.org/10.1007/978-981-10-6544-6_34

relatively new field of research in the domain of Natural Language Processing and comes at the intersection of linguistics and cognition. For seamless human computer interaction, it is important to understand and automate the process of metaphor comprehension. Metaphor detection is the first step towards achieving the goal of automated metaphor comprehension.

Prior works in metaphor detection have predominantly focused on feature based techniques with emphasis on psychological features, also known as conceptual features like *imageability* [1, 20], *abstractness* [2, 19], and *familiarity/conventionality* [3, 22] to identify metaphors in text. It is quite evident that the familiarity or imageability of a word or a phrase is often subjective. Furthermore, these properties depend on the context and semantics of their associated text. As a result, these concepts are associated with a degree of vagueness and relative interpretation. Labov introduced the concept of vagueness in the meaning of a word [4]. He points out that it is a region rather than a point where a word gradually shifts from being relevant to irrelevant. Let us consider another sentence to illustrate this hypothesis:

He is an *old* man. (b)

The term *old* in (b) does not indicate a specific age, rather it represents a continuum with a varying degree of oldness. It thus makes sense to emulate the human mind within a framework that supports vagueness in order to analyse overlapping concepts derived from human language. Zadeh proposed Fuzzy logic as extension of classical set theory to model real world problems in a realistic manner [5]. Unlike classical mathematics that takes a deterministic world view, fuzzy logic enables us to reason about the rules and parameters that govern a system while taking into account the inherent inaccuracies and uncertainties that are typical of a practical world.

So far, prior works on metaphor detection have modelled conceptual features such as *concreteness* or *imageability* by either assigning them numeric values or by categorizing them into classes using pre-defined thresholds. In this paper, we use MRC psycholinguistic Database (MRCPD) [6] to extract the numeric values of psychological properties annotated with terms/phrases and map them onto a set of linguistic variables. We develop a fuzzy framework based on the Mamdani Model [7] for binary classification of text into 'metaphorical' or 'literal'. We conduct experiments using the R package *frbs* [8] to analyse the efficacy of the proposed approach.

The remainder of the paper is organized as follows. Section 2 provides an overview of existing work in the domain of metaphor detection. We explain our proposed fuzzy-driven approach in Sect. 3. In Sect. 4, we present experiments and results conducted over a dataset of nominal metaphors. This is followed by the conclusion and pointers towards future work in Sect. 5.

2   Related Work

In this section, we provide a brief glimpse to previous work in metaphor detection. One of the earliest approach to identify metaphors is based on violation of *Selectional preference* given by Wilks [9]. It is based on the hypothesis that a linguistic element prefers arguments of a certain semantic class *e.g.* one such pair of sentences which illustrates this preference is:

Do not *eat* my ice-cream. (c)
Do not *eat* my head. (d)

Here in (c), the verb, *eat* is paired with an object *ice-cream* which belongs to semantic class, *food* whereas in (d), it is paired with another object, head which falls in semantic class, *body*. The former sentence is literal whereas the latter indicates an incongruity.

Martin [10], Fass [11] and Mason [12] proposed approaches to identify metaphors based on the concept of violation of selectional preference. Birke and Sarkar proposed Trope Finder (TroFi) system to recognize verbs with non-literal meaning using clustering [13]. Gedigian et al. introduced usage of knowledge resources like WordNet [15] to detect metaphorical verb usage in a text [14]. Likewise, Krishnakumaran and Zhu proposed an approach on the basis of violations in co-occurring noun and verb phrases using WordNet hierarchies [16]. Shutova et al. used a clustering technique on the basis of hypothesis that a target concept associated with the same source concept are more likely to co-occur in similar lexico-syntactic environments [17].

A conceptual metaphor explains an abstract concept using a relatively concrete concept [18]. By the term concrete, we mean a well-defined and highly structured concept. Turney et al. showed that a metaphorical usage is directly correlated with the degree of abstractness in a word's contextual usage [19]. Tsvetkov et al. [20] and Bracewell et al. used the concept of hybrid feature set by using features such as imageability and abstractness [1]. Klebanov et al. evaluated the effect of concreteness as a feature for metaphor detection and demonstrated its significance in identifying metaphors [2]. Gargett and Branden proposed to improve the process of metaphor detection using sensory features from Affective Norms for English Word (ANEW) and imageability [21]. In [22], Rai et al. proposed to identify metaphors using conditional random fields and evaluated the impact of different feature set such as conceptual, affective and contextual features in metaphor detection. They showed that inclusion of conceptual features such as concreteness and imageability improves the coverage of identified metaphors.

Our work is different from previous work with respect to approach and inclusion of degree of vagueness as an attribute. We represent a feature such as imageability using linguistic variables and membership function which allows overlapping between continuous concepts.

3   Methodology

We now elaborate upon our fuzzy driven approach for metaphor detection. The proposed approach is sub-divided into 3 stages namely *data processing, feature extraction and model building*.

3.1   Data Processing

This step involves pre-processing text to represent input sentences in the required format for the subsequent feature extraction phase. We use a dependency parser to extract subject and object from the sentence. In this work, we experiment with our proposed scheme by applying it on text containing nominal metaphors. Hence, the primary processing step involves removing sentences which do not follow the *<subject, to be, object>* format.

3.2 Feature Extraction

We use MRCPD [6], a large psycholinguistics database to extract psychological features of words and phrases. The features extracted have numerical values ranging from 100 to 700. We first normalize them to be in range [0, 1].

1. **Imageability** refers to the ability of a word to evoke a mental image. For example, *Cooking* is a more imageable concept than *thinking*. We define Imageability, *I* as a fuzzy subset, with linguistic values {*very low, low, average, high, very high*}.
2. **Concreteness** for a word is defined in terms of its ability to refer to aspecific or a concrete concept. Abstractness is inverse of concreteness. For example, *Truck* is more concrete than *vehicle*. We define Concreteness, *C* as a fuzzy subset with linguistic values {*very low, low, average, high, very high*}.
3. **Familiarity** refers to the feeling of knowing a word or the concept represented by the word. *e.g. sun* is a more familiar concept than *nucleus*. We define Familiarity, *F* as a fuzzy subset, with linguistic values {*very low, low, average, high, very high*}.
4. **Meaningfulness** is a measure of the association of a given word with other words. For example, *bread* is more meaningful than *sourdough*. We define Meaningfulness, *M* as a fuzzy subset, with linguistic values {*very low, low, average, high, very high*}.
5. **Affectiveness** is the degree of how affective a word is. A word is said to be affective if it denotes an emotion, sentiment or mood. It has been shown that a metaphor is rarely without any emotion [23]. Rai et al. indicated a correlation between affective words and metaphors in [22]. Thus, we incorporate this feature to analyse its impact in identifying metaphors.

For example, consider the sentence:

The economic policy *strangulated* the open market. (e)

Here, the verb *strangulated* in (e) is used metaphorically with an implicit negative sentiment. We define Affectiveness, *V* as a fuzzy subset, with linguistic values {*very weak, weak, average, strong, very strong*}.

3.3 Model Building

We employ the Mamdani model [7] for creating fuzzy rule based system for metaphor detection. This model entails four components namely *fuzzification, knowledge-base, inference engine* and *defuzzifier*. The fuzzification component converts crisp inputs into linguistic values using a membership function. The knowledge-base consists of fuzzy definitions of defined concepts and rules constructed with T-norms and S-norms. The Inference engine performs reasoning using fuzzy rules derived from the training dataset and inputs. The last component, Defuzzifier converts the linguistic decision values to crisp decision values.

Let X be a set, then a fuzzy subset A of X is defined by a membership function, μ_a. $\mu_A(x)$ gives membership degree of x in A. The choice of an appropriate membership function is dictated by the nature of input and the complexity of the problem at hand. In our case, we contend that the Gaussian membership function is well suited to the very smooth transitions in concepts that emanate from human language. We did experiment with different membership functions to verify our contention as reported in the next section.

The Gaussian membership function is defined as $f(x; \sigma; c) = \dfrac{e^{-(x-c)^2}}{2\sigma^2}$, where c and σ are parameters of the Gaussian distribution. Since we are performing binary classification, a class label, $y \in \{1, 2\}$ where '1' indicates metaphorical and '2' stands for literal sentence. We use the Wang-Mendel's technique based on Mamdani model to generate fuzzy rules from training data [24]. We use Zadeh implication with 'MIN' function as T-norm and 'MAX' function as S-norm for fuzzy rule generation.

4 Experiments and Results

We used the R package *frbs* V3.1-0 [8] available in CRAN repository to implement Wang and Mendel's technique for generating fuzzy rules [24]. For our experiments, we used the list of '*Target*' sentences given under heading '*Stimulus*' from the dataset used by Thibodeau and Durgin [3] to create a dataset of 150 sentences with equal number of metaphorical and literal instances. We divided the randomized dataset into training and testing datasets in equal ratio.

The crisp inputs for the first four features listed in Sect. 3.2 were extracted using MRCPD and mapped to the linguistic terms defined therein. For the feature *Affectiveness*, we used the ANEW database [25] which annotates each word with its degree of affectiveness. We evaluated our model using the classification metrics *accuracy, precision, recall* and *F-score*. F-score is the harmonic mean of precision and recall.

Table 1. Impact of fuzzy features on Metaphor Detection

Model	MF	A	P	R	F1
SVM (crisp model)	NA	77.34	72.5	82.86	77.34
Fuzzy model #Linguistic variable = 3	Gaussian	65.34	58.82	85.71	69.77
	Trapezoid	77.34	75	77.17	76.06
	Triangle	62.37	56.37	88.57	68.89
Fuzzy model #Linguistic variable = 5	**Gaussian**	**78.67**	**72.09**	**88.57**	**79.49**
	Trapezoid	62.37	64	45.71	53.34
	Triangle	73.33	65.95	88.57	75.61
Fuzzy model #Linguistic variable = 7	**Gaussian**	77.34	73.68	80	76.71
	Trapezoid	65.34	57.89	94.28	71.74
	Triangle	68	73.91	48.57	58.62

Legends: MF-Membership Function; A-Accuracy; P-Precision; R-Recall; F1-F score

We analysed the effect of parameters such as type of membership function and number of linguistic variables. We conducted the experiments over different membership functions namely *trapezoid* and *triangular* to understand their effect on the generated model. We compared the proposed model with crisp features on Support Vector Machine based classifier (*Polynomial Kernel and C = 1*) available in the R package *kernlab* [26].

The results for our experiments are summarised in Table 1. We observe that our proposed fuzzy model with Gaussian membership function and 5 linguistic values performs the best with an F-score of 79.49%. The number of fuzzy rules generated using Zadeh implication is 69.

We analyze the effect of parameters such as type of membership function and number of linguistic variables. We conduct the experiments over different membership functions namely trapezoid and triangular for analyzing their effect on the generated model. We compare the proposed model with crisp features on Support Vector Machine (SVM) based classifier (*Polynomial Kernel and C = 1*) available in the R package '*kernlab*' [25].

The graph for membership functions is shown in Fig. 1. The crisp model shows comparable performance with respect to accuracy and precision. However, it is worth

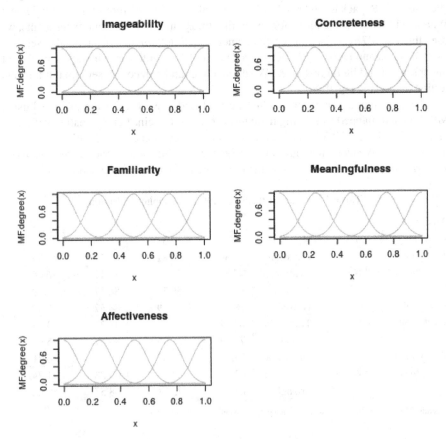

Fig. 1. Membership function for linguistic variables defined in Sect. 3.2

noting that inclusion of fuzzy features have shown significant improvement of 6% in recall over crisp model. This indicates that an overlapping representation of features is more suitable to expand the coverage of metaphor detection. We also find that performance of a fuzzy model vary according to the type of membership function and granularity of linguistic values. Gaussian distribution is a more suitable representation when size of linguistic variables $>=5$. The proposed model performs the best when the number of linguistic values is 5 *i.e.* succinctly retain vagueness and overlap between different classes without being too specific or generic about the value of features.

5 Conclusion

In this paper, we acknowledged the aspect of the inherent vagueness that is present in psychological features such as *Imageability* and *Concreteness*. We proposed a fuzzy rule based framework based on Mamdani's model to identify metaphors in a text. We used linguistic variables to precisely model the overlap and uncertainty in the features. The experimental results indicate that fuzzy logic is a promising avenue to explore the concepts such as metaphoricity and emotions embedded in a metaphor. In this work, we restricted our experiments to nominal metaphors. There is a plenty of scope for further experimentation on studying the impact of fuzzy features on different types of metaphors.

References

1. Bracewell, D.B., Tomlinson, M.T., Mohler, M., Rink, B.: A tiered approach to the recognition of metaphor. In: Computational Linguistics and Intelligent Text Processing, pp. 403–414. Springer, Heidelberg (2014) doi:10.1007/978-3-642-54906-9_33
2. Klebanov, B.B., Leong, C.W., Flor, M.: Supervised word-level metaphor detection: experiments with concreteness reweighting of examples. In: NAACL HLT 2015, p. 11 (2015)
3. Thibodeau, P.H., Durgin, F.H.: Metaphor aptness and conventionality: a processing fluency account. Metaphor Symb. **26**(3), 206–226 (2011)
4. Labov, W.: The boundaries of words and their meanings. In: Bailey, C.-J.N., Shuy, R.W. (eds.) New Ways of Analyzing Variation in English. Georgetown University Press, Washington, DC (1973)
5. Zadeh, L.A.: Fuzzy sets. Inf. Control **8**(3), 338–353 (1965)
6. Wilson, M.D.: The MRC psycholinguistic database: machine readable dictionary, version 2. Behav. Res. Methods Instrum. Comput. **20**(1), 6–11 (1988)
7. Mamdani, E.H.: Application of fuzzy algorithms for control of simple dynamic plant. Proc. Inst. Electr. Eng. **121**(12), 1585–1588 (1974)
8. Riza, L.S., Bergmeir, C.N., Herrera, F., Benitez, J.M.: frbs: Fuzzy Rule-Based Systems for Classification and Regression in R. American Statistical Association, Alexandria (2015)
9. Wilks, Y.: Making preferences more active. Artif. Intell. **11**(3), 197223 (1978)
10. Martin, J.H.: A Computational Model of Metaphor Interpretation. Academic Press Professional, Inc., Cambridge (1990)
11. Fass, D.: met*: a method for discriminating metonymy and metaphor by computer. Comput. Linguist. **17**(1), 4990 (1991)
12. Mason, Z.J.: CorMet: a computational, corpus-based conventional metaphor extraction system. Comput. Linguist. **30**(1), 23–44 (2004)

13. Birke, J., Sarkar, A.: A clustering approach for the nearly unsupervised recognition of nonliteral language. In: Proceedings of EACL 2006, pp. 329–336 (2006)
14. Gedigan, M., Bryant, J., Narayanan, S., Ciric, B.: Catching metaphors. In: Proceedings of the 3rd Workshop on Scalable Natural Language Understanding, New York, pp. 41–48 (2006)
15. Princeton University: AboutWordNet: WordNet. Princeton University (2010). http://wordnet.princeton.edu
16. Krishnakumaran, S., Zhu, X.: Hunting elusive metaphors using lexical resources. In: Proceedings of the Workshop on Computational Approaches to Figurative Language, Rochester, NY, pp. 13–20 (2007)
17. Shutova, E., Sun, L., Korhonen, A.: Metaphor identification using verb and noun clustering. In: Proceedings of the 23rd International Conference on Computational Linguistics. Association for Computational Linguistics (2010)
18. Lakoff, G., Johnson, M.: Metaphors We Live by. University of Chicago Press, Chicago (1980)
19. Turney, P.D., Neuman, Y., Assaf, D., Cohen, Y.: Literal and metaphorical sense identification through concrete and abstract context. In: Proceedings of the Conference on Empirical Methods in Natural Language Processing, pp. 680–690. Association for Computational Linguistics (July 2011)
20. Tsvetkov, Y., Boytsov, L., Gershman, A., Nyberg, E., Dyer, C.: Metaphor Detection with Cross-Lingual Model Transfer. Language Technologies Institute, Carnegie Mellon University, Pittsburgh (2014)
21. Gargett, A., Barnden, J.: Modeling the interaction between sensory and affective meanings for detecting metaphor. In: NAACL HLT: 2015, p. 21 (2015)
22. Rai, S., Chakraverty, S., Tayal, D.K.: Supervised metaphor detection using conditional random fields. In: Proceedings of the Fourth Workshop on Metaphor in NLP, NAACL-HLT 2016, pp. 18–27 (2016)
23. Rentoumi, V., Vouros, G.A., Karkaletsis, V., Moser, A.: Investigating metaphorical language in sentiment analysis: a sense-to-sentiment perspective. ACM Trans. Speech Lang. Process. 9(3), 6 (2012)
24. Wang, L.-X., Mendel, J.M.: Generating fuzzy rules by learning from examples. IEEE Trans. Syst. Man Cybern. 22(6), 1414–1427 (1992)
25. Bradley, M.M., Lang, P.J.: Affective Norms for English Words (ANEW): Instruction Manual and Affective Ratings, pp. 1–45. Technical report C-1. The Centre for Research in Psychophysiology, University of Florida (1999)
26. Zeileis, A., Hornik, K., Smola, A., Karatzoglou, A.: Kernlab - an S4 package for kernel methods in R. J. Stat. Softw. 11(9), 1–20 (2004)

Author Index

Printed in the United States
By Bookmasters